# Archaeology of the Chinese fishing industry in colonial Victoria

Alister M Bowen

Studies in Australasian Historical Archaeology
Volume 3

Australasian Society for Historical Archaeology

SYDNEY UNIVERSITY PRESS

Published 2012 by SYDNEY UNIVERSITY PRESS
University of Sydney Library
sydney.edu.au/sup
In association with the Australasian Society for Historical Archaeology
asha.org.au

© Alister M Bowen 2012
© Australasian Society for Historical Archaeology 2012

Reproduction and Communication for other purposes

Except as permitted under the Copyright Act, no part of this edition may be reproduced, stored in a retrieval system, or communicated in any form or by any means without prior written permission. All requests for reproduction or communication should be made to the Australasian Society for Historical Archaeology at the address below:

Sydney University Press
Fisher Library F03
University of Sydney
NSW 2006 AUSTRALIA

Email: sup.info@sydney.edu.au

**National Library of Australia Cataloguing-in-Publication entry**

| | |
|---|---|
| Author: | Bowen, Alister M |
| Title: | Archaeology of the Chinese fishing industry in colonial Victoria / Alister M Bowen. |
| ISBN: | 9781920899813 (pbk) |
| Series: | Studies in Australasian historical archaeology; v.3. |
| Notes: | Includes bibliographical references. |
| Subjects: | Fisheries--Victoria--History--19th century. |
| | Chinese--Victoria--History--19th century. |
| | Victoria--Social life and customs--1834-1900. |
| | Victoria--Economic conditions--1834-1900. |
| Dewey Number: | 994.503 |

# AUSTRALASIAN SOCIETY FOR HISTORICAL ARCHAEOLOGY EDITORIAL BOARD

Dr Eleanor Conlin Casella, Senior Lecturer, University of Manchester, United Kingdom

Dr Mary Casey, Director, Casey & Lowe Pty Ltd, Sydney, NSW

Dr Sarah Colley, Senior Lecturer, University of Sydney, NSW

Emeritus Professor Graham Connah, Australian National University, ACT

Dr Martin Gibbs, Senior Lecturer, University of Sydney, NSW

Dr Michael Given, Senior Lecturer, University of Glasgow, United Kingdom

Dr Grace Karskens, Associate Professor, University of New South Wales, Sydney, NSW

Dr Tracy Ireland, Assistant Professor, University of Canberra, ACT

Dr Susan Lawrence, Associate Professor, La Trobe University, Melbourne, Victoria

Dr Jane Lydon, Australian Research Council Future Fellow, Monash University, Melbourne, Victoria

Professor Tim Murray, Dean, Humanities and Social Sciences, La Trobe University, Melbourne, Victoria

Dr Charles Orser, Distinguished Professor Emeritus, Illinois State University and Curator of Historical Archaeology, New York State Museum, USA

Dr Caroline Phillips, Honorary Research Fellow, University of Auckland, New Zealand

Dr Jon Prangnell, Senior Lecturer, University of Queensland, Queensland

Dr Neville Ritchie, Waikato Conservancy, Department of Conservation, Hamilton, New Zealand

Dr Ian WG Smith, Associate Professor, University of Otago, New Zealand

Dr Iain Stuart, Principal, JCIS Consultants, Sydney, NSW.

# MONOGRAPH EDITORS

Dr Martin Gibbs

Dr Peter Davies.

# ABOUT THE SERIES

The *Studies in Australasian Historical Archaeology* series is designed to make the results of high-quality research in historical archaeology available to archaeologists, other researchers, students and the public. A particular aim of the series is to ensure that the data from these studies are also made available, either within the volumes or in associated websites, to facilitate opportunities for inter-site comparison and critical evaluation of analytical methods and interpretations. Future releases in the series will include edited and revised versions of Australasian higher-degree theses, major consultancy projects and academic research and commissioned studies on other topics of interest.

# CONTENTS

| | |
|---|---|
| **ABOUT THE SERIES** | **III** |
| **CONVERSIONS** | **XIII** |
| **ACKNOWLEDGEMENTS** | **XIV** |
| **CHAPTER 1 INTRODUCTION** | **1** |
| Background | 1 |
| Aims and questions | 3 |
| Significance | 4 |
| Data sources | 4 |
| Previous research | 5 |
|     History | 6 |
|     Historical archaeology | 7 |
|     Social archaeology | 8 |
|     Methodological and theoretical background | 9 |
|     World-systems and postcolonial theories | 9 |
|     The theory | 10 |
|     Class | 11 |
| Monograph outline | 12 |
| **CHAPTER 2 HISTORY OF COMMERCIAL FISHING IN AUSTRALIA** | **14** |
| Australian Aboriginal fishing | 14 |
|     Aboriginal fishing technology | 14 |
|     Adoption and adaptation | 15 |
| The European fishing industry | 15 |
|     Fishing methods | 15 |
|     Importance | 17 |
|     Australia | 17 |
| Victoria's commercial fishing history | 20 |
|     Eastern Victoria | 20 |
| Coastal South Gippsland | 21 |
|     The Kurnai people | 21 |
|     European discovery of Gippsland | 23 |
|     Early settlers and cattle | 24 |
| Port Albert | 24 |
|     Commercial fishing | 25 |
|     The Chinese at Port Albert | 27 |
|     Historical documentation | 29 |

## CHAPTER 3 THE CHINESE IN CHINA AND VICTORIA — **31**

The Chinese fishing in China — 31
China's social situation and aspects of culture — 34
    Social situation — 34
    Aspects of culture in China and abroad — 36
    Merchant involvement — 38
Chinese social organisation in Victoria — 40
    Occupational change — 44

## CHAPTER 4 THE CHINESE IN VICTORIA'S FISHING INDUSTRY — **46**

Location — 47
    New South Wales — 47
    Northern Territory — 47
    South Australia — 48
    Tasmania — 49
    Victoria — 50
Internal structure — 55
Chinese fishing and fish curing — 58
    Chinese fish-curing methods — 61
    Economics — 63
    Market locations — 66
    United States of America — 69
    Overview of Chinese fish-curing operations — 70

## CHAPTER 5 EXCAVATION AT CHINAMAN'S POINT — **72**

Site Selection — 72
    Site description — 73
Methodology — 76
Excavation — 77
    Gutter system — 77
    Excavation area 1 — 78
    Excavation area 2 — 80
    Excavation area 3 — 80
    Excavation area 4 — 82
    Jetty remains — 84
Results — 84

## CHAPTER 6 ARTEFACT ANALYSIS — **87**

Artefact collectors — 87
Analysis methodology — 87
Architectural/Structural — 90
    Fasteners — 90
    Materials — 93

| | |
|---|---|
| Domestic | 94 |
|     Cooking | 95 |
|     Food | 96 |
|     Discussion | 100 |
|     Food storage | 101 |
|     Furnishings | 107 |
|     Liquid storage | 108 |
|     Tableware | 119 |
| Industrial | 123 |
|     Fishing | 123 |
|     Recording | 126 |
|     Slag | 128 |
|     Tools | 128 |
| Personal | 131 |
|     Buttons | 131 |
| Recreational | 131 |
|     Opium smoking | 132 |
| Unidentified | 139 |
| Conclusion | 139 |
| **CHAPTER 7 OCCUPATION DATES AND SITE INTERPRETATION** | **141** |
| Occupation dates | 141 |
| Dating method | 141 |
| Historical setting | 141 |
| Chinese ceramics | 142 |
| Datable artefacts | 142 |
|     Nails | 142 |
|     Clothing buttons | 143 |
|     Window glass | 143 |
|     Bottle glass | 144 |
|     European ceramics | 145 |
|     Discussion | 146 |
| Site interpretation | 146 |
|     Broader overseas Chinese community | 146 |
|     Site workings | 147 |
|     Number of occupants | 149 |
|     Site activities | 150 |
| **CHAPTER 8 CONCLUSION** | **153** |
| Hypothetical re-creation | 154 |
| **BIBLIOGRAPHY** | **157** |

# LIST OF TABLES

## CHAPTER 4 THE CHINESE IN VICTORIA'S FISHING INDUSTRY

| | |
|---|---:|
| Table 4.1 The beginning, boom and end period for Chinese fish-curing establishments in Australia. | 70 |
| Table 4.2 A percentage estimate of the total quantities of fish sold in Victoria and New South Wales combined by European and Chinese fish dealers during the late 1860s. | 71 |

## CHAPTER 5 EXCAVATION AT CHINAMAN'S POINT

| | |
|---|---:|
| Table 5.1 Main artefact categories by number and weight from gutter system. | 78 |
| Table 5.2 Main artefact categories by number and weight from excavation area 1. | 78 |
| Table 5.3 Main artefact categories by number and weight from excavation area 3. | 82 |
| Table 5.4 Main artefact categories by number and weight from excavation area 4. | 83 |

## CHAPTER 6 ARTEFACT ANALYSIS

| | |
|---|---:|
| Table 6.1 Breakdown of artefact material types, numbers and weight. | 90 |
| Table 6.2 Chinaman's Point site artefact densities. | 90 |
| Table 6.3 Breakdown of retained and discarded metals. | 91 |
| Table 6.4 Minimum number of metal fasteners. | 92 |
| Table 6.5 Window-glass type and amounts. | 94 |
| Table 6.6 Number, weight and location of recovered animal bones. | 97 |
| Table 6.7 Faunal distribution across the site. | 97 |
| Table 6.8 Type, number of sherds, MNI and location for Chinese stoneware vessels. | 103 |
| Table 6.9 Colour, number of shards, number of base types, MNI and MNI percentages for glass containers. | 108 |
| Table 6.10 Colour, form, MNI and MNI percentages for cylindrical, square and polygonal glass containers. | 109 |
| Table 6.11 Chinaman's Point bottle glass distribution. | 109 |
| Table 6.12 Minimum number of European compared to Chinese alcohol bottles. | 111 |
| Table 6.13 Green aqua bottle glass attributes. | 111 |
| Table 6.14 Amber bottle glass attributes. | 114 |
| Table 6.15 Aqua-blue/light blue bottle glass attributes. | 115 |
| Table 6.16 Clear bottle glass attributes. | 117 |
| Table 6.17 Chinese liquor-bottle and spouted-jar fragment quantities. | 118 |
| Table 6.18 Type, number of sherds and MNI for Chinese *tz'u* ceramics. | 120 |
| Table 6.19 Chinese celadon bowl rim diameters and quantities. | 120 |
| Table 6.20 Chinese bowl fragments displaying either the double happiness or three friends pattern. | 121 |
| Table 6.21 Type, number of sherds and MNI for European ceramics. | 123 |
| Table 6.22 Type and number of recovered buttons. | 131 |
| Table 6.23 Representation of opium-smoking equipment. | 132 |

## CHAPTER 7: OCCUPATION DATES AND SITE INTERPRETATION

| | |
|---|---|
| Table 7.1 Colour, number of shards and MNI for glass bottles. | 144 |
| Table 7.2 Breakdown of datable glass bottle shards. | 144 |
| Table 7.3 Breakdown of datable European ceramics and their percentage of the total ceramic collection. | 146 |
| Table 7.4 Theoretical model for the activities conducted, equipment required and the archaeological evidence recoverable from commercial fishing sites. | 151 |

# LIST OF FIGURES

## CHAPTER 1 INTRODUCTION

| | |
|---|---|
| Figure 1.1 Map showing east coast of Victoria. | 2 |
| Figure 1.2 Map of Port Albert region. | 2 |

## CHAPTER 2 HISTORY OF COMMERCIAL FISHING IN AUSTRALIA

| | |
|---|---|
| Figure 2.1 Gill-net designs. | 16 |
| Figure 2.2 An early form of European drag net. | 16 |
| Figure 2.3 Two methods of seine netting. | 17 |
| Figure 2.4 A drift net being set. | 17 |
| Figure 2.5 Australian colonial fishing vessels and crew. | 18 |
| Figure 2.6 A nut-cracker hand winch. | 19 |
| Figure 2.7 A mangle hand winch. | 19 |
| Figure 2.8 'The old fish track' route. | 21 |
| Figure 2.9 The waterways of south Gippsland. | 22 |
| Figure 2.10 Indigenous Kurnai women fishing. | 22 |
| Figure 2.11 Indigenous Kurnai people with European-style clothing, bark canoes and European fishing nets. | 23 |
| Figure 2.12 Indigenous Kurnai people with European fishing nets, bark canoes and a European-style boat. | 23 |
| Figure 2.13 An early-style Australian oyster dredge. | 26 |

## CHAPTER 3 THE CHINESE IN CHINA AND VICTORIA

| | |
|---|---|
| Figure 3.1 Map of Canton (Guangdong). | 31 |
| Figure 3.2 A fish cut into strips. | 34 |
| Figure 3.3 The British bombing of Canton during the first Opium War from 1839 to 1842. | 35 |
| Figure 3.4 An 1866 wood engraving of Lowe Kong Meng. | 38 |
| Figure 3.5 Wood engraving of Chinese immigrants. | 40 |

## CHAPTER 4 THE CHINESE IN VICTORIA'S FISHING INDUSTRY

| | |
|---|---|
| Figure 4.1 Known Chinese fish-curing establishments in New South Wales. | 47 |
| Figure 4.2 The Moo Tai Mue Chinese fishermen's temple. | 48 |
| Figure 4.3 The only known Chinese fish-curing establishment in South Australia. | 49 |
| Figure 4.4 Known Chinese fish-curing establishments in Tasmania. | 49 |
| Figure 4.5 Two wood engravings of Chinese fishermen. | 50 |
| Figure 4.6 Chinese fishermen at Long Chinaman's Beach, Wilson's Promontory. | 51 |
| Figure 4.7 Map of South Gippsland waterways showing Fahey's Point. | 52 |
| Figure 4.8 Plan drawing of site at Fahey's Point. | 52 |
| Figure 4.9 Shaving Point, Metung. | 53 |
| Figure 4.10 Location of known and inferred Chinese fish-curing establishments in Victoria. | 54 |
| Figure 4.11 Known regions of Chinese fish-curing activity in Australia. | 55 |
| Figure 4.12 B Robert's engraving *Chinese fishing by moonlight* c. 1873. | 59 |
| Figure 4.13 The Australian schnapper (*Chrysophrys guttulatus*). | 60 |
| Figure 4.14 Common Australian squid (*Sepioteuthis australis*). | 61 |

| | |
|---|---|
| Figure 4.15 Australian abalone (*Haliotis naevosa*). | 62 |
| Figure 4.16 An 1886 wood engraving by D Syme, titled *Chinese fisherman's hut: holiday tour round Port Phillip*. | 63 |
| Figure 4.17 Two Chinese hawkers in Australia and picture by H Livingstone 1886, titled *Chinese carrying shoulder baskets, the Rocks Sydney*. | |
| Figure 4.18 Two varieties of the American sturgeon fish. | 69 |

## CHAPTER 5 EXCAVATION AT CHINAMAN'S POINT

| | |
|---|---|
| Figure 5.1 Survey map. | 72 |
| Figure 5.2 Map of the east coast of Victoria. | 73 |
| Figure 5.3 Map of the Port Albert region. | 74 |
| Figure 5.4 Vegetation cover on the Chainman's Point site area. | 74 |
| Figure 5.5 The rapidly eroding condition of Chinaman's Point. | 75 |
| Figure 5.6 Plan of the Chinaman's Point site. | 75 |
| Figure 5.7 Map detailing the gutter system, excavated trenches in the gutter system and site excavation areas 1, 2, 3 and 4. | 76 |
| Figure 5.8 Cross-section of gutter system showing soil matrix and artefact zone. | 77 |
| Figure 5.9 Schematic diagram showing stratigraphy and Harris matrix for area 1. | 79 |
| Figure 5.10 A common 19th-century European iron-hooped 164-litre wooden barrel cask. | 79 |
| Figure 5.11 Stratigraphy and Harris matrix for area 2. | 80 |
| Figure 5.12 Cross-section of excavated post remains. | 80 |
| Figure 5.13 Plan diagram and photograph of excavated area 3. | 81 |
| Figure 5.14 Low fish-drying racks. | 81 |
| Figure 5.15 Schematic diagram showing stratigraphy and Harris matrix for area 3. | 82 |
| Figure 5.16 Bottle glass displaying hinged-breakage patterns. | 83 |
| Figure 5.17 Schematic diagram showing stratigraphy and Harris matrix for area 4. | 84 |
| Figure 5.18 Site reconstruction. | 86 |

## CHAPTER 6 ARTEFACT ANALYSIS

| | |
|---|---|
| Figure 6.1 Site grid and one-by-one metre breakdown used for artefact province details. | 88 |
| Figure 6.2 One-page example of the Chinaman's Point artefact catalogue. | 89 |
| Figure 6.3 Square shaft, cut plate, rose head nails. | 92 |
| Figure 6.4 Location map for Moruya to Bermagui, South Coast, New South Wales. | 93 |
| Figure 6.5 Hand-moulded mud brick. | 94 |
| Figure 6.6 Common 19th-century cast iron spout. | 95 |
| Figure 6.7 Robust pouring spout. | 95 |
| Figure 6.8 Curved cast iron cooking pot fragments. | 96 |
| Figure 6.9 Stumpy iron pot feet. | 96 |
| Figure 6.10 Metacarpus. | 98 |
| Figure 6.11 Cattle long bone. | 99 |
| Figure 6.12 Cask hoop (with rivets). | 102 |
| Figure 6.13 A Chinese-style timber cask. | 102 |
| Figure 6.14 Chinese spouted jar and Chinese wide-mouthed shouldered jar. | 103 |
| Figure 6.15 Drawing of a wide-mouthed shouldered jar. | 104 |
| Figure 6.16 Chinese globular jar and straight-sided jar. | 104 |

Figure 6.17 Fragments of unglazed lid/shallow bowls. 105
Figure 6.18 The two most common types of Chinese ginger jar. 105
Figure 6.19 Chinese ginger jar rim fragments. 106
Figure 6.20 Base fragment of common European bung jar. 107
Figure 6.21 Suspected box hasp. 107
Figure 6.22 Map of Gippsland's main colonial goldfields. 111
Figure 6.23 Deliberate modification marks on bottle base fragments. 112
Figure 6.24 Reconstruction of oil lamps. 113
Figure 6.25 Inkwell. 114
Figure 6.26 Three common types of aqua-blue or light blue applied single-bottle collars or finishes. 115
Figure 6.27 Medicinal vials. 116
Figure 6.28 A Chinese liquor bottle. 118
Figure 6.29 Chinese spouted jar and fragments. 119
Figure 6.30 Three sizes of Chinese celadon bowl. 120
Figure 6.31 Manufacture marks in the foot ring of celadon bowls. 121
Figure 6.32 Chinese *tz'u* shards. 121
Figure 6.33 Chinese spoon sherds. 121
Figure 6.34 Two separate decorative forms of barrel-shaped Chinese teapot sherds. 122
Figure 6.35 European plate ceramics. 123
Figure 6.36 Corroded anchor remains. 124
Figure 6.37 Mass of oil-based paint. 125
Figure 6.38 Deliberately burred copper nails. 125
Figure 6.39 Selection of lead net sinkers. 126
Figure 6.40 Corroded balance scales. 127
Figure 6.41 Broken slate pencil and writing board. 128
Figure 6.42 Spent bullet cartridge. 129
Figure 6.43 Corroded and broken section of a bayonet or sword blade. 129
Figure 6.44 Corroded Chinese-style metal cleaver. 130
Figure 6.45 Glass and metal buttons. 131
Figure 6.46 Opium smoking pipe, bowl and other parts. 133
Figure 6.47 Common opium smoking bowl shapes, designs and artefacts. 134
Figure 6.48 Opium-bowl connectors. 135
Figure 6.49 Two typical opium-lamp types. 135
Figure 6.50 Typical opium-lamp shades and opium-lamp shade fragments. 136
Figure 6.51 Modified bottle bases for the purpose of opium smoking. 137
Figure 6.52 Potential method of modified bottle-base use. 138
Figure 6.53 Reinforcing strips and other opium-can pieces. 139
Figure 6.54 Opium cans modified into 'funs trays'. 139

## CHAPTER 7: OCCUPATION DATES AND SITE INTERPRETATION

Figure 7.1 Selection of common nail types from Australian sites. 143
Figure 7.2 Base. 145
Figure 7.3 Turn marks visible on a shard of amber-coloured bottle glass. 145

# CONVERSIONS

## MONEY

One pound (£1) equals 20 shillings (20s).
One shilling (1s) equals 12 pence (12d).
One guinea equals 21 shillings.
In 1966 when Australia adopted decimal currency, one pound equalled two dollars.

## DISTANCE

One mile equals 1.6 kilometres.
One yard equals 0.91 metres.
One foot equals 30.48 centimetres.
One inch equals 25.40 millimetres.

## WEIGHT

One pound (lb) equals 454 grams.
One stone equals 6.36 kilograms.
One ton equals 1.01 tonne.
One hundredweight (cwt) equals 112 lbs.

# ACKNOWLEDGEMENTS

Acknowledgements deservingly go to the team of volunteer archaeology students from La Trobe University who accompanied me into the field to assist with the excavation. This enthusiastic team consisted of: Lance Wackett, Fay Norton, Siobhan Paterson, Neil Dudley, Tyson White, Rupert Mann, Demi Paps, Julia Malloni, Chris Kaskadanis, Katie Kligerman, Jodi Turnbull, Kerrie Hamilton, Boheme Rawoteea, Katarina Audy, Lisa Amore, Kate Smith, Rhonda Naser, Aaron Chettle, Bethany Hassold, Vanessa Flynn, Anne-Louise Muir, Ashley Bannister and Janine Major.

To help catalogue the large number of artefacts recovered from the site, a number of volunteer archaeology students from La Trobe University assisted. Acknowledgements for students (who turned up more than twice to help in the laboratory) go to Jacqui Tumney, Tierney Rose, Paul Freestone, Eleanor Lancaster, Asher Ford, Allison Frost, Neil Dudley, Linda Pellin, Heather Bice, Jess Reid, Therese Hammond, Tyson White, Ruth Rawlings, Rupert Mann, Mel Taylor, Erica Downard, Sarah Hunter, Joseph Brooke, John Gilding, Demi Paps, Robyn Buckley, Julia Malloni, Chris Kaskadanis, Katie Kligerman andrew Prentice, Jodi Turnbull, Kerrie Hamilton, Matthew Barker, Rachel Johns, Boheme Rawoteea, Katarina Audy, Fay Norton, Sandy Norton, Jonathan Lushey, Aaron Chettle, Janine Major, Vanessa Flynn, Jessie Walker and Helene Athanasiadis.

Bill Black granted me unrestricted access to the Port Albert Maritime Museum archives, introduced me to numerous long-term Port Albert residents, was very helpful with local historical information and also allowed me to camp on his land during many field reconnaissance missions. I am likewise grateful to the many retired and working Victorian fishermen and their families who spent hours of their time relaying otherwise unobtainable personal knowledge and industry-related information.

Susan Lawrence, my primary supervisor, is worthy of great praise for so skilfully guiding me through the many stages of this work. My co-supervisor Tim Murray gave sound advice on completing such a project and also commented on draft chapters. Rudy Frank from La Trobe University was extremely helpful with all field, laboratory and technical work and beyond. Peter Davies reviewed this monograph and gave helpful advice. Barbara, John, Margaret and Adrian Bowen are my family and their encouragement always helped. My sister Margaret painstakingly read and gave comment on draft chapters. My two children Harriet and Hugh were with me throughout and gave pleasurable respite from the hours of study. Samm Julian Curtis put up with my study regime and with me during her teens. My partner Carol Julian commendably endured all and gave rock-solid support throughout.

During the course of this research countless people willingly and enthusiastically assisted me in innumerable ways. It is simply not possible to recognise (individually) all these people here and to relate their good deeds. These people know of my appreciation to them and I trust that this broad acknowledgment is adequate.

I thoroughly enjoyed this project and am very grateful for the support I received; the original thesis and this subsequent monograph could not have been completed without it. Thank you.

# CHAPTER 1

# INTRODUCTION

*While they are making a power of money they are doing good to the fishermen of the district.*
(*The Gippslander* 1865, November 10)

## BACKGROUND

During the 1860s, most Melbourne and Sydney-based European fishermen were earning approximately £50 per year (*Gippsland Times* 1879, May 21). In this same period, some Chinese people working in Australia's colonial fishing industry were earning that much every day (*Votes and Proceedings of the New South Wales Legislative Assembly* 1879–80, vol. 3: 1224). In fact, as will be shown, during the 1860s, one Chinese fish dealer in Australia (and there were many) earned over ten times more money from fish sales annually than both Melbourne and Sydney's fish markets combined. The Chinese involvement in Australia's colonial fishing industry was much bigger than previously realised.

The majority of Chinese people who migrated to Victoria in the colonial period were impoverished lower-class men who came predominantly from the province of Guangdong, Fujian and the island of Amoy (Willard 1923: 12; Cronin 1982: 17). In each of these Chinese regions, fishing has historically played a major economic role (Choi 1975: 5). With the influx of Chinese miners to Australia during the gold and later tin rush period (from 1851 to approximately the early 1880s), some must have possessed knowledge of fishing and so instead of mining, they fished, bought fish and supplied fresh and cured fish (a cultural preference) to their fellow Chinese countrymen. Their aim was to meet the enormous demand for fish, which they knew (perhaps from experience during the 1849 Californian gold rush) would be created by the Chinese gold miners. This satisfied a culturally important component in the Chinese diet.

Written histories, newspaper reports and official documents from the mid-1850s reveal the large scale on which Chinese fish curers were operating, not only in Victoria, but also in Tasmania, South Australia, New South Wales and the Northern Territory. It appears that wherever large numbers of Chinese people gathered in Australia, Chinese fish curers began operating from the nearest coastline (and probably, but yet to be investigated, from inland Australian waterways).

Transport of fresh fish to market during the 19th century was the biggest factor hampering development in Australia's fishing industry. Ice was unavailable before approximately 1880 (depending on region) and transport to market by boat or horse and cart was expensive, time consuming and unreliable, particularly in bad weather. It was common for whole catches of fish to be condemned because of putrefaction before a market was reached. In areas distant to market, European commercial fishing operations – which relied on the sale of fresh fish – were simply not a viable option.

Chinese cured fish lasts several months, effectively eliminating any problems of putrefaction before market. To supply the thousands of Chinese gold miners in colonial Australia (Census figures show over 38 000 in 1861) with cured fish, Chinese fish curers required huge quantities of fresh fish. To supplement their own catches, they would purchase almost all fish brought to them, so creating a new and reliable market outlet for fish. Chinese fish curers established themselves close to existing European fishing stations (to facilitate easy purchase of fish) and in remote, coastal regions (to exploit waters teeming with fish that had never before been commercially fished). This stimulated the movement of European fishermen into regions previously regarded as unsuitable for commercial fishing and led to a significant increase in European fishing activities.

With minimum cost to themselves, fishermen could row or sail their catch directly to a Chinese fish-curing camp and receive payment immediately. Through this new market, Chinese fish curers contributed to the growth and continuation of Australia's fishing industry and to Australia's economy more broadly. This project uses historical archaeological methods to investigate Chinese involvement in Australia's colonial fishing industry, specifically, in Victoria.

Victoria was the first Australian region in which Chinese curers were active. Chinese fish curers established themselves around the shores of Port Phillip Bay and in areas distant from Melbourne such as Corner Inlet, Port Albert and Metung (figure 1.1).

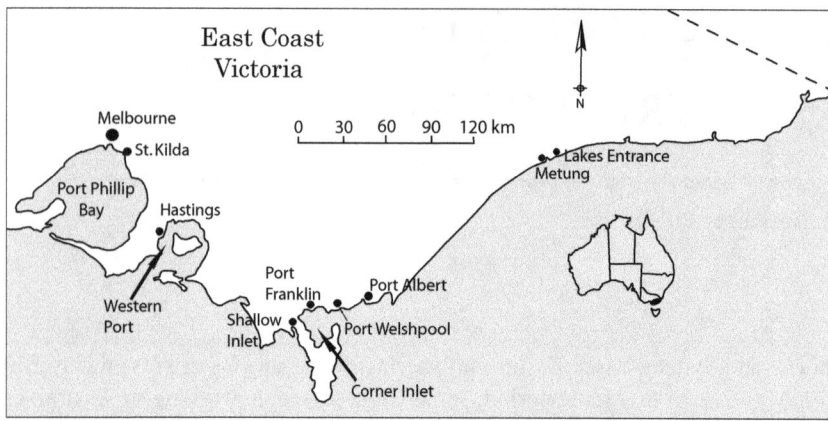

Figure 1.1 Map showing east coast of Victoria and areas of importance in this study.

Many coastal locations in Victoria have experienced environmental change, the development of new industries, land subdivisions, marina developments and tourism, all of which are detrimental to archaeological investigation. Nevertheless, physical evidence for a colonial period Chinese fish-curing establishment was located near the coastal town of Port Albert on a headland called Chinaman's Point (figure 1.2). Port Albert has a small population, has not been greatly affected by tourism or land development and maintains a long association with the fishing industry. As part of this project, the Chinaman's Point site was archaeologically excavated.

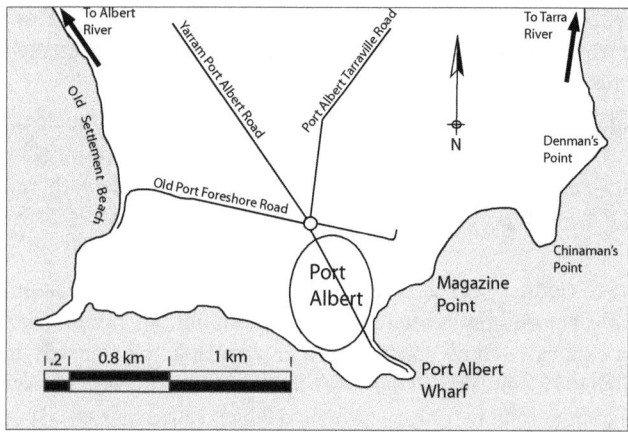

Figure 1.2 Map of Port Albert region showing Chinaman's Point, where evidence of a Chinese fish-curing site was located (see figure 1.1 for location reference to Port Albert).

A surface scatter of Chinese-style ceramic and glass artefacts, lead net sinkers, dilapidated boat parts and other colonial period remains revealed solid evidence of a Chinese fish-curing site. Together with this material record, the place name 'Chinaman's Point', historical newspaper reports and land title documents confirm that this site was occupied by Chinese people involved in Victoria's colonial fishing industry.

The site represents the only remains of Chinese fish-curing activities found during extensive field research in eastern Victoria. It also provides the only material evidence of Chinese fish-curing activities currently known in Australia and what is believed to be the only archaeologically excavated Chinese fish-curing site in the world (a Chinese shrimp curing site was excavated in California, see Schulz & Lortie 1985). Historical documentation and the site's material remains reveal a detailed picture of how these establishments worked, how the occupants lived, internal and external relationships associated with fish-curing activities and the links between such sites and the wider local, regional and global overseas Chinese communities during the Australian colonial period.

This previously unexplored aspect of overseas Chinese activity in colonial Australia has prompted questions regarding the nature of colonial encounters and the consideration of more theoretical aspects of overseas Chinese society. This project takes a step back from the standard broad colonial encounters framework of changing social organisation. Instead, it considers Chinese fish-curing establishments at the micro-community level, investigating the strategic actions of Chinese individuals and the social structures of small groups that combine to influence change. This has led to the identification of significant aspects of overseas Chinese communities in colonial Australia including their social and economic organisation and the impetus and consequences of cross-cultural (Chinese–European) interactions.

A common method of Chinese emigration was the 'credit–ticket' system (Campbell 1969: 2–3; Richardson 1982: 2). Under this scheme, wealthy Chinese individuals paid passage for an individual or group to emigrate. The passage recipients were then bound to work solely for their creditor until the passage was paid, or more commonly for a specified period. The importance of this debt bondage system to Chinese activities in colonial Australia has been underestimated in the relevant literature. The credit–ticket system, together with binding Chinese cultural kinship methods of social organisation was central to the functioning of Chinese fish-curing operations – and overseas Chinese activities generally – in colonial Australia. After the initial gold-rush period, the kinship system continued unchanged. However, the credit–ticket system for labour procurement became less important, prompting a significant change in the overseas Chinese system of social organisation.

This project conceptualises, investigates, tests and further develops theories regarding the internal dynamics of small groups of overseas Chinese people in colonial Australia. It allows a much broader perspective on the complexities of the overseas Chinese population and their social and economic support systems, social divisions (including aspects of power) and inter-group relationships. Three broad categories of overseas Chinese class rankings have been identified in colonial Australia: a wealthy minority of influential elite (the merchants), a broad range of middle-class workers/headman (the merchant aspirants) and the lower ranking workforce majority (the lower classes).

Evidence from the Chinese fish-curing establishment excavated for this project and investigation of historical documentation has brought to light previously unknown details of the colonial period overseas Chinese community. This project attempts to explain the Chinese involvement in Victoria's colonial fishing industry and to better understand how overseas Chinese communities in colonial Australia operated and coexisted with existing populations. The conceptual and theoretical base of this project revolves around social organisation and interaction themes.

It is hoped this research will hold intellectual interest across a range of disciplines as well as for the general public. Archaeology, although an integral component, will not rule this text. Instead, it will be used in conjunction with a wide range of sources not only to provide a good understanding of Chinese fish-curing activities in colonial Victoria, broader Chinese activities in colonial Australia and an appreciation of Chinese–European colonial encounters, but also to provide a more comprehensive and accurate picture of the Chinese experience in colonial Australia.

## AIMS AND QUESTIONS

To help focus this research, a number of aims and questions have been formulated. Little is currently known about Chinese fish curers in colonial Australia. Consequently, the initial aim is simply to obtain an understanding of Chinese involvement in Victoria's fishing industry, from commencement to the end of the Chinese fishing era. Traditional Chinese fishing and fish processing techniques encompass a number of traditional practices. It is interesting to examine whether these were put into operation unchanged in a new and unique Australian environment. Accordingly, the second aim is to obtain an indication of the methods the Chinese in Victoria used to procure and cure fish. With no detailed descriptions of colonial period Chinese fish-curing establishments (in Australia or elsewhere), the third aim is to examine the layout, structure, function and associated material culture of Victorian Chinese fish-curing sites. The final aim is to use historical documents and material remains to investigate aspects of social organisation and economic interactions of Chinese people in colonial Victoria.

The internal workings of Chinese society in colonial Australia and the implications for both Chinese and non-Chinese populations are a general theme of this research. A number of questions are posed to bring together different areas of existing research on the Chinese in colonial Australia. It is commonly acknowledged that the large number of Chinese people arriving in Australia during the gold-rush period were extremely well-organised and were typically under the supervision of a commanding 'headman'. However, information regarding the manner in which Chinese fish curing gangs established themselves and functioned in Australia's fishing industry is completely absent from the historical record. Therefore, a question asked in this research is: was Chinese fish curing an organised component of Chinese involvement in the gold rush, or does it represent a separate economic activity? This project also considers the mutually beneficial relationships between colonial period European and Chinese populations. The question is asked: how important was the Chinese involvement to the growth and survival of Victoria's fishing industry? Other questions, answerable more readily from the Chinaman's Point excavation than from historical documents, are: what activities actually took place at a

Chinese fish-curing site? What did these establishments look like? How many people did they take to operate? How did they function? Over what period did they work? What is the material culture like? Realising each of these aims and answering these questions will go a long way towards building a picture of the Chinese fish curers, their lives and life systems in colonial Australia.

## SIGNIFICANCE

The significance of this research is in its potential to reveal unknown aspects of Australia's colonial past and some of the influences of the Chinese in the development of Australia. Chinese involvement in Victoria's colonial fishing industry has not been researched previously. Similarly, there has been very little archaeological or historical research on this topic in Australia more broadly, or in Britain or Europe. In the United States, the topic has received slightly more attention. For example Nash (1973), Melendy (1984), Schulz & Lortie (1985), Roeder (1993), Kemp (1996), Lee (1999) and Berryman (1999) each discuss Chinese participation in California's early fishing industry. These studies, however, tend to focus on the shrimp and abalone fisheries rather than fish with scales and provide limited detail on Chinese fishing methods, fish curing procedures, social and economic themes or lifestyle patterns.

Due to the demanding nature of commercial fishing, people in this industry led and continue to lead very busy lives. Perhaps this explains why they rarely documented or relayed to others the events, activities and details of their industry. As a result, purely historical or anthropological methods are inadequate for exploring Chinese involvement in Victoria's early fishing industry. The presently untapped nature of this topic is demonstrated by the limited available literature.

Michael Lorimer (1984) completed a Masters thesis in history concerning aspects of historical fishing in New South Wales from 1850–1930. While Lorimer's research focuses predominantly on European fishing technology, he does discuss Chinese fishing in colonial New South Wales. Lorimer's work represents the only academic literature to acknowledge (in more than just a brief mention) Chinese involvement in Australia's early fishing industry. Possibly, this has been overshadowed by interests in prehistoric fisheries, or historical sealing and whaling activities. In *Digital Dissertations* on the database *Proquest*, 14 anthropological and eight historical (no archaeological) dissertations relating to aspects of historical fishing, mostly from Japan, Malaysia, the United States and Europe (the database does not include Australia) are registered from 1970 onwards. Searches of electronic and hard copy journals (from 1970 to present) have revealed no archaeological, anthropological or historical articles relating to Chinese involvement in Australia's early fishing industry. This current blind spot in our knowledge has limited the potential of Australian historical archaeology to "make its contribution to the history of Australia in the modern world" (Murray 2002:12).

Some documentary reference to Chinese fishing activities in Australia does exist, although it is generally limited to small sections in local history books. For example, Adams (1990) and Glowrey (2000) attribute small sections of their books to fishing in Victoria and acknowledge Chinese participation. Bennett (2002) gives an excellent history of Melbourne's fish markets and this work represents one of the better available references. Ellis & Lee (2002) provide a good although very general account of the early fishing industry in Gippsland, compiled from interviews with working and retired fishing people, some of who briefly discuss early Chinese involvement.

This monograph presents a better understanding of Chinese activities in colonial Australia, the physical and social mechanisms driving these activities and some of the processes that have helped shape present-day Australian society. In delving into unknown aspects of Australia's past, the project "answer[s] specific historical questions" (Lawrence 1998: 9), enables "the building of new theories" (Murray & Allen 1986: 90) and contributes to knowledge of colonial fishing and Chinese people in Australia. In a broader sense, this work is significant in further developing historical archaeology in Australia.

## DATA SOURCES

Research techniques in historical archaeology are interdisciplinary, permitting the use of a wide range of methods and resources in collating and evaluating information for this project. Primary and secondary historical texts, pictorial and oral histories and material remains are principal sources used to draw out information.

Many details of Chinese people in colonial Australia were never recorded in English. Accordingly, what cannot be located in primary documents or proven archaeologically is now either totally lost, within the realm of inferred theory or possibly exists in Chinese language sources. This is especially the case with Chinese people in Victoria's fishing industry, as the industry employed relatively few men, took up little physical space in very marginal areas and generally attracted little attention outside of the Chinese community. The fragmentary sources that do exist are extremely valuable to understanding this part of Australia's history.

The most significant of these sources are a number of Victorian and New South Wales royal commissions and parliamentary enquiries. During the mid to late colonial period, royal commissions were the standard means used by colonial authorities to investigate developments in industry and new technologies (Frost and Harvey 1997: 431). A small number of these investigations relate specifically to the colonial fishing industry and have proved to be the best source of written information on the Chinese and their fishing activities. Colonial authorities typically targeted people working in the fishing industry as their primary information source, subjecting them to lengthy interviews, which were fully transcribed. In these dialogues, fishermen (predominantly European) often refer to Chinese involvement in the fishing industry. This has resulted in the preservation of some excellent first hand information. Of particular interest is an 1880s royal commission into the state of and prospects for New South Wales fisheries, during which an English-speaking Chinese fish curer was interviewed. The fish curer provided invaluable insight into this Chinese activity in colonial Australia. Another inquiry of note is an 1892 Victorian Legislative Assembly report into Victoria's fishing industry, in which European fishermen in the Port Albert district answered questions relating directly to the Chinese fish curers at Port Albert.

Attempts by Christian missionaries to convert or simply communicate with the Chinese in colonial Australia have also resulted in the production of a small body of useful literature. In regard to the Chinese presence in colonial New Zealand, the best known source is the diaries of the Reverend Alexander Don (1894–1911). No missionary-derived New Zealand or Australian documents are known to exist specifically in relation to Chinese fishermen or fishing activities. There is, however, a four-part report on the situation of Victoria's Chinese residents by Reverend W. M. Young, completed in 1868 (reproduced in full by McLaren 1985). Young's work gives important insight into the activities of the Chinese population in Victoria during the colonial period.

Other good sources of information have come from columns in colonial newspapers, especially local papers such as the *Gippsland Guardian, Gippsland Standard, Gippsland Mercury* and *The Gippslander*. General accounts from European travellers such as Wheelwright (1861: 248), who befriended or simply observed Chinese people engaged in fishing activities, are also of interest. Newspapers and general historical and first-hand accounts have been used with great caution in this project, as they tend to be influenced to some degree by the writer's own beliefs and prejudices.

A good deal of historical text concerning Port Albert, Victoria and the overseas Chinese is in the State Library of Victoria and the Victorian Public Records Office. Some relevant documents are in the National Library of Australia. The local Port Albert Museum is a valuable source of more obscure literature such as unpublished local histories, personal diaries, early nautical charts and local official documentation.

A broad understanding of related topics such as the traditional cultural practices, material culture, architecture and technology of Chinese people in Australia, New Zealand, the United States and China was facilitated through literature including dissertations, archaeological reports, papers and official documents.

A wealth of material remains were archaeologically surveyed and excavated from the Chinese fish-curing establishment at Port Albert. These artefacts comprise a major source of information. In many instances, individual or groups of artefacts provide solid evidence of a particular aspect of overseas Chinese life in colonial Australia. The collection as a whole is used to develop theories concerning the site's importance – both during its period of operation and currently. The material remains play a key role in forming hypotheses regarding Chinese social organisation in Victoria. Through comparing the full spectrum of datable remains from the site with primary and other historical documentary sources (discussed in chapter 2 and chapter 6), the Chinese occupation period at Chinaman's Point is estimated to have been from the early 1860s to the early 1900s.

Oral evidence was gathered whenever possible. Due to the period under investigation, oral information can only be third generation oral history. In the coastal towns of Victoria, third generation fishing people were able to supply a good deal of information on the overseas Chinese fishermen – from preferred fish types to fish-curing processes – and upon further documentary and field investigations, it was surprising how often this information proved to be accurate.

## PREVIOUS RESEARCH

Historical and to a lesser extent historical archaeological texts relating to the overseas Chinese in Australia, New Zealand and the United States constitute a major source of information for this project. The term 'overseas' Chinese is a modern expression of identity, referring to people with a Chinese cultural background and homeland who live (temporarily or permanently) outside of China (Chun 1996: 122). American historical literature has also been of great comparative value. General historical and archaeological literature on the overseas Chinese in the United States is too vast and not central enough to this project to warrant a detailed review. It is suggested that Melendy (1984), Schuyler (1980), Wegars (1993), Lydon (1999: 179–202) and Schulz and Allen (2004) are good starting points for new researchers to the American texts in this field.

Chinese people have travelled and migrated to many world regions during the past few centuries. To understand properly this 'global culture' requires research at a local, site-specific level and in the wider regional, state, national and global context. This is not to argue for a single global interpretation of any consistencies, but to establish points of reference to assist in identifying similarities and differences (Schuyler 1970; Karskens 1999b: 121; Lydon 1999: 179–235; Lawrence 2003: 3). Documentary evidence has been gathered from as broad a geographical range as possible in order to facilitate a contribution to historical archaeology in the international setting.

In Australasia and regions north of Australia, Chinese people have settled in Thailand, Malaysia, Indonesia, the island of Borneo, the Philippines, Papua New Guinea, Australia, New Zealand and many of the small islands and atolls in between these. In these regions – and elsewhere – Chinese people have turned their hands to a surprising array of social and economic roles (Schulz and Allen 2004: 1). Researchers such as Jackson (1970) and Wu (1982), present patterns of similarities in the way Chinese people settled and entered the workforce in various Australasian locations. However, the knowledge of overseas Chinese activities throughout these regions is incomplete. Accordingly, until similarities in the actions of overseas Chinese people in Australasia have been established historically and archaeologically, it is not accurate to refer to the activities of one group in one area as being general to Australasia – except in referring to very broad circumstances. Throughout this text, comparisons of Chinese activities are drawn predominantly from China, the United States, Australia and New Zealand. The term 'Australasia' has not been eliminated, but is restricted in use to reference only broad patterns of activity.

The following is a selective overview of early historical and historical archaeological literature on the overseas Chinese in Australia. A full understanding of the literature becomes clear as topics are further explored and arguments developed.

## History

The history of Chinese people in Australia has certainly not been ignored and there is an abundance of literature regarding their colonial presence. It would be impractical to attempt an exhaustive discussion of these general works. Therefore, a selection of the writings significant to this study will be considered. Some regionally specific publications that list documentary sources of Chinese history in Australia are also available. Two relatively recent and good literature guides – particular to New South Wales – are Young and Barneveld (1997) and Bagnall (2000).

A variety of noteworthy literature is contained in Choi (1975), Yong (1977), Price (1978), Markus (1979), Cronin (1982), May (1984) and Andrews (1985). These are very good in the quantity and quality of information concerning historical matters such as Chinese emigration, lineage systems, movement patterns, logistics, family ties, merchants, hostilities and Australian government regulations and the Chinese reaction to them. Such early works will always be a valuable aid to investigators of Chinese history in Australia. However, as noted in more recent literature, these early investigations are limited in the scope and nature of information provided and often portray quite narrow and Eurocentric points of view (Lydon 1999: 199; Chan 2001: 3).

In a very significant review article, Cushman (1984) was the first to bring attention to a heavy academic focus on Australian attitudes towards incoming Chinese and the colonial government's legal reaction to their presence. This narrow historical focus tended to result in broad generalisations. The overseas Chinese were portrayed in a very submissive light, as victims of Australia's restrictive laws and whose principal actions were in response to these laws and the persistent racism they encountered. Cushman (1984: 101) argued that scholars should strive to "establish the characteristics of these societies as individual entities" and thereby obtain a deeper understanding of the Chinese experience in Australia. Encouraged by Cushman's ideas, Australian historians began looking more critically at the available literature and in doing so, greatly altered lines of investigation in this field.

Historical research on the overseas Chinese in Australia became much more productive and a myriad of Chinese-related themes came under examination. Topics such as lifestyle, customs, values, social and economic structures, Chinese literature sources and importantly, individual Chinese people, became popular.

Increasingly, historians began to understand that the overseas Chinese in Australia were not one homogenous group of Asian people, but were ethnically, socially and economically diverse. By the early 1990s, a greater depth of understanding had been achieved in regard to past Chinese communities, behaviour, lifestyle and the Chinese contribution to Australian society.

This fertile refocus of inquiry created a good deal of scholarly interest Chan (2001: 3) described it as "something of a revolution in scholarship". Research conferences, workshops, museum displays, government-funded projects, several doctoral and masters dissertations and a number of very good publications on Chinese activities in Australia appeared after 1990.

The key recent development to note is the major shift in research focus. Initial work in the early-to-mid 1980s gave a relatively narrow perspective, shedding limited light on Chinese activities in Australia. From approximately 1985 to 1995, the investigation of a much broader range of topics allowed a better understanding of the internal workings of colonial Australian Chinese communities, lifestyle complexities and culture. Methods now used by historians such as analysing current Chinese communities in China and elsewhere, exploiting Chinese literature sources (in Australia and China), critically examining colonial court proceedings, royal commissions and other primary records, understanding the subjective nature of documents and undertaking very focused topical research, have brought new substance and credibility to the gathering and interpreting of historical information.

At the same time, the dynamic methods employed by modern historians are not exclusively responsible for the current insight into past Chinese communities in Australia and do not always take into account broader research areas. After much scholarly debate, it is now generally accepted that to gain the fullest possible understanding of Australia's past, an interdisciplinary approach should be taken (Carment 1993: 139; Orser 1996: 10; Pedrotta and Romero 1998: 127). Professional historians are trained to identify, examining and decipher broad historical perspectives, while the expertise of historical archaeologists lies in very detailed analysis of particular sites. Ian Jack (1993: 131) puts it this way:

> historical archaeology is most useful to historical understanding in the context of a single, puzzling, insufficiently documented site and in the study of the most anonymous sectors of society.

This statement underlines the value of historical archaeological methods in considering overseas Chinese sites in Australia, especially in this study of a previously undocumented colonial Chinese fish-curing site and its occupants.

Historical archaeology and historical research in Australia have passed through many parallel stages of growth. The following is an account of the development of historical archaeological research on the overseas Chinese in Australia and New Zealand. It also explains why a social and economic theoretical base is appropriate for this project.

## Historical archaeology

Historical archaeological studies on Chinese activity in Australia have been under way for over 20 years. The earliest located work is an excavation in 1982 by Ian Jack of a Chinese garden site in north Queensland, followed by a 1983 study by Peter Bell on Chinese mining sites in the Pine Creek district of the Northern Territory (cited in Bell et al. 1993: 8; Jack et al. 1984).

For the next ten years, Jack's excavation remained the only academically based archaeological project on the Chinese in Australia (Bell 1996: 13). More common, however, were archaeological consultant projects generally resulting from heritage conservation requirements or as a component of environmental impact statements. The level of information obtained during this period was accordingly limited by the financial constraints of contract work. Nevertheless, contract work has resulted in many basic but useful research designs, simple site identifications, surface collections and inventory lists. Regrettably, archaeological contractors have largely ignored the task of setting up and testing new theoretical constructs or testing previously established archaeological hypotheses, so limiting the usefulness of their site explanatory analysis. Bell (1996: 13) then Lydon (1999: 191) and most recently Ritchie (2003: 4) have each commented on the superficial nature of this early archaeological work on the Chinese in Australia.

The initial inadequacies of historical archaeology in Australia were not limited to Chinese themes, but reflected Australian historical archaeology more broadly. Concern about the value of historical archaeology in Australia was first voiced in the early 1980s by Birmingham & Jeans (1983). Also in 1983, Connah expressed alarm about 'stamp-collecting' in Australian historical archaeology, arguing that practitioners were merely gathering information and not continuing with further analysis. The challenge was taken up and over the next ten years historical archaeology in Australia began moving out of a predominantly 'record and describe' methodology to a more 'problem oriented' form of research using 'open ended' questions (Connah 1998: 3; Mackay & Karskens 1999: 112). Practitioners developed new research methods, enabling archaeology to "actually contribute to our understanding of Australian history" (SM Jack 1993: 124; Connah 1998: 3). Many published works have considered how historical archaeology in Australia can continue to move forward as an intellectual discipline (for example Byrne 1996–97; Mackay 1996; Karskens 1996–97, 1999c; Lydon 1999).

New research methods in historical archaeology complement the investigative approaches that historians are now employing. Much of the relevant literature discusses the need for historians and historical archaeologists to work more closely (see for example SM Jack 1993: 128; Carment 1993: 141; I Jack 1995: 21). Historical archaeologists generally consult the work of historians to enable a greater depth of understanding in their archaeological projects. More importantly, however, historical archaeologists are now beginning to adopt the research techniques of historians together with their own increasingly dynamic systems.

However, besides notable exceptions such as Staniforth and Nash's (1998) porcelain/trade analysis, Lydon's (2001) work on social networks, Smith's (2006) analysis of social and economic aspects of overseas Chinese in southeast New South Wales and Muir's (2007) study of Chinese urban identity, most work so far on the archaeology of the overseas Chinese in Australia and New Zealand involves identifying and interpreting markers for ethnicity and acculturation. This is also an overwhelmingly dominant theme in the American archaeological literature on overseas Chinese communities (Voss 2005: 426; Orser 2004: 86).

Ethnicity, as defined archaeologically and as recognised in the material record, poses a problem-oriented research area for historical archaeologists (Chan 1995: 420). To counter inconsistencies in interpreting expressions of cultural traits, Lydon (1999) suggests that symbolic expressions of culture need to be placed in the context of individual or small group experiences, rather than considering cultural identities as a whole.

Whether smaller ethnic group identities – as opposed to Chinese generally – can be distinguished through archaeology remains a point of debate (see for example Smith 1998: 8–11; Lydon 1996: 21). The Chinese association with Victoria's fishing industry represents an ethic minority group (Chinese) working in an industry dominated by an ethnic majority (Europeans). While the excavated fish-curing site presents an opportunity to further investigate aspects of ethnicity, this has already attracted considerable attention in the archaeology of the overseas Chinese. The narrow focus on ethnicity has to some extent limited the type of research questions so far asked in archaeological studies. Although ethnicity remains important, it is now time for other major conceptual approaches – such as social and economic aspects and the results from cross-cultural encounters – to be explored.

A further factor in the "large gap in our knowledge of the Chinese experience in Australia" (Lydon 1999: 192) is that research undertaken so far revolves around a limited number of Chinese activities such as mining, market gardening and urban activities. Many areas of Chinese activity in colonial Australia – that may also be recognisable archaeologically – remain to be examined. For example, in 1868 Reverend W Young (who had lived in China for seven years and who had a good knowledge of the Chinese in Victoria) wrote a report on the Chinese population in Victoria that contains a section on common Chinese industries. Surprisingly, Chinese were identified as shopkeepers, market gardeners, barbers, butchers, carpenters, tailors, doctors, tobacco growers, sheepshearers, bakers, blacksmiths and fish mongers (cited in McLaren 1985: 31–58).

Consideration of new areas of Chinese social organisation and economic activities, such as fish curing, are essential to broadening current knowledge of Australian history and will enable new research to move beyond previous ethnicity-based studies. The Chinese fish curers in Victoria were financially motivated and were reliant on both Chinese and European networks for the supply, sale and distribution of their product. Accordingly, these Chinese fish curers are an important medium for studying the dynamic nature of intercultural encounters and social and economic activities in colonial Australia.

Examination of a small industry such as Chinese fish curing will also contribute to the ongoing need in modern archaeology for further theoretically based thematic investigations. To achieve meaningful results, an interdisciplinary approach that combines historical, archaeological, anthropological, sociological, economic, geographic and other methodologies as appropriate, will be used.

## Social archaeology

The social organisation and economic interactions of overseas Chinese people in colonial Australia provides the theoretical framework for this project. Social and economic themes concerning Chinese and non-Chinese interaction in colonial Australia have to date attracted little archaeological attention, although Lydon (1999) explores a broad range of contacts between Chinese and European people, including some economic activities.

Historians have shown somewhat more interest in social and economic themes, including McGowan (2005) in his paper on the economic contribution and social status of Chinese miners in colonial Australia and Frost (2002) in his discussion on Chinese entrepreneurship in early Australian farming enterprises. Other relevant literature usually only makes brief generalisations, for example on European perceptions that Chinese people were taking too much gold out of the country, were too greedy, too numerous, sold gold of dubious quality or were depriving Europeans of a livelihood (McGowan 2005: 19–20). Rarely do Australian, New Zealand or American-based studies examine situations where Europeans benefited through their interactions with Chinese populations (Voss 2005: 426).

Other researchers have focused on the complex relationships between ethnicity and culture or expressions of culture and cultural change (see for example Schuyler 1980; Ritchie 1986; Piper 1988; Wegars 1993; Upton 1996; Smith 1998; Jones 1999; Lydon 1999: 18; Stein 2005: 8–9). This current project examines the past social organisation and interactions of an incoming group to Australia (the Chinese) and the resultant cross-cultural (Chinese–European) encounters. Archaeological and historical information will be used to develop and test hypotheses regarding the Chinese system of social order in colonial Victoria, especially where social and economic factors are decisive.

## Methodological and theoretical background

American archaeologists would classify the line of study in this project as 'colonial encounters', which cover cultural contacts from prehistory (ancient state/empires) to the present (historic European nations) (see for example Trigg 2003; Gosden 2004; Dietler 2005; Gasco 2005; Rogers 2005; Schreiber 2005 and Stein 2005). In Australia, the much narrower study area of 'contact archaeology' is designed to examine Indigenous Australian–European interactions during the period of initial contact. Australian archaeologists have yet to place a classificatory name on endeavours to explore the myriad of complex cross-cultural relationships that occurred after initial Aboriginal–European contact. This is a period when people of many nationalities migrated to Australia, especially during Australia's gold rush years of 1850 to 1900.

Tens of thousands of Chinese people arrived in Australia during the 1850s and lived in company with the existing European and Aboriginal population. This differs from the usual perception of a colonial encounter (or colonialism), as involving a group of people (usually European) occupying and ultimately dominating a less technologically developed population. Lightfoot (2005: 210) argues the futility of prolonging such a narrow perspective of colonial contact in archaeology, asserting "we do great injustice to the study of cross-cultural variation by attempting to pigeonhole our case studies into a few discrete colonial types". There are many promising areas in this realm of colonial period studies such as class divisions, cross-cultural contact, demography, consumerism, social and technological development, acculturation, diaspora and economics. This is especially the case with a mid-industrial, mixed nationality society such as Australia during the gold-rush period.

Australian archaeologists have often incorporated colonial encounter research (generally of the mid-colonial period) into social archaeology, a component of historical archaeology. However, archaeological methodological practices for studying colonies, their establishment, how they were maintained, expanded or abandoned and associated social activities (especially as a cross-cultural phenomenon) are rather hazy and lack any solid theoretical or comparative framework (Stein 2005: 4; Rogers 2005: 353). This is particularly the case in Australia and to some extent in America. The social processes of Chinese or European groups are too complex to contemplate in a single model or even in one project. Two current archaeological methods for examining colonial contacts – world-systems theory (see Wallerstein 1974; Kardulias 1999) and postcolonial theories (see Said 1978; Gosden 2004) – will be combined to identify and investigate social and economic aspects of the 1850 to 1900 Chinese–European contact period in Australia.

## World-systems and postcolonial theories

The two methods are complementary. World-systems examines broad, long-term global trends in colonialism. Its original purpose was to help explain why separate societies living in similar environments developed differently over the same period and in turn to identify what processes contributed to the rise of power and uneven divisions of wealth, labour and resources (Gasco 2005: 71). These research methods enable major stages and broad trends in societal advancement to be identified (such as the rise of Europe during the last 500 years) thus opening avenues for researchers to conduct valuable comparative work with other world regions. World-systems theory therefore allows a better understanding of long term, global patterns in human history (Gosden 2004: 12). In contrast, postcolonial theory is concerned with events of colonisation and resultant cross-cultural phenomena. It seeks to explain social change by focusing on local agents, particularly the culture, actions and reactions of colonising and colonised societies (Stein 2005: 17). However, due to the complexities of human interactions, neither method is entirely satisfactory from an archaeological point of view. This has prompted recent developments in the study of colonial encounters (Gosden 2004; Stein 2005).

While world-system theories are useful in explaining the long-term effects that Europen colonisation has had on colonised populations and how modern capitalist civilisations have developed (Gasco 2005: 71), the model is moulded through the narrow experience of European expansion and therefore takes a Eurocentric stance. The world-systems model neglects the roles of the colonised people and so limits consideration of the labyrinth of colonial interactions (Dietler 2005: 58). In particular, factors such as unique cultural group reactions, the roles of existing local cultural systems, consequences of changing identity and consideration of material objects tend to be ignored and colonised people are seen as passive victims of global expansion (Nash 1981; Wolf 1982; Gosden 2004: 7: Gasco 2005: 71; Rogers 2005: 335).

Postcolonial theory, although opposite in approach to world-systems theory, also lacks any detailed consideration of the value of material remains (Gosden 2004: 7). In focusing on the actions (or level of resistance to colonisers) of individuals and small groups within a society, postcolonialists view social actions and culture as the most important agents in shaping a colonised society. Thomas (1994: 9) comments that postcolonial ideas are about local histories, not global theory. This suggests that postcoloial theory could be useful in examining the Chinese in colonial Australia.

Gosden (2004) and Stein (2005) share the view that a general theoretical understanding of colonisation is best obtained through a comparative approach. Gosden's approach is based on postcolonial thought, but is enhanced by an understanding of the material record of interactions. He also includes archaeologically-identified local variations and inconsistencies within a comparative framework. This facilitates the identification of broad consistencies in colonisation processes, as well as more subtle variations brought about by differing local situations (Gosden 2004: 24).

Establishing the social and economic characteristics (or survival strategies) of past societies is of key interest to anthropologists, historians, archaeologists and the wider-ranging social sciences. Although economic activities are often an exclusive focus of archaeological research (not incorporated into larger themes), economic activities are considered in this project as just one component of social archaeological research.

## The theory

In exploring and interpreting the often ambiguous history of social interactions, the range of research avenues available to historical archaeologists gives the discipline considerable advantages compared to other social sciences. Long-distance movement of people, behaviours and material culture can be identified through artefacts or expressions of culture that do not belong to the region or society under examination (Adams 1974: 240; Gilchrist 2005: 331). In regard to the Chinese fish curers of Port Albert, domestic and industrial artefacts, ground features, structural evidence, oral evidence, historical documentation and theoretical deduction suggest the Chinese were involved in complex local, regional and global interactions. This evidence will be used to identify social aspects of Chinese people in Port Albert and the wider Victorian region and to theorise on the types of social interactions that were occurring during Australia's colonial period.

Archaeological theory is appropriately one of the most heavily discussed and critiqued areas of the discipline. Two theoretical approaches – processual and post-processual – have been instrumental in the development of social archaeology. In parallel with the development of historical archaeology was the founding of 'processual' or appropriately termed 'New Archaeology' in the 1960s. This line of research emphasises a functionalist explanation of past social processes and cultural evolution and focuses on the wider processes in human interactions (as opposed to the actions of small groups or individuals). New Archaeologists such as Binford (1962; 1965; 1972) place importance on the use of precise and repeatable methodologies. Material and empirical archaeological remains and comparative analysis are used to identify relationships within and between cultural systems. The processual movement facilitated major scientific advances in archaeological thinking and also acted as a springboard for progress in social reconstruction and historical archaeology generally (Orser 2002: 468).

The methodologies of processsual archaeology fuelled archaeological debate and facilitated the development of post-processual archaeological theory. While post-processual theory also uses material and ephemeral remains to suggest meaning (such as cultural identity, social practices and events), it is primarily concerned with using material remains to provide a dynamic historical and archaeological interpretation of small groups and individuals (Bahn 1992: 406). With a strong focus on social topics such as identity and economic interaction, post-processual theories provide a local/regional picture of social factors in past human societies (Orser and Fagan 1995: 276).

Both processual and post-processual movements remain relevant to modern archaeology. Cultural and social systems are complex, highly changeable and often difficult to decipher through one set of theoretical concepts. To reconstruct the social interactions of a small minority group of individuals – the Port Albert fish curers – and postulate on the social organisation of a much larger group – the Chinese in Victoria and in Australia more broadly – both processual and post-processual archaeological theories will be combined with the current broad, multi-disciplinary methods of historical archaeology.

The Chinese fish curers of Port Albert had many mutually beneficial levels of social interaction with European and Chinese people. They purchased large quantities of fresh fish from Europeans and made business arrangements to have their product of dried fish transported to Melbourne, interstate and international destinations. The fish curers also would have purchased some of their domestic and industrial supplies from within the local and regional area. Such contact was, strictly speaking, strategic action grounded in occupational necessity. Through these functional interactions the fish curers would have known – probably quite well – all of the fishermen in the district, the harbour masters, pilots, shipping agents and the general store owners. These interactions would have contributed to their everyday social integration.

This reasoning may be taken further. Through their business dealings, the fish curers at Port Albert may have come to enjoy friendly social relations with local European people. Such situations have been documented elsewhere in Australia. For example in 1898, Tam Sie, a very successful Chinese farmer in Queensland, earned great respect from the non-Chinese community and from colonial authorities for his contribution to the development of regional farming (Shen 2001: 50). Also, Frost (2002: 127) describes two colonial instances in Victoria's north-eastern region where farming partnerships between Chinese and European people resulted in annual harvests of high quality tobacco and hops. Interestingly, Frost notes that in each instance the Chinese received a higher percentage of the annual net profits than their European partners. Lydon (1999: 57–58) argues that through Chinese industries such as vegetable selling in Sydney's Rocks area, Chinese and European people developed friendly associations, often exchanging gifts.

Certainly these brief examples represent a different relationship to the ones generally documented between the European and Chinese populations. The Australian gold-rush period provides a useful opportunity for historians and archaeologists to explore the unique character of contact between various cultures in a colonial setting. This project forwards the theory that, during Australia's colonial gold-rush period, Chinese people in Victoria maintained a much greater complexity of social networks – between themselves and with European people – than previously known. The intricacies of these social situations and the cultural mechanisms sustaining them can be explored through the use of a theoretical archaeological framework.

## Class

Social stratification, as defined by Orser and Fagan (1995: 200) refers to a society comprising of two or more differently ranked social, economic or other groups of people. Theories will be developed concerning three broad, often competing, categories of capitalist Chinese society: a minority economic and social elite, a growing number of middle-class merchants and the lower ranking workforce majority. Overseas Chinese society in Australia and in Australasia more broadly, displayed class rankings through occupation and wealth. Importantly, an indication of class can often be discerned through material remains at archaeological sites. Several researchers (such as Horsely 1879; Oddie 1961; Jones 1990; and Gungwu 1992) have identified select aspects of overseas Chinese elite, middle merchants and the working class during colonial times.

An examination of these social classes will enable a more detailed understanding of Chinese social organisation and economic activities in colonial Australia. Arguments will be forwarded regarding power relations, scale, function and responsibilities of social units in overseas Chinese communities. Theories are developed on how and why Chinese people were able to obtain and sustain niche positions in commercial ventures, how the Chinese fared economically, coordinated labour, organised commodity transport and utilised family and kinship connections and the nature of Chinese interactions with each other and with European people.

Stein (2005: 7) notes rewarding results obtained by recent American research of colonial encounters which acknowledged the postcolonial notion that

> social structure and the strategic actions of individuals or small groups plays a major role in
> reproducing and changing social organisation of complex societies.

While the validity of this approach is demonstrated in his recent publication (Stein 2005) and other studies (such as Stein 2002; Lightfoot et al. 1998; Wells 1998), the situation of overseas Chinese in colonial Australia demands a step back from the broader issue of changing social organisation. Researchers of Australian colonial social themes in a Chinese–European cross-cultural context first need to identify the social structures and strategic actions of Chinese individuals and small groups that have combined to create change. Only then can broader social interaction between colonial period Chinese and Europeans be considered in comparative studies of other complex societies.

The approach taken in this project complements and actively takes forward the widely accepted concept that Australian historical archaeology must seek "an inside view denied us by standard historical accounts" to allow us to "grasp the full nature of our colonial past" (Mackay & Karskens 1999: 111). This project further explores early migrant activities and how the Chinese lived, utilised resources and became integrated into Australian colonial society.

## MONOGRAPH OUTLINE

The following section provides a summary of the remaining chapters in this study.

Chapter 2 concerns the history of commercial fishing in Australia. It begins with a discussion on Australian Aboriginal fishing practices before European settlement, their adaptation of technology after European contact, the entry of Aboriginal people into commercial fishing activities and the resultant impact on Indigenous culture. This history is important as it shows the colonial European fishing industry was open to anyone with the knowledge to catch fish. A background to Britain's early fishing industry then acts as an introduction to the colonial fishing industry in Australia, with a focus on Victoria and more narrowly coastal Gippsland. This leads to discussion on the fishing methods used in Australia and the importance of the fishing industry to Victoria, east Victoria and the town of Port Albert. Lastly, general information is provided on coastal south Gippsland, including its Indigenous population, European discovery and history of settlement and a brief introduction to overseas Chinese activity in this region.

Chapter 3 commences with an examination of China's 19th-century fishing industry. It discusses the importance of fish in the Chinese diet, aspects of the organisation of commercial fishing activities in Kwangtung Province and the various methods used to catch fish in this region. This is followed by discussion on relevant aspects of 19th-century Chinese culture, traditional Chinese social structure and elements of Chinese social organisation in China and other world regions. The ways in which Chinese social organisation and labour utilisation functioned in colonial Victoria and Australia generally is then examined. The chapter concludes that the original systems of social organisation of overseas Chinese people in colonial Australia underwent considerable transformation, taking on aspects of the host culture.

Chapter 4 presents a thorough examination of the documentary evidence concerning Australia's colonial Chinese fish curers and their involvement in commercial fishing activities. To make clear the interpretive process, the amount of primary versus circumstantial evidence is discussed explicitly. Evidence of overseas Chinese fish-curing activities in New South Wales, the Northern Territory, South Australia and Tasmania is explored, before a more detailed examination of the situation in Victoria. This reveals a far greater level of Chinese participation in Australia's colonial fishing industry than previously realised and sheds light on many answers to the questions asked in this project.

Chapter 5 discusses the field methodology and archaeological results of site survey and excavation at the Chinaman's Point site. Initial survey work enabled a detailed plan of site boundaries and established the main physical and cultural features of the site. A thorough surface collection and excavation of four site areas yielded a good representative sample of the material equipment required to maintain a colonial period Chinese fish-curing site. A detailed account of each excavated area is given along with the excavation results. The recovered material remains assist in evaluating the contribution the Chinese fish curers made to Victoria's colonial fishing industry.

Chapter 6 describes, analyses and interprets the artefacts recovered from Chinaman's Point. This reveals the methods Chinese fish curers used to sustain a livelihood, the domestic and industrial equipment required and the living conditions, consumption patterns and recreational activities at the site. Distinct artefact types and distribution densities reveal different site activity areas and assist comparative analysis with other overseas Chinese sites in Australia and elsewhere. In general, the artefacts are seen as evidence that the site was one working component of a much larger, largely homogeneous overseas Chinese community in colonial Australia.

Chapter 7 is comprised of two main sections: consideration of the site occupation period and an interpretation of the site. The first section examines the full spectrum of datable material remains from the site and compares these with primary and other historical documentary sources. The aim is to date, as accurately as possible, the occupation period at Chinaman's Point. The chapter's second half discusses the more significant information gained from the artefact analysis. This is followed by an examination of the relationship between the Chinaman's Point fish-curing establishment and the broader overseas Chinese community. The evidence for site ownership, identity of the labouring workforce and the possible number of site occupants are discussed.

The activities performed on site are then summarised, followed by an examination of fish-curing methods and the equipment this required.

The final chapter brings together the evidence from all avenues of inquiry, including in-text discussions used in this project. The conclusions confirm the significant contribution this project makes to the historical understanding of the Chinese experience in colonial Australia, especially regarding Chinese involvement in Victoria's fishing industry.

# CHAPTER 2

# HISTORY OF COMMERCIAL FISHING IN AUSTRALIA

For thousands of years, colonising groups have utilised marine environments to provide subsistence resources. Indigenous groups were the first people to exploit Australia's fish resources. Aboriginal people harvested food from their marine surroundings and shared the rewards within their own tribal groups. After European colonisation, new concepts of marine exploitation were introduced into Australia. Non-Aboriginal people harvested Australian waters in much greater quantities than had previously occurred, bartering or selling their catch within their own settlements for personal gain. Indigenous Australians soon adapted their own more prudent fishing methods to begin catching surplus fish, which they bartered or sold to European people.

The ease with which Aboriginal Australians entered the European fishing industry is significant, as it shows that any person with the knowledge to fish could participate through simply catching and selling fish. To the buyer, it was irrelevant who caught the fish – the product remained the same. The intensity of any exploitation is proportionate to demand and as Australia's population increased, so did the demand for ocean resources.

As Victoria's gold rush in the 1850s gained momentum, the demand for fish grew to voracious levels. This created an opportunity for people of various nationalities – including Chinese people – to enter Victoria's commercial fishing industry. During this period, Victoria's south Gippsland region emerged as an important supplier of fish. A history of south Gippsland focuses on the then-remote town of Port Albert, which was central to the establishment and growth of Gippsland commerce. In time, Port Albert developed a strong local fishing industry including – as a key part of the industry – a Chinese fish-curing establishment.

A broad history of fishing in Britain and Australia provides a context for discussion of early Chinese involvement in Victoria's fishing industry. It also demonstrates the enterprising atmosphere of the times. People could work hard and prosper in fishing. The Chinese fish curers at Port Albert became an integral part of the area's commercial fishing industry – with local, regional and international implications. The historical background presented in this chapter includes aspects of a much broader history of fishing. Further detail can be found through the references cited in this chapter.

In Australia's colonial period, wives occasionally paired with their husbands to fish commercially, but an individual woman or a female crew have not been historically identified. As this project is concerned only with the colonial period when men were the predominant fishing people, the term 'fisherman' seems most appropriate – except when referring to Aboriginal fishing practices.

## AUSTRALIAN ABORIGINAL FISHING

### Aboriginal fishing technology

Many archaeological excavations of prehistoric sites throughout the world reveal evidence of fish consumption (Balme 1983; Bowdler 1993). Methods used to catch these fish are generally difficult to discern and are rarely researched in detail (Colley 1983: 162).

Archaeological investigations in Australia often show evidence that Aboriginal people exploited fish (Dargin 1976; Walters 1987; Haysom 1999). Middens containing considerable quantities of shell and fish remains – dating to 36 000 BP – reveal that Aboriginal people consumed and used fish long before European settlement (Bowler et al. 1970; Bowler 1976: 57; Bowdler 1993: 61; Johnston 1993: 197).

Balme (1983) conducted a study of fresh water-fish remains from Aboriginal sites in western New South Wales, noting not only a dominance of the species golden perch, but also that remains were restricted to a particular size perch. Coleman (1980) noted the same occurrence with the marine fish flathead and bream from midden analysis in eastern New South Wales. Both researchers concluded the select species and size restrictions represent the use of nets – either gill or drum nets – to catch fish.

In 1790, Reverend J. G. Wood described Australian Aboriginal people using a net in a similar manner to that of a seine net (circling a net around a school of fish) (Roughley 1953: 324). Dargin (1976: 25) describes drag nets, 12 ft (4 m) long and 4 ft (1.2 m) deep, made of thin, strong twine, constructed from the inner bark of a kurrajong tree. He suggests that Aboriginal men swam or waded through water with a net stretched between them to catch fish.

The prehistoric remains of several hundred stone walls designed as fish traps are evident in the Darling River and fishhooks made of shell and bone have been recovered from middens on the northeast coast of New South Wales (Bowdler 1976: 253; Dargin 1976: 32). Wicker traps resembling a basket or round cage have been recorded ethnographically, along with the Aboriginal catching of fish by hand, poisoning, diving, brush fencing and most commonly spearing (Bowdler 1976: 249; Colley 1987: 16).

The evidence presented above is adequate to demonstrate that before European settlement and at the time of first contact, Aboriginal people used fish as a food source and their fishing techniques incorporated a range of nets, hook, line and various types of traps.

## Adoption and adaptation

A strong feature of Aboriginal culture is the sharing of subsistence resources (Flood 1980: 100). Fishing was conducted on a subsistence exchange basis, where the acquisition of fish and its distribution occurred in accordance with strict obligations to share. While male and female group members participated in the catching of fish (depending on region and fishing technique), their individual activity was for the benefit of the general society (Bowdler 1976: 249–51). Accordingly, in Aboriginal society there was no 'sale' or commercialisation of fish. On occasion, fish may have been used for exchange with neighbouring groups. However, this did not reflect a desire for gains that would reward the individual alone (Patel 1989: 54). Aboriginal fishing in prehistoric Australia was not a capitalistic venture (Haysom 1999: 25).

It is interesting from the point of view of imitation and transfer of cultural objects and ideas between two communities to examine how Aboriginal society adapted – and how fishing practices made the transition – to a set of new, European, technologies and ideas.

Prehistoric Aboriginal and colonial-period European cultures both used fishing hooks. European hooks were made from metal, whilst Aboriginal hooks were constructed from a variety of materials, predominantly shell and bone (Walters 1987: 22). Both were successful in catching fish, although shell hooks took considerable time to manufacture whilst metal ones were mass produced and arrived in Australia in bulk (Roughley 1953: 324; Pearson 1983: 49). During the colonial period, Aboriginal people began using metal fishhooks and other utensils introduced by Europeans. Time previously spent making a shell hook could now be put towards other pursuits, prompting a shift in social structure and providing the means for a cultural change in the patterns of coastal Aboriginal people (Das and Kolack 1989: 2; Bimber 1994: 84). Bowdler (1976: 251–54) discusses this situation, arguing that after the introduction of metal fishhooks, fishing with hook and line altered traditional Aboriginal fishing patterns from a mixed sex activity (depending on region) to a predominantly male task.

The time saved making traditional fishhooks could potentially be put towards catching more fish, which would create a surplus that could be sold for money or exchanged for more time-saving equipment. In accordance with Hughes' (1994: 102) concept of 'technological momentum', it is speculated that the introduction of the metal fish-hook contributed to the transition of Aboriginal society from an egalitarian to a hierarchical social order. This situation can be seen on the New South Wales coast at Jervis Bay, where the Jerringah Aboriginal community changed their ancestral fishing traditions to fit a European monetary economy (Egloff 1993: 8). By the 1860s, six Jervis Bay Aboriginal fishing families were considered professional fishers and were catching enough fish to sell at the fish markets in Sydney (Nugent 1980: 8). In 1876, two of these fishermen, Sadler and Timbery, asked the Australian Government for a fishing boat. Four years later they received it:

> The Boat is a splendid one, fitted with every appliance and a suitable fishing net completes the outfit ... their business in selling fish will bring the blacks frequently into town. (*The Wollongong Argus* 1883, April, in Organ 1990: 342)

This demonstrates the ease with which many Aboriginal people entered commercial fishing. All that was required was the knowledge to fish and a small amount of fishing equipment. Similarly, the European population could enter into commercial fishing simply with the knowledge to fish and the ability to acquire a small rowboat and net. Fish were an abundant natural resource during the colonial period and cost very little to catch. Despite its early reputation as a low paid, difficult and dangerous occupation, a small percentage of people including Aboriginal, European and Chinese found it an excellent industry in which to establish themselves with few start-up costs.

# THE EUROPEAN FISHING INDUSTRY

## Fishing methods

From the fifth century AD there are records of ancient Greeks, Romans and Phoenicians using gill nets (figure 2.1) to catch fish (Roughley 1953: 200). Drag nets towed behind a sail boat – an earlier form of the modern trawl – were in use by 952 AD in the English Channel (figure 2.2) (Daumas 1969: 479). Seine netting (figure 2.3) and drift netting (figure 2.4) also have a long history – over nine hundred years – of recorded use in British waters (Roughley 1953: 201). Rich concentrations of plankton and other marine biomass are present along the west coast of Scotland and in the English Channel (Banbury 1975: 172). This source of nutrients has ensured a liberal supply of fish, which in part accounts for the early development of advanced British river and ocean-going fishing vessels (Robinson 1987: 2). When British people colonised Australia, they naturally placed the same importance on catching fish – and used the same fishing methods – as they had done in Britain. Modern fishing techniques in Australia were in large part transferred from Europe during the first few years of colonisation.

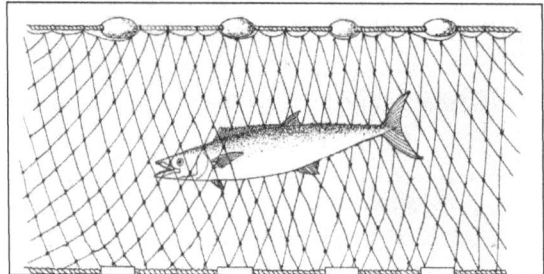

Figure 2.1 Gill-net designs have changed little over the centuries.

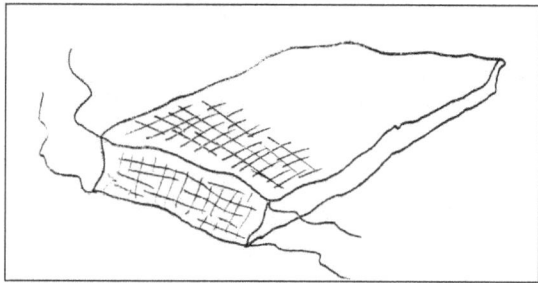

Figure 2.2 An early form of European drag net.

Fishing methods in Britain, from at least the fifth century AD, consisted of nets, line with hooks and traps. The remains of tidal salmon traps in Britain indicate that trapping was also a common means of catching fish (Jenkins 1974: 40). Garratt (1989: 2) discusses wicker pot traps of various sizes that were used for centuries to catch fish in Britain.

Historical evidence from the 12th century AD indicates that the town of Birdpot on the south coast of England was a major manufacturer of flax and hemp used for fishing nets and line (Jenkins 1974: 67). It is difficult to establish when the widespread use of metal fish hooks by Europeans began. Metal fish-hooks have been in use from the Bronze Age, as demonstrated by Coles & Coles' (1989) discussion of bronze hooks from an excavation at Cortaillod-Est in Switzerland (cited in Fallowfield 2001: 12). Initially, steel was probably prohibitively expensive and iron insufficiently ductile for fish hook production (Diderot 1959: 184; von Brandt 1972: 41). However, by 1607 iron fish hooks were in use, as evidenced by their archaeological recovery from an early colonial settlement at Jamestown, in Virginia, US (Schmidt 2006: 84). During the mid 1700s, good quality pins were manufactured from brass in Britain (Berg 1994: 268) and this material was probably also used to make fish-hooks. A note from British explorer and scientist Joseph Banks to the British Government indicates metal fish hooks were in common use by 1779. The note suggests that during sea voyages, metal fish hooks made an excellent bartering tool for acquiring fresh supplies from island inhabitants (Martin 1978: 23).

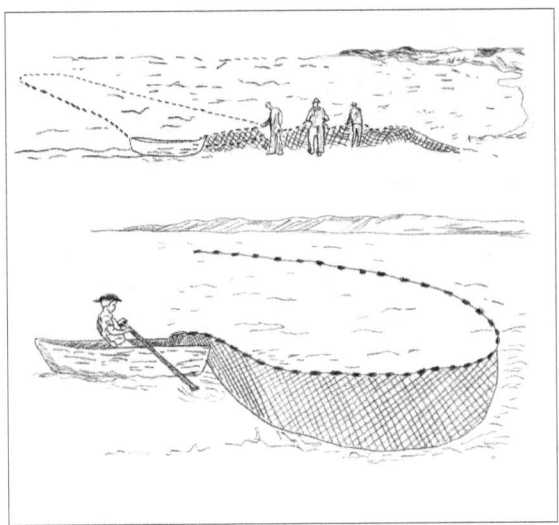

Figure 2.3 Two methods of seine netting: hauling a net into a shore line (top), also known as beach hauling, and hauling a net into a boat (bottom).

Figure 2.4 A drift net being set.

## Importance

The importance of commercial fishing in Britain's social and economical history is demonstrated by the continuous development in techniques and the detailed laws concerning fishing that have been in place since the 12th century AD (Daumas 1969: 482).

For centuries fish has been a vitally important source of protein for the people of Britain. As early as the 12th century AD, British fishing boats were sailing 40 miles offshore to fish in the deep waters of the North Sea (Banbury 1975: 173). Fresh inland waterways, tidal rivers, close to shore seas and distant deep oceans were all targeted by British fisheries and fish was a much more common meal than today (Dickinson 1987: 1; Palmer and Neaverson 1994: 29). Fresh or dried and salted fish has been the staple of marching armies, explorers, slaves, the incarcerated and the poor. More recently, with Britain's early 1800s population explosion, the famous British fish 'n' chip shops often provided a cheap, hot, nutritious meal for families without the regular means to cook (Goddard and Spalding 1987: 11). Whole British regions such as Plymouth, Scarborough and Whitby have, at various periods, been dependant on the catching and trading of fish (Dickinson 1987: 7).

It could be expected that when British people arrived in Australia, they brought with them their fishing traditions and technology. Interestingly, European and pre-contact Aboriginal fishing methods are remarkably similar, with three dominant techniques persisting to the present – nets, hook and line and traps.

## Australia

The first commercial exploiters of marine resources in Australia appear to be the Indonesian trepang fishermen from Makassar. Trepang (a type of sea slug also called *bêche-de-mer*) were harvested by hand in shallow coastal waters along Australia's northern coast, then cured through a process of boiling and sun-drying (Cooke 1987: 7). In MacKnight's (1976) detailed history of the Makassan trepangers, he suggests they began annual trepang harvesting voyages to the Northern Territory in about 1700 AD (MacKnight 1976: 1). During the trepang season – from late December to mid-April – between 200 and 350 tons (dry weight) of this highly valuable marine resource would be processed and traded as a delicacy throughout the Indonesian archipelago and into mainland China (MacKnight 1976: 15; Campbell 2002: 72).

In 1770, when Captain James Cook first voyaged to Australia on the *Endeavour*, part of his exploration instructions were to test waters for fish resources (Dunn 1991: 36). For this task he carried on board a number of fishhooks, lines, drag nets and seine nets (Dunn 1991: 59). Similarly, cargo manuscripts for the First Fleet to Australia reveal that fishing lines, hooks, nets, needles and twine were deemed necessary for the establishment of a new colony (Martin 1978: 24). It was inevitable that European people would transfer their ideas, values and technology to their new surroundings. Some of this technology was transported in the physical form, but most of it, as McNeil (1988: 75) has argued, would have been cultural, technological and social knowledge.

John Palmer, a purser on board the *Sirius* in 1789 (he later became the commissary in charge of food distribution), documented that 1000 lb of fish was eaten weekly in the new settlement. Fish was an easily obtainable and cheap source of food for the British colonists. The authorities encouraged convicts to eat fish by issuing 6 lb of fish as a substitute for one pound of salt pork (Ollif and Crosthwaite 1977: 60). Karskens (1997: 207) discusses the keen eye that convicts had for making a profit. As free settlers began arriving in Australia, convicts with knowledge of how to fish probably sold or bartered their catch within the settlement and many would have continued fishing upon their emancipation. These actions would place fishing among the first market-based, economic activities in Australia.

Unlike Britain's large ocean going fishing fleets, Australian colonial fishing boats were comparatively small. In Australia, the standard fishing vessel was a small boat manned by two or three people (figure 2.5) and estuary, beach and inshore locations were the common fishing grounds. Cohen discussed this in 1892:

> Unlike the fishermen in other countries, in this Colony the prolific waters of the surrounding oceans are in great measure ignored in favour of the harbours and rivers and other shallow waters abutting the coast. (Cohen, 1892: 7)

Figure 2.5 Australian colonial fishing vessels and crew typically fished estuary and inshore locations. Image from Garran 1886.

This focus on inshore fishing can be attributed to the East Australian Current, which flows along the east and part of the South Coast of Australia carrying large quantities of plankton, fish larvae, mollusc larvae, crustaceans and other nutrients into the relatively shallow waters of the Australian continental shelf and inland waterways (Hutchins and Swainston 1986: 7; Bennett 1974: 230; Pownall 1979: 12). The rich variety of marine species supported by the current eliminated the need to hunt deep-water fish and facilitated the establishment of efficient inshore fishing operations.

Fishing methods were suited to estuary, beach and lake species. Hooks were used with line and nets were hauled into a boat or into shore by hand or hand-operated winches (figure 2.6 and 2.7). The types of fish targeted included sea mullet (*Mugil cephalus*), bream (*Acanthopagrus butcheri*), luderic (*Girella tricuspidata*), sand whiting (*Sillago ciliata*), sand flathead (*Platycephalus bassensis*) and eastern salmon (*Arripis trutta*) (Hutchins and Swainston 1986).

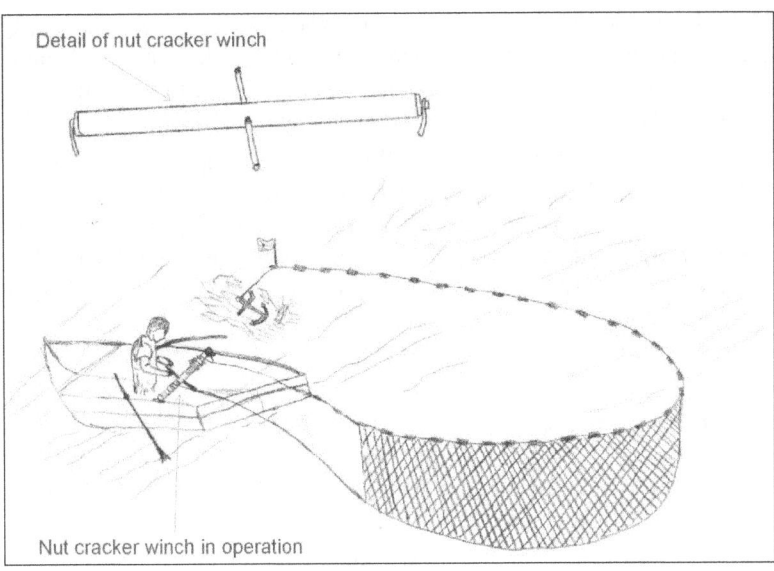

Figure 2.6 A hand winch used for hauling fishing nets into a launch, often called a nut cracker. On either end of the winch, steel pins fit into the oar rowlock holes. Ropes tied to the net ends are placed on the timber shaft and the centre handle is turned to haul the net towards the boat.

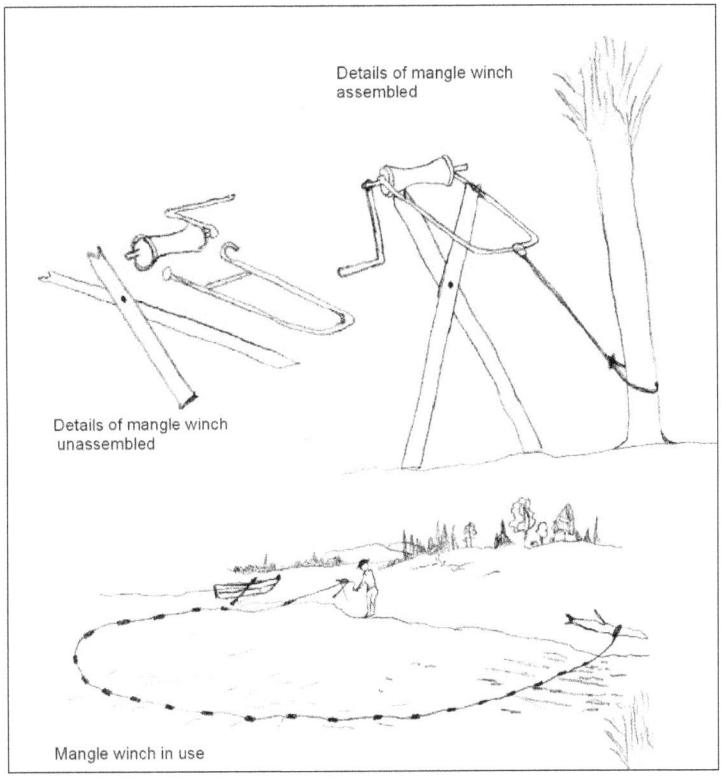

Figure 2.7 A hand winch used for hauling in fishing nets from the shoreline, often called a mangle, is set up in operational position. A rope attached to the net is wrapped around the centre dolly and the handle is wound to winch the net into shore.

Fish was seen as a virtually inexhaustible source of food and employment for the colonies. In 1892, Frank Farnell MP made this statement about the colony's fishing industry "instead of 800 or 900 men, we ought to have thousands of men employed in this business" (*Votes and Proceedings of the New South Wales Legislative Council,* Papers Laid Upon the Table 1892: 5590). In 1894, he argued that commercial fishing should be a topic of national importance, as it was adding wholesome food and considerable wealth to Australia (*Votes and Proceedings of the New South Wales Legislative Council,* Report from the Fisheries Commission 1894: 1439).

From the late 1800s to early 1900s, fishing developed into a major Australian industry. An increasing number of commercial fishermen – predominantly Australian Aboriginal people and immigrants from China, Italy, Greece and Britain – ensured a healthy industry, including equipment manufacturers, distribution agencies and markets (*Sydney Morning Herald* 1915, January 23).

In 1915, the New South Wales state government established the NSW State Trawling Industry, aimed at exploiting deep-ocean fish resources to supply a growing demand for fresh, affordable fish to government institutions and the public (*Sydney Morning Herald* 1915, March 20). Three ocean trawlers containing the most modern trawling technology were brought from England to ensure the success of the new industry (*Sydney Morning Herald* 1915, January 23). While early operations proved very promising, after ten years of poor administration, over-expenditure and general mismanagement, a royal commission closed the industry and sold all the equipment to private enterprise, where it was used to develop what is now one of Australia's largest primary industries (Secomb 1995: 41).

Fish remains recovered through archaeological excavation confirm the establishment of deep-ocean fishing. For example, from the Rocks area in Sydney, Karskens (1999a: 94) reported that only shallow water and estuarine fish species were represented in early 19th-century archaeological assemblages, while later 19th- and 20th-century assemblages contained shallow water and deep-ocean fish species.

In 2007, commercial fishing is Australia's fifth most valuable rural industry after wool, beef, wheat and dairy (www.affa.gov.au, 7 May 2007).

## VICTORIA'S COMMERCIAL FISHING HISTORY

Commercial fishing in Victoria began soon after European settlement in the mid-1830s. Fishermen lived in huts at Fisherman's Bend on the Yarra River and from here fished the Port Phillip Bay waters. Government Surveyor Robert Russell set aside a general market reserve slightly west of Princes Bridge and commercial fishermen would row or sail up the Yarra to this market, blowing a horn to announce their arrival with fresh fish (Bennett 2002: 3). Any evidence of fishing huts and the open market place has long since disappeared with the development of the city of Melbourne.

During the 1850s, the gold rush fuelled an enormous increase in Victoria's population. This led to a greater demand for food including relatively cheap sources of protein such as fish. About 20 boats were fishing commercially in Port Phillip Bay during the 1840s and by the mid-1850s numbers had risen to approximately 170 boats (Bennett 2002: 6). This led to fears that Port Phillip fish stocks were becoming depleted, prompting fishermen to move to the sheltered bays and harbours east and west of Melbourne.

### Eastern Victoria

For reasons of practicality, this project focuses predominantly on eastern Victoria. Western Victoria's fishing history is discussed briefly in chapter 4, mainly in relation to Chinese fishing activities. The first coastal bays exploited by fishermen east of Melbourne were those of Western Port (see location map Figure 1.1). Commercial fishing was underway in this area by the 1840s, as indicated by newspaper reports that Thomas and James Wren were running horse-drawn fish carts from Hastings (then King's Creek) to Melbourne markets (*Peninsula Post* 1917, October 26). Laden with up to one hundred baskets of fish and drawn by three horses, spring carts would travel in the cool night air to reduce spoilage of the fresh product (*Illustrated Australasian News* 1880, February 16).

A cartage industry quickly developed, with fish transported to Melbourne markets and the carts returning with merchandise for the distant settlements (Bennett 2002: 16). The carts travelled from Western Port through Frankston, Mordialloc, Carrum Swamp, Cheltenham, Beaumaris, Brighton and through to Prince's Bridge. This track became known as 'the old fish track' and was the forerunner to today's Nepean Highway (figure 2.8) (Bognuda and Moorhead 1981: 34).

Ice was largely unavailable before approximately 1880 – depending on region as the Patent Ice Company was operating in Geelong by 1862 (Aspinall 1862: 120) – and transport of fish to market by steamboat or horse and cart was expensive, time consuming and unreliable in inclement weather (Bennett 2002: 6). As commercial fishing moved further from Melbourne, transport of fish to market before the flesh putrefied became the main obstacle for Victoria's rural fishing industry.

From the mid-1800s, many small settlements around Western Port Bay, such as Phillip Island, Crib Point, Bittern, Hastings, Tyabb, Cannons Creek, Warneet and Tooradin were to some extent dependent on fishing. Many commercial fishermen used coastal sailing boats for trading as well as for fishing, thereby facilitating the development of these small settlements into larger townships (Capps 1994: 141; Little 2004: 7).

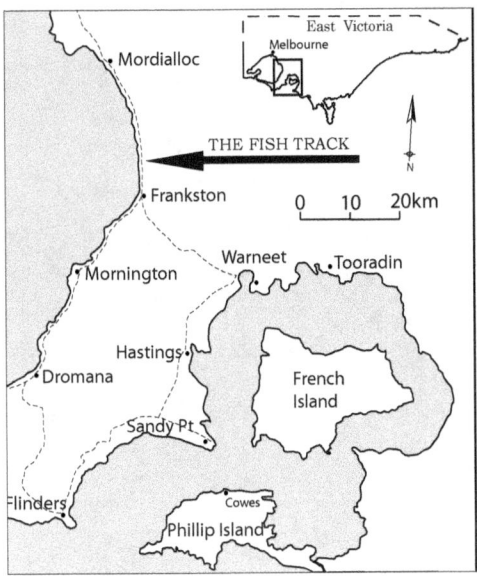

Figure 2.8 Dotted line indicates 'the old fish track' route taken by horse-drawn fish carts travelling to and from Melbourne markets. Route details from Bognuda and Moorhead 1981: 34.

Field reconnaissance (by the author) in 2003 revealed that archaeological evidence of past European fishing activities has survived around Western Port including isolated slipways, wharf timbers and concrete ice boxes (in common use by the 1890s) and more complete fishing stations that reveal the multifaceted workings of European fishing sites. Surface examinations, documentary and oral evidence suggest these sites date to approximately 1870–1910 (Bognuda & Moorhead 1981: 72; Woolley 2003 pers. comm.; Johnstone 2002 pers. comm.). Earlier fishing sites would have been positioned in the main settlement area, where over time archaeologically damaging development has occurred. It is possible the identified sites may have been subject to successive occupation, in which case excavation or archival research may reveal earlier dates.

By the 1860s, an ever increasing demand for fish and fears of depleting fish stocks again prompted fishermen to move eastward, this time to the Gippsland region (Ellis & Lee 2002: 4).

## COASTAL SOUTH GIPPSLAND

The Gippsland coast consists of a series of lakes, rivers, estuaries and inlets covering approximately 20 500 km$^2$ of tidal waterways (Barr 2000: 1). South Gippsland's geology comprises a bedding of Mesozoic tectonic belt (mainly consisting of cretaceous sediments) that extends across southern Victoria and onto the continental shelf (Singleton 1973: 129, 133). In the late Pleistocene period, a siliclastic barrier (sand dune) system was deposited along the Gippsland coast and formed a series of estuarine lakes. Fluvial sediments became trapped by the lakes and created coastal swamp deposits. During the late Quaternary period more sand was deposited along this coastline, forming the beginnings of the present-day Gippsland Lakes and beaches (figure 2.9) (Birch 2003: 355–56).

### The Kurnai people

Long before its official European 'opening' in 1841, the Gippsland region provided hunting and fishing grounds for the Indigenous Kurnai people. The Kurnai group consisted of five related tribes, each occupying their own separate region of Gippsland but sharing the same basic socio-cultural characteristics (Howitt 1904: 134; Barr 2000: 1). In the early 1840s, Charles Tyers, the Commissioner of Crown Lands, estimated there were approximately 1000 Kurnai people living in and around the Gippsland coastal region (Tyers in Bride 1969: 233). The Port Albert region was populated by the Brataualung tribe of Kurnai people whom, in 1841, Tyers estimated to number 300 (cited in Mulvaney & Colson 1971: 301). The Brataualung exploited the resources of Gippsland's waterways and from bark canoes they speared, netted, trapped and hooked fish (Synan 1989: 2). The tribal name Tatungalung – neighbours to the Brataualung – attests to their use of marine environment as 'Tatungalung' means "men of the sea" (Howitt 1904: 77).

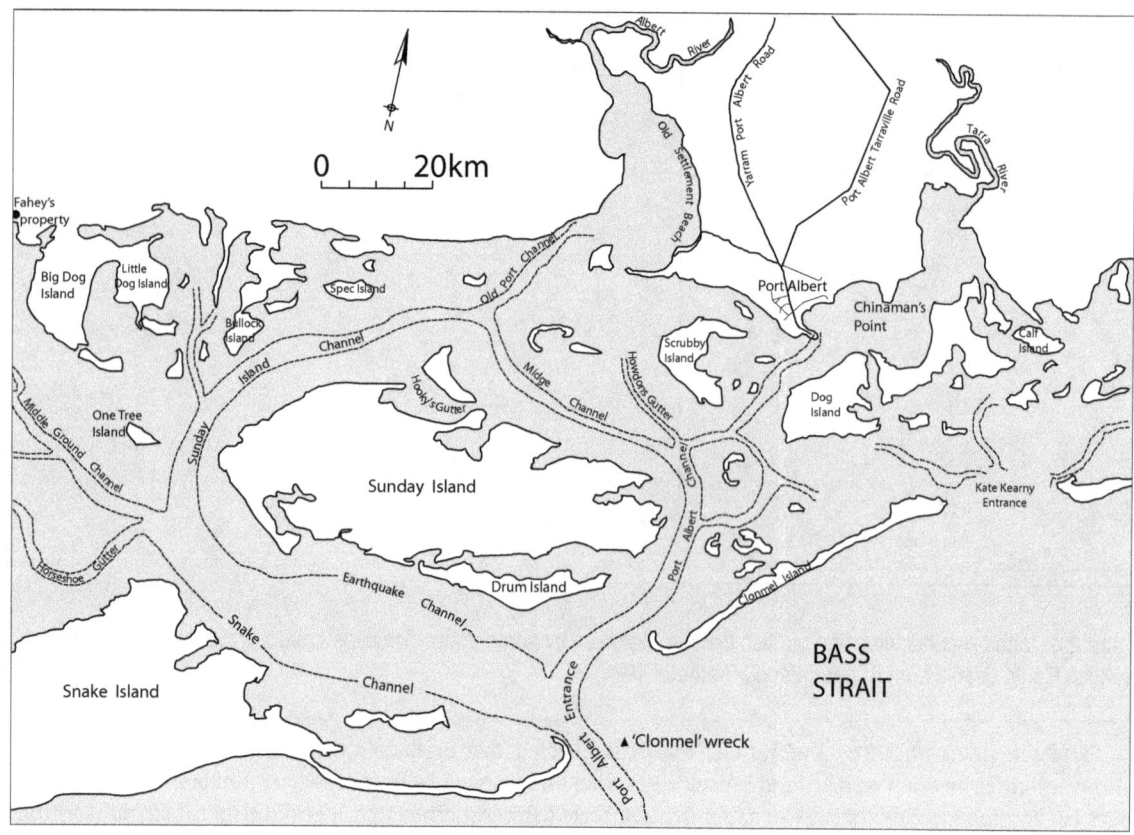

Figure 2.9 The waterways of south Gippsland directly relevant to Port Albert and the Chinaman's Point fish-curing establishment.

Figure 2.10 Indigenous Kurnai women fishing from bark canoes on Lake Tyres just east of Lakes Entrance in Gippsland (see location in figure 1.1). Wood engraving by Samuel Calvert 1869. La Trobe Picture Collection, State Library of Victoria.

After European contact, the Kurnai quickly learned how to fish for financial gain. Writing of the Kurnai, Wells (1986: 45) states, "Sometimes Aboriginals would sell fish, too, when they needed cash". An engraving from the *Illustrated Australian News* on April 24 1869 shows Kurnai women fishing from bark canoes (figure 2.10). The reporter states these women often sold fish in the towns around Gippsland's lakes, "about 20 lb weight being given for six-pennyworth" with which they purchased "small supplies of tea, sugar, tobacco and a few other luxuries" (also Attwood 1984). Further pictorial evidence from the 1870s shows Kurnai people dressed in European clothing and standing in a traditional bark canoe containing a large European-style fishing net (figure 2.11). Another photograph from 1912 shows a group of eight Kurnai – men and women – who have been fishing with European style nets from three traditional bark canoes and one European style row boat (figure 2.12). This indicates that the Kurnai, like other Australian Aboriginal people, adapted their traditional fishing techniques to fish commercially.

Figure 2.11 Indigenous Kurnai people wearing European-style clothing and using European type fishing nets (seen in centre of first canoe) from traditional bark canoes. Photograph by NJ Caire, 1886. La Trobe Picture Collection, State Library of Victoria.

Figure 2.12 Indigenous Kurnai people wearing European-style clothing and using European-type fishing nets (visible in first and second canoe), traditional bark canoes and one European style boat (to back of picture) c.1912. Hendrie Hamilton collection, State Library of Victoria.

## European discovery of Gippsland

The European discovery and settlement of Gippsland has been discussed adequately by other researchers such as Cuthill (1959); Lennon (1975; 1998), Clements & Richmond (1968), Bognuda & Moorhead 1981, Cox (1890), J Adams (1990) and A Adams (1997). Therefore, the region's European history will be conveyed here in a succinct manner. Captain Cook documented sailing past the area in April 1770, but did not attempt a landing (Martin 1978). The explorer George Bass sheltered on the eastern side of Wilson's Promontory in February 1797 and documented the entrances to what are now Corner Inlet and the Port Albert waterways (Le Cheminant 1978: 14). Over the next 40 years, sealing and whaling crews frequented the region, establishing temporary bases and leaving archaeological evidence of their activities (Townrow 1997; Lennon 1998: 64). These were most likely the first Europeans to explore South Gippsland's coastal inlets. Some Gippsland areas closer to Melbourne, such as Port Franklin, had intermittent settlement from 1836 by timber cutters exploiting the great southern forests (Doran 1954: 1).

There is debate about the first European 'officially' to discover the Gippsland region. In 1840, two explorers, Count Paul Strzelecki and Angus McMillan, were separately engaged in exploring Gippsland for quality livestock pastures and suitable access routes into the region (Cuthill 1959: 9; Watson 1984: 115). After several long and difficult expeditions both men were successful in locating fertile country, large fresh water rivers and overland access points in and out of the region. However, Strzelecki was the first publicly to report – in the *Port Phillip Herald* of 23 June 1840 – the region's livestock potential, calling it Gipps' Land after Governor Sir George Gipps.

Word of the lush, arable country spread rapidly among farmers and squatters, but the rugged country between Melbourne and Gippsland hindered the region's development. By way of chance, the wreck of a 700 ton steamship, the *Clonmel*, played a role in developing this region.

Travelling from Sydney on 2 January 1841, the *Clonmel* was wrecked near the entrance to Port Albert (Cox 1890: 12). Captain Lewis (a harbour master in Port Phillip Bay) was in charge of one of several vessels that assisted in rescuing the *Clonmel*'s passengers. Motivated by Strzelecki's account of Gippsland, Captain Lewis took the opportunity to inspect the region's waterways and returned to Melbourne with stories of a huge navigable inlet, deep waters and sheltered passages (*Port Phillip Patriot* 1841, January 7).

It was only a matter of days – 16 February 1841 – before a group of Melbourne businessmen engaged in the cattle industry chartered a vessel and began systematically exploring the region's waterways for a satisfactory shipping harbour (Adams 1990: 9). The group established themselves on the eastern side of the Albert River and called their site 'Albert Town' (Cuthill 1959: 11; Halstead 1977: 22).

### Early settlers and cattle

A deep shipping channel was located a short distance east of Albert Town and by late 1841, trade was conducted from this location, called Shipping Point (Lennon 1975: 85).

By late 1843, a rudimentary overland stock route had been established (Cuthill 1959: 22). Thousands of sheep and cattle were driven overland to Gippsland, fattened into prime animals and then shipped by sea to market (Maddern 1965: 107; McMahon 1966: 58). As profits from Gippsland's fertile pastures increased so did general interest and on 28 November 1845, the *Port Phillip Herald* announced a new road to Gipps' Land, stating the journey from Melbourne now took less than four days in a wheeled vehicle – horse drawn.

A small community sprang up at Shipping Point, which was now private land that had been purchased from the Crown in 1843 by a Major Davidson (*Gippsland Standard* 1914, June 5). Turnbull, Orr and Co (a land, cattle and shipping company) purchased Shipping Point – now commonly called Port Albert – from Davidson in late 1844 (Adams 1990: 17). Sea transport from Melbourne to Port Albert was cheaper, more comfortable and generally much quicker than by overland road, which reinforced the usage and importance of Port Albert's harbour (Clements and Richmond 1968: 131).

By 1845, Port Albert had a resident population of 28, supported a number of general stores, good stockyards, a hotel and a customs office. It was visited by trading vessels 69 times that year and exported 10 440 lb of wool, 6 973 sheep and 1 912 head of cattle (Pearson 1992: 2; Daley 1928: 40). The new settlement was developing into a busy town.

## PORT ALBERT

Industries such as timber cutting, wattle bark stripping (for natural tannins) and farming contributed to the development of Port Albert (Dow 1995: 10). However, it was the livestock industry – fresh and salted meat, tallow, hides and skins – that really established Port Albert as a major colonial port during the 1840s to the early 1860s.

Port Albert was three days sailing from Hobart, giving it a geographical advantage as the closest mainland port and therefore able to offer cheaper transport rates (*Port Phillip Patriot* 1842, August 29). Gippsland graziers saw their opportunity and began exporting livestock to Hobart, finding it a highly profitable market due to the growing number of convicts transported there (Lennon 1975: 103, 105; Clements & Richmond 1968: 132).

By 1850, large quantities of building and general supplies were coming into Port Albert and large numbers of livestock were going out. As the only dock and safe harbour in Gippsland, Port Albert was a busy port, supporting a relatively large – although scattered – regional population (Baggaley 1984: 4). The port had become a vital market depot and distributing centre for the Gippsland region and wider eastern Victoria.

Things were not all easy, however, as by the late 1840s, good quality livestock from Melbourne and Geelong began dominating sales in Van Diemen's Land. From 1848 to the early 1850s the Californian gold rush – known as the 'Californian trade' – took many livestock and general trading vessels away from Australia, again hampering Port Albert's development (Bateson 1963: 159). Nevertheless, by 1857, Port Albert had a residential population of 211 people and had become an established port, with the livestock industry as its main economic base (Adams 1990: 41). Then came Gippsland's gold rush and Port Albert really began to boom.

In 1851, large gold deposits were found in Victoria and gold fever struck the colony. Ballarat, Mount Alexander and Bendigo were the first regions to develop major goldfield diggings (Birrell 1998: 15). The

'Gippsland rush' began more slowly, with initial gold discoveries at Omeo in 1851 by Reverend (and geologist) W. B. Clark (Porter 1977: 114). Omeo was remote and rugged country, but gold was a powerful incentive. Food, clothing and mining equipment were carted by bullock-drawn wagons and packhorses from Port Albert 290 km over the mountains (Adams 1997: 6). Other Gippsland goldfields soon opened such as Boggy Creek and Merrijig in 1856, Crooked River in 1860, Woods Point in 1861, Jordan River in 1862 and Walhalla in 1864 (Caldow 2003: 7; Clements and Richmond 1968: 132). Port Albert became the gateway to Gippsland's goldfields and economic development increased rapidly around the livestock, gold and transport industries.

During this period – mid 1850s to early 1860s – a small fishing industry developed at Port Albert (*Gippsland Standard* 1894, May 5). Fish was sold door-to-door within the local region, but the market was only small and could not support industry expansion (*Gippsland Standard* 1888, September 5). Accordingly, fish were packed in wicker baskets – often with wet ferns to keep them cool – and sent on steamers and sailing vessels (at cheap return cargo rates) to markets in Melbourne (Clements and Richmond 1968: 132; Loney 1982: 51). Although the 20-hour sea trip to Melbourne often left fish in a decomposing, un-saleable condition, with a bill for transport still owing (*Gippsland Times* 1889, August 23), small profits to the fishermen were achieved and the industry continued (*Gippsland Times* 1866, May 1).

By the early 1860s, Port Albert's future looked assured. Livestock, gold, forestry and now fishing were contributing to the town's prosperity. In 1862, Port Albert even rivalled Port Phillip Bay in the number of ships entering its harbour, with some people believing the area would overtake Melbourne to become a capital city (Pearson 1992: 2). However, from the mid 1860s Port Albert's development took a series of downward turns.

As Melbourne grew, so did its demand for Gippsland's meat and timber, which was now frequently transported overland, reducing Port Albert's trade (Clements and Richmond 1968: 133). Convict transportation to Van Diemen's Land ceased in 1853 and by 1860 the small number of convicts still held there did not require imported meat supplies (Caldow 2003: 6). With the Australian and, from 1862, New Zealand gold rushes in full swing there was still a huge demand for Gippsland's livestock (*Gippsland Guardian* 1864, January 1). However, in February 1864, the livestock disease pleuro-pneumonia was detected in Gippsland cattle and the export of livestock came to an instant stop (*Gippsland Guardian* 1861, July 5; Caldow 2003: 6).

Although Gippsland's gold deposits were not of the best quality – £2 12s per ounce compared to £3 18s 9d on Central Victorian goldfields – they were plentiful and thousands of miners travelled through Port Albert on their way to the gold regions of north Gippsland (Daley 1960: 61). Such a large movement of people northwards created considerable incentive to locate a shipping port closer to the goldfields than Port Albert. In April 1858, Malcolm Campbell – motivated by the promise of huge profits through the transport of miners and their supplies – became the first person to sail safely through the entrance to the Gippsland Lakes, 200 km northeast of Port Albert (Bull & Williams 1967: 25; Barr 2000: 4). From the late 1850s to early 1860s, numerous reports appear in the *Gippsland Guardian* and the *Gippsland Times* of wrecked or lucky escapes for trading vessels attempting to pass through this entrance. Regardless of the dangers, by 1864, steam and sail vessels regularly navigated the Gippsland Lakes' natural opening to the sea (Clements & Richmond 1968: 134). The 'Lakes' became the new entry point for Gippsland's inland regions and Port Albert lost its status as the gateway to Gippsland (Bird 1987: 2).

By 1864, Port Albert's situation was dire. Gippsland's diseased livestock were barely worth boiling down for tallow, improved overland routes through Gippsland were reducing the port's use and the goldfields trade vanished when shipping bypassed the town. Port Albert's boom years were over. On 4 February 1865, the *Gippsland Times* confirmed Port Albert had "yielded up the ghost and there has been a general exodus of population". A similar comment appeared in the *Gippsland Times* on September 1 1868: "if it was not for the weekly arrival and departure of the steamers and our personal squabbles, there would be little stirring". Newspapers advertised firms that were "late of Port Albert" as many businesses simply went with the trend, packed up and moved northeast to the Gippsland Lakes. Within three years of its peak in 1863, Port Albert's residential population had dropped by 83% from approximately 211 to 36 (Butler's Gipps Land and Wood's Point Directory 1866). Port Albert's continuing existence was largely due to the small but stable fishing industry that operated from its harbour (Clements & Richmond 1968: 132).

## Commercial fishing

Dredging oysters in south Gippsland's waterways was initially more lucrative than fishing and several small craft were in profitable employment dredging and conveying oysters from Corner Inlet to the Melbourne markets (*The Port Phillip Patriot and Melbourne Advertiser* 1843, October 23). Dredging for oysters was so popular that within 12 years – from approximately 1842 to 1854 – the region's natural oyster beds were completely destroyed (*Gippsland Guardian* 1862, February 7; *Gippsland Mercury* 1892, July 23). Over the coming decades, several attempts were made to establish new oyster beds but, besides a brief recovery in 1860, all attempts were unsuccessful (*Gippsland Times* 1889, August 23). The prolific use of small oyster dredges, designed to be towed behind a small sail vessel, became obvious during fieldwork in 2003. Many of the fishermen interviewed within the Corner Inlet/Port Albert area had an old oyster dredge – used by their fathers or grandfathers – lying in their shed, under a water tank or rusting away in paddocks (figure 2.13).

Figure 2.13 An early-style Australian oyster dredge. These dredges were designed to be towed behind a small sail vessel and were used extensively in the Gippsland waterways (scale in 50 mm increments).

As with Britain's early fishing industry, people in the Port Albert region often mixed farming and fishing to sustain a livelihood (Wells 1986: 45; Dickinson 1987: 3; Capps 1994: 56). A small, but increasing number of fishermen settled around the Gippsland waters, making a living by catching and selling fish locally and, when suitable transport was available, at the Melbourne markets.

From the mid-1840s to the mid-1850s, ships were frequently arriving at Port Albert, but not to a regular timetable. Fish could not be stored while waiting for transport to market. Therefore, Port Albert's shipping arrangements were not favourable for the development of commercial fishing activities. The Victorian Directory for Country Districts and Smaller Townships lists no full-time fishermen living at Port Albert in 1851 (cited in Cox 1995: 47–49).

On 6 June 1856, the *Gippsland Guardian* published an electoral register, for selected Gippsland towns, in which one fisherman was listed as living in Port Albert. However, people mixing farming and fishing probably only listed their main occupation, which would most likely have been farming, thereby under-representing the extent of fishing activities.

By 1864, Port Albert's once regular shipping trade had slowed considerably (Lennon 1975: 211). Turnbull, Howden and Co. purchased a steamer called the *Ant* and began a weekly, on a set timetable, Port Albert–Tasmania–Melbourne passenger and cargo run (Adams 1990: 71). This enabled – for the first time – the regular transport of fish from Port Albert to Melbourne markets. Regular shipping columns in the *Gippsland Guardian* indicate that within a year, other steamers (those involved in the Gippsland Lakes trade) also began a weekly stop at Port Albert (*Gippsland Guardian* 1865, April 7; *Gippsland Times* 1871, September 5; Loney 1982: 51). These vessels were actively seeking cargo, giving fishermen increased opportunity – and competitive rates – to transport their fish to market.

From 1864 to approximately 1880 (with the arrival of rail) these vessels provided a suitable – and usually on time – means to transport fish to market. Fishermen could fish all night before the arrival of the steamer, then have their fresh catch loaded in the morning for transport to Melbourne. Even with this regular service, condemned fish tickets were common and Gippsland fishermen had a long-standing complaint about high fish cartage fees and low financial returns (*Gippsland Times* 1889, August 23).

Jock Carstairs, a Gippsland fisherman in the early 1870s stated that

> I have known as many as 400 baskets of fish condemned in one week, during the hot weather and the freight had to be paid, at times two men would be £20 in debt for their weeks work.
> (cited in Gunson 1996: 41)

Despite the risks, there seemed to be a never-ending supply of fish to catch and regular transport offered potential for profits. The *Gippsland Guardian* of 27 April 1866 confirms this by reporting that

> By every steamer leaving our port [Port Albert] no one can help noticing the increasing supply of fish forwarded from here to Melbourne.

## The Chinese at Port Albert

Small groups of Chinese cooks, shepherds and farm labourers had worked on Gippsland properties before Victoria's gold-rush period (Adams 1997: 2). Gold enticed the first substantial number of Chinese people into Gippsland. In 1859, a small group of Chinese miners were working the Omeo field and by 1863, their numbers had risen to approximately 600 (Daley 1960: 67). The majority of these Chinese miners would have travelled through Port Albert to reach the goldfields.

The following section acts as a brief introduction to Port Albert's Chinese fish curers and is intended to facilitate further discussion of the development of Port Albert's fishing industry. Documentary evidence for the arrival and departure of the fish curers in Port Albert is also discussed. Insight into their operations, evidence of their fishing and curing activities and their contribution to the fishing industry is discussed in detail in chapters 3 and 4.

In 1861, overseas Chinese numbers in Victoria were estimated at 24 724 (Cronin 1982: 136). Chinese fish curers had probably been involved in Victoria's fishing industry – predominantly around Port Phillip Bay – since 1855. In the early 1860s, a group of Chinese fish curers arrived in Port Albert, stimulating further growth of the fishing industry. The Chinese remained the best market outlet for Port Albert's fishermen for the next 20 years (*Gippsland Standard* 1894, May 5). While the Chinese did catch fish themselves, their major contribution to Port Albert's fishing industry was in purchasing quantities of fish from European fishermen for curing. With Port Albert industry in a slump, the market created by the Chinese curers played a crucial role in the town's economic development. Port Albert was again growing in importance, this time as a fishing port. In 1880, the Great Southern Railway began servicing the Gippsland region, creating a new option for cartage of fish to market which lasted until the 1930s, when cheaper refrigerated road transport began to dominate fish cartage. By 1881, Port Albert's permanent population had risen to 148 (Adams 1990: 112), approximately 40 of whom were fishermen.

With the growing market for fish – which by the late 1860s included local residents, the Chinese fish curers and Melbourne markets – Port Albert's fishing industry began to take off. Commercial fishing techniques comprised simple nets, hooks and line. As fishermen stayed close to shore, even a small rowboat or sailboat was suitable for fishing (*Gippsland Standard* 1894, May 5; Baggaley 1984: 5). Hook and line fishermen usually worked alone, targeting snapper and flathead (Wheelwright 1861: 249). Net boats generally had a crew of two, sometimes three and caught a variety of fish types (*Gippsland Times* 1879, May 21).

The *Victorian Fisheries Act 1859* required professional fishermen to register their name, place of residence and where they kept their nets (Baggaley 1984: 4). For the Port Albert region, unfortunately, none of these colonial records have survived. In an 1892 parliamentary inquiry into Victoria's fisheries held at Port Albert, fisherman George Smith states there were about 25 fishing boats and 50 fishermen operating from Port Albert (*Votes and Proceedings of the Victorian Legislative Council* 1892). When questioned by the Parliamentary Committee on the types of fish caught in Corner Inlet/Port Albert waterways, local fishermen Joseph Cripps replied "mullet, garfish, pike, flathead and indeed all kinds of fish" (*Votes and Proceedings of the Victorian Legislative Council* 1892; Pearson 1992: 11; *Gippsland Times* 1892, July 8). These would also have included whiting, salmon, trevally, bream, snapper and two favourites of the Chinese, flounder and calamari squid (*Votes and Proceedings of the New South Wales Legislative Assembly* 1879–80, vol. 3: 1225).

The Port Albert Fisherman Association's minutes book for 1894 indicates that 32 boats were fishing in the Port Albert region at that time (Minutes Port Albert Fishermen's Union 1894). This suggests that good financial gains were achieved through commercial fishing at Port Albert.

William Carstairs, a Gippsland fisherman, commented on 12 November 1878 that he and his fishing partner's catch for that week consisted of 59 baskets of fish – approximately 1 ton – sent by steamer to Melbourne markets. From this catch 13 baskets were condemned, for the remaining 46 baskets he received £14 2s, cartage and a sales commission cost £11 5s 7d, leaving a net profit of £2 16s 5d to be shared between the two fishermen. Carstairs noted this was a poor week's catch and suggested his personal wage averaged out annually to approximately £5 per week (*Gippsland Times* 1879, May 21).

Over the next 14 years, profits from fishing do not appear to have risen. Of the 18 Port Albert fishermen interviewed for the 1892 parliamentary committee, each suggested their fishing profits could vary from £1 to £5 per week. The main complaints of the fishermen were that their fish often reached market in an unsaleable condition and that fish transport costs, agent commissions and market dues were too high.

When the Chinese fish curers established themselves at Port Albert, the fishermen's problem of condemned fish and market-related fees were greatly reduced. Without any cost to themselves, fishermen could sail or row their catch over to the Chinese camp – one kilometre by water from the Port Albert wharf – and receive payment immediately. Reminiscing about the early 1860s, a writer for the *Gippsland Standard* (1944, July 7) commented:

> They were an asset to Port Albert fishermen, because, when a haul of fish could not be sent
> away owing to transport difficulties, the whole catch was sold to the Chinamen at £4 a ton.

Compared to William Carstairs receiving £2 16s 5d in 1878 for a ton of fish sold at Melbourne's market, the Chinese curer's rates seem very attractive. Another writer for the *Gippsland Standard* on 5 May 1894, suggests that in 1864 the Chinese were paying from £6 to £8 per ton and sometimes as much a £9 for sought after varieties. On 26 June 1866, the *Gippsland Guardian* commented that about half the fish caught at Port Albert was going to the Chinese curers.

During their first few years of curing operations in Port Albert – approximately 1860 to 1875 – Victoria's gold rush was in full swing and cured fish would have been in great demand by Victoria's Chinese population. A writer for the *Gippsland Standard* in 1894 (described only as 'One Who Was There'), wrote that

> they [the Chinese fish curers] came to Port Albert and Port Welshpool and were open to buy
> all the fish they could get ... the Port boats ... generally made a fair cheque out of them.
> (*Gippsland Standard* 1894, May 5)

The ready market provided by the Chinese fish curers would have been a strong incentive for fishermen to move into the Port Albert region. Historical newspapers show that steamers were carrying tons of fish every week from Port Albert to Melbourne, but there were significant risks involved. The Chinese fish curers would almost certainly have been the preferred market. This suggests a limit to the quantity of fish the Port Albert curing establishment could process, forcing European fishermen to send a portion of their catch to Melbourne markets via steamer.

By the early 1880s, Victoria's gold was dwindling and many of the Chinese miners had returned to China (Oddie 1959: 22). Rail had come to the Gippsland region, offering another, although relatively inconvenient, option for cartage of fish to Melbourne. After much government debate over the best rail route, the line bypassed Port Albert, going instead through the township of Sale, 85 km north-northeast of Port Albert. By 1891, a line was opened from Sale to Alberton, approximately four miles inland from Port Albert (Adams 1990: 111). To make use of the rail line, fish from Port Albert had to be taken to the railway station, creating extra cartage expenses, greater risk of damaged fish due to increased handling and no great reduction on the number of fish condemned each week at Melbourne markets (*Gippsland Times* 1891, March 16). Although cartage options had increased and the Chinese fish curers intake would have decreased (due to a reduced Chinese presence in Victoria), the curers still remained a valuable part of Port Albert's fishing industry.

In 1892, Port Albert fishermen were receiving – depending on season, quality and type of fish – an average of 2s 3d per basket of fish sold at the Melbourne markets, with expenses of approximately half basket value still to be deducted (*Votes and Proceedings of the Victorian Legislative Council* 1892). After costs, the price received was approximately £5 per ton. The best price recorded during the 1892 Fisheries Commission inquiry was an average of 19s on 14 baskets of fish – probably in-season flounder. Such sales demonstrate why fishermen continued sending bulk fish to Melbourne markets, as in this case, approximately £10 full profit was obtained for one ton of fish. As the waters were still abundant with fish, wastage through the condemning of fish was acceptable, so long as a few shillings of profit were made.

During the 1892 Fisheries Commission inquiry, William Fitz reveals the value of having two major market outlets – Chinese fish curers and Melbourne markets – for fish:

> last week we sent up 200 baskets [by steamer] and all were condemned ... There has been
> a fish-curing establishment here belonging to Chinamen. This is an instance; we sent 200
> baskets by steamer [about 3.5 tons receiving profit of approximately £10] and brought a ton
> to the Chinamen and received £8 16s for it. That is how we keep our heads above water.

The steamer services were only a viable option for Port Albert fishermen if large quantities of fish were sent to Melbourne markets. Fish not condemned would cover the expenses for fish that were condemned and with luck profits would be made. The Chinese curers could not process such bulk tonnage, but delivered the fishermen with guaranteed good profits, thereby facilitating the development of Port Albert as a fishing port.

The Fisheries Commission inquiry shows that, as late as 1892, Chinese fish curers were still a valuable part of Port Albert's fishing industry. The Chinese continued buying and curing fish at Port Albert into the early 1900s. By this time, with the mining days over, easy access to ice for preserving fish and good transport options, the curing camp probably only consisted of a couple of Chinese men, seeing out their twilight years as best they could.

Through written histories, newspaper reports and official documents, the following section suggests periods of Chinese occupation at Chinaman's Point. This information will initially be used independently of the material record – which is discussed (in regard to dating) in chapter 7.

## Historical documentation

General local histories provide useful information that can assist with dating archaeological sites. However, care must be exercised, as these often rely on human memory and subjective interpretations (S Jack 1993: 125). Contemporary newspaper reports are a slightly better source of information, but should not be fully trusted in isolation. While newspapers discuss local events and provide firm dates, details are often slanted towards the writer's own opinion. When written local histories are used in conjunction with newspaper reports, reliable information can result. Official documents such as licence fees, land tax payments, court proceedings and royal commissions are generally a reliable source of historical documentation.

It would be expected that a number of Chinese people establishing a fish-curing camp within full view of the township would attract the attention of the local newspaper. A lengthy article appeared in *The Gippslander* (1865, November 10) when a group of Chinese people began curing fish at Hastings in Western Port Bay. However, no similar article has been located for the arrival of Chinese fish curers in Port Albert. It is suspected the event was reported, but the relevant edition became one of the many newspapers or historical documents that have since disappeared through fire, neglect or some other agent.

Clements and Richmond (1968: 132), when writing on industry and trade networks in Port Albert between 1840 and 1866, give the earliest date so far located for the fish curers at Port Albert. They state, "Chinese fish curers began operations in the town in 1860 and the importance of the industry steadily increased". Unfortunately, Clements and Richmond give no indication of where they obtained this information.

On May 5 1894, a writer for the *Gippsland Standard* newspaper – described only as One Who Was There (mentioned above) – discusses Port Albert's early fishing industry and in doing so supplies the second earliest documented date for Chinese fish curers at Port Albert.

> About the year 1860 the first of the Chinamen curers started to cure fish and gave from
> £6 to £8 per ton. But it was not until a few years later, 63–64, when the schnappers were
> getting scarce in Port Phillip Bay, that they bought any great lot.

As this article was written in 1894 and reminisces about a period thirty years before, it would be dubious material to specifically date the site on. However, the article gains credibility through another newspaper article. One Who Was There's article refers to a Chinaman fish curer known as 'Old Daddy'. In 1867, the *Gippsland Guardian* ran a short story concerning "a Chinaman familiarly known as Old Daddy" who had gone missing in his small boat in the Port Albert region. After three days, a search party was sent out and Old Daddy was found safe and sound. This article reveals two relevant aspects of information. Firstly, a Chinaman in a small boat is likely to have been a fisherman; secondly, the name 'Old Daddy' has now been associated twice with Chinese and fishing (once to the actual curers) in Port Albert during the 1860s.

Bailliere's Post Office Directory lists Shuo Yet as a fisherman living at Port Albert in 1870. No Chinese fishermen other than the curers from Chinaman's Point are known to have resided at Port Albert. The directory gives no details of where in Port Albert Shuo Yet lived. Therefore, although tantalisingly close to hard evidence that this man was part of the Chinaman's Point group, this information can only be used to add weight to the existing data.

Capps (1994) published extracts from the diaries of Richard Smith, an ex-convict who took to fishing at Port Albert in 1865. Capps does not precisely date the diary entries, however, in the early 1870s while writing about teaching his sons to fish, Smith mentions that

> After an hour we went back to the marker floats and hauled in the net. In that short time we
> caught 20 fish and the boys reckoned it was great. I had learnt a lot from the Chinese. (Capps
> 1994: 56)

It is very likely that Smith is referring to the Port Albert Chinese fishermen, again placing Chinese fishermen in this vicinity during the early 1870s. Smith's diaries were consulted directly. Unfortunately, their deteriorated condition renders them almost impossible to read – giving reason for Capps's unspecified date entries.

On March 4 1884, the *Gippsland Standard* had this short note: "Large hauls of fish at Port Albert. Five tons sold to Chinamen on eastern beach at £6 per ton". Chinaman's Point is east of Port Albert and, although an earlier occupation date can be inferred from the previous references, this report is the first of a number of reliable dates for Chinese occupation at the fish-curing camp.

In 1887, Ah Hoo paid the Department of Lands and Survey £2 7s 5d for a fisherman's residence licence at Long Point (Chinaman's Point was formerly called Long Point), then again on 19 February 1889, only this time he was a year overdue and was required to pay £5 to keep the licence current. No further documents are available until two years later when Hop Sing paid £1 15s for the same fisherman's residence site, which he kept until 31 March 1892. The next relevant document, dated 26 December 1893 states, "the fisherman's site has been abandoned, Hop Sing left here about 12 months ago" (PROV, VPRS 5357/P0000, unit 5899).

In 1892, the Legislative Assembly of Victoria ordered a progress report into the fishing industry of Victoria. A number of Port Albert fishermen were interviewed for the report on 6 July 1892 including William James Fitz who, when asked how much his average earnings were, responded:

> I think I average about £10 per month. The reason we can drag on those number of years
> without a railway was because we had the Chinamen to sell our fish to.

Fitz was then asked if the fish-curing establishment was still there and he answered, "Yes. Sometimes we get £6 and sometimes they get full up and we have to stop home" (*Votes and Proceedings of the Victorian Legislative Council* 1892: 111). Fitz's statement relays three important aspects of information: the site was still in use as a commercial fish-curing establishment in mid-1892; the term 'Chinamen' and 'they' suggests more than one person occupied the site; and during this later period the site's capacity to cure fish was limited.

Ah Hoo then reappears and is listed in 1896 as paying only five shillings for a fisherman's residence licence and again on 8 January 1897 and on 9 May 1898. Things are then quiet for another six years when Ah Hoo is again listed as paying a land residence licence of £1 5s for the Chinaman's Point site, paid in full on 16 March 1904, thereby obtaining legal occupation of the site until March 1905 (PROV, VPRS 5357/P0000, unit 5899). A land residence licence, as opposed to a fisherman's residence licence, may suggest Ah Hoo was now only living at the site and was no longer involved in the fishing industry.

This examination of secondary historical documentation enables an initial site-establishment period to be estimated at between 1860 and 1870. Solid primary documentation confirms Chinese occupation at the site in 1884 continuing sporadically until 1905.

This chapter has facilitated an understanding of fishing in Australia from before European colonisation to the establishment of a stable fishing industry. Discussion on Gippsland and the town of Port Albert has provided an understanding of the region and its changing social and economic status prior to the establishment of a stable fishing industry.

This chapter has also given an introduction to Port Albert's Chinese fish curers, including how their activities impacted the local fishing industry and their period of operation. The European fishermen were not making large profits from their commercial fishing activities. The Chinese fish curers, through providing a reliable local market and having a steady demand for their cured product (the Chinese goldminers), were probably doing quite well financially and were almost certainly making more money than their European suppliers.

Who were these Chinese fish curers? What was their background? What do we really know about them and their activities in colonial Victoria? The following chapter discusses in more detail the Chinese in colonial Victoria and chapter 4 details their involvement in commercial fishing activities.

# CHAPTER 3

# THE CHINESE IN CHINA AND VICTORIA

This chapter examines the fishing industry in China before and during the peak periods of Chinese emigration to Australia in the early 1850s to mid 1860s. For the same period, it discusses Chinese social structure and relevant features of Chinese culture and then examines various aspects of Chinese social organisation in colonial Victoria. This acts as a backdrop for chapter 4, which identifies evidence for the first appearance of Chinese fish curers in Australia and then Victoria and how these establishments operated.

## THE CHINESE FISHING IN CHINA

Historical records show that during Australia's gold-rush period a small number of Chinese emigrants arrived from the Shantou (near Canton Province) and Fukien (in the south-east) regions (Choi 1975: 78–79). However, the majority – over 90% – came from south Canton Province in southeastern China (more correctly referred to as Guangdong or Kwangtung) and spoke variations of the Cantonese dialect. In particular, they came from rural areas surrounding Canton city and the Pearl River delta (figure 3.1). A number of Hakka people were also amongst this population (Cronin 1982: 17; Brienes 1983: 3). The Hakka are native to central north China, but became displaced in the 13th century and migrated to south China, where they maintained a separate language (Mandarin form) and culture (Choi 1975: 3).

Figure 3.1 Map of Canton (Guangdong) and surrounding region (dark grey indicates major rivers and bodies of water) (top) and map of China in relation to Australia (bottom).

Kwangtung has a large marine environment with networks of rivers, canals and lakes including the huge Pearl River delta. Fish is a dietary staple and fishing plays a major economic role in this region (Choi 1975: 5; Brienes 1983: 26). Many Chinese people who immigrated to colonial Victoria would have fished the waters of their home province and been quite familiar – at least by sight – with Chinese commercial fishing activities. An old Chinese adage, "Salted fish and green vegetables is cause for contentment", attests to the importance of fish in Chinese culture (Kan & Leong 1963: 121). To gain an understanding of the Chinese processing and use of fish products and the techniques likely to have been transferred to Victoria, it is useful to examine past Chinese fishing activities in China with a focus on Kwangtung.

There is strong evidence that Chinese people have a long history of eating fish as a source of dietary protein (Anderson and Anderson 1977: 334). In 1972, the tomb of the wife of a Chinese lord, Li-ts'ang, who ruled over the Ch'ang-sha Hunan district of China from 193 to 186 BC, was archaeologically excavated. The tomb revealed several vessels containing a variety of preserved foods, including fish (Yü 1977: 55). These remains demonstrate that for at least 20-one centuries Chinese people have been preserving fish, in this case bream, perch and three types of carp – each probably considered among the best eating fish of the time. In an 1849 Prices of Provisions catalogue for a Shanghai market, bream was by far the most expensive fish for sale (*Chinese Repository* magazine 1849). Located with the food vessels in Li-ts'ang's wife's tomb were 321 inscribed bamboo cards containing details of the preserved foods, notably that the fish had been cured by salting the flesh and then drying it in the sun (Yü 1977: 55–57).

During his 12th-century travels through China, Marco Polo observed that the Chinese fishing industry was highly developed and well organised (Cutting 1955: 50). In Kwangtung, fishing has remained a major industry. During the 1950s, inshore fishing based at small villages was noted by Ward (1954: 195–96) to be more common than ocean fishing based at larger coastal ports. Chinese inshore fishing relates well – for comparison purposes – to Victoria's colonial fishing scene.

Chinese people harvest thousands of different fish species and other aquatic animals from their ocean, rivers, lakes and ponds. Artificial propagation of fish in ponds had been successfully practiced in China for centuries, long before European people used such techniques (Brienes 1983: 27). During the Ching dynasty (1644 to 1911), a period of great poverty in Kwangtung (Anderson 1970: 3), the most sought after fish were bream, carp, mullet, sole and squid (Diamond 1969: 16; Schafer 1977: 102). Fresh-water fish were eaten as close to capture as possible and were preferred by the wealthy minority. Salt-water varieties were typically cured and consumed by the Chinese majority (Anderson & Anderson 1977: 335; Colquhoun 1883: 78).

Chinese fishing methods have remained largely unchanged over centuries and lineally across the Chinese land mass (Abbott 1883: 456; Diamond 1969: 1). This uniformity over time and distance enables 20th-century research – such as by Firth (1946), Ward (1954; 1959), Diamond (1969) and Anderson (1970) – to provide a good indication of Chinese fishing practices on the Pearl River delta in the Ching dynasty.

Some relatively recent references are used here as main sources of information, especially in regard to overseas Chinese activities in Australia, such as Chan (1997); Lydon (1999); Williams (1999); Chan, Curthoys & Chiang (2001) and Wang (2003). Each of these is discussed in the 'Previous research' section of chapter 1. However, to examine select aspects of 19th-century Chinese people, their lives, lineage systems, family ties, merchant activities, hostilities and emigration practices – mainly within China, but also abroad – the earlier works of Oddie (1959), Choi (1975), Watson (1975), S Wang (1978), Mei (1979) and G Wang (1991; 1992) were found to be most useful.

The references which have been most valuable for this project and which are most often cited in the literature on China's 19th-century social situation and aspects of culture are Choi (1975) and Wang (1978). Both of these give excellent background to the situation in China leading up to the Australian gold-rush period, the Chinese migration/immigration to Australia and systems of overseas Chinese organisation in Australia.

Cronin's (1982) work – although now largely superseded by newer research projects such as Wang (1992), Chou (1995) and Curthoys (2001) – has also been used in this chapter. This is due partly to her useful overview of Chinese involvement in Victoria's gold rush, but also for her original discussions on Chinese organisation in Victoria, Chinese–European interactions and the activities of Chinese merchants.

Social ranking in traditional Chinese society places fishermen in the lowest occupational class (Diamond 1969: 3). Both Anderson (1970: 7) and Diamond (1969: 3) suggest this low social status may be partly due to a general perception about their relative lack of economic opportunity and a belief that fishing is contrary to the Confucian value of preserving life.

Chinese commercial fishing activities were generally conducted by a family unit, which was often extended to include patrilineal kin i.e. a man, his wife, their children and the wives and children of their married sons – all living together either on their fishing boat or in a hut directly on the water margins (Ward 1954: 208). Whether living on boats or on land, every fishing family had a village base, of which there are a very large number dotted around the waters in Kwangtung (Ward 1954: 196). Men did the fishing, net making and maintenance, while women managed the house and children; and both men and women participated in sorting and curing fish (Ward 1954: 204). The hiring of extra men was common, but these too were generally patrilineal kin – i.e. relatives having the same surname as the owners – and would work, eat and live with their employers (Ward 1954: 209). An interesting point noted by Ward (1954: 197; 1959: 44) is that most Kwangtung fishing villages included a number of Hakka families that were engaged mainly in farming, but sometimes fished or were employed on fishing boats.

Fishing families often lived in perpetual debt, securing money loans or item credits through their local fish merchant, who was usually a relative or who had kinship relations within the fishing village (Ward 1959: 44). No bank or collateral guarantee was needed, money was lent or credit given on the basis of personal relationships (Ward 1954: 211). The system was one of association and applied to most commercial activities in Kwangtung – not only for fishing families. The crucial factor was to be associated with a group. Without the connection of a home village, fishing families would be unable to obtain loans, credit or even sell their catch to market.

As with fishermen in other countries, the Chinese fished predominantly with nets, traps and lines with hooks (Colquhoun 1883: 209; Ward 1954: 196; Von Brandt 1972). Inshore fishermen fished in pairs from small row or sail boats and often at night with a lamp hung over the bow to attract fish (Ward 1954: 202–03). A common Chinese fishing method – established in the Sung dynasty (960–1298) – is the use of cormorant birds, which are trained to catch fish and take them to their master (Davis 1844: 161; Gudger 1926: 6). These fishing methods had been practiced over generations and were highly refined and efficient. Ward (1954: 200) suggests that the most important task of the Kwangtung fishing people was the curing of fish, as the bulk of all catches were sold cured.

An American adventurer travelling through China in 1876 indicated that the Chinese fishing villages "surpass all others in abominations of sight and smell" (*The Living Age* 1876: 817). In this aspect at least, Chinese fish-curing establishments in Victoria appear similar, as after visiting a Chinese fish-curing establishment at Metung in Gippsland, a writer for the *Gippsland Mercury* on 20 May 1879 commented that his senses had been assaulted and the establishment "forcibly reminded one of the hovels in Little Bourke Street".

During the Ching dynasty, curing processes allowed fish to be stored and transported to inland mountainous regions of China and provided a means of dealing with seasonal fish surpluses (Firth 1946: 10). Cured fish contains higher protein levels than fresh fish (as adding salt to fish flesh and then drying it creates amino acids which increases protein levels) and has acted as a food staple for Chinese people, often representing the only animal protein in a standard diet of rice and leafy vegetables (Herklots & Lin 1964: 6; Anderson 1970: 7; Wang 1920: 293).

For the fisherman, curing is a serious business, requiring the utmost attention to produce the best product. In English language literature there are a small number of eyewitness accounts of Chinese people curing fish. However, information on methods of fish curing is scarce and it is not known how fish were cured during the Ching dynasty. The techniques generally referred to by travellers include that fish was salted and then dried in the sun, just dry salted, just dried in the sun, or pickled in salty brine and then dried in the sun. A common term in historical literature is 'cured and dried fish' which is ambiguous as it may refer to two separate methods or to fish that was cured (in a brine or dry salt) and then dried.

Firth's 1946 anthropological study of a Malay fishing village gives the earliest written indication in English of how Chinese people cured fish – not actually in China, but at least for Chinese people in an Asian country. Firth notes that in many East Asian regions fresh fish industries tend to be managed by the "natives", while fish curing is conducted entirely by Chinese people (1946: 12, 14). The various types of cured fish products observed by Firth were prawn paste, pickled anchovies (placed in large baskets of salt), salted fish paste, spiced pickled fish (placed in containers with spices and salt), strip cured fish (the whole fish is cut into strips, held open by a hoop and hung in the sun for several days) (figure 3.2) and most commonly, salted and dried fish (Firth 1946: 218–20). For the salted and dried product, fish were gilled and gutted, soaked in salty brine and placed on timber or bamboo trays to dry in the sun (Firth 1946: 219). The New South Wales 1880 Fisheries Inquiry and a newspaper article in the *Bendigo Advertiser* (1857, January 5), suggest the Chinese fish curers in Australia also used this method, as at least in some cases, they split the fish down the backbone, salted and then dried them in the open air. They also pickled fish in casks or barrels (*Votes and Proceedings of the New South Wales Legislative Assembly*, vol. 1 1880: 1224; *Bendigo Advertiser* 1857, January 5).

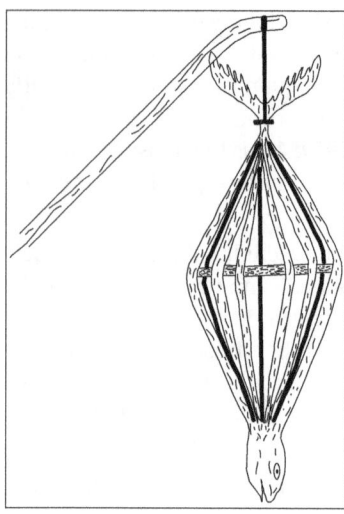

Figure 3.2 A fish cut into strips, held open and hung in the manner of strip curing.

In almost every country that has an important fishery, cured or processed fish makes up the largest measure of fishery products (Jarvis 1950: 2). The industry is driven by a wide range of forces that are sometimes of such social and economic importance that countries have gone to war in order to retain or secure fishing grounds and fish-curing locations. The following section facilitates an understanding of why and how Chinese people sought opportunity overseas and gives insight into the cultural systems they brought to Victoria.

## CHINA'S SOCIAL SITUATION AND ASPECTS OF CULTURE

Kwangtung's numerous and densely populated rural villages were underpinned by large family clans of common lineage – or kinship – groups (Choi 1975: 10). The kinship system of social organisation was – and to an extent still is – central to the unity and functioning of Kwangtung society (Choi 1975: 9).

Each clan was ruled by a kinship leader who took counsel from headmen and used a series of administrative advisers to keep him informed of events that may have bearing on his own clan (Moore and Tully 2000: 4). In the Pearl River delta region, there was great diversity within local cultures and social traditions, which often varied even within one village (Chan 2001: 8). Nevertheless, common lineage over centuries promoted a strong sense of social unity. Clan finances were generated by an internal system of land rent and various taxes. Wealth was channelled back into the community to improve collectively held land, assist primary food production and to build and maintain education facilities, communal religious temples and other benefits shared by clan members (Jackson 1970: 47). Kinship leaders also brought social cohesion to the clan, including providing advice on personal matters and adjudicating in conflicts between clan members (Moore and Tully 2000: 4; Chou 1995: 62).

During the latter half of China's Ching dynasty, however, a number of factors combined to make Kwangtung a more unpleasant and dangerous place to live.

### Social situation

Predominantly due to the fertile flood plains, Chinese people have historically considered Kwangtung a regional safe haven. For this reason – and over centuries of changing Chinese dynasties – defeated emperors, loyal soldiers and displaced people have migrated to Kwangtung (Choi 1975: 4). Choi (1975: 9) discusses a number of 'push factors' in the exodus of people from China during the second half of the 19th century, notably poverty, land shortage, political instability, banditry and natural climatic disaster. Population increase had taken its toll on land availability, land fertility and water resources, plunging many into poverty (Greif 1974: 5). By the mid 18th century, Kwangtung was supporting some 14 million people and population levels were still rising (Durand 1960: 247). Throughout the mid 19th century, drought and floods further reduced land availability and fertility and intensified poverty (Yarwood and Knowling 1982: 166).

District clans struggled to control the remaining fertile land on the Delta flood plains and hostility between Kwangtung clans grew into fierce and prolonged fighting (Choi 1975: 8). Warlords, rebel armies and bandits roamed the region and homelessness and starvation were common (Greif 1974: 6–7). Most fertile land regions in

China were experiencing similar instability, reducing the option of simply moving out of the troubled Kwangtung (Choi 1975: 9). By the mid 19th century, the population in Kwangtung had swelled to approximately 30 million people, placing the region among the most heavily populated in China (Durand 1960: 247).

During the long periods of political instability, violence and famine, Kwangtung villages came under yet another threat – pirates engaged in the opium trade. From the late 18th century, British traders exchanged opium from India for Chinese silver – China's standard currency – and Chinese-grown tea (Adams 1997: 2). Huge quantities of opium entered Kwangtung illegally through Hong Kong harbour and were distributed by smugglers throughout China (Greif 1974: 6). The vast sums of money involved in opium trading corrupted many imperial officials and clan leaders, who hoarded profits for personal gain. Others used opium money to hire mercenary fighters to protect clan interests (Greif 1974: 7–8; Choi 1975: 11).

Opium running and addiction compounded Kwangtung's instability and the province sank into further social and economic crisis (Choi 1975: 4). The imperial Chinese Government in Peking (Beijing) acted by seizing and destroying 20 000 chests of British-owned opium and passing harsh laws to punish drug dealers (Adams 1997: 2). Far from pacifying the situation, the British Government – not wanting to lose the lucrative opium trade – launched the first Opium War, lasting from late 1839 to mid 1842 (figure 3.3). China lost the war, plunging the nation into further financial and political turmoil and enabling corruption and banditry to flourish (Greif 1974: 7). The Opium War also forced China to open the ports of Canton, Foochow, Ningpo, Amoy and Shanghai to British and other foreign trade (Chang 1968: 91; Mei 1979: 469). This greatly increased the number of foreign vessels entering Chinese ports and gave many desperate people a means of transport out of China (Wang 1988: 109). From the end of the first Opium War in 1842, small-scale but persistent Chinese emigration was underway (Chang 1968: 90; Wang 1988: 116; Jones 1990: ix). Long-standing Chinese imperial laws prohibiting emigration – a crime punishable by death – were relaxed in 1860 and annulled in 1893.

Figure 3.3 The British bombing of Canton during the first Opium War from 1839 to 1842. Image from Ridpath 1899.

After the first Opium War, social and political unrest continued. Large unruly groups of impoverished people travelled the countryside, seeking food and other commodities by attacking villages, small towns, rich families and government food-storage compounds (Choi 1975: 8). The differences between rich and poor were already stark, but became further emphasised by the Ching Government's oppressive military action against the destitute Kwangtung people. Civil unrest intensified and rural populations rebelled against the Ching Government. Known as the Taiping Rebellion, this tumultuous period lasted from 1851 to 1864 (Lazarus 1975: 358; Mei 1979: 473).

In the midst of this rebellion, another war over opium erupted in 1856, social chaos deepened and the Ching Government came close to collapse (Choi 1975: 17). By the end of 1864, poor living conditions, natural disaster and fighting had claimed an estimated 20 million lives (Wang 1978: 12; Horsfall 1985: 7). The Chin Government, victorious in the Taiping Rebellion, immediately began a lengthy campaign of rebel executions, which resulted in the loss of approximately another one million lives (Wakeman 1966: 136–50; Mei 1979: 437).

Against this background, Choi's 'push factor' seems hardly descriptive enough. An early Chinese emigrant from Kwangtung to the Australian goldfields, Lum Khan Yang, gave his reason for seeking opportunity overseas:

> Our money and property were plundered, we had not the means of purchasing a morsel to
> put in our mouths and there appeared no way by which we could extricate ourselves from
> poverty ... We happily heard intelligence regarding a new gold-field in an English colony.
> (*The Wesleyan Chronicle*, 1859 February, cited in Nicholas & Sheehan 2002: 10)

From approximately 1830, developing markets (mostly under British influence) in, for example, North and South America, Cuba, Peru, West Indies, Jamaica, Hawaii and Australia welcomed cheap labour to clear land, set up basic infrastructure and perform general manual labour. Contract workers from Kwangtung had been providing a portion of this labour for over a decade (Chang 1968: 91). Then, in 1849, the Californian gold rush began, followed two years later by the discovery of gold in Australia. Leaflets circulated in Kwangtung by Chinese merchants and shipping companies advertised the opportunities provided by the goldfields. Persistent emigration from Kwangtung after 1849 suggests that these opportunities were attractive to Kwangtung people. Tens of thousands of southern Chinese people left to seek their fortunes, not necessarily from gold, but in the gold-rush countries. This was the origin of Chinese emigration to Australia, California and other world regions.

## Aspects of culture in China and abroad

The number of people who left China to seek their fortunes abroad during the 19th century is unclear (Choi 1975: 22; Wang 1978: 268). As a very broad approximation, between 60 000 and 80 000 Chinese people entered Australia during the colonial period (Wang 1978: 269; Markus 2001: 69), some 200 000 to 300 000 went to the United States and a further 150 000 travelled to various other non-Asian regions such as Hawaii, Papua New Guinea and New Zealand (Chang 1968: 99, 103; Stapp 1990: 82). Wang (1978: 308) estimates that 2 355 000 Chinese people left China via seaports between 1840 and 1900.

The kinship system is central to understanding Chinese social behaviour in foreign countries (Cronin 1982: 19; Wu 1982: xi). In particular, Chinese men were responsible for the survival and future wealth of their clan (Yarwood and Knowling 1982: 166). The decision to leave China was not one for the individual to make, but a carefully thought out, serious family affair, initiated as a means to generate family capital (Cronin 1982: 19; Choi 1975: 13). When permission was given for a clan member to work overseas, the emigrant was under obligation to transmit a large portion of earnings back to their immediate family in China, which was beneficial to the clan more broadly (Wu 1982: 93; Chou 1993: 76). Clan officials, a headman or merchant of the same kinship would arrange groups from ten to one hundred or more people to emigrate at a time and would often travel personally with the party (Wang 1978: 99–101; Choi 1975: 81).

A credit–ticket system was commonly entered into, where the headman or a merchant paid passage for an individual or group. The recipient was then bound to work solely for their creditor under debt bondage until the passage plus interest was paid or more commonly for a specified period, usually one year (Cronin 1982: 18) – although Wang (1978: 305) suggests credit–ticket payments could take several years. The credit–ticket system operated as a labour recruitment scheme and had been in use in China from approximately the mid 1700s (Campbell 1969: 2–3; Richardson 1982: 2). Yong (1977: 1) suggests that some 80% of Chinese people who travelled to Victoria during the gold-rush period did so under the credit–ticket system. Wang (1978) provides the most informative evidence concerning the Chinese credit–ticket system, suggesting that

> most so-called Chinese free emigrants borrowed their passage money from others and were
> bound by invisible agreements to work for their creditors for a certain time. Evidence shows
> that only a very small percentage of them, such as rich merchants, physicians and so on,
> came out of China on their own account. (1978: 89)

The indebted contractor usually received rations, accommodation and possibly a small wage, but the profits of their labour all went to their passage creditor (Cronin: 1982: 19).

The use of the credit–ticket system in Australia can be identified in an 1858 New South Wales select committee into Chinese immigration. A Chinese merchant, Chin Ateak, is asked how an individual Chinese person would secure the labour of some 30 Chinese men (in China) to come and work in Australia. He answers:

> Suppose they do, they write an agreement in a house and the 30 men put their names to it;
> the man who advances the money sends a head man with them and when they have paid
> back the money to him they can go back to China if they like; but if they do not clear the
> money they must dig. (*Votes and Proceedings of the New South Wales Legislative Council*
> 1858, vol. 3: 19)

Family loyalty is an integral part of Chinese culture and emigration was managed within the bounds of such kinship obligation (Choi 1975: 10; Chou 1995: 60; Chan 2001: 9). Binding kinship obligations were not simply to work and send money home. The Chinese individual was – from birth to death – influenced by senior members of their family, especially on major concerns such as education, choice of marriage partner, place of residence and, importantly, occupation (Choi 1975: 9–10; Moore and Tully 2000: 4). As put by Coolidge (1909: 7, cited in Brienes: 1983: 4):

> No Chinaman acts alone; always he expects to act and live subject to the limitations and cooperation of his family, his village relations, his society and his guild. As a citizen he has great freedom; as an individual he is entangled in a thousand customs, rules and regulations which, though voluntary, he regards as absolutely binding.

The situation is also noted by Chan (1997: 200, cited in Chan 2001: 9):

> The lone migrant is seemingly set free to go off home ground, into the air, like a kite – but not without the family pulling the string ... The migrant thus experiences the family in his everyday sojourning life as a real factor, sometimes seeing it as a liability, a constraint, other times as a source of strength and enablement.

Cronin (1982: 18) cites Tao & Leong (1915: 68) who state,

> Our ephemeral self is nothing; it is for the good of our ancestors, our immediate parents and our descendants that we work, we drudge and even we die.

It is often suggested in historical literature that all Chinese immigrants to Australia – aside from some merchants – were headed for the goldfields (see for example Wang 1988: 109; Chou 1995: 60, Adams 1997: 3; Williams 1999: 20; Curthoys 2001: 103). Only after failing at mining – it is generally suggested – did some Chinese people enter other occupations such as market gardening, shop keeping and fish curing (Horsfall 1985: 118; Loh 1989: 10; Curthoys 2001: 115–16). While the number of Chinese people in occupations other than mining did increase during Victoria's later gold-rush period (discussed later in this chapter), the assumption that all Chinese people initially came to mine for gold may not be accurate.

A large influx of people into any area requires the establishment of basic infrastructure and supplies such as accommodation, food, clothing and equipment. It is often acknowledged that Chinese people in colonial Australia were remarkably self-sufficient, rarely buying supplies from European merchants on the goldfields or otherwise (Cronin 1982: 21–31; Jones 1990: 26; Williams 1999: 11–12; Lydon 1999: 69; Curthoys 2001: 107). As noted by Brienes (1983: 5) in reference to Chinese social organisation in California, "the Chinese were truly remarkable for their resistance to the essentially English-based model surrounding them". Cronin (1982: 21–22) argues that Chinese people already established in Victoria provided for the needs of new Chinese arrivals to Victoria. Such an organised system would certainly require a permanent workforce of people who were not working on the goldfields.

Greif (1974: 29) examines the establishment of Chinese infrastructure during the initial period of Chinese mining in New Zealand (1866–1867), finding that by the time miners arrived, Chinese market gardeners had already purchased fertile land and were growing produce that was intended exclusively for their countrymen.

There is other evidence that Chinese people prepared for an influx of miners into Australian regions. In regard to the Palmer goldfields in Queensland, Kirkman (1984: 169) cites newspaper reports from 1873 (one year before the Chinese 'rush') that Chinese gardeners were planting vegetables in the area. In late 1874, Chinese doctors, hoteliers, storekeepers and other merchants set up businesses in the major settlements on the Palmer fields, then "suddenly in 1875 a damburst of immigrants direct from China occurred" (Kirkman 1984: 169–170).

Wang's (1978: 117) study of Chinese emigration suggests that arrangements for Chinese people arriving to mine for gold in Australia were kept totally in the hands of Australian-based Chinese firms. Wang (1978) credits Lowe Kong Meng (figure 3.4), a prominent Chinese merchant based in Melbourne, as shrewdly designing and organising the entire Chinese immigration to northern Queensland. Wang (1978: 117) also suggests Lowe Kong Meng had a major role in facilitating Chinese business in Western Australia, Tasmania and New Zealand. This is consistent with the traditional Chinese system of using cooperative enterprise to advance group social and economic interests (Jackson 1970: 48). In an overseas setting, this helped Chinese people to become self-sufficient and to remain independent from European systems.

Researchers have acknowledged the diversity of overseas Chinese occupations (see for example Williams 1999: 6; Stapp 1990: 81–84; Wang 1978: 89–93). However, the implications of the credit–ticket system that required most Chinese immigrants to Victoria – and to Australia more broadly – to work at least their first year overseas under the control of their passage creditor and then to work as directed under kinship obligation, has not yet been recognised in relevant literature. Moreover, the historical evidence for early Chinese primary industry, their cooperative enterprise, the desire to be self-sufficient and the Chinese influence in the development of colonial Australia makes the Chinese system of labour usage in Victoria – and overseas countries – a significant issue which demands further examination.

Figure 3.4 An 1866 wood engraving of Lowe Kong Meng in his mid 30s. Image from the *Illustrated Australian News* 1866, September 27.

Chinese labour systems in colonial Victoria are difficult to determine. Research is hampered by a lack of colonial-period Chinese written records and the apparently deliberate efforts by colonial-period Chinese people to hide their social organisation and structures (Cronin 1982: 1). To better understand Chinese micro-society – such as a fish-curing establishment – the modern researcher must conduct cautious interpretations of contemporary records often written by a misinformed, culturally unfamiliar and generally antagonistic European population (Cronin 1982: 1). The Chinese system of labour usage in colonial Victoria that is suggested here and backed up where possible is forwarded as the most likely scenario of how their systems may have functioned. In addition, as the intended occupation of Chinese people entering Victoria during the gold-rush period would have varied – for example, from merchant, headman, miner, even temporary sailor or goods smuggler – the following discourse is not intended to be inclusive of every Chinese person in Victoria.

The system of delegated occupation suggests that Victoria's Chinese population may not have all gone to the goldfields in the hope of 'striking it rich'. A select minority – people with particular skills such as vegetable growing, fish curing, retail experience and cart/bullock drivers – would have been more valuable to creditor and common kinship goals not as miners, but as suppliers of essential goods.

This Chinese system of labour utilisation – although without creditor involvement – has been noted on a smaller scale among other groups of overseas Chinese people. For example, in an early study of Chinese fishermen in Perak, Malaysia, Dew (1891: 107) discusses how one fisherman out of a team of six (each on a similar share of profits), always stayed at the base camp to keep house, tend the garden and cook meals. Piper (1984: 9) and Butler (1977: 29) discuss similar practices among Chinese miners in New Zealand. Common kinship obligations and a cultural understanding that individual efforts were for the benefit of all, facilitated strong group cohesion. These factors, including indebted labour usage, enabled the kinship system to operate smoothly amongst overseas Chinese people (Chou 1995: 64).

## Merchant involvement

Chinese merchants in Australia participated heavily in the credit–ticket system (*Votes and Proceedings of the New South Wales Legislative Council* 1858, vol. 3; Wang 1978: 117) and therefore had at their disposal a supply of very flexible labour. By delegating more or fewer workers to specific tasks, potential avenues of economic gain in Australia could be tested and then either exploited or abandoned – a particularly useful tactic with fleeting or fluctuating markets which the Chinese were very good at identifying (Inglis 1975: 73; Omohundro 1977: 117; Wu 1982: 105; Frost 2002: 124).

The credit–ticket system also assisted to raise the social status of the Chinese merchant class (Wang 1992: 188). The traditionally low status of Chinese merchants reflects the Confucian value that an individual should not endeavour to become rich through entrepreneurial activities (Wang 1992: 310). This places merchants near the bottom of the traditional class structure, which includes, in order of importance, scholars and officials, peasants, artisans, merchants and shopkeepers and the lower classes in undesirable occupations such as fishermen, servants, gravediggers and prostitutes (Wang 1992: 238; Diamond 1969: 21).

After the first Opium War and southern China's increased contact with the outside world, merchants found an improved market for import/export activities. This enhanced merchant wealth, enabling them to inject more finance into their kinship system. This would have been highly regarded according to Confucian philosophy that values "philanthropy towards the needy and loyalty to the clan-village", effectively raising the social status of merchants (Wang 1992: 238, 310). As identified by Hwang (1976: 6), Wang (1991: 186) and Lydon (1999: 68–69), Chinese merchants overseas began actively developing their philanthropic activities as a strategy to achieve a higher status. High social status gave merchants power over their fellow overseas countrymen, which in turn facilitated more wealth. By favouring certain people in business endeavours, the merchants broadened their *guanxi* network. *Guanxi* is a Chinese cultural system structured around kinship and locality ties) where a favour given represents a favour owed (Praetzellis & Praetzellis 1997: 282, Lydon 1999: 80–85, Stockman 2000: 85–90). As put by Yang (1994: 123):

> It is a rule that the larger one's guanxi network and the more diverse one's guanxi connections
> with people of different occupations and positions, the better becomes one's general
> manoeuvrability in society and with officialdom to obtain resources and opportunities.

Chinese merchants involved in the credit–ticket system – now with increased social status and *guanxi* contacts – would have also acquired some influence over kinship officials in China. The overseas merchant could now – if desired – use their social position to encourage particular workers to stay with them after they had repaid their passage debt. These people may have been placed in a position of elevated authority such as a headman of a working group and/or given the opportunity to establish their own commercial enterprises, enabling them to climb the Chinese social ladder and begin merchant activities themselves. As stated by Wang (1992: 311), "Each merchant earned his initial success through his own efforts, with the support of his family, local links and trade organisations."

Shipping records from the 1850s onwards show that regular shipments of preserved foods and other cargoes were arriving in Victoria from Asian regions (Syme 1987). Newspaper reports and other historical documents reveal that from the mid-1850s, Chinese people in Victoria operated businesses such as market gardens, rice mills, fish-curing establishments, butcheries, tobacco farms, commercial hotels, boarding houses and general supply stores (Choi 1975: 30; Cronin 1982: 23–28; Williams 1999: 20). Chinese people involved in these businesses were obviously not working as miners and were likely subject to the Chinese social system. As with 80% of the Australian Chinese population, they were probably under debt obligation. These kinship ties – and merchant control – meant that Chinese people working in supply/demand occupations were not general retailers, but were meeting the needs of their own group (Macgregor 1998: 26).

This kinship trade is well-established in Chinese cultural traditions that require commerce to be conducted primarily within family circles in order to facilitate loyalty to lineage and brotherhood trust and to maintain kinship connections (Wang 1992: 310). Lydon (1999: 81) has noted this system was active amongst Sydney's Chinese population:

> The Chinese merchants of George Street were nodes in a wide-cast net of business and trade,
> kinship, native-place and neighbourhood ties, patterned on Chinese family structure.

In this way, Chinese people in Victoria were able to remain self-sufficient, survive better physically (through fresh food supplies) and be more economically productive than many of their non-Chinese colleagues, including those working on the goldfields (Curthoys 2001: 105).

There is potential for further research into the 'on-the-ground' systems that Chinese people used to distribute commodities throughout Victoria. Initially, it is important to emphasise three factors. First, some Chinese merchants had a great deal of labour at their disposal. Second, that through the kinship system, an individual Chinese person's occupation in Victoria could be controlled, and third, that there was likely a substantial number of Chinese people in Victoria who never worked on the Victorian goldfields, but who instead formed part of the working infrastructure supporting Chinese endeavours to build wealth through gold. This non-mining overseas Chinese population is referred to in Reverend Young's 1868 report into the

Chinese population in Victoria. The report lists a broad range of Chinese occupations in Victoria, all of which were a component in supplying commodities to the Chinese mining population, for example shop managers, market gardeners, butchers, tailors, shoemakers and hawkers (Young 1868 cited in McLaren 1985).

Chan's (2001: 9) statement that overseas Chinese people sometimes saw lineage obligation as a liability and a constraint could suggest that many Chinese men longed to be part of the goldfield excitement but were instead obligated to work in supporting occupations.

For the general Chinese workforce in Australia, merchants acted as the overarching link to all that was Chinese, especially the kinship system. Catering for over 42 000 Chinese people – the approximate number in Victoria during the late 1850s (Choi 1975: 20; Wang 1978: 275) – would have been a substantial endeavour, requiring considerable organisation. Merchants underpinned overseas and Australian trading networks, acted as banking agents and loan creditors, mediated in bureaucratic procedure and offered lodgings, employment, working equipment and much more (Lydon 1999: 84). It is likely they also undertook the vast organisational effort required to assemble, feed, transport and place in suitable occupations the thousands of Chinese people entering Victoria during the gold-rush period. This makes their importance to the early Chinese social system in Victoria paramount.

## CHINESE SOCIAL ORGANISATION IN VICTORIA

Between 1848 and 1852, Australian colonies were also involved in the Chinese labour trade (Curthoys 2001: 104). With the British Government's abolition of slavery in 1833 and the end of convict transportation to New South Wales in 1840, Chinese labourers were seen, mainly by pastoralists, as a reliable, cheap solution to the shortage of labour in Australia (Daley 1932: 23; Choi 1975: 18). The first major group of Chinese people to enter Victoria were part of this labour trade system. They consisted of 123 male labourers who arrived on the *Phillip Lang* from Hong Kong in 1848 (Wang 1978: 272; McLaren 1985: x).

Due to European difficulties in pronouncing and spelling Chinese names, official government registries for Chinese people entering colonial Victoria are incomplete and confusing (Williams 1999: 85–87). Therefore, the majority of Chinese labourers who entered Victoria during the gold-rush period remain nameless (figure 3.5).

Figure 3.5 Wood engraving of Chinese immigrants arriving in Little Bourke Street, Melbourne, 1866. Image from the *Illustrated Australian News* 1866, September 20.

Census details suggest that merchants made up approximately six to eight percent of Chinese people in colonial Victoria (Williams 1999: 94; Couchman 2001: 126). Cronin (1982: 26) indicates there were between thirty and forty Chinese merchants living in Melbourne during the gold-rush period. The *Sydney Morning Herald* (1861, May 11) reported that the Chinese merchants were:

> generally clever fellows in their way – are possessed of some capital and as *sine qua non* have scraped together sufficient English to enable them to act as interpreters.

Chinese merchants often had their names recorded properly, are better represented in historical records and were more accepted by the Australian population than the Chinese working class (Oddie 1961: 69; Cronin 1982: 78). Due to these factors, Chinese merchants have less anonymity than most Chinese people in colonial Victoria and, along with their dominant position in overseas Chinese communities, make promising research subjects, especially in regard to social and economic factors influencing colonial Australia.

It is useful to examine two of Melbourne's leading Chinese merchants: Louey Ah Mouy (often written Louis Ah Mouy) and the previously mentioned Lowe Kong Meng.

In 1851, Louey Ah Mouy was brought to Melbourne under contract to Captain T. Glendinning (Daley 1932: 24). At this time, Louey Ah Mouy was a 24-year-old carpenter from Toishan in the Sze Yap district of Kwangtung (Pike 1974: 19). He was contracted by Glendinning to build six houses with Singapore oak. On completion of his contract, Louey Ah Mouy decided to stay in Victoria and work for himself (Cronin 1982: 26).

By 1852, Louey Ah Mouy would have been aware that Victoria was stirring with the excitement of gold discoveries. Familiar with China's social situation, cultural practices and kinship system, he would have realised there was money to be made if he could finance Chinese labourers to Victoria. Louey Ah Mouy sent letters to his home village in China relating the news of gold discoveries (Pike 1974: 19). These letters have often been regarded as triggering the Chinese gold rush to Victoria (Pike 1974: 19). *The Shipping Gazette* and *Sydney General Trade List* show that 129 Chinese people arrived in Victoria by sea in 1852 (cited in Wang 1978: 268). It is likely they were, as suggested by Cronin (1982: 16) "The first emigrants, an advance party of young 'respectable' Chinese". In March 1854, the *Rose of Sharon* landed another 503 Chinese people in Melbourne (*Sydney Morning Herald* 1854, March 7). If Yong's (1977: 1) and Wang's (1978: 90) claim is accurate that 80% – possibly more – of Chinese people entering colonial Victoria were under the credit–ticket system, this shipment contained more than 400 indebted labourers. By the end of 1854, approximately 5000 Chinese people had entered Victoria by sea (Moore & Tully 2000: 4); perhaps 4000 of these were indebted labourers. In the following five years, over 40 000 Chinese people entered Victoria, creating an enormous source of merchant-friendly labour. It would have been logical and cost-effective to create an infrastructure of transport, market gardens and fish-curing establishments to support this influx of people.

Historically, it is known that Louey Ah Mouy accompanied a Chinese labouring crew to Victoria's Yea district, probably between 1852 and 1854, and struck rich gold deposits (Pike 1974: 19). It is possible that he engaged some of his workers to prepare market gardens and other basic infrastructure in anticipation of the next wave of Chinese immigrants. Within a year, 19 of these first Chinese goldminers returned to China to flaunt gold, purchase equipment and recruit more labourers for Victoria (Cronin 1982: 16). In late 1852, Louey Ah Mouy established a cartage business and merchandise store in Swanston Street, Melbourne, selling goods imported from Asia and other parts of the world (Pike 1974: 19; Cronin 1982: 20, 28; Macgregor 1998: 26).

Cronin (1982: 20) states that it was 'widely rumoured' – although no hard evidence has been located to back her claim – that Louey Ah Mouy was heavily involved in the credit–ticket system. Within a few years he had used Chinese labour to build and operate a rice mill in Flinders Street and establish profitable gold mines in the Victorian districts of Yea, Ballarat, Mount Buffalo, Bright and Walhalla (Oddie 1961: 68). He also held shares in other mining ventures in Australia and overseas, invested heavily in Victorian real estate and was a large shareholder and a chairman of Melbourne's Commercial Bank of Australia (Pike 1974: 106; *Gippsland Guardian* 1866, May 11). Louey Ah Mouy died in Melbourne in 1918, aged 92, a wealthy and respected man.

Lowe Kong Meng (figure 3.4) was born into a wealthy Chinese family from Penang, in present day Malaysia, although his lineage could be traced to the Sze Yap district near Canton (Leavitt 1888: 98). He was well-educated and spoke both French and English fluently. In 1853, he travelled to Victoria and spent three months working as a gold digger (Cronin 1982: 28). After carefully assessing the Victorian situation, Lowe Kong Meng left Australia for India, returning to Victoria in 1854 with his own sailing ship and a good supply of trading commodities (Leavitt 1888: 98; Pike 1974: 106; Cronin 1982: 28). At this time he was only 20-four years old and would have almost certainly been acting with the support of his wider family. He opened a tea and merchandise store in Little Bourke Street, purchased six more ships – all registered to the Port of Melbourne – engaging one in the Torres Strait with the trepang industry – sea slugs were a delicacy in Asia – and keeping the rest constantly trading between Melbourne and China (Oddie 1961: 68; Cronin 1982: 28). Like Louey Ah Mouy, Lowe Kong Meng is presumed to have paid passage for thousands of Chinese people to come to Victoria (Cronin 1982: 20), furnishing himself with a steady supply of labour. Vivian (1985: 9) cites evidence from *The Examiner* (1870, October 15) of Lowe Kong Meng's use of Chinese labour. The article states that Lowe Kong Meng provided James Peters of Tasmania with 19 experienced gold diggers from Ararat, Bendigo and New Zealand, offering up to two thousand more Chinese men if desired.

Lowe Kong Meng would have needed a considerable workforce to support the mining claims and companies which he owned and others in which he held major shares such as the Kong Extended Gold Mining Company, Kong Meng Gold Reef, Kong Meng and Columbia Tribute Gold Mining Company, New Kong Meng Company, Madame Bent Gold Mining Company, Midas Consols Gold Mining Company and the hugely rich Majorca mine (Oddie 1961: 68; Cronin 1982: 28; Kyi 2004: 62). Lowe Kong Meng also held major shares in, and was a chairman of, the Commercial Bank of Australia in Melbourne, represented a major Chinese insurance company, was part-owner of a sugar conglomerate and owned businesses in Queensland, Darwin, New South Wales, Western Australia and New Zealand (Pike 1974: 106; Oddie 1961: 68; *Gippsland Guardian* 1866, May 11). He invested heavily in land, purchasing large blocks at Brighton, Toorak, Malvern and St Kilda, where he employed Chinese labour to grow bulk vegetables, fruit and tobacco (Oddie 1961: 68; Cronin 1982: 28). Interestingly, there was a large Chinese fish-curing establishment at St Kilda (Horsfall 1985: 119) and although the owner is unknown, it was quite possibly under the control of Lowe Kong Meng.

Early in Victoria's gold rush, three dominant – although separate – Kwangtung language/district associations emerged: the Sze Yap representing the 'Four Districts' of Toishan, Sunwuui, Hoiping and Yangping; the Sam Yap representing the 'Three Districts' of Nanhai, Punyu and Shunte; and the Heang-San, a minority group possibly of Hakka people (Young 1868 cited in McLaren 1985: 49). These grew rapidly to contain thousands of associates and – like an extended kinship membership – provided social protection, support and identity (Wang 1978: 116). These associations were not unique to Australia, but appeared wherever large numbers of Chinese people settled. Each association had direct antecedents in China (Armentrout-Ma 1983: 107).

The Chinese merchant class established themselves at the head of these district associations, directing the members and controlling many aspects of their economic system (Oddie 1961: 67; Wang 1978: 117; Stapp 1990: 84). Upon arrival in Victoria, new Chinese immigrants were met by district association members and taken to a Chinese tent city 'beyond the town' where they were lectured on life in Victoria, issued with working equipment, then left in the care of their creditor's headman who told them where they would work (Crawford 1877: 27; Wang 1978: 115; Cronin 1982: 22). Wang (1978: 102) suggests the Chinese immigrants to Victoria

> were all in parties under headmen until they could repay their passage ... These headmen were sometimes creditors themselves but more generally were sent by an agent [Chinese merchant] to look after the party.

For the indebted labourer, there were three broad occupation possibilities. The first was mining, the second was employment in the produce and supply industries, the third was to be socially connected enough to be set up as a merchant store owner. Some merchant store owners became wealthy and socially influential, others remained small-time business people and some went bankrupt. Stapp's (1990: 335) study of a Chinese mining community in Idaho, United States, suggests that merchant stores either sold a poor range of cheap goods, or a large range of necessities and luxury items. It is not known if Chinese store owners – in the United States or Australia – actually owned the products for sale or were simply working for wealthier merchants. Whatever the case, three distinct Chinese social class types become evident in colonial Victoria: the wealthy and influential leading merchants, a broad range of middle-class merchants and headmen and the majority working-class labourers.

Each of the larger Victorian goldfields were comprised of several individual (spatially separate) villages where Chinese people lived, worked and were dependent on their own district groups. In Beechworth, Horsham, Bendigo and Ballarat, the Hakkas, Sze Yap and Sam Yap each had separate merchandise stores, vegetable gardens, butchers, barbers, cook-shops, opium establishments and religious temples (Young 1868 cited in McLaren 1985). They also had independent systems of transporting imported goods, fresh agricultural supplies and cured products such as fish and tobacco from Melbourne to the various goldfields (Cronin 1982: 22–23).

Through appointing Chinese people to undertake specific tasks according to who they did or did not favour, Louey Ah Mouy, Lowe Kong Meng and other Chinese merchants shaped the early (1850s to 1870s) Chinese communities in colonial Victoria.

Where major economic opportunities emerged, such as the Victorian gold rush, it appears that the first Chinese person or group of people to set themselves up as merchants and encourage other Chinese people into the region often ended up with the largest pool of available labour. These merchants became the wealthiest class and would then employ and do business favours for the next, aspiring, class of merchants (Oddie 1961: 69), thereby creating a functional and self-sufficient social system. In this way, Louey Ah Mouy and Lowe Kong Meng established themselves as leaders in Victoria's colonial Chinese society. The system outlined above – especially the techniques of social survival and methods for procuring and utilising labour – has been noted among Chinese settlers in other parts of the world, both before and after the Chinese arrived in Victoria. Four brief case studies will be used to add weight to the suggestions above.

Many researchers have discussed Chinese merchant activities in the United States in the 19th century and merchant control over the labouring Chinese population. Mei (1979: 475–76), for example, argues that merchants were the first Chinese people to immigrate to California, where they immediately engaged in all manner of trade, opened stores and organised others to sell Chinese groceries and daily necessities to incoming Chinese. Stapp (1990: 325–46) indicates that the Chinese mining population in Idaho was grouped into social clan units that were fully controlled by a higher organisational class – presumably the Chinese merchants. Armentrout-Ma (1983: 110), mentions that the earliest merchants in San Francisco held authority over and dominated Chinese community leadership. Rohe (1982: 9), commenting on the journey by Chinese miners to the goldfields, suggests that "Commercial agents or storekeepers in constant contact with the headquarters of their district companies directed the movement". Similarly, Mark and Chih (1982: 56) comment that "Merchants controlled the clan and district associations ... Their power gave them jurisdiction over most aspects of the lives of Chinatown's working men".

These researchers acknowledge the control that Chinese merchants had over the Chinese working population, but fail to discuss the role of merchants in organising labour to set up initial infrastructure such as market gardens and fish-curing establishments. Taking Wang's (1992: 301–12) description of overseas Chinese merchants – that merchants went abroad to seek trade opportunities – into account, the early Chinese merchants in the United States would have almost certainly identified opportunities to supply their compatriots with goods and services and directed a portion of their available labour to this end.

Omohundro (1977: 116) briefly describes Chinese labour organisation in the Philippines, noting that people indebted to Chinese merchants were mostly basic labourers. Omohundro (1977: 116) and Campbell (1969: xvii) observe that these labourers were frequently loaned out to work for other merchant kinsman elsewhere in the Philippines, suggesting that indebted overseas Chinese workers had close connections with their merchant bosses, were highly mobile and worked at whatever occupation was assigned to them. Wang (1978: 92) discusses Chinese people in California and refers to the credit–ticket system, stating that "After arrival in California, migrants remained directly indebted to the brokers, either working for the agents on mines or hired out to employers".

Between approximately 1790 and 1820, West Borneo was host to a Chinese gold rush. In a study of cultural geography, Jackson (1970) has detailed social patterns of Chinese organisation on the West Borneo goldfields. This region was not under direct European rule until the 1850s and gold mining and goldfield administration was predominantly in the hands of Chinese Kwangtung villagers (Jackson 1970: 2). Each of the West Borneo fish-curing locations were settled by separate kinship and district association units (*kongsis*, or 'ritual brotherhood') held together by common bonds of kinship, loyalty and economic interests (Jackson 1970: 62; Wang 2003: 71). Kinship headmen, traders and merchants occupied positions of influence within the *kongsi* communities (Jackson 1970: 63). Each *kongsi* goldmine was comprised of groups of miners, shop owners, farmers, fishermen and tradesmen. Jackson (1970: 64–65) notes that the non-mining population was integral to each *kongsi*'s gold mining activities and held the same organisational position as miners. Each member of a *kongsi* was subject to taxes relative to their occupation, but everyone received a share of the gold profits (Jackson 1970: 64–65). The system described by Jackson suggests that those involved in non-mining occupations such as farmers and fisherman were part of an integrated group pursuing wealth through gold.

Wu (1982) discusses the migration of Chinese people to New Guinea and examines aspects of their social organisation. From 1889 to 1901, a German company engaged some two thousand Chinese labourers – predominantly from Kwangtung – to experiment in New Guinea with coconut and tobacco farming (Wu 1982: 17). The farming projects failed. In 1901, approximately 150 Chinese people chose to remain in New Guinea as free settlers (Wu 1982: 19). Wu states that when subsequent work opportunities arose in New Guinea, the settlers sent messages back to China asking brothers, cousins and other clan or lineage members to join them. Then, "when newcomers arrived, the established pioneers became patrons for them, acting as leaders as well as protectors" (Wu 1982: 52).

Ah Tam was one of the earliest Chinese settlers in New Guinea and became a leading figure in the community. Using Chinese kinship connections, Ah Tam recruited labour to promote his commercial ventures. By 1910, his business interests included a wholesale and retail store, two ship building yards, a hotel, several agricultural plantations, a gambling establishment, a brothel and an opium house and he owned every building in Chinatown (Wu 1982: 52). While nothing is mentioned of Ah Tam paying for passage of immigrants, Wu notes that Ah Tam was a large employer and, for an initial period, paid very low wages to the new Chinese arrivals.

Further discussion of overseas Chinese social systems and use of labour can be found in Willmott (1960) for Indonesia, Moench (1963) for Tahiti, Inglis (1975) for Papua New Guinea and Watson (1975) for England.

In each case, for Victoria or elsewhere, by drawing on the kinship system, a set of ready-made contacts was available through which credit, import/export commodities and labour resources could be obtained. Importantly, kinship obligations through the credit–ticket system facilitated a willing and cheap labour source. This, it is suggested, is the major factor in enabling Chinese people in Victoria to operate as a self-sufficient minority and turn local economic possibilities into capital. As argued by Wang (1978: 310),

> the whole system of Chinese emigration was actually an organised international trade. The poor, innocent Chinese labourers were only the commodities from which the merchants concerned made their great profit.

## Occupational change

The Chinese labour systems discussed above were used in Victoria for only a relatively limited period, from the arrival of Chinese gold-rush immigrants in the early 1850s to approximately 1870. By 1870, declining gold yields in Victoria, racially restrictive Victorian immigration laws – in place since 1855 – and Chinese kinship pressures for male family members to return home, were quickening the outflow and slowing the inflow of Chinese people in Victoria (Choi 1975: 26). Victoria's Chinese population had peaked at 42 000 in the late 1850s, then dropped to below 18 000 by 1870 and continued to fall at an approximate rate of 500 per year for the rest of the century (Horsely 1879: 417; Choi 1975: 20, 22). By the end of 1888 – the height of anti-Chinese sentiment – there were only around 3500 Chinese people working as goldminers in Victoria (Oddie 1959: 19). By 1901, numbers had dwindled to some 1200 (Choi 1975: 29). Most of Victoria's existing Chinese population would have long completed their period of passage debt by this time. The initial commercial boom of Victoria's gold rush was over and the Chinese community in Victoria was in decline (Chou 1995: 59). With more Chinese people leaving Victoria than were arriving, the credit–ticket system would have been supplying only a small number of labourers to support merchant entrepreneurial activities. At the same time, the huge infrastructure set up by Chinese merchants to supply Chinese miners became less important as mining populations decreased.

Kwuangtung remained a troubled province, with Chinese people in Victoria still under kinship obligations to support family back in China. The ideal for most lower-class Chinese goldminers had always been to return to China when their family's economic circumstances had stabilised (Brienes 1983: 7). On failing to 'strike it rich' through gold – as was often the case – many Chinese miners in Victoria began pursuing a new range of occupations to allow them to continue to send regular remittance money to family in China (Oddie 1961: 65; Choi 1975: 29; Chou 1993: 70–75). This is evident through census reports that show in 1861, 80% of Chinese people in Victoria were employed as miners, dropping to 74% in 1871, then to only 25% in 1891 (Census of Victoria 1861, 1871, 1891). The Chinese people in Victoria were no longer pursuing wealth through gold, but nor were they left penniless from their mining activities as is often suggested in historical literature (see for example Cronin 1982: 60). McGowan (2005) argues that when gold was plentiful, many Chinese goldminers in Australia had done quite well financially and could be classified in the 'middling' as opposed to the lower classes.

With reduced profits from mining, Chinese people turned to other labour-intensive occupations such as market gardening and tobacco farming, previously occupied by the debt-obligated new Chinese immigrants. Individuals or small groups of kinship and district-associated people entered into occupations that provided adequate income to continue remitting money to China. Chinese people also started providing services, selling products and working for non-Chinese people in positions such as general farm labourers, seasonal harvesters, sheep washers and shearers, scrub clearers/tree ring barkers, cooks, servants, hawkers, boot makers and tailors (Oddie 1961: 66; Chou 1993: 65). However, in the initial post-mining period, it was to market gardening that many Chinese people turned in order to earn a small but steady income (Baker 1985: 37; Adams 1997: 20; Wegars 2003: 70–71).

After the 1870s, Chinese market gardeners comprised 30% of the Chinese population and became the principal vegetable growers for Victoria (Clowes 1911: 196). Chinese gardeners planted crops that were popular in European diets and with Melbourne's increasing population, due initially to the gold rush and then to the building boom of the late 1870s through the 1880s. They were making sizeable profits catering to non-Chinese consumers (Chou 1993: 65; Wilton 2004: 27). By the late 1880s Chinese people also dominated laundry services and furniture and cabinet-making industries (Oddie 1959: 81, 86), then in the early 1900s Chinese retail stores and restaurants became popular among Chinese entrepreneurs.

The fundamental elements of Chinese social organisation in colonial Victoria, however, continued unchanged. The kinship system was dominant, district associations remained central and merchants acted as community leaders. Commerce was still predominantly conducted within the family unit, which enabled kinship merchants – through their *guanxi* favour and money-lending abilities – to continue to control many aspects of Chinese economic activity in Victoria. However, the days of large numbers of Chinese labourers working to support the Chinese presence on the Victorian goldfields were over.

The system discussed above is also relevant to Chinese fish-curing operations in Victoria. It is speculated that these establishments were initially owned by Chinese merchants and operated by indebted credit–ticket labourers, possibly with a kinship obligated headman. Cured fish was sold to independent Chinese miners and used as a food source for the large numbers of indebted Chinese labour under merchant control. In regard to the Port Albert fish-curing establishment, when mining activities slowed and Chinese miners began drifting into other occupations, two or three Chinese people may have leased or had some other arrangement with the owning merchant to take over fish-curing activities.

To obtain the best possible understanding of the ownership, operation and labour force of the Port Albert Chinese fish-curing establishment, it is useful to examine the entry of Chinese people into Australia's fishing industry and evidence of other fish-curing establishments in Australia and elsewhere.

# CHAPTER 4

# THE CHINESE IN VICTORIA'S FISHING INDUSTRY

A central argument of this investigation is that Chinese fish curers facilitated the development of Victoria's colonial fishing industry. This chapter examines documentary information concerning Australia's colonial Chinese fish curers to build a case for that argument (material remains are discussed in chapter 6). A range of hitherto unexplored questions concerning the activities of Chinese fish curers in colonial Australia are answered. For example, how extensive were their operations? During what period and where did they operate? Is there evidence for individual ownership of fish-curing establishments? Did Chinese people themselves fish? What were their fish-curing methods? Did their methods differ from non-Chinese fishermen? What were the market outlets? What quantities of fish were cured? Were good profits made?

Extensive desktop and field research in Victoria has recovered a good quantity of documentary information, mostly in the form of government literature, newspaper reports, diaries and oral histories. Many written histories and some scholarly works briefly mention the Chinese fish curers in Australia, including Cooper (1931), Hibbins (1984), Fitzgerald (1996), Williams (1999), Bennett (2002) and Hill (2004). Such literature often contains un-referenced information or is narrowly based on a few well-known newspaper articles or on the 1880 royal commission into the New South Wales fisheries. For this reason, this chapter predominantly uses primary sources, including an 1858 New South Wales Legislative Council report on Chinese immigration, 1861, 1879 and 1891 parliamentary debates on matters concerning the fishing industry, 1866 statistical returns from Tasmania's House of Assembly, an 1871 and an 1883 government-funded report on the fisheries of New South Wales, 1880 and 1919 royal commissions into fishing industry activities, an 1892 royal commission on Alleged Chinese Gambling and Immorality, an 1892 Legislative Assembly progress report upon the fishing industry of Victoria and 52 separate Australian colonial newspaper reports. Further historical material yet to be discovered may in future shed new light on Chinese fishing activities in Australia. In order to provide an accurate description of Australia's Chinese fish-curing industry, quotations from primary sources have been used as much as possible. Where necessary, the reliability or speculative nature of references will be assessed.

The most substantial academic comment on the Chinese fish curers in Australia is in Michael Lorimer's 1984 masters thesis on the technology used in and practices of the New South Wales fishing industry from 1850 to 1930. However, Lorimer's dissertation contains only one page of general information on the Chinese fish curers in colonial New South Wales and uses the 1880 royal commission and one newspaper article – the *Australian Town and Country Journal* (1870, July 9) – as a reference base.

The 1880 royal commission is the most informative and reliable source of information on the Chinese fish curers in Australia. Even so, royal commissions, parliamentary debate or official government reports must be considered in the context of the thinking of the period and possible individual prejudices of the authors.

New South Wales, Victorian and South Australian parliamentary debate also provide good evidence. Occasional references to the location and period of occupation of Chinese fishing sites can be found in government land tax and rate book records; although names – other than 'Chinaman' – are often unrecorded. Occupations, however, are frequently documented. General writings from the colonial period contain some useful information, but are often very subjective.

Chinese fish-curing establishments must have been a curious irregularity to the non-Chinese population. Perhaps for this reason, newspaper reports proved an abundant source of information about the role of Chinese people in Australia's early fishing industry.

The *Geelong Advertiser* (1865, January 16) observes that the fishermen of Melbourne's Port Phillip Bay are "made up of Italians, Dutchmen, Frenchmen, Chinese, Maori and others". The term "and other" would likely include British, German, Swedes, American, Greek and Australian Aboriginal people, all of who were involved in Australia's colonial fishing industry. As these 'other' fishermen were mostly of European background, to distinguish Chinese fishermen from non-Chinese fishermen the term 'European fishermen' will be used, except in reference to Aboriginal fishermen.

# LOCATION

## New South Wales

Documentary evidence from New South Wales, Victoria, the Northern Territory, South Australia and Tasmania indicates that Chinese fish curers were active in many Australian and nearby regions. Lorimer (1984: 93) suggests that when European fishermen from Sydney began to seek fishing grounds further from the metropolitan area, they often found large, already well-established Chinese fishing settlements. Parliamentary debate on Australia's fishing industry mentions that, from the early 1860s, many coastal regions of New South Wales such as Port Stephens, Newcastle, Lake Macquarie, Lake Illawarra, Hunter River, Twofold Bay, Jervis Bay, Merimbula and Coila Lake had Chinese fish-curing establishments (*Votes and Proceedings of the New South Wales Legislative Assembly* 1879–80, vol. 1: 670–78) (figure 4.1). Scrutiny of the local histories and newspapers for these areas would undoubtedly reveal further hints of the Chinese fish curers' presence. More direct evidence comes from a Chinese merchant, Chin Ateak (sometimes written Chen Ah Teak). When questioned by the royal commission of 1880, Chin Ateak states that approximately 20 years previously, he "had stations" himself and also received Chinese cured fish from other stations at each of the regions mentioned above (*Votes and Proceedings of the New South Wales Legislative Assembly* 1879–80, vol. 3: 1224). In addition to this, the *Sydney Morning Herald* (1861, April 6) noted that on the shores of Sydney's Pittwater region there was "a small colony of Chinamen, who live in tents and are engaged in curing fish".

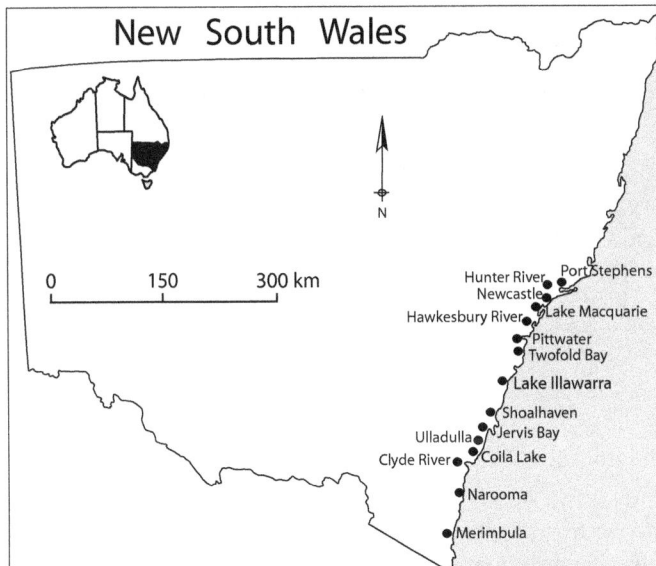

Figure 4.1 Known Chinese fish-curing establishments in New South Wales. Based on newspaper reports and the 1892 royal commission into the fisheries of New South Wales.

These references suggest that Chinese people operated an extensive fishing industry in New South Wales during the colonial period. In 1871, Alexander Oliver, a former fisheries inspector, was engaged by the government to enquire into the industrial progress of the New South Wales fisheries. Oliver (1871: 789) reports that the fishing grounds between Sydney and Newcastle "once supported more than 200 Chinese curers" and gives their decline as a "consequence of the falling off of the Victorian demand for cured fish". Later in this chapter, the approximate tonnage of fish handled annually by the Chinese fish curers in New South Wales is compared to that of European fishing activities, with very unexpected results.

## Northern Territory

In 1873, goldmining activities in the Northern Territory were gaining momentum and supplies came mostly from Darwin – then known as Palmerston. Kirkman (1984) and Jones (1990) have undertaken well-referenced research on Chinese activities in this region. By 1874, Chinese people were mining extensively in the Northern Territory and, not surprisingly, a Chinese fishing and fish-curing industry was established at Palmerston (Jones 1990: 24). On 1 June 1878, *The Northern Territory Times* commented,

> There are some people that are beginning to like John Chinaman – they get fish, prawns and
> fine vegetables, &c, which they could not procure awhile ago at any price.

The only known picture of a Chinese fishermen's temple in Australia (known as Moo Tai Mue Chinese Temple), comes from Fisherman's Beach at Palmerston, dated simply "before 1900" (figure 4.2).

Figure 4.2 The Moo Tai Mue Chinese fishermen's temple. The picture was taken in Darwin before 1900. Spillett Collection, Northern Territory Library.

Lack of water during the Northern Territory's dry season slowed Chinese mining operations. At these times, the Palmerston Government often provided Chinese miners with relief work, which paid a small wage and food rations (Jones 1990: 23). Part of the weekly rations included 3 ¾ lb of salt fish. It is highly likely that this product was Chinese cured fish, revealing a situation possibly unique to Australia where the government purchased produce from Chinese fish curers.

## South Australia

Chinese fish curers were active in South Australia from at least 28 May 1864, as evidenced in a column in *The Argus*:

> Fish Curing – Somewhat a novel exportation from South Australia to Victoria has taken place during the past few weeks ... By the Coorong, from Melbourne, there arrived some two months back four Chinamen, who brought a boat and a remarkably long seine, with which they located close to the Semaphore Jetty ... very many tons [of fish] have already been forwarded to the neighbouring colony, to be used as food by the Mongols on the various diggings ... In addition, however, to this branch, that of schnapper curing is carried on by the same men, who received fresh accession to their forces by three more arriving by last week's steamers.

This may be an example of a Chinese merchant using a ready supply of labour to test – and then if results were favourable, to exploit – a resource area. At the very least, the article from *The Argus* is good evidence that Chinese fish curers readily located themselves wherever there were fish and they did not – as did Europeans at the time – consider distance from market a constraint (figure 4.3).

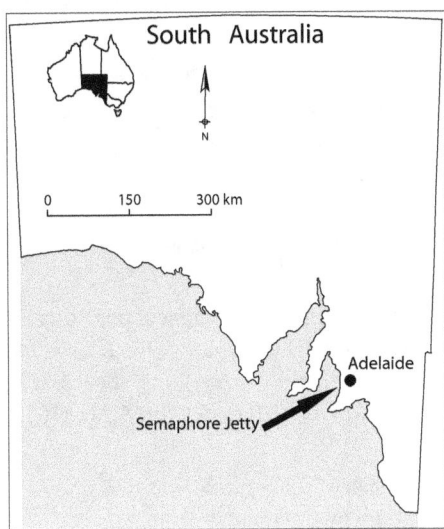

Figure 4.3 The only known Chinese fish-curing establishment in South Australia.

## Tasmania

The main period of Chinese immigration to Tasmania was from 1875 to 1890 (Vivian 1985: 1), when Chinese people were attracted by gold and tin resources. Before this time, however, the Chinese had other interests in Tasmania. On 30 November, 1860, the *Hobart Town Advertiser* reported that near the Franklin Wharf "several" Chinese had "commenced curing cray fish for the Melbourne Market. These fish they either catch, or purchase from any one willing to catch them". Parliament of Tasmania statistical returns (*Votes and Proceedings of the Tasmanian Legislative Council* 1886, vol. 13) show that in 1866, £460 of cured fish were exported from Tasmania to Victoria and £190 to New South Wales – revealing that the Chinese curers were making considerable sums from their industry. During this period European fishermen in Victoria averaged an annual wage of £250 (*Gippsland Times* 1879, May 21).

In June 1872, *The Examiner* wrote:

> Ah You a Chinese fisherman, arrived from Melbourne with his party last week and he proceeded to Ilfracombe with the intention of establishing a fishing station and fish-curing depot in that locality.

Historical studies conducted by Harrison (2006: 1) on Maria Island revealed that Ah Sin Yung, Sing and Chan worked as abalone gathers and curers, sending the cured product to Victoria. Finally, the Tasmanian census of 1881 shows one Chinese fisherman and two fish curers working near Dunalley at the mouth of Blackman Bay (figure 4.4).

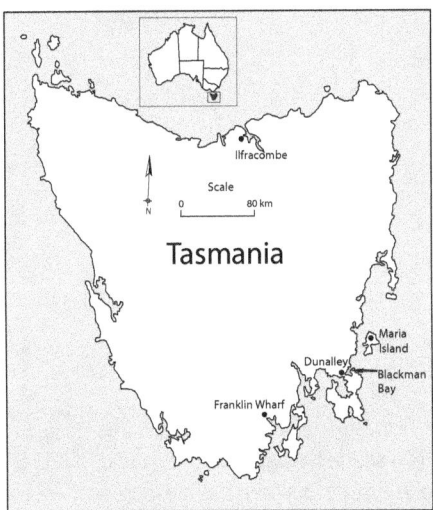

Figure 4.4 Known Chinese fish-curing establishments in Tasmania.

## Victoria

As this project focuses on Victoria's Chinese fish curers, a comprehensive discussion of site locations is warranted. The earliest located evidence for Chinese involvement in Australia's fishing industry – besides the trepang industry – comes from Victoria on 8 November 1856, when the *Bendigo Advertiser* reported that "It may not be generally known that several Chinese have established at St Kilda a fishery and fish-curing establishment". Three months later on, 5 January 1857, the *Bendigo Advertiser* states,

> The enterprise of the Chinese has of late displayed itself at St Kilda, Geelong and Schnapper
> Point in the establishment of curing-houses for the various fish found in the Bay.

From early 1857, newspaper articles on Chinese fish-curing activities in Port Phillip Bay appear periodically (see for example the *Geelong Advertiser* 1857, January 12; 1862, November 1865, January 16; *Illustrated Australian News* 1866, September 20). Engravings of Chinese people hauling fishing nets onto the beach at St Leonards (Geelong) and between Sandridge and St Kilda appeared in the *Illustrated Australian News* (1870, January 24; 1873, December 4) (figure 4.5). The 1873 report stated the

> party of Chinese fishermen pursuing their occupation on the beach ... are not very
> communicative. They live cheaply; carry on their fishing, as well as all their other industrial
> pursuits.

Extensive field research around the shores of Port Phillip Bay has revealed no surviving material evidence of Chinese fish-curing activities.

Figure 4.5 Two wood engravings of Chinese fishermen hauling in seine nets, Victoria. The scene at St Leonards (Geelong) (top) appeared in the *Illustrated Australian News* 1870, January 24. The scene between Sandridge and St Kilda (bottom) appeared in the *Illustrated Australian News* 1873, December 4. La Trobe Picture Collection, State Library of Victoria.

Surprisingly, no historical or material evidence has been located for Chinese people fishing on Victoria's west coast, although it is likely the Chinese were actively fishing and curing fish in this region. Stan Evans (2003) undertook a history of this region's fishing industry – with a focus on Port Fairy – in which no evidence of Chinese fishing activity was noted. In contrast, good quantities of historical evidence demonstrate the presence of Chinese fish curers along Victoria's east coast.

Working predominantly from the oral histories of fishermen at Phillip Island, John Jansson (2004) documents that William Richardson, a Phillip Island fisherman in the 1870s, "bought his first boat from a Chinese fisherman who had a house on the foreshore land west of Cowes" (see location Figure 4.10). This information was corroborated during interviews for this study with third-generation Phillip Island fishermen Ted Walton, Les Findlay and Jim Osterlund. However, subsequent field research in the area was hampered by recent housing developments and no material evidence of Chinese fishing activities was located.

Wells (2001), quoting from the personal notes of Peggy Banks, an early resident in Victoria's Warneet region, notes that

> Chinaman Island to the south of Warneet is separated from the mainland by only a narrow channel ... many years ago some Chinese fishermen lived and fished there ... they dried them and sent them to China.

Although field research on Chinaman Island revealed colonial period material remains, there was nothing to suggest a Chinese occupation. The island's name and oral history strongly suggest Chinese influence, although further evidence is required to confirm the presence of Chinese fish curers at this location.

Further east from Warneet, *The Gippslander* (1865, November 10) reported:

> A party of Chinese last week started a fish-curing establishment on the beach at Hastings and on Wednesday last no less than two and a half tons of fish were taken there to be cured.

The place names Chinaman's Creek, Johnny Souey Cove and Long Chinamen's Beach suggest Chinese fishing people were also active around the shores of Wilson's Promontory. In a written history of this area, Peterson (1978: 10) states that Long Chinaman's Beach was named "in memory of six Chinese men who drowned in that Bay", but unfortunately does not reference the information source (figure 4.6). More reliable written evidence of Chinese people fishing at Wilson's Promontory comes from the *Gippsland Guardian* (1865, April 7) which states that on 12 April, the SS *Ant* "called at Sealer's Cove and landed there a boat and a party of Chinamen".

Figure 4.6 This presumably depicts Chinese fishermen at Long Chinaman's Beach, Wilson's Promontory. Image from Peterson 1978: 10.

On 19 January 1866, the *Gippsland Guardian* cited a case where the Collector of Customs was called out to investigate a complaint that Chinese men based at Shallow Inlet were fishing with "nets of a finer mesh than was allowed by law". "A boat was dispatched to seize the illegal nets", but on investigation, no unlawful fishing equipment was found and the complaint was put down to jealousy at the success of the Chinese fishermen.

Writing on the beginnings of Port Welshpool, Collett (1994) states that

> Port Welshpool dwindled, until by 1871 it had only three houses and one tent, with 19 inhabitants, including four Chinese men who lived by the beach and the small jetty built in 1862, catching fish.

It is unfortunate that in this generally well-referenced book, Collett fails to cite where this information came from. Another reference for Chinese fish curers at Port Welshpool comes from the *Gippsland Standard* (1894, May 5), which reports, "there was a party of Queenscliff Chinamen fish curers came to Port Albert and Welshpool". When interviewed in 2003 for this project, many of the old residents of Port Welshpool indicated that there had been Chinese fish curers living in the area. However, perhaps due to land development, field research revealed no material remains of Chinese activities at Port Welshpool.

Efforts made in this project to locate physical remains of Chinese fishing activities have been hampered by scanty, misleading or lost written records. In view of this, collating oral evidence with field reconnaissance is often the best method of locating sites. Around the Port Albert waterways this was done with some success. Norie Rossiter and Jock Greenaway, both long term residents of the south Gippsland district of Hedley, gave oral evidence in 2003 of a Chinese fish-curing camp at Fahey's Point slightly west of Nine Mile Creek (figure 4.7). Subsequent field research revealed a small quantity of colonial period material remains. No distinctly Chinese artefacts were located, however there was an assortment of timber post remains and three purposely dug ground trenches – approximately 600 mm wide, 600 millimetre deep and 7 m long – running at right angles to the shore line (figure 4.8). Local residents could not put a purpose to the trench system. However, over a year later in 2004, Jimmy Robinson – a third-generation south Gippsland fisherman – relayed that his father had told him Chinese fish curers sometimes salted fish in purposely dug trenches, such as those described above. A historically identified Chinese fish-curing site in Tasmania's Dunalley region contains a trench system very similar to that described above (Ben Morphett 2006 pers. comm.). Very dense coastal tussock grasses at Fahey's Point possibly hide the Chinese artefacts required to conclusively link this site with Chinese fish-curing activities. Archaeological excavation may also confirm Chinese occupation of the site.

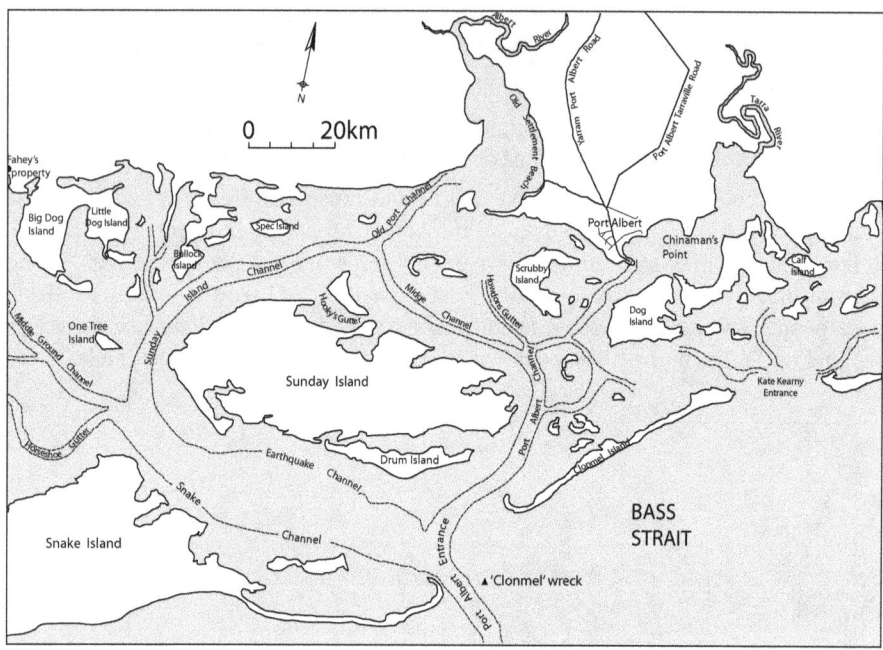

Figure 4.7 Map of South Gippsland waterways showing Fahey's Point (top left of map, labelled 'Fahey's property').

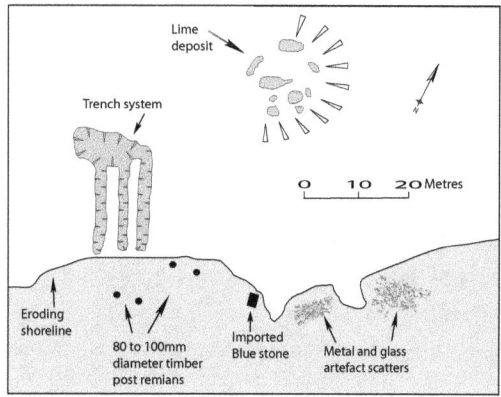

Figure 4.8 Plan drawing of site at Fahey's Point.

Albert Clark, a third-generation Port Albert fisherman interviewed for this project in 2003, gave oral evidence of a Chinese fishing camp slightly west of Port Albert on Drum Island (figure 4.7 for location of Drum Island). Subsequent field research on the island revealed – through scatters of Chinese-type ceramics – definite evidence of Chinese occupation, although no evidence of fishing or fish-curing activities was apparent. Chinese people living so close to the Port Albert fish-curing establishment that is the subject of this research were almost certainly fishermen supplying fish to the curers and possibly also sending fresh fish to Melbourne markets.

A report in the *Gippsland Guardian* (1867, July 1) mentions a "familiarly known Chinaman" who "left his mates on Sunday Island and proceeded in a small boat to the Port [Port Albert]". Sunday Island is only metres away from Drum Island and the two islands may even have been joined in 1867. Days later his boat was found anchored but empty in the mouth of Kate Kearney Channel and it was assumed the Chinaman had fallen overboard and drowned. Police made enquiries and it was discovered, "in about four feet of water at low tide … the Chinaman had found his way to some of his own countrymen who reside on the island". This report indicates first, that there were Chinese people living on Sunday Island. As Sunday Island had no fresh-water supply it is unlikely they were market gardeners and so quite likely were fishermen. Secondly, the phrase "some of his countrymen" implies a group of – or at least more than two – Chinese people were living on one of the several islands near Kate Kearney Channel, which is the eastern sea entrance to Port Albert (figure 4.7 for location of Kate Kearney Channel). Both Lennon (1973: 197) and Peterson (1978: 9) suggest that Chinese people had fishing camps on many of the islands between Wilson's Promontory and Port Albert, but it is not known where they obtained this information.

The Port Albert Chinese fish-curing establishment – the focus of chapters 5, 6 and 7 – originally came to my attention through oral evidence and was located through subsequent field research. Associated historical literature and material evidence for this site will be discussed in detail in the following chapter.

One of the very few examples of pictorial evidence for a Chinese fish-curing camp in Victoria – or Australia more broadly – is an 1886 photograph of an establishment at Metung, formerly Rosherville (figure 4.9). A reporter for the *Gippsland Mercury* (1879, May 20) visited the camp, stating "and here we saw a Chinese fishing camp … the men were civil and obliging enough and showed us a lot of fish". The *Bairnsdale Advertiser* (1955, September 5) ran a series of articles written by an early resident of Metung, Rowland Bell. Bell writes that one of the Metung fishermen "was a Chinaman named Ah Sing". In October 1928, Bell wrote an article for the local Metung paper *Every Week* in which he notes the Chinese camp was "the fishing camp of Ah Sing and Co." and goes on to mention there were "six Chinese" working and living there.

Figure 4.9 This NJ Caire photograph c. 1886 of Shaving Point, Metung, probably unintentionally captured part of the Chinese fish-curing establishment, identifiable predominantly through the low fish-drying racks visible in the right portion of the picture, but also through newspaper reports and oral histories. La Trobe Picture Collection, State Library of Victoria.

When interviewed by Ellis & Lee (2002: 32), Jack Allen, a third-generation Metung fisherman, stated:

> there were quite a few Chinese around Metung [approximately 1860 to 1900]. I've heard my grandfather talking about them too. He said they'd sing as they hauled their nets in. There'd be four or five of them on the end of the nets, singing away in Chinese.

Again in Ellis and Lee (2002: 46), Bill Farquhar a former fishermen of the Gippsland lakes, said,

> Old Joe Bull, he'd tell me about how the Chinese used to carry these great big heavy baskets of fish … in Bancroft Bay and the little creek up in the corner of it, we found all these fish scales many feet deep. Where the Chinese had sat … and scaled them.

Another third-generation Metung resident, Peter Bury, interviewed in 2003 for this project, also claimed to have seen these fish scales and gave what he believed to be their exact location. However, extensive auger test pitting in this region revealed no evidence of fish scales or Chinese fishing activities. This may be due to the constantly shifting bodies of sand moving the location of the evidence or possibly because oral history is not always precise.

There is unambiguous evidence of 11 Chinese fish-curing establishments in Victoria and suggestions of a further five (figure 4.10). Solid historical evidence for Chinese fish-curing activity in New South Wales, Northern Territory, South Australia, Tasmania and Victoria (figure 4.11), leaves no doubt that Chinese people were heavily involved in Australia's colonial fishing industry. As further historical evidence is recovered, the locations of other Chinese fish-curing establishments in Australia are likely to be identified. Wheelwright (1861: 248) wrote of Victoria: "on every [European] fishing station along the coast Chinamen are camped, who buy the fish from the boat and salt them on the spot".

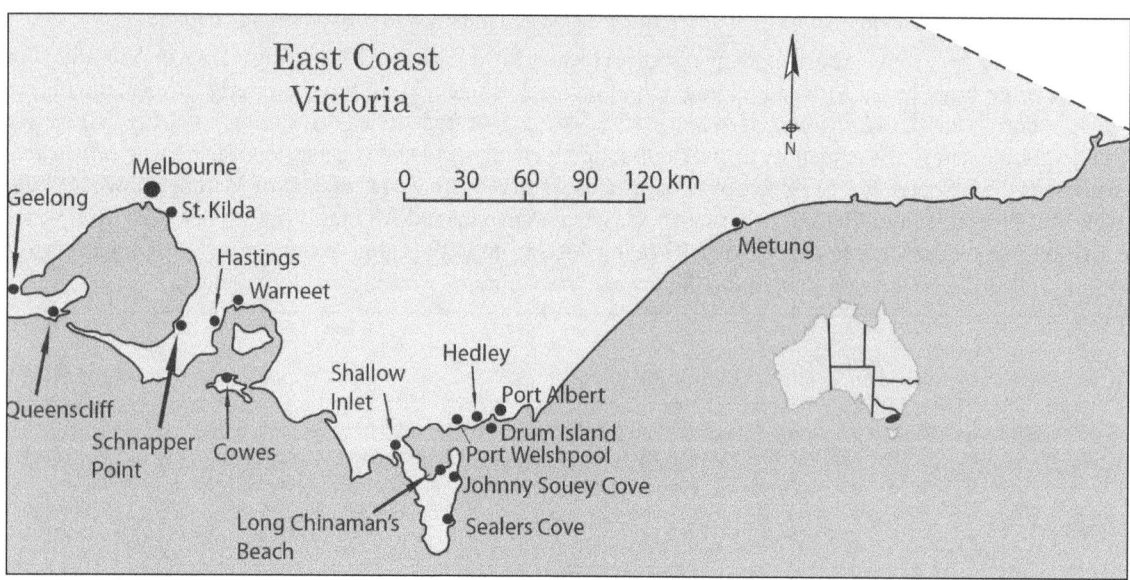

Figure 4.10 Location of known and inferred Chinese fish-curing establishments in Victoria. Based on newspaper reports, local histories, field reconnaissance and the 1892 select committee upon the fishing industry of Victoria.

Figure 4.11 Darkened areas indicate known regions of Chinese fish-curing activity in Australia.

## INTERNAL STRUCTURE

The labour structures i.e. owner/employer and headman/labourer relationships of Chinese fish-curing establishments in Australia may never be entirely understood. Nevertheless, by working through the available literature, some basic knowledge can be ascertained.

When *The Argus* (1864, May 28) reported on Chinese fish-curing activities at Semaphore in South Australia, it was noted that

> There appears to be one amongst them who directs the whole operation and whenever
> any inquires are made he, in rather indifferent English, is remarkably willing to afford
> information.

This suggests – at least at this establishment – that the common Chinese practice of a headman overseeing operations was observed among fish curers. As this particular headman spoke a little English, he may have been an aspiring merchant already on the lower rungs of this class.

In the *Australian Town and Country Journal* of 9 July 1870, a reporter describes the Chinese fish-curing camp at Lake Macquarie – established in approximately 1863:

> I arrived at the house of Mr. Ah Tie (the principal boss of the whole concern) ... From the
> lips of Ah Tie I learnt that altogether there are about 17 Chinamen engaged in the work of
> catching and curing fish on the lake. Of this number nine are under the leadership of Mr
> Ah Tie, while the remaining eight acknowledge as their chief a highly intelligent-looking
> individual rejoicing in the name of Hop Lung. The respective parties of Messrs. Ah Tie and
> Hop Lung live about half-a-mile apart.

Separate camps probably represent different Chinese kinship association groups or possibly members of the same kinship group owned or financed by different Chinese merchants. Again, the apparent ability of the headman to speak English suggests that Ah Tie may have been a (lower-class) merchant.

The living arrangements at the Lake Macquarie camp appear unusually attractive:

> They [the camps] have each two or three very comfortable slab cottages, well lined and
> shingled and perfectly weather tight, which is more than can be said of all the European
> dwelling-houses on the lake.

This suggests that the headmen of these camps may have had some wealth themselves or a generous merchant financer. Further evidence of a possible higher authority is the mention of Ah Tie's "account-book, into which every consignment of fish was duly and carefully entered". Account books are common business items but – particularly given the care with which Ah Tie maintained his accounts, it is conceivable that Ah Tie had a superior to whom he reported business quotas, dividends or commissions. Should any such written records survive, they would provide an invaluable insight into Chinese fish-curing activities in colonial Australia.

The *Sydney Morning Herald* (1861, April 6) reports that Sydney's Pittwater region had a "colony of Chinamen, who live in tents and are engaged in curing fish". Anderson (1920: 174) expands on this – presumedly through oral history – by indicating that the fish-curing camp "belonged to a Chinese firm ... The manager Ah Chuey was a Chinese gentleman, much respected by residents". This suggests the camp was part of a larger business and Ah Chuey was almost certainly a kinship or district associate of the business owner. Although Ah Chuey's exact employment details are unknown, it is likely he was placed as headman at the fish-curing establishment by his employer. This would have given him an income and an opportunity to become a merchant himself. In 1861, the Chinese labourers at the camp were quite likely to have been under credit–ticket obligation to Ah Chuey's employer.

Evidence of fish-curing establishments being owned by Chinese merchants and of labourers working under an obligation to their employer can be found in the 1880 royal commission. T Curtis, a fisherman, was asked, "You were fishing a long time at Port Stephens and there were Chinamen there that took your catch?" Mr Curtis replied "Just so". Mr Curtis was then asked, "Were those fish despatched to the diggings, or to Chinese merchants in Sydney for despatch there?" Mr Curtis answered, "Both ways; one Chinaman that I was fishing for belonged to a Melbourne merchant" (*Votes and proceedings of the New South Wales Legislative Assembly* 1880, vol. 3). This suggests that the Chinese fish curer was working under some form of ownership or obligation, quite likely the credit–ticket system. The fact that he was working at Port Stephens but "belonged" to a merchant in Melbourne demonstrates that distance was not a major obstacle to Chinese fish-curing activities in colonial Australia. It may also show that credit–ticket labourers could be farmed out to merchants in other parts of Australia – as described by Omohundro (1977: 116), for Chinese labour organisation in the Philippines (previously discussed in chapter 3).

In the royal commission (1880: 1224–26), the Chinese merchant Chin Ateak provides further evidence of merchant ownership of fish-curing establishments. The questioning begins:

> [Q] What is your name? [A] Chin Ateak. [Q] You are a merchant? [A] Yes. [Q] We want to ascertain something of the fish trade; you have had something to do with it, have you not? [A] Yes. [Q] For a long time? [A] Yes. [Q] Will you mention when it was you carried on the trade and where? [A] Port Stephens, Lake Macquarie, Jervis Bay and Merimbula – Twofold Bay, before we put a station there to catch fish. [Q] At all those places you had stations to procure fish? [A] Yes.

The wording "before we put a station there" suggests Chin Ateak was working with other people, but his relationship to these people is unclear. Regardless, it is unlikely that Chin Ateak worked at all these establishments himself and must have had others administering and labouring for him.

The questions continue:

> [Q] That is some years ago? [A] Yes, nearly 20 years ago. [Q] And when did you give them up? [A] I gave them up, oh, long ago – nearly eight years ago [approximately 1872]. [Q] But you had some Chinese fishers? [A] I had at some places Chinese fishermen and at some places the Europeans.

Chin Ateak's answers suggest that he owned these camps.

From the information available, it can be ascertained that, at least in some cases, Australian Chinese fish-curing establishments were most likely owned by Chinese merchants who staffed their operations with a headman and a team of working-class labourers. In one instance only – the 1880 royal commission – does the evidence suggest an indebted labourer worked at a Chinese fish-curing establishment. Until further evidence comes to light, this remains the principal evidence for merchant use of indebted labour in the fish-curing industry.

Chin Ateak's exit from fish-curing activities in the early 1870s is consistent with an increase in Chinese market gardening at this time. After the 1870s, Chinese gardeners had an advantage over fish curers, as garden produce could be sold to European customers, whereas Chinese cured fish had no European demand. For example, the 1880 royal commission states the Chinese fish curers at Nelson Bay "catch their own fish here and preserve it after their own detestable fashion" (*Votes and Proceedings of the New South Wales Legislative Assembly* 1879–80, vol. 3: 1135). When the same royal commission interviewed the fisherman G Newton, he was asked, "Do you know whether their preserved fish are purchased or liked by Europeans?" He answered, "I do not think so; they are not fit for Europeans … anybody who saw the Chinamen cure the fish would not, I am sure, eat them" (*Votes and Proceedings of the New South Wales Legislative Assembly* 1879–80, vol. 3: 1200). In 1871, a government official, Alexander Oliver, reported on the condition of the New South Wales fisheries, stating:

> The mode of curing adopted by the Chinese, however relished by their countrymen in Victoria, is sufficiently revolting to European tastes to exclude the article from general consumption … the flesh in the dried state is always more or less cheesy (1871: 785)

With a declining Chinese population in Australia and no European market, Chinese fish-curing establishments became less viable. Oliver's (1871: 789) comments in this regard are illuminating:

> Those [fishing grounds] near Lake Macquarie only a few years ago gave occupation to several gangs of Chinese curers and would do so now, but that this industry ... is in a very depressed state in consequence of the falling off of the Victorian demand for cured fish.

In questions answered by Chin Ateak during the 1891–92 Royal Commission on Alleged Chinese Gambling and Immorality – almost a decade after the royal commission into the fishing industry – the change in preferred Chinese economic activities can be clearly seen (*Votes and Proceedings of the New South Wales Legislative Assembly* 1891–92, vol. 8). The questioning starts:

> [Q] What business are you in? [A] I keep a lot of gardeners. [Q] How many Chinamen have you in your employ? [A] I used to have half a dozen in some places, a dozen in others and smaller numbers elsewhere; about fifty altogether. [Q] How much do you pay them? [A] I give each man £40 a year, except the head man, who gets £50. [Q] And they feed themselves? No? [A] I pay for their food too. It costs about 10s a week per man.

Chin Ateak's move from fish curing into market gardening reflects the general decline in fish-curing activities after 1870 and the ability of Chinese merchants to adapt to the economic circumstances at hand.

Chinese fish curing did persist in Australia – although on a smaller scale – well after the 1870s, as will be shown at the Port Albert site and as is evident in an 1891–92 royal commission into the fisheries of New South Wales. In this report WM Boyd, the Assistant Inspector of Fisheries for Lake Macquarie states, "There is only one camp of these men [Chinamen], five in number, with one boat, who send their fish to Sydney and Newcastle" (*Votes and Proceedings of the New South Wales Legislative Assembly* 1891–92, vol. 7: 294). As far as can be established, this was the last group of Chinese fish curers operating in New South Wales, a stark contrast to earlier periods when the fishing grounds just between Sydney and Newcastle "once supported more than 200 Chinese curers" (Oliver 1871: 789). How many individual fish-curing establishments this represents is difficult to determine. Nevertheless, some indication of the number of Chinese people required to work a Chinese fish-curing establishment can be ascertained.

When a reporter for the *Illustrated Australian News* visited the Chinese fish-curing establishment at St Kilda Beach on 4 December 1873, he noted "The fishermen number about 16". At Lake Macquarie in 1870, Ah Tie had nine Chinese workers at his curing camp and Hop Lung had eight (*Australian Town and Country Journal* 1870, July 9). At Mount Eliza in Victoria, the *Bendigo Advertiser* of 7 March 1857 reported "four Chinese established themselves in the neighbourhood as fish salters and curers". At Schnapper Point in Victoria in 1857 there were "forty men (all Europeans or Americans) engaged in catching schnapper and selling them to the two Chinamen who reside there" (*Bendigo Advertiser* 1857, January 5). The curing site at Semaphore Jetty in South Australia had seven Chinese people working there (*The Argus* 1864, May 28). From this information, it appears that at establishments where Chinese people fished and cured fish, up to 16 Chinese workers could be employed, but for operations that only cured fish, two to four Chinese people were sufficient.

Some evidence exists to suggest that after the 1870s, fish-curing establishments tended to be owned by individuals or groups rather than by merchants who controlled headmen and labourers. This is also the case for Chinese market gardens, as argued in chapter 3.

In Wilton's (2004: 27) discussion on Chinese market gardens in Victoria, she suggests that after the 1870s,

> Often, a market garden was set up as a cooperative venture between a number of men. This meant that as one partner returned to China or moved on to seek other work, someone could be brought in to replace him.

Using oral evidence, Williams (1999: 42) suggests that during the late 1800s, Sydney's Chinese market gardeners were also pursuing cooperative venturers:

> Most of these gardens were leased by groups of 5 to 10. Such arrangements suited people who would go to China for a year or two. When they did so their share was passed on to another gardener and taken up again on return.

The 1880 royal commission into fisheries reports that in New South Wales, "A considerable gang of Chinamen is always located at Nelson Bay and as soon as one lot returns to its native country another takes its place" (*Votes and Proceedings of the New South Wales Legislative Assembly* 1879–80, vol. 3: 1135). While the evidence is not conclusive, it seems likely that, as merchants abandoned their interests in cured fish, some fish-curing operations may have been taken over by individuals or groups and run along the same lines as Chinese market gardens in Australia.

# CHINESE FISHING AND FISH CURING

Most written histories assume that Chinese fish curers in colonial Australia did not fish themselves, but instead purchased fish from European fishermen (see for example Hibbins 1984: 46; Fitzgerald 1996: 69; Bennett 2002: 9). As was noted in chapter 3, this was largely not the case. The other common misconception is that Chinese fish curers smoked their fish (see for example Halstead 1977: 32; Synan 1989: 161; Collett 1994: 50). Primary documentation confirms that Chinese people did fish commercially in colonial Australia and indicates that salting and pickling were the main methods used to cure fish. Material evidence for this will be examined in chapter 6.

For comparative purposes, Ward's (1954: 202–03) account of fishing methods in China in the 1950s is instructive. Ward indicates the most common form of fishing in China, that she witnessed, was netting from boats, principally purse-seining where fish are encircled by a net and long-lining, however,

> almost all fishermen from time to time will engage in hand-lining and trapping ... They do their fishing in pairs and usually by night ... bright kerosene lights are used to attract the fish.

Diamond (1969: 13) notes that Chinese fishermen in Taiwan most often use a beach seine. A boat is used to encircle fish with a net some 900 ft long and the boat then rows back to shore where the net is hand-hauled by long ropes onto the beach.

When the reporter for the *Australian Town and Country Journal* (1870, 9 July) visited Ah Tie and Hop Lung at Lake Macquarie, he noted:

> Attached to the fisheries are four long-boats of about 18 feet keel and any number of nets, the construction of which is rather peculiar, inasmuch as they can be used separately in shallow water, or unitedly in deep water, interlinked together so as to form one immense net.

*The Argus* (1864, May 28) reports the Chinese fish curers at Semaphore, South Australia had "brought a boat and a remarkably long seine".

The *Illustrated Australian News* (1873, December 4), in an article on Chinese fishermen at St Kilda, reports:

> Net fishing is what they are engaged in at the moment – a style of fishing in which our Mongolian immigrants appear to be most at home. The nets vary in length from forty to eighty fathoms [264 to 480 ft] having inch mesh ... The fishing is chiefly carried on at night, or early morning.

This article also contains a wood engraving of Chinese fishermen hauling a net onto the beach at St Kilda (figure 4.12).

Colonial-period literature often blames Chinese fishermen for destroying fishing grounds by using too-small net mesh, which "destroy large quantities of the spawn and young ... and a hundred times more fish than they caught" – and nets that are too long (*Votes and Proceedings of the New South Wales Legislative Assembly* 1879–80, vol. 1: 678). This criticism can be seen to varying degrees through the 1880 royal commission. For example, Richard Seymour, Sydney's Inspector of Nuisances and the auctioneer in charge of the Eastern Fish Market was asked by the royal commission (1880, vol. 3: 1151) if the Chinese fishermen in New South Wales were harmful to the industry. Seymour answers:

> [A] Well, the fishermen during the winter months generally grumble about the Chinamen, because they pick up a class of fish they have no right to. [Q] How do they fish? [A] With nets. [Q] Have you heard that they fish with six nets together? [A] I have heard so.

The same committee asked Hugh Logan, a New South Wales fisherman, if

> [Q] The young fish are put back in the water [by Europeans]? [A] Yes, – although the Chinamen are doing more to injure the fishery trade than any people on earth; they are catching all the small fish, sweeping them up with the close [seine] nets. (*Votes and Proceedings of the New South Wales Legislative Assembly* 1879–80, vol. 3: 1265)

A fisherman, William Boyd, answered in a similar fashion:

> [Q] I suppose it is chiefly net-fishing in Lake Macquarie? [A] Yes, principally ... The way those Chinamen slaughter them with their nets, when they get fishing, is something frightful. (*Votes and Proceedings of the New South Wales Legislative Assembly* 1879–80, vol. 3: 1256)

Figure 4.12 B Robert's engraving *Chinese fishing by moonlight* c. 1873. La Trobe Picture Collection, State Library of Victoria.

Boyd goes on to give the most detailed description so far located regarding the manner in which Chinese fishermen used fishing nets in colonial Australia. He also suggests that European fishing methods were equally as damaging to fish stocks as those used by the Chinese. The question was asked:

> [Q] But did they [the Chinese] use the small mesh? [A] The smallest mesh was a 2-inch mesh, not as small as Europeans use. [Q] What sort of net did they [the Chinese] use? [A] About 300 fathoms long [1800 ft] and 30 feet deep in the bunt. [Q] And they passed that round the fish in the deep water? [A] Yes … They would shoot down between 30 and 40 feet of water and then the net would sink down until they came to shallow water. [Q] Did they sink the net in deep water and haul it into shallow water? [A] Naturally it would sink itself. It was not corked the same as our nets. [Q] And they used to pull it ashore? [A] Yes; ten men hauled it, five on each side. They would shoot out of two boats … and then they would haul into the land, on the beach. [Q] Do you think that lessened the numbers of the fish very much? [A] Oh, bless you yes. You can only catch small schnapper now; but our fishermen cause more destruction to the lake than the Chainmen did, with those small meshes; they have ruined the lake. (*Votes and Proceedings of the New South Wales Legislative Assembly* 1879–80, vol. 3: 1257)

In these instances, Chinese fishermen appear to have used a similar method to net fish as was used in China. The description of Chinese fishermen sinking a net fully before dragging it to shore differs from European methods only in that during Australia's colonial period, European fisherman used net floats to keep a portion of their nets on the water's surface. Other fishing methods used by Chinese fishermen in Australia, as reported in the various government documents and newspaper reports, appear similar to European methods of the times. Both Chinese and European fishing techniques appear to have been detrimental to fish populations.

The *Illustrated Australian News* (1873, December 4) reports on the species of fish that the Chinese in Melbourne's Port Phillip Bay were catching: "The fish caught by them [Chinese fishermen] are mostly flounders, garfish, flathead, salmon trout, silver fish and mullet". The *Australian Town and Country Journal* reporter (1870, July 9) at Lake Macquarie states that

> [The] principal kinds of fish cured by the Chinamen are schnapper, bream, whiting, flat-head and mullet; but Messer. Ah Tie and Hop Ling are not at all particular and it is very rarely that they catch a fish they cannot make use of in one form or another.

The evidence shows that Chinese curers were procuring a portion of the fish they cured by fishing, themselves, with nets.

Firth (1946: 13, 14), Inglis (1975: 71) and Omohundro (1977: 115) have noted that in regions other than China overseas Chinese people often employed locals as basic labourers. In colonial Australia, Chinese fish curers supplemented their own catches by purchasing fish that Europeans had caught with nets and by line and hook. Oliver (1871: 788) notes that in New South Wales,

> there are and will continue to be found, prolific fishing grounds without number, many already known to the schnapper and net fishermen, who, at various times and often in most unexpected places, have plied their trade for the supply of Chinese curers.

Schnapper (figure 4.13) is caught predominantly by line and hook and, as will be shown, was highly desired by Chinese people in colonial Australia. As far as can be ascertained, the Chinese fish curers did not engage in line fishing for schnapper themselves. Rather, they purchased schnapper from European fishermen, perhaps because the resource-intensive nature of line-and-hook fishing made it more economical to use local fishermen for this task.

Figure 4.13 The Australian schnapper (*Chrysophrys guttulatus*). Image from Roughley 1953: 76.

When fisherman Thomas Curtis was interviewed for the 1880 royal commission he was asked:

> [Q] Can you give us an idea of what line fish you could have got in the early times, or even now for the Chinamen? [A] I did very well with the Chinamen there. Some days 18 or 20- five dozen of schnapper and other days from three or four or five dozen. It always paid. [Q] The Chinamen only took a limited quantity? [A] As many as we could catch. [Q] If ten boats could have fished there the Chinamen would have all the fish that were caught? [A] Yes. (*Votes and Proceedings of the New South Wales Legislative Assembly* 1879–80, vol. 3: 1181)

Fisherman Michael Salomon was then interviewed:

> [Q] Did you ever fish for the Chinese? [A] Yes. [Q] You were largely engaged at one time schnapper-fishing? [A] For the Chinamen – Yes. (*Votes and Proceedings of the New South Wales Legislative Assembly* 1879–80, vol. 3: 1186)

George Newton gives a similar story:

> [Q] Have you ever been engaged in the services of Chinamen? [A] Yes. [Q] What fish did you catch for the Chinamen? [A] Schnapper principally. [Q] How many fishermen were engaged in that occupation? [A] I have known as many as about 20 boats to be engaged by the Chinese [in Broken Bay, NSW]. [Q] Would they take all the fish that you brought to them? [A] Yes. (*Votes and Proceedings of the New South Wales Legislative Assembly* 1879–80, vol. 3: 1200)

The same pattern of European hook-and-line fishermen selling to Chinese curers was apparent in South Australia, as reported in *The Argus* (1864, May 28):

> In addition, however, to this branch, that of schnappers-curing is carried on by the same men [Chinese men] ... In order to procure a better supply, all fish that comes to their net, as well

as any other kinds purchasable at £6 per ton. This offer enlisted some Europeans, who have driven a fair trade in consequence, bringing to the Semaphore Jetty beautiful samples of the finer description of schnapper.

In Victoria, the *Bendigo Advertiser* (1857, January 5) reports that

The enterprise of the Chinese has of late displayed itself at St Kilda, Geelong and Schnapper Point in the establishment of curing-houses for the various fish found in the Bay ... At Schnapper Point this singular people appear to be conducting this branch of industry on a large scale. Not less than a dozen boats with crews from 20 to forty men (all Europeans and Americans) being engaged in catching schnapper and selling them to the two Chinamen who reside there.

Chinese fish curers were procuring – through a purchasing arrangement – a significant number of schnapper from European fishermen. The quantities of finance generated by European fishermen and Chinese fish curers will be discussed in the 'Economics' section of this chapter.

## Chinese fish-curing methods

Other fish were just as important to the Chinese curers as schnapper. The desirability of different sorts of fish depended to a large degree on how well they cured. Chinese methods of curing also varied according to fish type.

In the 1880 royal commission the Chinese merchant Chin Ateak gives an insight into the types of fish Chinese curers preferred for curing and their methods of curing:

[Q] Was it any particular kind of fish? [A] Yes, some schnapper and net fish. [Q] All mixed together? [A] Not all mixed. [Q] You separated them? [A] Yes. [Q] And those were salted and dried I suppose? [A] Salted and dried; some dried and some they call pickled fish, put in a cask or barrel. [Q] What are considered the best fish for salting? [A] Schnapper ... you can salt schnapper at any time; you can use them – they keep longer – not spoil much. [Q] Pickled? [A] No, another kind of fish make pickle. Only make tailor and like the mullet. [Q] For the use of your countrymen I suppose? [A] My countrymen – Yes ... only smoked fish Europeans use.

Considering that large quantities of schnapper must have been caught and cured, it is surprising to discover that Chinese people considered schnapper a low-grade eating fish. When asked if he ever sent cured schnapper to China, Chin Ateak responded, "No, in the China market cheaper – only cheap fish". Schnapper appears to have been sought after by Chinese curers in Australia because – as Chin Ateak says "It is very easy salting the schnapper ... they keep longer – not spoil much" (*Votes and Proceedings of the New South Wales Legislative Assembly* 1879–80, vol. 3: 1224–26).

The Chinese curers also processed a wide variety of other fish and shellfish. Chin Ateak suggests that Chinese people considered squid (*Sepioteuthis australis*) (figure 4.14) to be the most valuable and best eating fish along with the "mutton-fish, with a big shell" – the Australian abalone (*Haliotis naevosa*) (figure 4.15). Speaking of the squid, Chin Ateak says, "At Melbourne plenty of that; schooner send plenty up ... that we call the best fish – the squid". When asked about the abalone, "What do you make of the inside?" Chin Ateak responds, "All the same – make soup ... the very best".

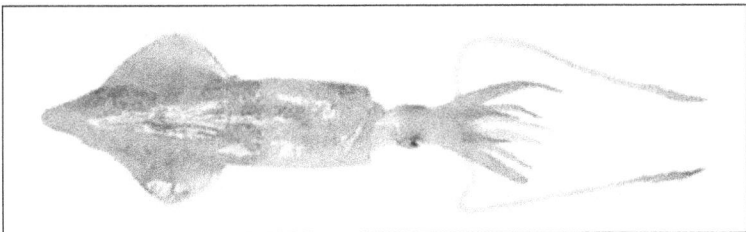

Figure 4.14 Common Australian squid (*Sepioteuthis australis*) Image from Vaughan 1987: 196.

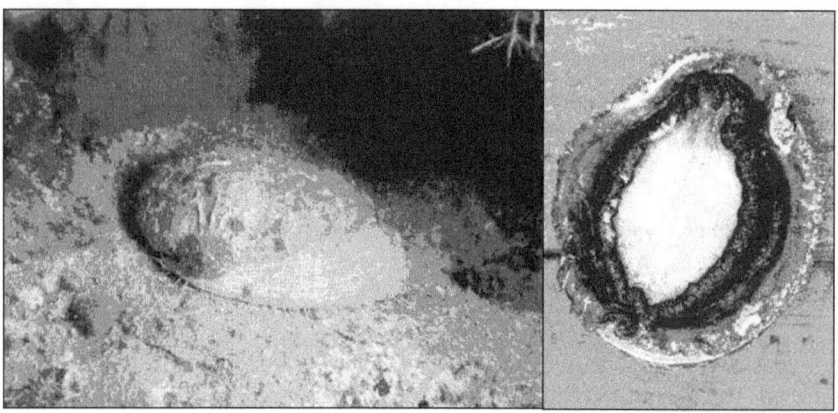

Figure 4.15 Australian abalone (*Haliotis naevosa*). Images from Vaughan 1987: 188.

The Chinese curers also targeted prawns and lobsters, as Chin Ateak indicates:

> [Q] Do you know what are called prawns here? [A] Yes. [Q] Do you ever purchase them for the trade? [A] Plenty, from the Hunter River and Newcastle and some are got up from Lake Macquarie ... we get them and mix them up with salt and make pickle, like a paste – like anchovy. [Q] And do you make use of the cray-fish – the lobster? [A] The lobster, yes ... we dry them ... send them to the country. [Q] Do you get a good price for them? [A] Just like the fish.

Chin Ateak describes how Chinese people in Australia ate the cured fish:

> [A] Only cook it with rice – on top of rice. [Q] Do they boil it? [A] Not boil it, only steam it, rice at the bottom and fish at the top; the steam comes up and cooks the fish and makes the rice to be done and the fish to be done too.

Chin Ateak's participation in the 1880 royal commission provides valuable details of Chinese fish-curing operations in colonial Australia. The accounts of European fisherman who fished for the Chinese curers and eyewitness descriptions from newspaper reporters are also good sources of information. For example, in the 1892 select committee on the fishing industry of Victoria, William Fitz answers questions on the Chinese fish curers at Port Albert. When asked, "How do they cure their fish?" he answers: "Salt them and dry them in the sun" (*Votes and Proceedings of the Victorian Legislative Council* 1892: 111). A writer reminiscing about his youth in Port Albert gives a more detailed description:

> We boys delighted to walk to Long Point, to see the Chinamen fishing and curing fish. They had long tables on trestles, on which the fish, gutted and split open, were laid to dry in the sun. The fish were closely packed in bags and sent by steamer to Melbourne. (*Gippsland Standard* 1944, July 7)

Oliver (1871: 785) also notes the use of bags for packing cured fish: "Fish have hitherto been salted chiefly by Chinamen for exportation to Victoria ... they are shipped in a dry state in bags". The *Bendigo Advertiser* (1857, January 5) reports that at Schnapper Point in Port Phillip Bay, Victoria, Chinese fish curers "split the fish in the usual fashion and after being cured, are spread out to dry upon the long kangaroo grass".

Two separate curing procedures were described at the fish-curing establishment in South Australia, for

> herrings, garfish, mullet, whiting, ruffs, flounder, salmon, cuttlefish, squid, silverfish ... [T]hey were indiscriminately cast into casks of brine and when a couple of days were past, they were removed and spread in the sun to partially dry ... After this they were stowed in casks fit for exportation. (*The Argus* 1864, May 28)

Schnapper appears to have been processed differently:

> [The] internal arrangement of the fish is partially removed, leaving the liver and roe attached, being cleverly split from the back. They are then thrown into a brine-cask and left for a few days, after which they are taken to the beach, cleanly scrubbed with small brooms and dried on the rushes. (*The Argus* 1864, May 28)

A similar method is described by fisherman George Newton, when asked by the New South Wales royal commission (1880: 1200), "Can you give us any idea of their mode of curing – what they did with the fish?", he answers,

> They split them and salt them and shove them into a cask ... at other times they would cut
> a little of the belly, take the inside out – just what they could reach – put a lot of salt in and
> stuff the fish into a cask.

The *Australian Town and Country Journal* (1870, July 9) gives a very good description of Chinese fish-curing methods, "The smaller varieties – such as perch, tailor, garnet, soles, herrings, &c, – are mostly converted into a kind of semi-liquid preserve". All other types of fish are:

> taken in baskets to the splitting-table: and after being there opened, headed and the back bone
> removed, they are passed on to another part of the establishment for salting ... and should
> only remain a certain number of hours or days – according to the kind of fish being salted –
> in pickle. After salting, the fish is placed in a large trough, filled with water, cleansing away
> superfluous salt, until at length it is laid on slabs or sheets of bark, to be dried by the sun. The
> labour spent on this part of the process is very considerable, each fish having to be shifted
> and turned an immense number of times before it is finally ready for packing for exportation.

The evidence above provides an understanding of the types of fish Chinese fish curers preferred, how they procured them and cured them and how they were eaten. A good indication has also been obtained as to which fish Chinese people considered the best for eating. From the curing methods described, it appears the Chinese fish curers in Australia produced two types of product: pickle-cured fish, which was packed into casks; and salted fish that was sun-dried and packed into bags. While slight variations in fish-curing methods were noted at different fish-curing establishments (figure 4.16), the end product was always either pickled or salted sun-dried fish.

Figure 4.16 An 1886 wood engraving by D Syme, titled *Chinese fisherman's hut: holiday tour round Port Phillip* shows fish hanging to dry in the open air. This is a variation to the horizontal drying racks represented elsewhere in Victoria such as at Chinaman's Point and Metung. La Trobe Picture Collection, State Library of Victoria.

## Economics

European fishing operations in colonial Australia generally involved two or three men making a basic living. In the later colonial era, with the advent of sea trawling, bigger boats and refrigerated, faster transport of fish to market, some European fishermen generated considerable wealth. An examination of how much fish the European fishermen and Chinese fish curers were processing annually and how they fared economically, produces some very surprising results.

Firth (1946: 220) indicates that for Chinese fish curers in Malaya, "the largest element in the 'profit' of the fish-curer is normally a return for the labour expended". It is difficult to estimate the costs that were involved in maintaining a colonial-period Chinese fish-curing establishment, largely because the cost of the various inputs – from labour usage to quantities of salt required – cannot accurately be ascertained. It is possible, however, to establish the amount and price of fresh fish sold annually through European markets and to compare these with the quantities and price of fish that Chinese people were curing.

Historical data from the period of peak Chinese activity in colonial Australia – the late 1850s to early 1870s (Cronin 1982: 140) – is instructive, as this is when Chinese cured fish would have been in highest demand.

Statistics from Sydney's fish market in 1870 show that just one and a half tons of fresh fish was sold per week, totalling 78 tons for that year for a population of 200 000 (Oliver 1871: 782–84). From contemporary market records and his own field research, Oliver estimates the annual value of this fish including all inputs from ocean to marketplace was about £6000 wholesale and £10 000 retail. This averaged £77 per ton, a huge mark up from the £2 to £7 per ton – after costs – that fishermen received for their catch (*Gippsland Times* 1879, May 21). As a comparison with later years, the New South Wales Legislative Assembly (*Votes and Proceedings of the New South Wales Legislative Assembly* 1891–92, Papers Laid Upon the Table: 279) recorded that in 1890 the total value of fish sold at Sydney's fish markets was £38 694 – no tonnage is recorded – which suggests that consumption of fresh fish in colonial Australia increased over time.

Statistical data for fish sales in colonial Victoria is scarce. From the information available, Victoria – with a population of 500 000 in 1862 – appears to have had a healthier appetite for fish than New South Wales, most likely due to Victoria's larger population. In 1866, the minutes from the Fish Market Committee show that on average, 11 tons of fish was sold through Melbourne's fish market each week; no sale prices are listed (Minutes of the Victorian Market Committee. Victorian Public Records Office (PROV), Series 4030, Unit 2 & 3: 102–58). Averaged annually, 132 tons of fish passed through the Melbourne fish market in 1866. Assuming that fish sale prices, transport and agent fees were similar between the two colonies, approximately £10 153 of wholesale and £16 923 of retail fresh fish was sold annually in Melbourne during the mid 1860s. As a comparison with later years, a royal commission into Victorian fisheries (1919) records that in 1918, £129 529 of fish was sold through the Victorian fish market (*Votes and Proceedings of the Victorian Legislative Council* 1919: 7).

Ten separate historical documents have been located that indicate Chinese fish curers would purchase from European fishermen as much fish as they could get (see for example *Votes and Proceedings of the South Australian Legislative Council* 1861: 857; *Votes and Proceedings of the New South Wales Legislative Assembly* 1879-80, vol. 3; *Votes and Proceedings of the New South Wales Legislative Assembly* 1879–80, vol. 1: 1181, 1200; *Geelong Advertiser* 1857, January 12; *The Argus* 1864, May 28). As there do not appear to be any official records of the quantity of fish that Chinese people caught themselves (they did not sell through European markets) or purchased from European fishermen, it is not possible to determine exactly how much fish Chinese people cured. However, Chinese cured fish was often transported between the Australian colonies by sea and records of ship cargoes, listed in the shipping intelligence columns of colonial newspapers, provide an indication of the quantities of fish cured by the Chinese (a topic discussed in more detail below).

The amount that Chinese curers paid European fishermen for fresh fish can be broadly ascertained through historical literature. For example, fisherman George Newton indicates that during the late 1850s to early 1860s, Chinese curers in New South Wales gave £14 6s per ton for schnapper, but by the late 1870 they were only giving £5 3s (*Votes and Proceedings of the New South Wales Legislative Assembly* 1879–80, vol. 3: 1200). Fisherman Michael Solomon commented that in the early days – the 1860s – the New South Wales Chinese curers paid £14 a ton for net fish (*Votes and Proceedings of the New South Wales Legislative Assembly* 1879–80, vol. 3: 1186). By the 1880s, however, the Chinese fish-curing industry was in decline and prices paid to European fishermen had fallen substantially. An article in the *Gippsland Standard* (1884, March) reports "Large hauls of fish at Port Albert. Five tons sold to Chinamen on eastern beach at £6 per ton". The *Gippsland Standard* (1944, July 7) – reminiscing back to approximately the 1890s – suggests the Chinese fish curers at Port Albert were paying £4 per ton for net fish at this time.

Some analysis of terminology and weights is useful. It has been shown that Chinese salted sun-dried fish was packed in hessian bags, sometimes called packages or written 'pkgs' and pickled fish was stored in timber casks (see for example Oliver 1871: 785; *The Argus* 1864, May 28; (*Votes and Proceedings of the Tasmanian Legislative Council* 1886, vol. 13: 36). Only one document has been located that indicates the weight of a bag of cured fish. This comes from the *Bendigo Advertiser* (1861, November 14), which reports an incident where two Chinese men stole a bag of cured fish from a Chinese store in Bendigo: "While Ah Chin came in and purchased 6d worth of opium the other [Ah Way] picked up a bag of fish 150 lb weight, which was by the side of the counter". It can only be assumed that bags of fish – like other bagged products such as salted beef or pork, tea, coffee, tobacco, fruit, flour and sugar (Pears Cyclopaedia 1905: 353; Barker 1882: 138–41) – were sold as a standard weight. There are 2240 pounds in a ton; so 15 bags of cured fish make one ton.

It must also be noted that salt sun-drying fish removes moisture content, leaving the fish from 30 to 60% lighter in weight than when fresh – depending on fish type (Cutting 1955: 183; Davis 1973: 10–11; Ashbrook 1955: 246). Calculations for this project average the weight of cured fish to 45% lighter than fresh fish.

The *Hobart Town Advertiser* (1860, November 22), recorded that on 15 November 1860, the ship *Wonga Wonga* transported the following quantities of Chinese cured fish from Sydney to Melbourne: "6 packages fish J. Chan; 42 packages fish, Lee See; 10 packages fish, Ah Cheong; 30 packages fish, Sam Ting; 44 packages fish, Chin Ateak". If one package of fish weighed 150 lb, in this shipment, five Chinese people forwarded 9 tons of cured fish from Sydney to Melbourne.

The *Wonga Wonga* features in the shipping intelligence columns as the main ship used for transporting Chinese cured fish cargoes from Sydney to Melbourne. The *Wonga Wonga* was a 681-ton coastal steamer. Sister ship to the *City of Sydney*, which also carried considerable quantities of Chinese cured fish, both vessels were owned by the Steam Navigation Company, a private organisation that comprised a number of directors and shareholders (Nicholson 1998: 474; www.pbenyon.plus.com/Gazette/Shipping_Steam/Wonga_Wonga_Maiden_Trip.html). It is conceivable that Chinese merchants had interests in the Steam Navigation Company, but no evidence of this has been located.

Shipping intelligence columns in colonial newspapers reveal that bulk quantities of Chinese cured fish were regularly transported between Australian colonies. To examine each colonial newspaper (between approximately 1854 to 1900) for ship destination and cargo types is beyond the scope of this project. However, even a brief review of two months (May and June) in 1861, a peak period of Chinese activity in colonial Australia, of the *Shipping Gazette* in *The Sydney Mail* (this newspaper had a reasonably regular shipping intelligence column) shows that Chin Ateak transported from Sydney to Melbourne 314 packages of dried fish and 41 casks of pickled fish, Foo Chong 28 packages of dried fish, Sal See 50 packages of dried fish, Sing Waa 41 packages of dried fish, Jon Fun 16 packages of dried fish, Hong Chow Ling 37 packages of dried fish, and Waa Lee 67 packages of dried fish and 36 casks of pickled fish. In total, for this two month period, 553 packages – 37 tons of dried fish or 53.5 tons of fresh fish equivalent – and 77 casks of Chinese cured fish went from Sydney to Melbourne. Taking into account only the packages of dried fish – as the weight of cured fish in casks is unknown – this 37 tons of cured fish is 1.5 times the amount of fresh fish going through the European fish markets in Sydney and Melbourne combined over any two months in the same period. Add these 37 tons – which is only the amount going from Sydney to Melbourne over eight weeks – to the unknown, but undoubtedly large quantities of fish that was cured (i.e. which did not get shipped between colonies and therefore cannot be traced) and consumed by Chinese people in New South Wales, Victoria, South Australia, Tasmania and at overseas locations and the significance of the Chinese contribution to Australia's colonial fishing industry becomes apparent.

By 1868, shipping intelligence columns show the volume of Chinese cured fish transported from Sydney to Melbourne had slowed to 48 packages during October and 68 packages in November, totalling 7.5 tons – 11 tons fresh equivalent. This amount – representing just a proportion of the total amount of fish cured by the Chinese in New South Wales – was similar to the quantity of fresh fish consumed by the whole population of Sydney over the same period.

Hop Lung and Ah Tie told the *Australian Town and Country Journal* (1870, July 9) that, when demand for cured fish was high during the 1860s, they would each send from Lake Macquarie to Sydney and Melbourne up to 70 tons of cured fish annually. This information is corroborated by the Hon. H Ayers, MP, who commented during the parliamentary debate on Chinese immigration (1861) that the Chinese living 120 miles north of Sydney (the Lake Macquarie region) "now exported [presumedly to Sydney and Melbourne] about 20 tons of fish per month" (*Votes and Proceedings of the South Australian Legislative Council* 1861: 57). This suggests that some 240 tons of cured fish – 348 tons fresh equivalent – was processed annually in this region alone.

Statistical returns for 1866 listed in Tasmania's parliamentary papers, show 266 packages of crayfish were exported to Victoria and a further 49 packages went to New South Wales. Uncured crayfish flesh would perish on such a voyage and as there are no records of European people curing crayfish, they almost certainly represent a product from the Tasmanian Chinese fish-curing establishments. Assuming fish and crayfish lost similar weight percentages during the curing process, 315 bags equates to 21 tons of cured crayfish, revealing that Tasmania was also supplying significant quantities of Chinese cured product to Victoria and New South Wales.

A report in the *Hobart Town Advertiser* on 30 November 1860 states that Chinese people at Fingal in Tasmania cure crayfish and "send them into the Melbourne market where they realize about one hundred pounds per ton". This price would have been achieved at the peak of the Chinese demand for cured fish during the 1860s. As with all commodities, prices for Chinese cured fish varied. When the royal commission of 1880 asked fisherman Thomas Curtis "Have you any idea of what price per ton they got for the dried and salted fish?" he replied, "About £70 a ton for them at one time" (*Votes and Proceedings of the New South Wales Legislative Assembly* 1879–80, vol. 3: 1186). Oliver (1871: 785) states that Chinese cured fish "in the piping times of gold-digging, frequently realized over £50 per ton". European smoked fish sold for approximately £16 per ton during the same period, but on the goldfields prices could reach £40 per ton (*Votes and Proceedings of the New South Wales Legislative Assembly* 1879–80, vol. 3: 1140).

Europeans ventured into fish curing – usually smoked fish – on a small scale. From approximately 1855 to 1863 James Meek smoked fish commercially at Curdie's Inlet near Warrnambool in Victoria (Duruz 1973: 43; *Warrnambool Examiner* 1863, November 8; 1864, February 9). For a short period during the 1870s Frank Koeing ran a fish-smoking establishment at Rosherville (Metung) in the Gippsland Lakes (*Gippsland Mercury* 1879, May 20). Due predominantly to the large labour input required, smoke curing fish was generally considered an unprofitable enterprise (*Votes and Proceedings of the New South Wales Legislative Assembly* 1879–80, vol. 3: 1140, 1204, 1267). John Massey's comments during the royal commission (1880: 1211) suggest the general opinion of European fishermen on curing fish: "[Q] When you get a large haul, do you cure the balance of the fish? [A] We let them go; it would never pay to cure them". Surprisingly, there appears to have been no effort to experiment with canned fish, despite a considerable market for canned fish products. The Statistical Register for New South Wales shows that from 1869 to 1897, £512 000 worth of canned sardines, ling and salmon was imported to Australia – approximately six times the value of fresh fish sold in New South Wales over the same period (*Votes and Proceedings of the New South Wales Legislative Assembly* 1879–80, vol. 1: 672).

In the 1880 royal commission, Chinese merchant Chin Ateak gives a broad indication of the quantities of cured fish he dealt with annually and the prices he received. When asked if he "found at one time there was a good trade to be done". He answered:

> Yes, a very good trade; there was a lot of people there and we sold two and three hundred tons a year ... In New South Wales some hundred tons and two hundred tons at Melbourne.
> (*Votes and Proceedings of the New South Wales Legislative Assembly* 1879–80, vol. 3: 1224)

Chin Ateak's annual sales amount to almost ten times the tonnage of fish sold through Sydney and Victoria's European markets combined. When asked if he "sometimes got very high prices in this country". He replied: "Yes ... One time up to £100 a ton". The mathematics is plain. In one year Chin Ateak could have made up to £300 000 from cured fish sales, much more than the fresh fish sales through Sydney and Victorian European markets and certainly a great deal more money that any European fishermen were making. Moreover, as seen through the shipping intelligence columns quoted above, there were other Chinese people dealing in cured fish, some of them shipping similar quantities to Chin Ateak.

The historical documents confirm that the Chinese fish curers in Australia were dealing in far greater quantities of fish than has ever before been acknowledged. As the various royal commission interviews with fishermen show, at one period – broadly from the late 1850s to early 1860s – a considerable number of fishermen in coastal Victoria and New South Wales fished for the Chinese curers. The Chinese fish curers were "conducting this branch of industry on a large scale" (*Bendigo Advertiser* 1857, January 5) and had "the whole of this trade in their own hands" (*Votes and Proceedings of the South Australian Legislative Council* 1861: 858). The Chinese contribution to Australia's colonial fishing industry was very significant.

As the Australian Chinese population dwindled, so did the price of Chinese cured fish. By 1870, the fish curers on Lake Macquarie reported they were receiving approximately £20 a ton for their product (*Town and Country Journal* 1870), compared to between £70 and £100 ten years previously. Oliver (1871: 785) states, "at present, the export trade is very limited and the price paid ... is not more than £16 to £18 per ton". In the royal commission of 1880, Chin Ateak also notes the downturn in sale prices, noting that in Sydney and Melbourne, cured schnapper would fetch £28 per ton and cured mullet would sell for £12 a ton. Chin Ateak – in 1880 – would pay, if someone would supply him, £28 per ton for shark fins, £50 per ton for squid and £84 per ton for abalone "for as much as you bring to me".

Reverend Young estimated in 1868 that Chinese market gardeners earned approximately £2 per week and a Chinese miner working for a Chinese company earned approximately £1 per week (cited in McLaren 1985: 39–40). During this period, European fisherman earned an average profit of £2 to £5 per week (*Gippsland Times* 1879, May 21). The hundreds of thousands of pounds sterling generated annually through Chinese cured fish was many times more than European profits from fish during the colonial period. The enormous market for Chinese cured fish is reflected in the observation in the *Bendigo Advertiser* (1857, January 13) that "The Chinese population employed on the diggings must be very fond of fish if they eat all that their brethren ... send to them".

## Market locations

The most obvious market for Chinese cured fish in Australia was the Chinese gold-diggers and associated infrastructure workers. Future discoveries of colonial-period Chinese documentation may provide an indication of exactly how much cured fish went to the goldfields. The next most likely market for Australian Chinese cured fish is China. Indeed, much of the Australian historical literature suggests a portion of Chinese cured fish was going to markets in China. Opportunistic markets would also have presented themselves, as shown in the section on the Northern Territory where cured fish was provided to government employees. The following section examines the market outlets for Chinese cured fish.

Many references have already been cited to show that Chinese fish curers in Australia sent a great deal of fish to Melbourne, much of which was destined for Victoria's goldfields. *The Gippslander* (1865, November 10) reported:

> The Chinese purchase the fish from the fishermen, cure them and forward them to Melbourne to their depot, whence the whole of the up country markets are supplied.

The *Bendigo Advertiser* (1857, January 5) reports in similar terms:

> We learn that this commodity [Chinese cured fish] is sent into the interior in large quantities, where it finds a ready sale among the Chinese population.

At Semaphore Jetty in South Australia, the Chinese curers forwarded their product to "the neighbouring colony, to be used as food by the Mongols on the various diggings" (*The Argus* 1864, May 28). Enormous amounts of cured fish were consumed in this fashion, first on the Victorian goldfields, then in New South Wales, Tasmania, the Northern Territory and elsewhere else in Australia where Chinese people worked and lived.

Another likely market outlet was the shipping industry, supplying rations for Chinese sailors and passengers travelling between China and Australia. When Chin Ateak was interviewed for the Chinese Immigration Bill 1858 he stated that ships coming from China usually carried between 400 and 500 Chinese men, but some carried as many as 1300 Chinese men (*Votes and Proceedings of the New South Wales Legislative Council* 1858, vol. 3: 18). The voyage between China and Australia took anywhere between 60 to 85 days, with crew and passengers receiving two meals a day, predominantly rice, salted fish and some salted vegetables (Wang 1978: 307). While arrangements for procuring Chinese ship provisions are not known, with large quantities of cured fish available in Australia, it is conceiveable that ship rations of salted fish were at least in part obtained from Chinese fish curers in Australia.

Firth (1946: 12) notes that Singapore was a heavy consumer of fish and a major distributing centre for fish. Sydney and Melbourne shipping arrival and departure notices support Firth's statement. In 1855, the *Glendaragh,* the *General Blanco* and the *Yarra Yarra* – regular vessels on the Australia–China trade route – each took cargoes of fish from Melbourne to Singapore and Hong Kong (Syme 1987: 321; 333; 343). Further evidence of the export of Chinese cured fish from Australia to Asian destinations is in Chin Ateak's testimony in the royal commission (1880: 1224). When asked "Did you ever send any [fish] to China?" he answered, "Yes, we sent some Mullet". "[Q] Do you Chinamen salt them? [A] Make pickle fish".

*The Shipping Gazette* in *The Sydney Mail* (1861, March 23) shows Chin Ateak exported on the *Antagonist* 12 casks of pickled fish to Hong Kong. On the same ship, he also exported 472 ½ ounces of gold. The *Shipping Gazette* (1861, 22 June) shows that Chin Ateak exported to Hong Kong – on the *Cyclone* – 603 tons of coal, 22 cases of copper, 1968.5 ounces of gold [worth approximately £7 874] and 47 bags of fish. The bagged fish indicates that Chinese fish curers did not only export pickled fish to China as Chin Ateak suggested in the royal commission of 1880.

*The Shipping Gazettes* confirm that, even though some cured fish was exported to China, Chinese people on the Australian goldfields, particularly in Victoria, consumed by far the majority of Chinese cured fish in Australia. Chinese fish curers would obtain and cure fish wherever a fresh source was available. Once cured, the product would be transported to wherever a suitable market outlet existed.

With ice still not in common use for fish preservation – this began approximately in the mid 1890s – the market for fresh fish was limited. Nevertheless, there is reference to Chinese people trading in fresh fish. A report in the *Illustrated Australian News* (1879, April 12) states:

> at the [fish] market during the auction sales ... the inevitable Chinaman may be seen in all his glory, but he has not yet elbowed the European sufficiently to be more than a subsidiary element in the crowd.

An article on Melbourne's fish market in *The Australasian Sketcher* (1876, March 18), however, report

> numerous Chinamen trotting to the [fish] market, swaying from habit, under their empty baskets ... they are amongst the most respectable of those present and without them the market would have but a poor chance of support.

In his 1868 report on the Chinese population in Victoria, Reverend Young comments that Chinese fish hawkers regularly purchased fish from the Melbourne fish market to sell in and around Melbourne. He also relays that "Mr. Ritchie, a fish salesman, stated to me that, for the last 20 years, the Chinese have been the chief support of the [fish] market" (cited in McLaren 1985: 60).

Similar to Chinese market gardening, Chinese people became more involved in fresh fish after the 1870s and began supplying to Chinese and European consumers. Freeman (1888: 158–65), writing generally of contemporary life in Melbourne, noted,

> Great numbers of the fish-hawkers are Celestials … One would scarcely credit the number of Chinese fish-hawkers there are if one did not see them together in the market. They have appropriated to themselves a kind of piazza on the right hand side as you go in, where they sort and divide their fish.

Working predominantly from newspaper articles, Bennett (2002: 23–24) devotes two pages to the Chinese fresh-fish hawkers of Melbourne; Brown-May (1998: 150) also acknowledges this activity. Both authors suggest that from approximately the 1870s to the early 1930s, Chinese hawkers purchased fish at the auctions and sold it on foot – like they sold vegetables – throughout the streets of Melbourne in the same way as European hawkers (figure 4.17). Given the clan-based nature of Chinese business, however, it is likely that Chinese fish hawkers had Chinese suppliers and were more heavily involved in the fresh fish industry than is so far recognised. This, however, is an area for future research.

Figure 4.17 Two Chinese hawkers in Australia (above). Picture from Freeman 1888: 158. Picture by H Livingstone 1886, titled *Chinese carrying shoulder baskets, the Rocks Sydney* (left). National Library of Australia, nla. pic-an 8870592.

## United States of America

In many ways, the Chinese involvement in Australia's early commercial fishing industry mirrors the American situation. As with Australia, Chinese immigration to the United States a was stimulated by the mid-19th-century gold rushes. In their new host society, many Chinese people took up niche economic positions in labour-intensive work areas such as market gardening and fishing.

Chinese participation in America's early fishing industry has received more scholarly attention – particularly in California – than it has in Australia. There is considerable scope for critical analysis of the American literature to compare Chinese fishing activities in the United States and Australia. To enable such a comparison, however, it is first necessary to establish a good understanding of Chinese fishing activities in Australia. On these grounds, this section will be brief.

The most informative literature on Chinese involvement in America's early fishing industry includes Goode (1884; 1887), Collins (1892), Wilcox (1893), Nash (1973), Melendy (1984), Lydon (1985); Schulz & Lortie (1985), McEvoy (1986), Collins (1987), Roeder (1993), Kemp (1996), Lee (1999); and Berryman (1999). Also of value is the joint project between Cornell University and the University of Michigan to establish the web site 'Making of America' (moa.library.cornell.edu/). This site consists of thousands of digitally scanned images, pages, books and serials, forming an excellent and indexed collection of primary sources relating to development of the infrastructure of the United States. Amongst these documents are many informative and easily accessible accounts of Chinese fishing activities in the United States.

A reading of some of the literature mentioned above demonstrates that the Chinese involvement in America's fishing industry was substantial. Chinese fish-curing operations began in California during the early 1850s. For approximately the first 20 years, Chinese people themselves fished to catch and cure whatever fish came into their nets. By the 1870s, specialised catching and curing camps were established to target individual fish species such as sturgeon (figure 4.18), herring, flounder, shrimp, abalone and squid (Collins 1987: 122; Nash 1973: 19–25). The literature suggests that only a small quantity of Chinese cured fish was consumed in the United States, the majority going to markets in China. The products were exported in both a dry state in bags and pickled in casks (Wilcox 1893: 188). Goode (1887: 809) used 1880 customs house records to estimate that US$229 858 worth of Chinese cured fish was exported from San Francisco to Hong Kong in that year. This is a substantial amount, especially considering that the retail value of all fresh fish sold in San Francisco fish markets during 1877 was only US$220 000 (*San Francisco Weekly Bulletin* 1878, January 6).

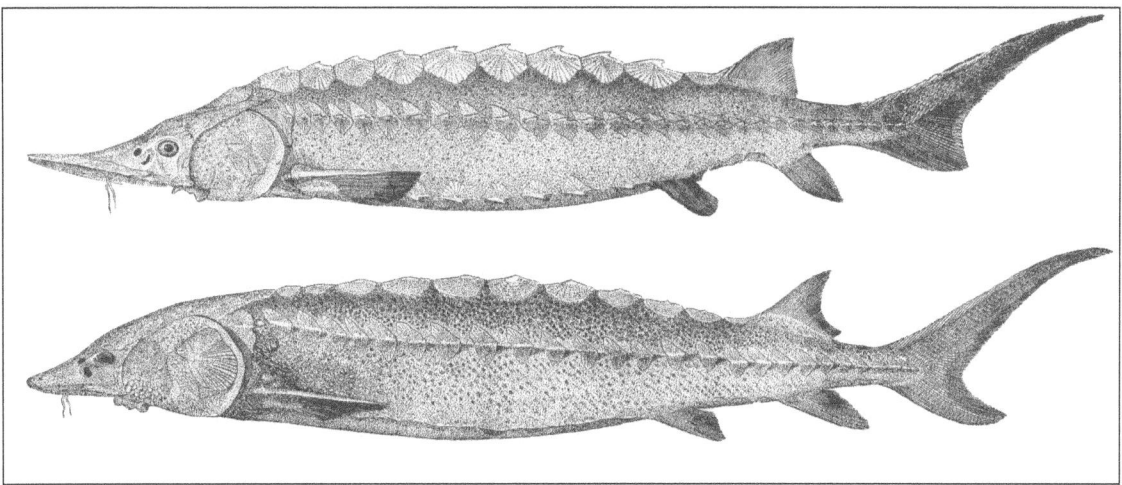

Figure 4.18 Two varieties of the American sturgeon fish targeted by Chinese fishermen in the United States of America. The lake sturgeon (*Acipenser rubicundus*) (top) and the shovel-nose sturgeon (*Scaphirhynchus platyrhynchus*) (bottom). Image from Goode 1884: 244.

As in Australia, the primary American literature records many complaints from United States fishermen about the methods Chinese people used to catch fish. For example, "Something should be done to put a stop to the wholesale destruction of fish by the Chinese ... No net of such fine mesh should be permitted" (*San Diego Union* 1889, February 6) and,

> They [Chinese fishermen] use fine mesh-nets, with which they sweep every part of the river
> ... so destructive has their fishing been on the Sacramento, that all the fish of that river
> except salmon are disappearing with unexampled rapidity. (Goode 1887: 738)

As with the European complaints about Chinese fishermen in Australia, the validity of these complaints in the United States is questionable.

Pictorial and documentary evidence from America's Chinese fishing history correlates with excavated material evidence from Australia. Through combining historical and archaeological evidence, material connections between the remains at Chinese fishing sites in the United States of America and Australia can be established. Evidence of this type will provide an important basis for studying the Chinese migrations during the colonial period including Chinese settlement patterns, areas of economic focus and evidence of individuals and their respective circumstances.

## Overview of Chinese fish-curing operations

Historical evidence for Chinese involvement in the colonial fishing industry demonstrated a far greater level of Chinese participation than previously realised. Chinese fish curers had extensive operations in Victoria and New South Wales and smaller but still very productive establishments in the Northern Territory, South Australia and Tasmania. In most of these regions, Chinese fish curers had established themselves well before local gold- or tin-mining operations began. This suggests the curers were there to gather and cure fish they knew would find a ready sale on the Victorian and New South Wales goldfields.

The earliest located documentary evidence for Chinese fish-curing operations in Australia is November 1856 at St Kilda in Victoria. The boom period for Chinese fish-curing establishments was from the late 1850s to the early 1870s (table 4.1). Documentary evidence has been located for the existence of 38 Chinese fish-curing establishments in Australia, but the actual number is probably much greater. By the late 1890s to early 1900s, a small number of curing establishments were still in operation – the last one was probably the Port Albert site which will be discussed in chapter 7.

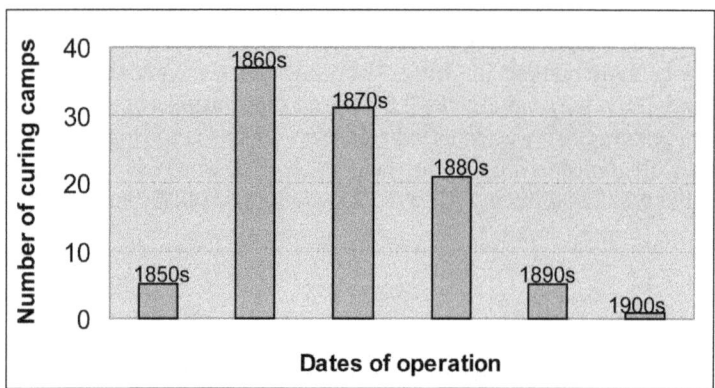

Table 4.1 Indicating the beginning, boom and end period for Chinese fish-curing establishments in Australia. Based on data from colonial-period royal commissions, newspaper reports and shipping intelligence columns.

Establishing a fish-curing operation in a location distant from the goldfields such as in Tasmania or South Australia does not seem like a random act by an out-of-luck gold miner. The available literature suggests that Chinese fish-curing establishments in Australia – from the late 1850s to early 1870s – were owned by a Chinese merchant and staffed by headmen and a team of working-class labourers. The logistical difficulties – such as obtaining necessary supplies, commodity exportation, then the further sale of cured products to the goldfields and overseas – involved in operating a fish-curing establishment suggests the involvement of Chinese merchants. Some evidence exists to suggest that indebted workers staffed these operations, but this is not conclusive.

Fish-curing establishments where Chinese people themselves fished required up to 16 workers. At curing establishments where fish was purchased from European fishermen, the Chinese component could be reduced to as few as two workers. As the Australian gold rush lost momentum and Chinese people began returning to China or seeking opportunity elsewhere, it appears that Chinese merchants reduced their interests in the fish-curing industry. This opened opportunities for Chinese individuals or small groups to establish themselves as owners of fish-curing establishments – though more modest operations than previously.

Chinese people themselves procured a portion of the fish they cured by fishing with nets. Their netting methods appear to be a mixture of techniques used in China and those already in use in Australia.

During a period when Australia's fishing industry was providing only a meagre wage for commercial European participants, the Chinese involvement opened further opportunities for European fishermen. Moreover, through purchasing fish from European fishermen, the Chinese fish curers facilitated the growth of Australia's early fishing industry. In places such as the Port Albert waterways and other regions close to European markets, the Chinese fish curers acted as a supplementary market for European fishermen. In other more remote regions such as the Gippsland Lakes and Lake Macquarie, where early commercial fishing was simply not viable due to transport difficulties, the existence of the fishing industry depended upon the Chinese fish curers purchasing fish from European fishermen.

There were slight variations in the fish-curing methods used at Chinese fish-curing establishments in Australia. In general, fish were placed in salty brine, then either dried in the sun or pickled in timber casks. These methods produced two separate products: salted sun-dried fish that was packed dry in bags, and pickled fish that was stored in casks.

A broad indication of how much fish was cured annually by Chinese people in Australia has been ascertained through documentary evidence – predominantly shipping intelligence columns. This reveals that the quantities of Chinese cured fish produced in Australia during the peak period of the mid 1850s to the early 1870s were far greater than the fresh fish markets operated by Europeans (table 4.2). Chinese people on the Australian goldfields and other Chinese people in Australia consumed the majority of cured fish, with a smaller portion exported to markets in China and elsewhere. Sale prices for Chinese cured fish and European-caught fresh fish were generally similar. Therefore, it was not the price of cured fish that generated large profit, it was the quantity of fish they were selling – literally hundreds of tons more than European sales of fresh fish. The sale of such large volumes generated substantial profits for the Chinese merchants who were dealing in fish. Taking a wider economic perspective, at least a portion of the money generated from Chinese fish-curing activities would have been circulated within Australia, thereby lubricating colonial economies.

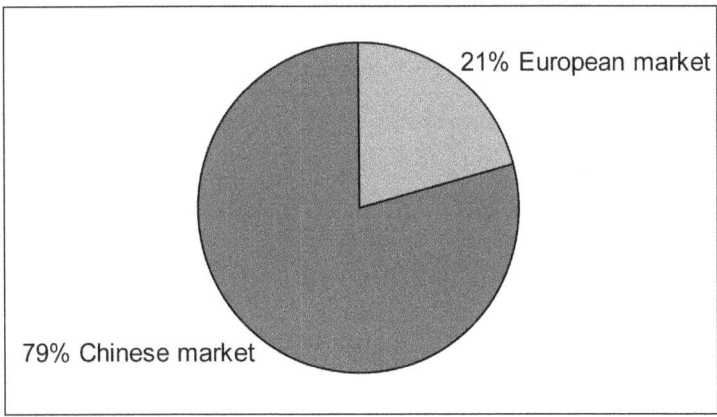

Table 4.2 A percentage estimate of the total quantities of fish sold in Victoria and New South Wales combined by European and Chinese fish dealers during the late 1860s. Based on data from colonial period royal commissions, newspaper reports, shipping intelligence columns and state fish market records.

Possibly from the beginning of Chinese fishing activities in Australia, but certainly by the late 1860s, Chinese people were selling fresh fish through European marketing systems. The door-to-door hawking of fish was limited to metropolitan regions and was possibly conducted by unsuccessful Chinese miners with connections in the Chinese fishing industry.

There are strong similarities between Chinese fishing activities in colonial Australia and colonial America. Greater volumes and accessiblity of documentary evidence on America's Chinese fish curers will facilitate a greater depth of knowledge and valuable comparative research between the Australian and American situations. Moreover, it will provide further information on the broader patterns of Chinese overseas migration.

The documentary evidence in this chapter is predominantly from primary sources. All material has been clearly referenced and is open to future researchers for reinterpretation. However, the facts and figures clearly demonstrate that Chinese fish curers were major players in Australia's colonial fishing industry.

# CHAPTER 5

# EXCAVATION AT CHINAMAN'S POINT

An understanding of the lifestyle, technology, artefact types and site layout at a colonial Chinese fish-curing establishment would not have been possible without archaeological excavation. Chapter 5 explains the excavation component of this project, including the rationale for site selection, a site description, the excavation methodology and an account of each excavated area and discussion of the results.

The excavation assisted to evaluate the contribution of Chinese groups to the establishment and continued development of Victoria's commercial fishing industry. Information from the excavation forms the basis – in later chapters – for an examination and understanding of Chinese fish curers in colonial Victoria. A detailed discussion and interpretation of the artefacts recovered from the site is the focus of chapter 6.

## SITE SELECTION

The abandoned site at Chinaman's Point, Port Albert, was identified through local oral histories, historical documentation and surface artefact scatters. It was subsequently recorded with Heritage Victoria as Heritage Inventory No. H8220-0011. The site contains the only conclusive evidence of Chinese fish-curing activity found during extensive field research in Victoria. There is currently no known material evidence of Chinese fish-curing activities elsewhere in Australia. Further investigation – i.e. excavation – was conducted to gain an understanding – through artefacts and ground features – of the working and living conditions for Chinese fish curers in colonial Australia.

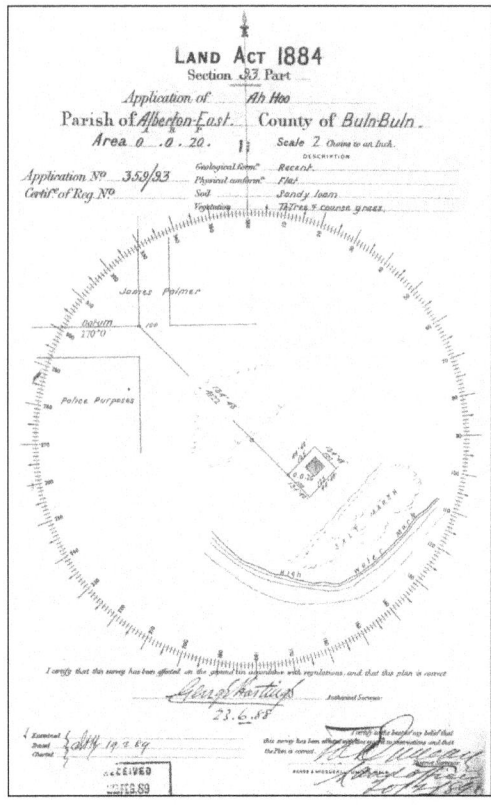

Figure 5.1 Survey map included in Ah Hoo's 1888 land title documents for Chinaman's Point (PROV, VPRS 5357/P0000, unit 5899).

A land titles document from 1888 indicates that Ah Hoo leased a one-acre site at Chinaman's Point as a fisherman's residence (PROV, VPRS 5357/P0000, unit 5899). The document includes a survey map with a compass bearing and datum marker indicating the position of the dwelling (figure 5.1). While the original ground datum – a timber post located 830 m north west of the site – was identified, tall eucalyptus trees and dense scrubby tea-trees hampered attempts to get an exact electronic measurement along the compass bearing from datum to house site. A measurement was taken by compass and tape measure, but due to the dense vegetation, salt marsh and mangroves, it was not possible to obtain an accurate location for the dwelling. There was also an absence of any visible house remains at the site. Nevertheless, the land title document provides a useful guide to the general location of the residential area, the former shoreline position and the physical ground environment during the occupation period – each of which assisted in the planning of fieldwork at the site.

## Site description

South Gippsland's geology is comprised of a bedding of Mesozoic tectonic belt – mainly consisting of cretaceous sediments – which extends across southern Victoria and out onto the continental shelf (Singleton 1973: 129, 133). In the late Pleistocene period (500 000 – 100 000 years ago), a siliciclastic barrier system (sand dunes) was deposited along the Gippsland coast and formed a series of estuarine lakes.

Fluvial sediments became trapped by the lakes to form coastal swamp deposits. During the late Quaternary period (approximately 50 000 years ago) more sand was deposited along this coast line, creating a layer of swamp between two sandy layers under the present day south-Gippsland lakes and beaches (Birch 2003: 355–56).

Chinaman's Point near Port Albert in south Gippsland (figure 5.2) was previously known as Long Point. Some time during the mid 20th century, well after the Chinese had abandoned the site, its name changed to reflect the former Chinese presence. The site is located at the end of Chinaman's Point, 1.6 km north-east of Port Albert, in the shire of Wellington, parish of Alberton East, county of Buln Buln and within the boundaries of Nooramunga Marine and Coastal Park – AMG co-ordinates: VICMAP Port Albert 8220-4-2, Zone 55, grid reference: 47465 571991 (figure 5.3).

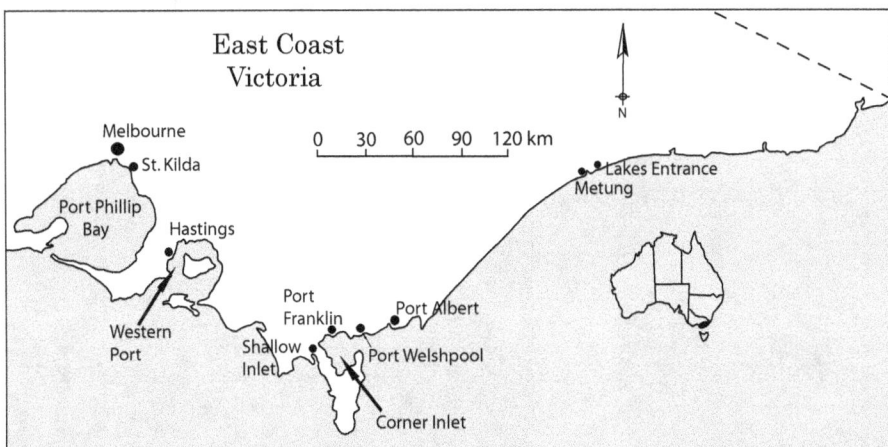

Figure 5.2 Map of the east coast of Victoria showing the location of Port Albert. Chinaman's Point is 1.6 km north-east of Port Albert.

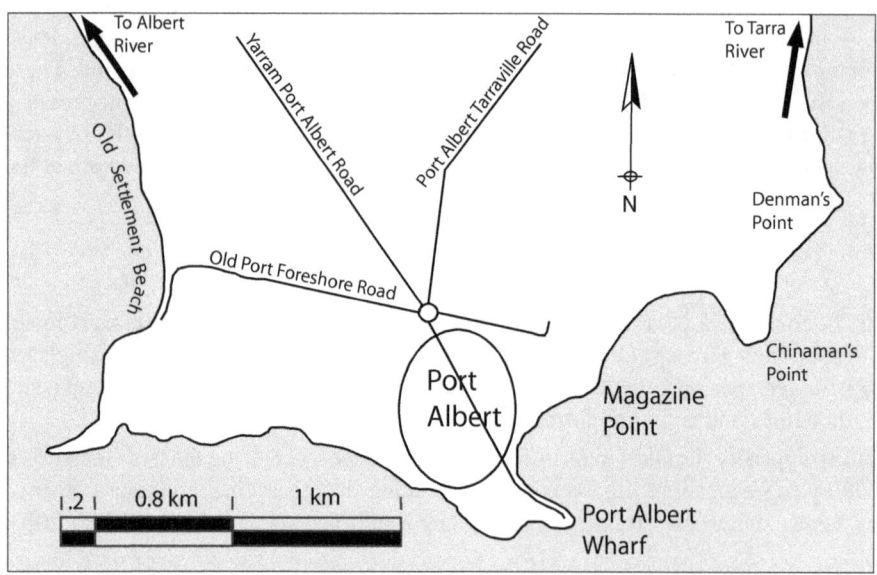

Figure 5.3 Map of the Port Albert region showing the location of Chinaman's Point.

The land narrowing to Chinaman's Point is made of alluvial sediments washed down from the Eastern Highlands to form an extensive flood plain, with sections of tidal swampy salt marsh, directly inland from the coastal sand-dune and lake systems. The soils consist of fine sands, silts and clays, covered with dense pockets of scrubby swamp paper bark (tea-tree) (*Melaleuca ericifolia*), swampy mangrove shrub and low-level coastal blue tussock grass (*Poa poiformis*) (Birch 2003: 557; Walsh and Entwisle 1994: 433). The final 70 m of Chinaman's Point – the site area – has a slightly higher elevation and therefore is not swampland or tidally inundated. This elevated ground has a thick cover of tussock grass with some pockets of tea-tree (figure 5.4). In this heavily vegetated state, ground visibility at the site is zero.

Figure 5.4 Vegetation cover on the Chainman's Point site area.

Test pits dug across the site showed the soil strata to be a fairly uniform three-unit stratigraphy. Surface layers consisted of approximately 40 to 80 mm – unit one – of brown (Munsell 10yr 3/2) humic loam. Below this was approximately 40 to 80 mm – unit two – of grey/yellow (Munsell 10yr, 7/8) sandy loam, with some clay content and leaching from the upper layer. This middle layer merged into tan-coloured (Munsell 10yr 6/1) clay – unit three – mottled with sandy dots, which continued to the bottom of the deepest test pit – 800 mm below surface level. Ground pH levels remain relatively neutral at 6 to 7.5, which, combined with moist soil conditions enabled good preservation of organic materials such as bone, leather and wood.

Where high tide meets the bank, the site is exposed to continuous wave action, resulting in a drop of approximately one metre between dry land and the sandy tidal zone that becomes exposed at low tide. Chinaman's Point is therefore a rapidly eroding headland only millimetres above high tide mark (figure 5.5). If sea levels rise just 50 cm over the next 100 years, wave wash and tidal movements will destroy archaeological evidence of past inshore coastal fishing activities world wide.

Figure 5.5 The rapidly eroding condition of Chinaman's Point (looking north).

By comparing aerial photographs taken in 1941 to ones taken in 2002 and using the lands title document from 1888, it is estimated that from 1865 to the present, some 100 m of Chinamen's Point has been washed away through erosion (figure 5.6). With this, literally thousands of artefacts have become dislodged from their *in-situ* positions and strewn across the site frontage by tidal movements. These artefacts include brick, imported stone, bone and hundreds of broken ceramic, glass and metal artefacts. Many of these confirm an association with Chinese people, including medicine vials, broken sections of opium smoking equipment, blue-green (celadon) ceramics, brown-green glaze Chinese earthenware and Chinese teapot ceramics. Ground holes – accompanied by broken artefacts – are prolific on the site surface, providing evidence of bottle-collector and artefact-scavenging activities. Artefact scavengers and their collections represent a potential resource that, to some degree, has been exploited for this project.

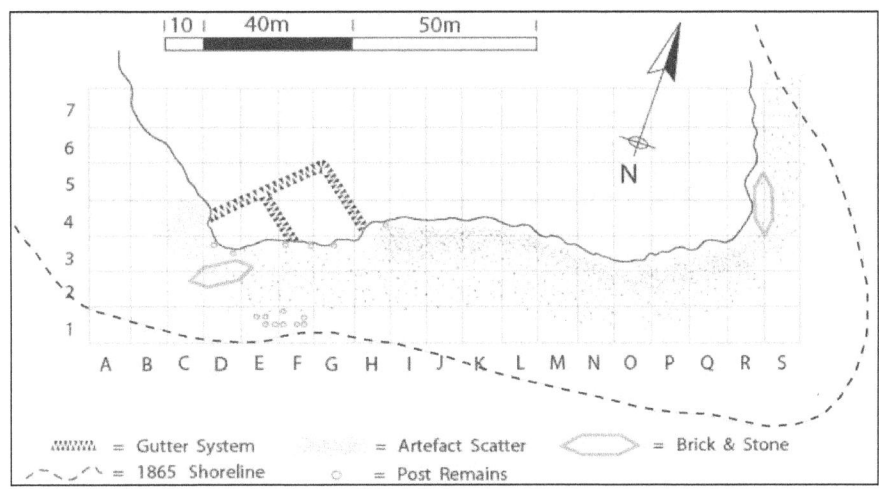

Figure 5.6 Plan of the Chinaman's Point site, including ten-by-ten metre grid system, site features and the estimated 1865 shoreline.

Three purposely dug, inter-joining gutters approximately 800 mm wide by 600 mm deep, encompassing 68 lineal metres of gutter and forming two segregated areas were identified, recorded and in part excavated (figure 5.7). These trenches – discussed later in this chapter – most likely represent a drainage system designed to keep the surrounding swamp away from the working and domestic areas of the site.

75

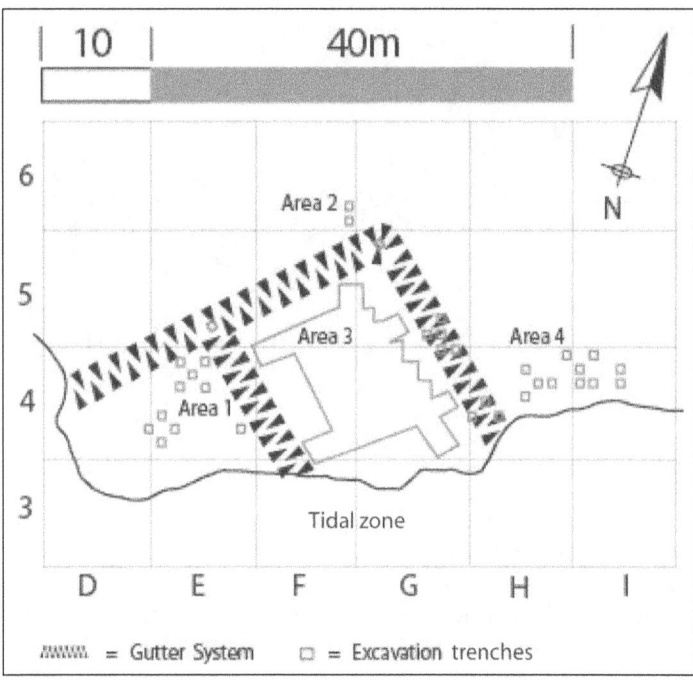

Figure 5.7 Map detailing the gutter system, excavated trenches in the gutter system and site excavation areas 1, 2, 3 and 4.

As domestic and industrial-type artefacts appear in the same localised area, it is believed the site represents both domestic and working spaces.

## METHODOLOGY

Archaeological excavation of the site began on 2 February 2004 and was completed on 28 February 2004. The excavation team consisted of volunteer students from the Archaeology Program at La Trobe University. The strategy was to identify areas of potential interest, clear surface vegetation, conduct surface collections, map the site and excavate – in order to recover artefacts and identify site features, then backfill all excavated soils and replant vegetation.

The site was occupied for an estimated period of 40 years, from the 1860s to early 1900, as discussed in chapter 7. This relatively short period suggests the stratification of cultural layers would be shallow. Lindsay Smith (1998: 65, 170) established that the average depth of cultural deposits at 6 separate excavations at historical Chinese mining sites in New South Wales was 150 mm. Peter Davies (Davies 2001a: 50) also found an average depth of 150 mm for historical material uncovered during excavations at the Henry's Mill site in Victoria. Similarly, Zvonka Stanin found cultural deposits petered out at a depth of 150 mm during her excavations of a Chinese site at Mt Alexandria, Victoria (Stanin 2004b: 34). My personal experience suggests that historical cultural material in Australia is generally not found lower than 200 mm – very occasionally at 300 mm – from the surface layer. Accordingly, it was anticipated that the cultural material would most likely be located within the top 150 mm of soil at Chinaman's Point. Given this, the technique of horizontal trowel excavation by squares on a grid layout was considered the most appropriate form of sub-surface investigation.

The site is 170 m long by 70 m wide. After carefully mapping the surface area using an electronic total station, string line and timber pegs, a ten-by-ten metre grid was set out over the entire site, including the artefact-littered tidal zone. The grid was labelled with an X and a Y axis: X representing one to seven and Y representing A to S (figure 5.6). In order to establish a reference datum, two stainless steel plates were engraved with 'CMP 2004' and set in concrete foundations on the exact intersections 5E and 5G of the site grid. This will allow any future archaeological investigators to lock exactly into the original grid system.

Test pits 200 by 200 mm were dug using a spade on dry land areas only at each intersection of the ten-by-ten metre site grid and the excavated soil was sieved for cultural material through 3 mm mesh. From this process, six areas of archaeological interest were identified: excavation areas 1, 2, 3 and 4, the gutter system and the site's tidal zone (figure 5.7).

Ground cover on the areas to be excavated was cut low with a brush-cutter, removed carefully by mattock and deposited at the site margin. As excavated areas were to be re-vegetated (an excavation permit condition from Parks Victoria), plants were stored with as little soil as possible attached to the root system, under hessian sheets and watered daily. A number of one-by-one metre excavation squares were set out and excavations by steel trowel continued downwards in 50 mm spits until culturally sterile layers were reached. All excavated material was dry-sieved through 5 mm sieve squares and deposited on a tarpaulin at the site margin. A portion of the excavated soil from each excavation trench was sieved through a 3 mm sieve. This confirmed that no smaller artefacts were present and that an adequate representation of cultural material was recovered through the larger 5 mm sieves.

Surface artefacts deposited on the tidal areas of the site had undergone considerable post-depositional movement through tidal action. With each new tide the sands shift, moving artefacts around, covering some with sand and uncovering others. The artefacts on the tidal perimeter of the site were scattered across a linear distance of approximately 200 m (figure 5.6). In these areas (i.e. the site's tidal zone) a surface collection was conducted on a daily basis and all visible artefacts were collected and bulk-bagged according to their ten-by-ten metre location.

In area 3, some bulk excavation was conducted by removing several two metre long and 50 mm deep strips using mattocks and shovels and sieving 25% of the excavated material. From the four excavation areas and the gutter system, 180 m$^2$ of ground area was excavated to varying depths of between 50 and 200 mm – one to four spits – totalling approximately 27 m$^3$ of excavated soil.

Recording of the excavation was conducted horizontally within the grid system and stratigraphically by spit and individual ground layer (natural stratigraphy). Each archaeological feature was allocated a context succession number that ran chronologically during the excavation period. Excavated trenches and features were photographed, drawn to scale and then mapped using a total station.

On completion of the project, all excavated soil was spread back over the areas by shovel, bucket and rake. Vegetation was then replanted and the slashed plant material laid down as ground mulch. Excavated artefacts were bulk-bagged according to their fabric and recorded by grid square and stratigraphic layer.

## EXCAVATION

Most cultural material was located within the first two soil units – one to three spits. This was also the case for materials located in the base of the gutter system, which besides already having a depth of between 600 mm to 800 mm from the ground surface level, still held artefacts within the first two soil units naturally deposited through aeolian forces (figure 5.8).

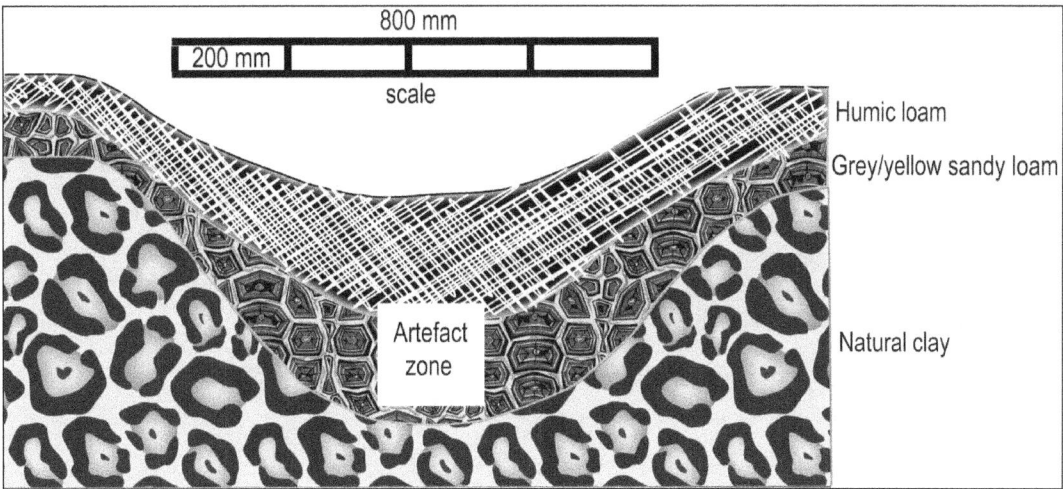

Figure 5.8 Cross-section of gutter system showing soil matrix and artefact zone.

## Gutter system

The 1888 land titles document indicated the area immediately south of the site had been a salt marsh (PROV, VPRS 5357/P0000, unit 5899) (figure 5.1). Cross-sections dug by the excavation team through the gutter system revealed the original gutter base had fallen away from the swamp. This suggests the system was designed to continuously drain the swamp area (as was and still is the custom in many regions of China) (Knapp 1989:

20, 68; Mote 1977: 197), effectively controlling this environment and preventing water from reaching the dry working areas of the site.

Ten one-by-one metre excavation squares were dug in the gutter system (figure 5.7), revealing a range of domestic artefacts including 256 bottle glass shards, 62 shards of Chinese ceramics, a glass button, three metal nails, two chicken bones, two fish bones, four cow bones and two sheep bones (table 5.1).

| Gutter system | Number of artefact fragments | Weight (grams) |
|---|---|---|
| Bottle glass | 256 | 2441 |
| Window glass | 0 | 0 |
| Ceramic | 62 | 214 |
| Bone | 10 | 79 |
| Brick | 8 | 185 |
| Leather | 3 | 17 |
| Nails | 3 | 8 |
| Spikes | 0 | 0 |
| Screws | 1 | 4 |
| Cask hoop | 85 | 361 |
| Nondescript metal | 217 | 368 |
| Total | 645 | 3677 |

Table 5.1 Main artefact categories by number and weight from gutter system.

## Excavation area 1

Within 4E of area 1, on the western limits of the gutter system, the only rewards from 11 one-by-one metre excavated squares were six round timber post remains (approximately 50 mm in diameter), five glass shards, two pieces of animal bone and scatters of heavily corroded metal fragments (2747 pieces, weighing 5452 kg) (table 5.2). Squares were excavated to depths of between 50 and 200 mm. The timber posts – well preserved underground – were made of tea-tree and had been axed to a sharpened point. This indicates the posts had been hammered into the ground rather than placed in a purposely dug hole and backfilled. They would not have stood higher than approximately 1.5 m (given they were hammered in) and were probably stay posts for drying fishing nets or supporting other lightweight items. The type of wood used for the posts – tea-tree – indicates that the site occupants obtained building materials from the immediate environment. Tea-tree, which remains prolific in this region, is a hard-wood resistant to salt environments and for these reasons was commonly used by fishing people as a building material during Victoria's colonial period (*Gippsland Times* 1879, May 21). The stratigraphy and Harris matrix for area 1 can be seen in Figure 5.9.

| Area 1 | Number of artefact fragments | Weight (grams) |
|---|---|---|
| Bottle glass | 5 | 73 |
| Window glass | 0 | 0 |
| Ceramic | 0 | 0 |
| Bone | 2 | 1 |
| Nails | 0 | 0 |
| Spikes | 0 | 0 |
| Cask hoop | 644 | 3947 |
| Nondescript metal | 2747 | 5452 |
| Total | 3396 | 9473 |

Table 5.2 Main artefact categories by number and weight from excavation area 1.

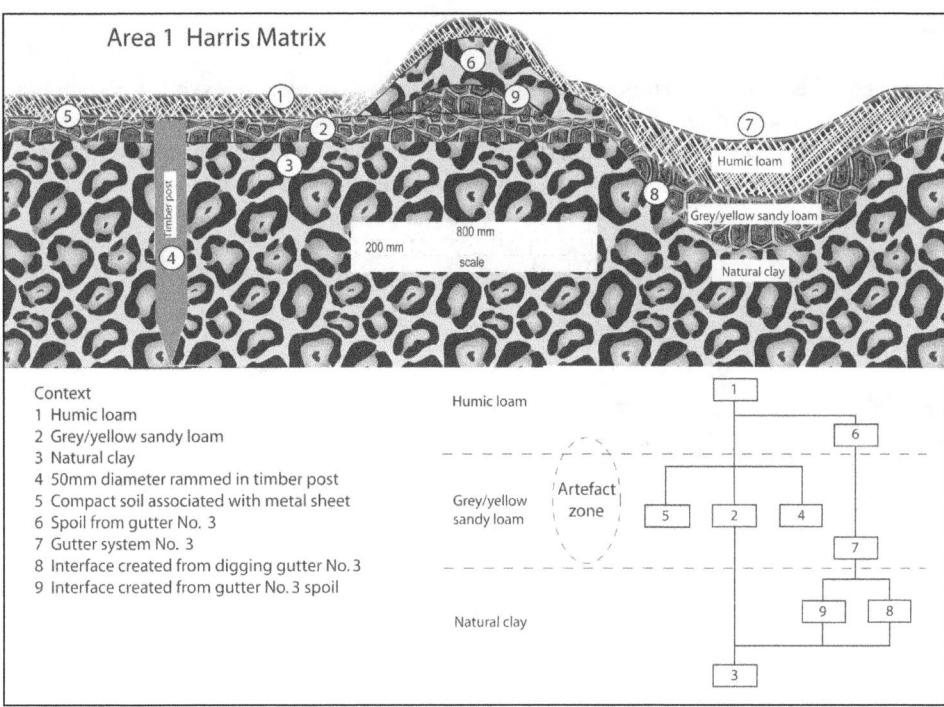

Figure 5.9 Schematic diagram showing stratigraphy and Harris matrix for area 1 (not to scale).

Many of the corroded metal fragments (644 pieces, weighing 3.947 kg) recovered from area 1 display a uniform width – 38 mm, 32 mm and 25 mm – and curvature. These match the 19th-century standard regulation widths for the top, middle and base hoops for wooden cask containers (Hughes 1926: 20). A cask is a generic term used to describe eight sizes of cylindrical wooden storage containers: the 745-litre leager, 500-litre butt, 372-litre puncheon, 245-litre hogshead, 164-litre barrel, 123-litre half, 82-litre kilderkin and the 41-litre firkin (Stevens 1894: 104). During the 19th century, casks were the most common container used to store and transport bulk items (figure 5.10). Casks with wooden hoops were constructed for holding dry or semi-liquid products and iron-hooped casks held liquids such as alcoholic beverages and vinegar (Staniforth 1987: 21). Timber casks likely represent a container for brining fish, as metal tubs would quickly rust and possibly taint fish flesh. Timber casks could be reused over long periods and may have been fitted with tight covers to reduce evaporation and dilution of the brine through rain water (Ashbrook 1955: 217). A number of metal rivets were found with the metal hoop-iron, consistent with the type of rivet used for storage casks. As limited domestic artefacts were recovered from area 1, this is thought to have been an industrial area, possibly for fish brining and drying nets.

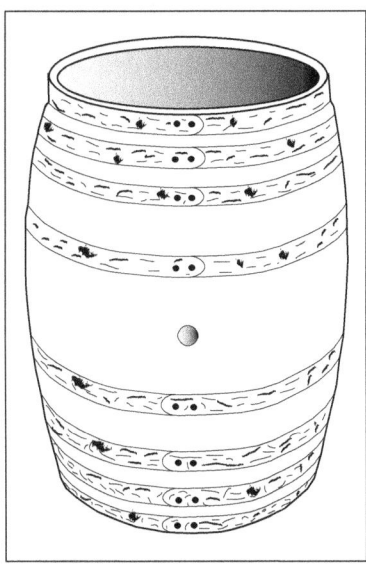

Figure 5.10 A common 19th-century European iron-hooped 164-litre wooden barrel cask.

## Excavation area 2

Excavation of area 2, outside the north-eastern boundary of the gutter system, was uneventful. Exploratory test pitting revealed a small fragment of celadon porcelain and one shard of light blue bottle glass embedded in the top soil layer. Two one-by-one metre excavation squares, dug to a depth of 100 mm, revealed – just below surface level – four small celadon shards and one piece of nondescript corroded metal. The area was recorded and then abandoned. The stratigraphy and Harris matrix for area 2 can be seen in Figure 5.11.

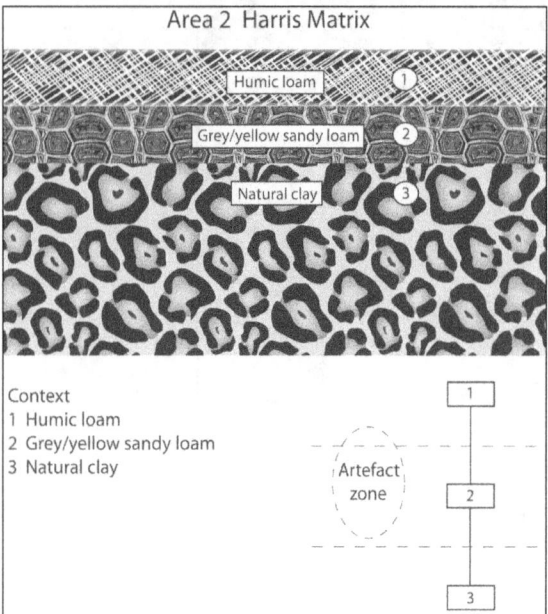

Figure 5.11 Stratigraphy and Harris matrix for area 2 (not to scale).

## Excavation area 3

Excavations began in the eastern perimeter of the gutter system by opening a one-by-one metre exploratory square. Four consecutive squares revealed very little of interest, however in the fifth square the remains of a 80 mm round post were uncovered. Further excavated squares revealed more post remains until, by using both one-by-one metre squares and some bulk excavation, 146 m² had been excavated, revealing the remains of 131 posts. Post circumferences ranged from 50 to 150 mm. In most cases, the posts appeared as vertical, circular tubes of dark humic matter encased in tan-coloured clay. Some posts had survived intact, providing evidence they were made of tea-tree and that the posts were cut by axe without a point, placed in a pre-dug hole and backfilled with clay from lower stratigraphic layers. Smaller 50 mm posts had been pointed by axe and rammed in beside larger posts, presumably to strengthen rotten or damaged supports. Cross-sections dug through the remains of three posts from different parts of area 3 reveal the posts were placed deep into the ground, the shallowest at 500 mm and the deepest at over one metre (figure 5.12).

Figure 5.12 Cross-section of excavated post remains. Note the rammed-hard backfilled clay at surface level and dark humic matter where post was positioned.

It is evident that the posts were placed in four distinct rows, each approximately 1.5 m wide and 15 m long (figure 5.13). The solid timber foundations had been designed to support a great deal of weight, but are unlikely to represent house supports as no floor horizon was visible in the soil matrix, no hearth was evident and there was a very poor representation of domestic artefacts.

Figure 5.13 Plan diagram (left) and photograph (above) of excavated area 3. Looking west towards Port Albert, the layout of uncovered posts remains is clearly distinguishable.

An 1880s photograph of Shaving Point at Metung, Victoria, shows a very small portion of a Chinese fish-curing camp in which long, low-level fish-drying racks can be seen (figure 5.14). Several references cited in chapter 4 suggest Chinese fish curers used racks to dry their fish. For example, in 1861, a *Sydney Morning Herald* correspondent visited a Chinese fish-curing establishment at Sydney's Palm Beach and reported the fish were dried in the open air on racks (*Sydney Morning Herald* 1861, April 6). Also, references to Chinese fish curers at Port Albert state that

> A number of Chinese settled at Long Point [now Chinamen's Point]. They bought fish at 7 pounds per ton, dried them on racks and sent them away by steamer. (Olson 1947: 118)

Figure 5.14 The previously shown NJ Caire photograph c. 1886 of Shaving Point, Metung, showing the low fish-drying racks visible in the right portion of the picture. La Trobe Picture Collection, State Library of Victoria.

The layout of the uncovered post remains, written accounts and the Metung photograph leave little doubt that area 3 represents the remains of a very sturdy fish-drying rack, built to take several tons of weight.

Other artefacts recovered from area 3 were 116 shards of glass, ten Chinese ceramic shards, five animal bone pieces, 1686 nondescript metal pieces (weighing 3.41 kg), nine metal nails and 144 pieces of metal cask hooping (table 5.3). The stratigraphy and Harris matrix for area 3 can be seen in Figure 5.15.

| Area 3 | Number of artefact fragments | Weight (grams) |
|---|---|---|
| Bottle glass | 116 | 1388 |
| Window glass | 0 | 0 |
| Ceramic | 10 | 194 |
| Bone | 5 | 54 |
| Nails | 9 | 24 |
| Spikes | 0 | 0 |
| Cask hoop | 144 | 946 |
| Nondescript metal | 1686 | 3410 |
| Total | 1970 | 6016 |

Table 5.3 Main artefact categories by number and weight from excavation area 3.

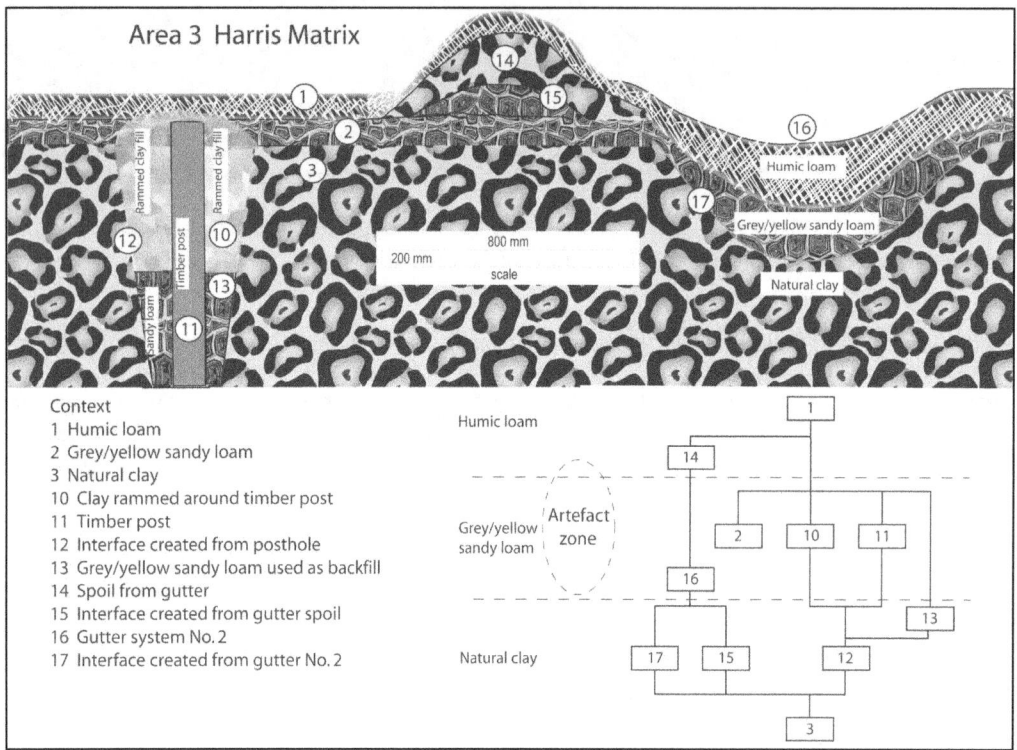

Figure 5.15 Schematic diagram showing stratigraphy and Harris matrix for area 3 (not to scale).

## Excavation area 4

This section includes discussion of excavated artefacts and artefacts collected from the site's tidal zone. Surface artefacts were densely scattered across the tidal zone immediately in front of excavation area 4 and many more artefacts were visible from the eroding shoreline in this area. A series of one-by-one metre excavation squares were opened 2 m in from the shoreline. Sub-surface layers in this area were particularly disturbed through bottle-collector and artefact-scavenging activities. Artefact types recovered from 11 excavation squares include 216 glass bottle shards, 23 glass window shards, 67 Chinese ceramic shards, nine bone pieces (sheep bone and teeth, butchered cow bone, chicken bone and fish bone), 762 metal pieces (weighing 821 kg), 39 metal nails, 14 metal spikes, 52 pieces of metal cask hooping, two sections of slate board, opium related utensils, cooking-pot pieces, lead net sinkers and numerous pieces of charcoal (table 5.4). These domestic artefacts, combined with the approximate house location obtained from the land title document, suggest that further excavation in this area may reveal the presence of one or more dwellings (although no such features were found during excavation).

| Area 4 | Number of artefact fragments | Weight (grams) |
|---|---|---|
| Bottle glass | 216 | 894 |
| Window glass | 23 | 86 |
| Ceramic | 67 | 864 |
| Bone | 9 | 28 |
| Nails | 39 | 48 |
| Spikes | 14 | 598 |
| Cask hoop | 52 | 311 |
| Nondescript metal | 762 | 821 |
| Total | 1162 | 3650 |

Table 5.4 Main artefact categories by number and weight from excavation area 4.

Artefacts found in the tidal zone appear to have originated from a central position in front of area 4 and been washed east by incoming tidal movements. Compared to the rest of the shoreline, the section adjacent to area 4 has experienced an increased rate of erosion. Surface finds in this area included a broken, homemade, handheld pick of a modern style, probably left by artefact collectors.

Breakage patterns in bottle glass found in the site's tidal zone has been used in conjunction with other evidence to suggest that the tidal zone bordering area 4 may have been a rubbish dump for the site. Approximately 45% of glass bottle shards recovered from the tidal zone display a hinged breakage pattern (figure 5.16). Hinged breaks are indicative of heavy, slow, outwards pressure (Cotterell & Kamminga 1990: 146; Dibble & Pelcin 1995: 429), although can also occur as a flaking error during the manufacture of glass and stone tools. It is hypothesised that empty glass bottles were discarded on a rubbish dump and as rubbish accumulated the glass was subjected to the slow, heavy pressure that would cause these hinged breaks.

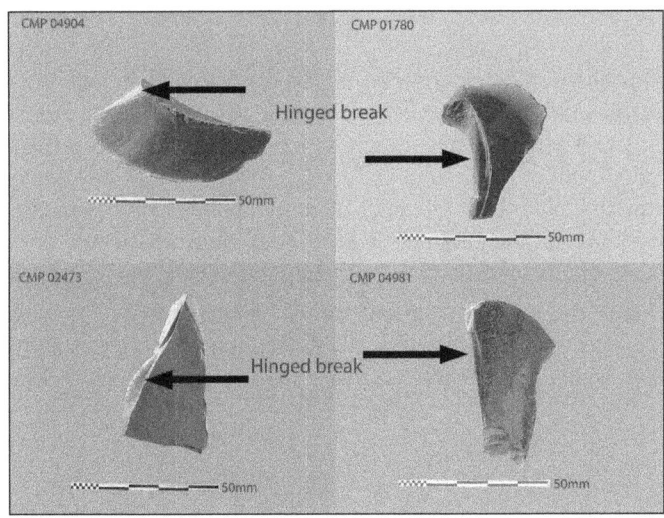

Figure 5.16 Bottle glass displaying hinged-breakage patterns.

In certain controlled experiments I conducted, a number of 19th-century square and cylindrical glass bottles obtained from a local market stall were subjected to long, slow, heavy pressure. Some bottles were placed in a vice at differing angles and slowly pressured – sometimes for days – until the glass broke. Other bottles had weight continuously loaded on top of them until they broke. Others were thrown against a wall, dropped on the ground or smashed with another object. While more scientifically controlled experiments would be useful to confirm the forces required to produce a hinged break in bottle glass, examination of the glass fragments confirmed Cotterell & Kamminga's and Dibble & Pelcin, findings that hinged breaks occur in bottles that have been broken through slow heavy pressure.

While Cotterell & Kamminga and Dibble & Pelcin experimented on flat plate glass in order to determine variability in flake morphology, experiments I conducted were on bottle glass in order to identify breakage patterns in discarded historical bottles. The long, slow, heavy pressure required to produce hinged breaks is consistent with the force applied to bottles in the middle or lower levels of rubbish dumps.

The hinged glass breakage pattern, the disturbed nature of area 4's sub-surface layers, the increased bank erosion, the discarded pick and the density of surface artefacts led to the conclusion that this area was probably a rubbish dump positioned beside or behind the site's residential area. This area has attracted the attention of bottle collectors and artefact scavengers who have dug at the bank and surface layers to retrieve material remains. The stratigraphy and Harris matrix for area 4 can be seen in Figure 5.17.

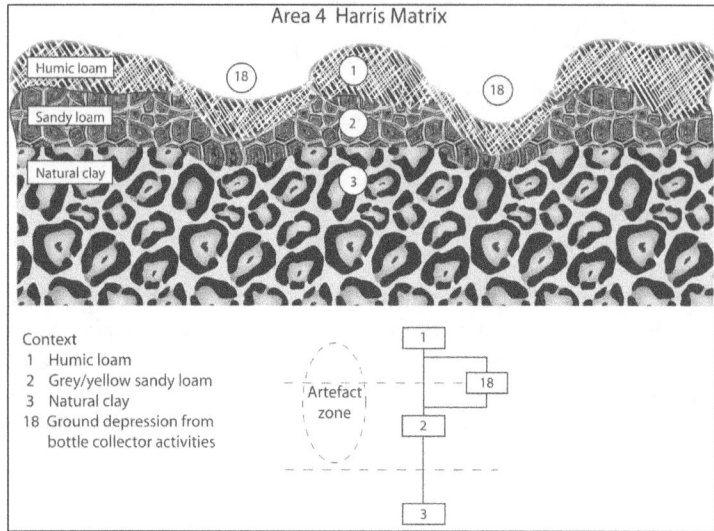

Figure 5.17 Schematic diagram showing stratigraphy and Harris matrix for area 4 (not to scale).

## Jetty remains

Through gently probing sub-surface layers within the tidal zone, a series of sub-surface post stumps were located, suggesting the remains of a jetty. Scientific analysis of the timber remains was not possible due to financial constraints. However, in this constantly wet environment the posts, including a series of milled hardwood stumps 150 by 35 mm (identified through timber hardnesss) and an assortment of tea-tree stumps from 40 to 80 mm diameter (identified visually through outer bark remains), were well preserved. The stumps lead out over the swamp area towards the deeper part of the channel. A jetty in this position would have allowed fishing boats to moor at the jetty and its occupants to walk over the swamp to the industrial site area.

Eight copper nails (used in boat construction as they do not rust) and 29 lead fishing net sinkers were recovered from surface and sub-surface layers of the site. Copper nails, net sinkers and the jetty remains suggest the site occupants probably had their own boats, fished with nets and took delivery of catches from other boats.

## RESULTS

The excavation of the site and examination of ground features and artefacts enabled an excellent understanding of the site's purpose and usage. The evidence shows that, while pursuing a livelihood from fish, the Chinese fished, bought fish, cured fish, constructed substantial infrastructure and, as evidenced in the gutter system, considerably altered the natural environment. The extent to which the site occupants themselves fished and their methods, remains unclear, although the presence of fishing-net sinkers and marine nails reveal that at least some of their activities involved the use of nets and boats.

The size of the drying rack suggests fish were cured on an industrial scale and that curing was done in the open air, unless new evidence comes to light suggesting the racks were enclosed or roofed. As few nails or fastening equipment were recovered from the drying rack area, the fish curers may have used traditional building techniques of mortice joints and lashing timbers together (Dumarcay 1991: 61). No fish scales and very few fish bones were recovered from the drying-rack area, suggesting that fish were scaled before drying and, if displaced from the rack, were considered valuable enough to be picked up and not left to rot on the ground.

Knowledge of whether fish was boned during the curing process is important for the future identification of fish remains from mining and other colonial-period Chinese sites in Australia. The *Australian Town and Country Journal* (1870, July 9) is the only located reference that suggests fish bone was removed, stating that at the Lake Macquarie Chinese fish-curing site "The smaller varieties [of fish] – such as perch, tailor, garnet, soles, herrings, &c, – are mostly converted into a kind of semi-liquid preserve". All other fish types are:

> taken in baskets to the splitting-table: and after being there opened, headed and the back
> bone removed, they are passed on to another part of the establishment.

Five other references regarding this stage of the curing process suggest that Chinese fish curers split the fish down the backbone (as opposed to removing the backbone) (*Bendigo Advertiser* 1857, January 5; *The Argus* 1864, May 28; Oliver 1871: 758; *Votes and Proceedings of the New South Wales Legislative Assembly* 1879–80, vol. 1: 1224; *Gippsland Standard* 1944, July 7). For example:

> the internal arrangement of the fish is partially removed, leaving the liver and roe attached,
> being cleverly split from the back. They are then thrown into a brine-cask and left for a few
> days. (*The Argus* 1864, May 28)

Some curing sites may have deboned their fish and not others. Alternatively, particular fish types only may have been deboned. Salmon (*Arripis trutta*) fish bone has been excavated from one colonial-period Chinese site at Butcher's Gully in Victoria (Stanin 2004a), which, due to the site's location (approximately 150 km inland from Melbourne), almost certainly represents a cured fish. At this time, no determination can be given as to whether fish was routinely deboned during the curing process. The discovery or absence of fish bone from future archaeological excavations at colonial period Chinese sites will help to answer this question.

Some metal fragment remains indicate that timber casks were present on the site. It is possible that casks were used for fresh-water storage, or to brine fish, or both.

The recovery of large amounts of Chinese artefacts suggests the site occupants had contact with people who traded in Chinese goods. Shipping records for the 1860s – previously discussed in chapter 4 – reveal that ships carried cured fish from Port Albert to Singapore and Hong Kong (Syme 1987: 321). Accordingly, it is likely some supplies came from Singapore and Hong Kong to Port Albert. Shipping records also show that cured fish was frequently shipped from Port Albert to Melbourne (Lennon 1973: 196), then probably taken to the goldfields.

Ample evidence of residential occupation of the site was recovered. However, as no remains of the dwelling shown on the 1888 land titles document are evident on the surface, in sub-surface layers or on the eroded areas of the site, the structure may have been a temporary or prefabricated structure. The Chinese use of prefabricated timber dwellings produced in China is noted in American colonial-period literature such as Borthwick (1857: 75) and Bowles (1866: 248–54). Also, Frost (1853: 100) states:

> The houses they [the Chinese miners in California] brought with them from China and which
> they set up where they were wanted, were infinitely superior and more substantial than those
> erected by the Yankees, being built chiefly of logs of wood, or scantling [planks of timber],
> from six to eight inches in thickness ... the roofs were constructed on an equally simple and
> ingenious plan and were remarkable for durability.

Similarly, Soule (1855: 387) writes of the Chinese in San Francisco: "Their dwellings, some of which are brought in frames direct from China and erected by themselves, are commodious ... and [they] live very comfortably". Accompanying the land title document of 1888 is the original hand-drawn surveyor's plan of the Chinaman's Point site in which the house is described as made of 'palings' (PROV, VPRS 5357/P0000, unit 5899). In Syme's (1987: 207, 232, 246) compilation of Victoria's shipping arrivals and departures during 1854 and 1855, there are several entries of 'houses' and 'wooden houses' among the cargoes exported from Hong Kong and Singapore to Melbourne. Therefore it is conceivable that the dwelling at Chinaman's Point was a prefabricated Chinese structure imported to Australia and – in this case – possibly dismantled when the site was abandoned (during the colonial period timber houses were commonly relocated or dismantled to be re-used for building material). The failure to locate any surface remnants of a domestic hearth area or the house itself may be explained through the dense site vegetation cover, site scavenging activities or a combination of both.

The artefact types, densities and positioning support the hypothesis that the tidal-zone artefacts originated from an eroded rubbish dump area, areas 1, 2 and 3 were industrial areas and area 4 was a domestic area (figure 5.18). Artefacts recovered from the surface collection are not considered to be *in situ*, but they do represent domestic and industrial components of the site. The jetty remains fit with the general documentary evidence to suggest that Chinese fish curers in colonial Australia had their own fishing boats and also took the catches of local European fishermen. As approximately only 3% of the site has been excavated, the land at Chinaman's Point still holds considerable potential to reveal further information concerning Australia's colonial Chinese fish curers and aspects of the industry they helped to create.

Figure 5.18 Site reconstruction based on archaeological and historical evidence. Painting by blaked beans design 2007.

# CHAPTER 6
# ARTEFACT ANALYSIS

Archaeological excavations at Chinaman's Point were conducted to obtain a representative sample of the material remains at the site. Through these remains information was sought on the methods the Chinese fish curers used to sustain a livelihood, the domestic and industrial equipment required, their living conditions, consumption patterns and recreational activities.

The excavated areas revealed a mix of industrial and domestic artefacts, although different areas of activity were apparent through artefact types and distribution densities. The recovered artefacts include deliberately discarded and accidentally lost industrial and domestic items. While some were located in a simple, single, *in situ* ground layer; others had eroded from ground layers of the site through wave action and been deposited within the site's tidal zone. None of the domestic remains could be directly connected to individual site occupants – known through historical documents – and therefore no attempt has been made to compare and contrast domestic artefacts to ascertain individual ownership or distinguish the roles of individuals.

As this research is the first of its kind in Australia, the industrial components from Chinaman's Point cannot be compared or contrasted with a similar body of material remains. Therefore, for the purpose of this research, the industrial remains from Chinaman's Point will be considered a standard collection of artefacts for a colonial Australian Chinese fish-curing site. The domestic artefact types from Chinaman's Point were found to be consistent with Australian colonial-period urban and rural overseas Chinese sites, enabling a good level of comparative analysis. The site's small size and isolation assists to provide a snapshot of a Chinese community in colonial Australia separate (but interlinked) to the overseas Chinese mining industry.

## ARTEFACT COLLECTORS

With the erosion of the bank at Chinaman's Point described in chapter 5 and the subsequent depositing of artefacts onto the tidal zone, thousands of artefacts became exposed to artefact collectors. People also retrieved artefacts by digging at the banks of the site. A walk through the residential streets of Port Albert reveals a myriad of Chinese style artefacts prominently displayed in kitchen and living room windows and in one case, hanging from a front-yard sculpture. Unusual looking objects, unbroken items and artefacts displaying Chinese characters would likely have been the first pieces collected. This is reflected in the poor representation of these artefact types recovered archaeologically from Chinaman's Point. Artefact collecting at Chinaman's Point has resulted in the loss of much scientific information and has made site interpretation difficult, especially in terms of estimating site population and gaining an understanding of how prolific certain industrial, domestic and recreational activities may have been.

## ANALYSIS METHODOLOGY

The artefact classification system devised for this project is based partly on the very adaptable historical artefact management tools presented in *The Canada Parks Service Classification System for Historical Collections* (1992) and partly on the artefact typology guide in Orser (1988: 233). To further aid in developing an appropriate classification system and to describe and archaeologically interpret artefacts from the Chinaman's Point site, a number of other artefact cataloguing and analysis guides were consulted, including South (1977), Sprague (1980–81), Davies & Buckley (1987), Orser (1989), Praetzellis & Praetzellis (1990), Adams & Adams (1991), Crook, Lawrence & Gibbs (2002), Casey (2004), Brooks (2005a; 2005b) and Crook (2005).

The artefact analysis aims to describe artefacts in a complete and organised manner, so that artefacts or groups of artefacts can be broken into variables that permit both a detailed analysis of the artefact assemblage – such as an individual tools usage or a description of fishing methods – and broad analysis – such as site demographics, activity areas or structural layout. The analysis also aims to identify artefacts of significance for more comprehensive examination. This will facilitate an understanding of the broader social and cultural framework of the assemblage and assist in an understanding of the people at Chinaman's Point.

The artefact classification system is broadly functional, concentrating mainly on material and form (rather than a fabric-based analysis) to interpret primary original artefact use. Detailed examinations of artefact attributes, manufacturing technologies and post-manufacture modifications have also in some cases been used to determine site occupation periods and possible artefact re-use functions (i.e. when artefacts were used other than for their original purpose). To identify the artefacts from Chinaman's Point, seven functional artefact categories are defined, each of which includes a number of more narrow sub-categories.

The categories are:

- *Architectural/Structural*. Artefacts originally created for the purpose of constructing dwellings or site features. Sub-category: fastener and construction material.
- *Domestic*. Artefacts originally created for the purpose of procurement, preparation and service of daily human food requirements and personal comfort. Sub-category: cooking, food, food storage, furnishing, liquid storage and tableware.
- *Industrial*. Artefacts originally created for the purpose of procuring and processing marine resources. Sub-category: fishing, recording, slag, tools.
- *Personal*: artefacts originally created for individual human use such as clothing and associated objects. Sub-category: button.
- *Recreational*. Artefacts originally created for individual or group enjoyment. Sub-category: opium smoking.
- *Unidentified*. Artefacts originally or subsequently created to serve a purpose that cannot now be determined. Sub-category: unidentified artefacts.

Recovered artefacts were cleaned in the field and bulk-bagged with other artefacts of the same fabric, grid square and stratigraphical layer. Bulk bags were assigned a five part identification code e.g. CMP-4G-IXh-2-3, where CMP represents Chinaman's Point, 4G the ten-by-ten metre grid square, IXh the one-by-one metre grid square, 2 the spit number and 3 the stratigraphical ground layer (figure 6.1). Bags were clearly labelled using waterproof, indelible, black pen (Artline Drawing System EK-238) on Tyvek waterproof labels. Complete or diagnostic items were separately bagged and tagged. Labels were placed inside artefact bags, or for objects such as bottles the labels were tied to the object with fine cotton string.

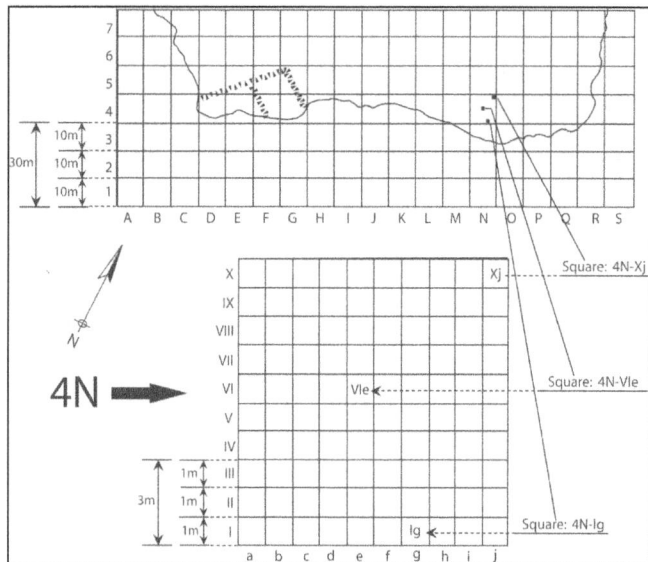

Figure 6.1 Site grid (top) and one-by-one metre breakdown (bottom) used for artefact province details.

Due to the site's coastal environment, recovered artefacts had been impregnated by salt and required salt leaching. Under the direction of Heritage Victoria's conservation department, artefacts were placed in synthetic mesh bags and immersed in fresh tap-water. Water was changed fortnightly from the time of recovery until the water the artefact was in had achieved a salt content reading of 20 parts per million or below. The final water change was conducted using purified water in which artefacts were submerged for another four-week period. Consequently, all artefacts were immersed in fresh water for approximately ten months. To ensure artefacts did not become damaged during transportation from the field and storage, plastic water-filled tubs were packed loosely with bagged artefacts and fitted with a strong lid. Wet polyethylene was used to cushion any loose and/or fragile artefacts.

Artefact cataloguing and analyses were conducted at La Trobe University's archaeological laboratories. In the laboratory, each artefact was reassessed and assigned a new double-sided tag. This tag displays the grid square and stratigraphic layer on one side and a Chinaman's Point accession catalogue number on the other side. After this was completed and conjoins between artefacts made where possible, all artefacts were placed in numbered archival Corflute boxes and submitted to Heritage Victoria's conservation laboratory in Abbotsford, Melbourne, where some significant artefacts underwent further conservation treatment and others went into storage.

Artefact information has been recorded in an accession catalogue using a Microsoft Access database. Each database entry includes the artefact number, object, an artefact description, date range (where possible), quantity, weight, province, material, sub-material, function, sub-function, identity, significance (site and state) and the archival box number (figure 6.2). For consistency in catalogue entries, drop down tables were developed within the database according to category. To facilitate artefact identification and retrieval, the accession catalogue was designed to allow all artefact entries – besides the general description – to be searched in individual fields. This also enables artefact properties to be broken into variables for detailed and complex queries – such as only white ware ceramic rim fragments with 50 mm diameters or broad levels of analysis – such as all ceramic of a certain ware.

### CMP 2004 Artefact Catalogue

Page 168

| Reg No | Object | Description | Date Range | Qty | Weight: g | Gr10 x10 | Gr1x 1 | Spit | Unit | D/R | Material | Sub-material | Function | Sub-function | Identity | Sig | Box No |
|---|---|---|---|---|---|---|---|---|---|---|---|---|---|---|---|---|---|
| CMP02506 | Base fragment from cylindrical bottle | 7.5cm base diameter, 34% complete, deep mechanical type push up | 1870 to 1920 | 1 | 61.0 | 4J | | SC | SC | R | Glass | Green/dark | Domestic | Liquid storage | Bottle | Low | 19 |
| CMP02507 | Base fragment from cylindrical bottle | 7.5cm base diameter, 27% complete, medium mechanical push up, sml mamelon | 1870 to 1920 | 1 | 76.1 | 4J | | SC | SC | R | Glass | Green/dark | Domestic | Liquid storage | Bottle | Low | 21 |
| CMP02508 | Fragment of bottle glass | Probably octagonal or hexagonal shape, 3mm thick glass | | 1 | 14.7 | 4J | | SC | SC | R | Glass | Clear | Domestic | Liquid storage | Bottle | Low | 27 |
| CMP02509 | Base fragment from cylindrical bottle | 8cm base diameter (bit oval), 25% complete, shallow mechanical push up, medium mamelon | 1870 to 1920 | 1 | 43.9 | 3K | | SC | SC | R | Glass | Amber | Domestic | Liquid storage | Bottle | Low | 1 |
| CMP02510 | Base fragment from cylindrical bottle | 8cm base diameter, 25% complete, medium depth mechanical type push up, medium mamelon | 1870 to 1920 | 1 | 17.4 | 3K | | SC | SC | R | Glass | Amber | Domestic | Liquid storage | Bottle | Low | 2 |
| CMP02511 | Base fragment from cylindrical bottle | Too small to be descript, possibly shallow push up, badly broken | | 1 | 7.6 | 3K | | SC | SC | R | Glass | Amber | Domestic | Liquid storage | Bottle | Low | 2 |
| CMP02512 | Fragment of bottle glass | Probably from hexagonal shape vessel, 6mm thick glass | | 1 | 18.7 | 4J | | SC | SC | R | Glass | Green/aqua | Domestic | Liquid storage | Bottle | Low | 47 |
| CMP02513 | Base fragment from cylindrical bottle | 7.5cm base diameter, 20% complete, shallow mechanical type push up | 1875 to 1920 | 1 | 68.4 | 4J | | SC | SC | R | Glass | Green/aqua | Domestic | Liquid storage | Bottle | Low | 4 |
| CMP02514 | Body fragment from cylindrical bottle | Non-descript, 6mm average glass thickness | | 7 | 76.3 | 3K | | SC | SC | R | Glass | Green/light | Domestic | Liquid storage | Bottle | Low | 59 |
| CMP02515 | Body fragment from cylindrical bottle | Non-descript, 3mm average glass thickness | | 8 | 29.0 | 3K | | SC | SC | R | Glass | Green/light | Domestic | Liquid storage | Bottle | Low | 59 |
| CMP02516 | Body fragment from square bottle | Flat shard, probably from dip mould, 4mm thick glass | | 1 | 3.4 | 3K | | SC | SC | R | Glass | Green/light | Domestic | Liquid storage | Bottle | Low | 51 |
| CMP02517 | Body fragment from cylindrical bottle | Non-descript, 3 to 5mm thick glass | | 1 | 6.1 | 3K | | SC | SC | R | Glass | Green/aqua | Domestic | Liquid storage | Bottle | Low | 46 |
| CMP02518 | Body fragment from cylindrical bottle | Rounded body has one flattened section, 6mm thick glass | | 1 | 32.3 | 3K | | SC | SC | R | Glass | Green/aqua | Domestic | Liquid storage | Bottle | Low | 46 |
| CMP02519 | Fragment of bottle glass | 3 sides from hexagonal bottle, 8mm thick glass | | 1 | 9.9 | 3K | | SC | SC | R | Glass | Green/aqua | Domestic | Liquid storage | Bottle | Low | 46 |
| CMP02520 | Base fragment from cylindrical bottle | 8cm base diameter, 12% complete, medium depth mechanical type push up | 1870 to 1920 | 1 | 16.0 | 4J | | SC | SC | R | Glass | Green/dark | Domestic | Liquid storage | Bottle | Low | 22 |

Figure 6.2 One-page example of the Chinaman's Point artefact catalogue.

In total, 29 030 separate artefact fragments, weighing 234.655 kg and representing 6335 accession catalogue entries were recovered from the site. The majority of artefacts – 21 838 artefacts, weighing 211.479 kg – came from surface collections conducted on the tidal area of the site (the tidal zone). The remaining 7192 artefacts – weighing 23.176 kg – were excavated from sub-surface ground layers. Twelve separate artefact materials are present in the assemblage: bone, brass, ceramic, copper, ferrous metals, glass, lead, leather, mortar, shell, slate and wood. The term sherd is used in conjunction with ceramics fragments and the term shard is used when referring to glass fragments. A breakdown of artefact material types, numbers and weight is in table 6.1. Artefact densities can be seen in table 6.2.

| Materials | Number of artefact fragments | Weight (grams) |
|---|---|---|
| Bone | 56 | 560 |
| Brass | 2 | 17 |
| Ceramic | 3110 | 14 298 |
| Copper | 41 | 79 |
| Ferrous metal | 11 825 | 42 780 |
| Glass | 13 660 | 17 4872 |
| Lead | 29 | 589 |
| Leather | 2 | 5 |
| Mortar | 6 | 16 |
| Shell | 10 | 87 |
| Slate | 6 | 12 |
| Wood | 283 | 1340 |
| Total | 29 030 | 23 4655 |

Table 6.1 Breakdown of artefact material types, numbers and weight.

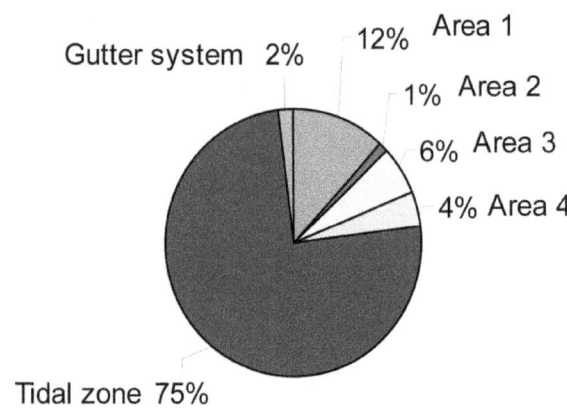

Table 6.2 Chinaman's Point site artefact densities.

## ARCHITECTURAL/STRUCTURAL

### Fasteners

Nails were the dominant type of fastener recovered from Chinaman's Point, although screws, spikes and washers were also found. Corrosion from the harsh marine environment hampered the identification and accurate sizing of many of the recovered nails. The largest nail size was approximately 75 mm long and 6 mm diameter – with diameter the most important determining factor. Smooth shaft ferrous metal fasteners exceeding these dimensions are classified as spikes. Two square shaft tack nails were recovered from the tidal zone, both approximately 25 mm long; one has a two facet chisel point and the other a four facet point. Two 25 mm diameter, machine-made, lead washers were also located in the tidal zone and could be associated with either boat maintenance or roofing nails.

Due to high levels of corrosion, some ferrous metal artefacts were deemed to have little or no archaeological value. It would be impractical to conserve and retain such artefacts. A sampling strategy that involved identifying and retaining the least corroded and most archaeologically informative pieces was employed to deal with the unidentifiable heavily corroded material. This resulted in a retention rate of approximately eight percent of metals. A percentage breakdown of retained and discarded metals can be seen in table 6.3.

| Metal form | Number of artefact fragments | Weight (grams) | Percentage |
|---|---|---|---|
| Nail | 319 | 1107 | 100 |
| Nail (retained) | 21 | 104 | 6.6 |
| Nail (discarded) | 298 | 1003 | 93.4 |
| Spike | 59 | 2992 | 100 |
| Spike (retained) | 7 | 557 | 11.9 |
| Spike (discarded) | 52 | 2435 | 88.1 |
| Screw | 8 | 103 | 100 |
| Rivet | 62 | 2231 | 100 |
| Rivet (retained) | 27 | 978 | 43.5 |
| Rivet (discarded) | 35 | 1253 | 56.5 |
| Cask strap | 2056 | 13 100 | 100 |
| Cask (retained) | 44 | 1016 | 2.1 |
| Cask (discarded) | 2012 | 12 084 | 97.9 |
| Cooking pot | 107 | 5440 | 100 |
| Drum plug | 65 | 122 | 100 |
| Drum rim | 20 | 113 | 100 |
| Lead | 29 | 589 | 100 |
| Slag | 279 | 754 | 100 |
| Slag (retained) | 4 | 14 | 1.4 |
| Slag (discarded) | 275 | 740 | 98.6 |
| Unidentifiable | 9286 | 16 229 | 100 |
| Unid. (retained) | 150 | 204 | 1.8 |
| Unid. (discarded) | 9136 | 16 025 | 98.2 |
| Total (retained) | 578 | 12 418 | 5.1 |
| Total (discarded) | 10 689 | 32 518 | 94.9 |
| Total | 12 290 | 42 780 | 100 |

Table 6.3 Breakdown of retained and discarded metals (Unid = Unidentifiable).

**Nails (ferrous)**

There are two problems in accurately dating nails recovered from historical sites in Australia. First, although a manufacture date can be roughly established from physical features, builders often held an initial prejudice against new nail types. This has created a time gap from when historical records demonstrate a nail was available, to when it was actually used in Australian structures. Second, due to the high price and scarcity of nails, builders often took nails from abandoned structures to re-use, creating a confusing chronological marker (Varman 1993: 182). Nonetheless, nails have proved to be one of the most common artefacts recovered from historical sites in Australia and are an important means of gathering historical archaeological information (Michael 1974: 99; Middleton 2005: 55, 61).

From 319 recovered iron nails, 233 are so corroded that identification to a specific type is not possible. The remaining 76 nails are recognisable and datable. Twenty are square/rectangle shaft, cut plate, rose head type nails that date from the 1840s until the 1870s (figure 6.3). The remaining 56 are hard drawn, round shaft, wire rose head type nails that date from 1853 to the 1890s (Varman 1980: 108) (table 6.4).

Spatially, the majority of nails were recovered east of square 3G within the tidal zone at Chinaman's Point. Excavated nails areas were centralised around 4G in area 3 and 4H of area 4, suggesting possible workshop areas or the position of a perished structure.

Figure 6.3 Square shaft, cut plate, rose head nails from the Chinaman's Point site.

| Metal fasteners | MNI | Site location |
|---|---|---|
| Square shaft rose head (retained) | 7 | area 4; TZ |
| Square shaft rose head (discarded) | 13 | area 4; TZ |
| Round shaft rose head (retained) | 6 | area 4; TZ |
| Round shaft rose head (discarded) | 50 | area 4; TZ |
| Unidentifiable nail (discarded) | 233 | area 4; TZ |
| Spike (retained) | 7 | area 4; TZ |
| Spike (discarded) | 52 | area 4; TZ |
| Tack | 2 | area 4; TZ |
| Screw | 8 | area 4; TZ |
| Washer (lead) | 2 | TZ |
| Total discard | 348 | area 4; TZ |
| Total retain | 40 | area 4; TZ |
| Total | 388 | N/A |

Table 6.4 Minimum number of metal fasteners (MNI = minimun number of individuals; TZ = tidal zone).

**Screws**

Eight screws are present in the assemblage. One is made of brass and the others are heavily corroded iron screws; all are designed to fasten into timber materials. Screw sizes range from 28 to 68 mm long and from 4 to 8 mm in diameter. These are standard type wood screws with a multitude of timber fastening applications such as securing internal or external shelving, frames, hinges and brackets.

Six screws were recovered from the tidal zone within squares 3G and 3P of the site grid. The remaining two screws – including the brass one – were excavated from area 4 of the site, one in the central region of area 4. Thus, the screws have very similar spatial positions to the recovered nails.

**Spikes**

Fifty-nine ferrous metal spikes were recovered. Thirty-eight of these have a square shaft that tapers to a two facet chisel point, with 12 of the 38 displaying a rose type head. Six of the spikes have round shafts with four facet points and unidentifiable heads; the remaining 15 spikes are too heavily corroded to have their attributes accurately recorded. All spikes range between 40 and 220 mm in length and 8 to 20 mm in diameter.

On the South Coast of New South Wales, between Moruya and Bermagui (figure 6.4), Bowen (1999: 64; 2003: 12) noted that spikes were commonly used by commercial fishermen to fasten together slipway timbers. Maintenance of boats is an ongoing task for any commercial fishing operation. Slipways were used to hold a boat out of water for maintenance purposes, necessary on average every six months. To construct a slipway, bearer timbers were placed parallel to the shore from below low tide mark to well above high tide mark. These were morticed to cradle timbers at a right angle to bearers and held together by steel spikes.

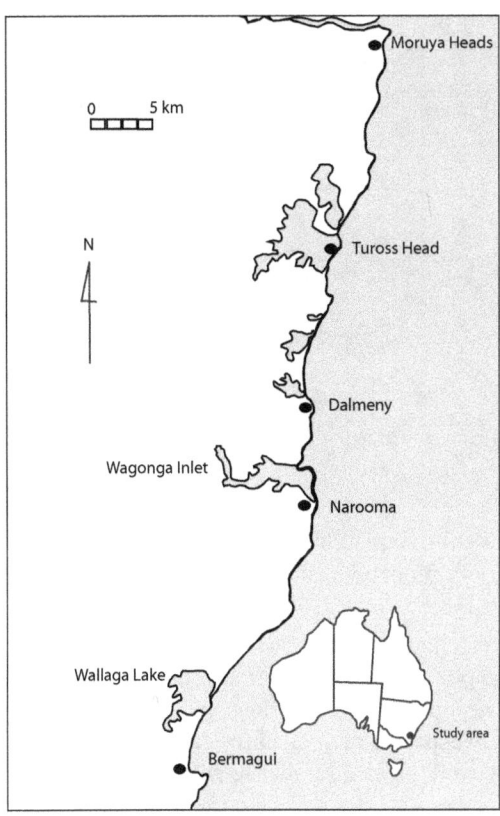

Figure 6.4 Location map for Moruya to Bermagui, South Coast, New South Wales.

Although no timber remains of a slipway are visible at Chinaman's Point, the recovery of metal spikes at an establishment where fishing boats were almost certainly present suggests slipways were in use at the site. The metal spikes – of a similar size to those found on the South Coast of New South Wales – were recovered within a localised vicinity, slightly east of area 4 in the tidal zone.

## Materials

A small representation of architectural and structural material was recovered from Chinaman's Point including brick, timber post remains, lead sheeting and window glass. Timber post remains in area 1 and 3 and those associated with the jetty in the tidal zone have already been discussed in the site description section of chapter 5.

### Bricks

With further settlement at Port Albert during the 1850s and 1860s, people desired permanent dwellings. To cater for this, a number of brick-making facilities were established in the region. For example, Henry Sherwood and Richard Huntington each operated a brick factory in the Tarraville area during the late 1850s and in the 1860s Samuel Taylor ran The Port Albert Brickworks located on the outskirts of town (*Gippsland Guardian* 1859, January 7; *Gippsland Guardian* 1860, September 21; Lennon 1975: 124).

Twenty-two brick objects, weighing 2702 g and representing a minimum number of 18 bricks were recovered in a fragmentary, deteriorating and fragile condition from the Chinaman's Point site. Most are hand moulded, uneven, poorly fired bricks of varying textures and range in colour from red/brown to orange/tan (figure 6.5). An estimate of the original brick sizes suggests their average square (head) end measurements were 75 mm thick by 100 mm wide. Length measurements were unobtainable. These dimensions do not match standard 19th-century British, American or Chinese brick sizes which were 65 thick by 115 mm wide (British), 55 mm thick by 100 mm wide (American) and 65 mm thick by 140 mm wide (Chinese) (Gurcke 1987: 118; Manson 1982: 13). Nineteenth-century Australian brick sizes did vary considerably (Stuart 2005: 83), however, as the standard brick sizes from other countries are not apparent in the sample from Chinaman's Point and as bricks were available locally, the Chinaman's Point bricks are probably not an imported variety. One brick fragment has a plain stamped frog or indent and is of superior manufacture quality – i.e. shows even firing – compared to the other recovered bricks.

Figure 6.5 Hand-moulded mud brick from the Chinaman's Point site.

The brick of superior quality from the site is likely to have been manufactured at one of the region's brick factories. The remaining poorer quality, non-standard sized bricks probably came from one of the informal, one-man brick-making operations that were also plentiful in the local vicinity (Adams 1990: 49, 120).

The bricks were not located in association with a hearth or other structural setting. Seven pieces were grouped together in the gutter system at the eastern end of square 5G. However, to function properly as a means of drainage, the gutter system would need to have been kept clear of obstructions, meaning these brick pieces probably represent displaced objects from the post-site occupation period. Three further brick pieces were excavated from area 4. The remaining 12 bricks portions were located randomly within the site's tidal zone.

**Lead sheet**

Two pieces of lead sheeting weighing a total of 292.3 g were recovered from the tidal zone and area 4 of the site. Both are 1.5 mm thick, approximately 80 mm wide by 150 mm long and rectangular in shape and have a series of 3 mm diameter nail holes spaced evenly around their entire perimeter. These two artefacts probably acted as water-resisting measurers, i.e. for flashing, or as subsequent building repairs to weatherproof a structure.

**Window glass**

One hundred and seven shards, weighing a total of 431 g and representing two types of window glass was recovered from the Chinaman's Point site. Sixty-three shards are of the crown type window glass dating from 1800 to 1870 and 44 shards are of the improved flattened cylinder type window glass dating from 1834 to 1910 (Boow 1991: 100–02). Eighty-four shards were recovered from the tidal zone and 23 were excavated from area 4 (table 6.5). Evidence from other overseas Chinese sites in Australia (Smith 1998: 65–82), New Zealand (Ritchie 1986: 149) and the United States (Sisson 1993: 56), demonstrates that overseas Chinese dwellings were generally constructed without windows. Therefore, these artefacts are a variation to the typical overseas Chinese site and suggest the presence of at least one relatively permanent domestic structure, with windows, at Chinaman's Point.

| Window | Type | Number of shards | Weight (grams) | Site location |
|---|---|---|---|---|
| Aqua tinge | Crown | 28 | 145 | area 4; TZ |
| Aqua tinge | Imp flat cylinder | 32 | 167 | area 4; TZ |
| Clear | Crown | 35 | 91 | area 4; TZ |
| Clear | Imp flat cylinder | 12 | 28 | area 4; TZ |
| Total | N/A | 107 | 431 | area 4; TZ |

Table 6.5 Window-glass type and amounts (TZ = tidal zone).

# DOMESTIC

Domestic artefacts include those associated with cooking, food, food storage, furnishings, liquid storage and tableware. These artefact types make up a sizable proportion – 5108 catalogue entries, representing 17 381 artefact fragments – of the Chinaman's Point assemblage, principally due to the large amount of bottle glass and ceramic fragments recovered from the site.

## Cooking

One hundred and seven metal objects, weighing 5440 g and including handles, rims, spouts, body fragments, base fragments, support legs and hooks were considered to be associated with metal cooking containers. All were recovered from within the tidal zone east of area 4 and are too corroded to enable even a rudimentary reconstruction through conjoining processes. There appear to be a minimum of two kettles, one cooking pot and one wok represented in the assemblage. There was no evidence of a cooking hearth, possibly due to erosion or to the common Chinese custom of using mobile clay stoves designed to allow easy removal upon site abandonment (Anderson & Anderson 1977: 365).

### Containers

The two kettles were identified through the recovery of two pouring spouts. One spout is of a universal pouring design and may be attributed to a number of robust 19th-century cast iron kettle types (figure 6.6). The second spout is of a similar design, but appears even more robust in construction (figure 6.7). As no similar design has been located for European pouring implements, it is speculated through site association that this spout may be of Chinese origin.

Figure 6.6 Common 19th-century cast iron spout from the Chinaman's Point site and the type of kettle it most likely represents.

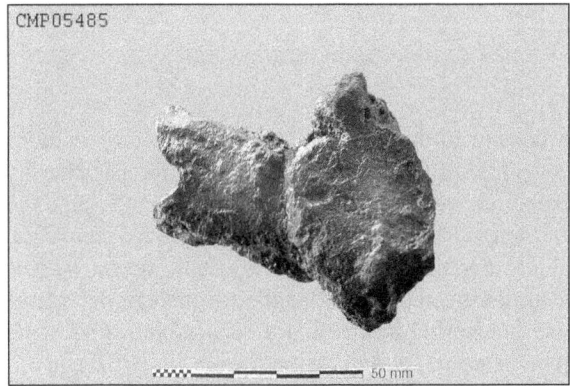

Figure 6.7 Robust pouring spout from the Chinaman's Point site, possibly of Chinese design and origin.

The thickness of the corroded metal enabled the cooking pot and kettle body fragments (6 to 12 mm thick) to be distinguished from the wok fragments which are approximately 3 mm thick. Differing curvatures of the thicker fragments – 150 and 200 mm diameters – show that either two separate cooking pot/kettle sizes are represented or that one of the objects was oval shaped (figure 6.8). The recovery of two stumpy iron pot feet suggests the cooking pot/kettle was manufactured in the standing tripod or four-leg style, popular in both Asian and European iron cooking vessels (figure 6.9). According to Anderson and Anderson (1977: 359), Lee and Lee (1979: 27), and Passmore & Reid (1982: 35), Chinese people did not tend to roast or bake food in their day-to-day cooking practices. Therefore, an iron pot would have been used for boiling rice, soups, stews and other liquid-based dishes and the wok for stir-frying, deep-frying, simmering and steaming. Kettles, pots and woks represent common kitchen implements in Chinese culture (Evans 1980: 90; Passmore & Reid 1982: 30).

Figure 6.8 Curved cast iron cooking pot fragments from Chinaman's Point suggest that oval-shaped cooking pots such as the one shown here may have been used at the site.

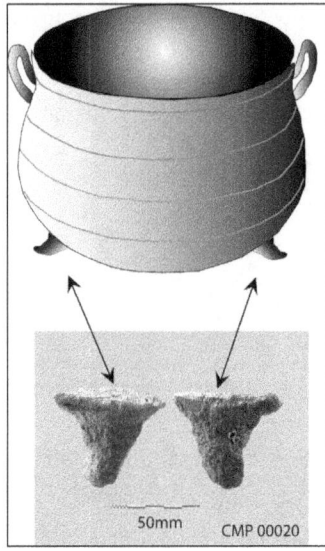

Figure 6.9 Stumpy iron pot feet from the Chinaman's Point site and a diagram of the type of vessel they most likely represent.

## Food

Bone and shell remains are the only evidence of food consumed at Chinaman's Point. All bone remains are believed to represent aspects of the diet of site occupants. Faunal remains are useful for deciphering cultural preferences, living conditions and the possible socio-economic status of the population (Schulz and Gust 1983: 44). Fifty-six bone pieces weighing 560 g and ten marine shells weighing 87 g were recovered. The bone and shell assemblage is analysed by individual taxa and then discussed as a single data set. This is intended to identify the full range of species and species components represented in the assemblage, determine the minimum number of each individual fauna, examine butchering and culinary aspects and offer some rationale for the assemblage. Faunal quantities and distribution across the site can be seen in tables 6.6 and 6.7.

Faunal specimens have been identified, described and analysed through the aid of documentary, pictorial and physical references such as in Levine (1921), Boessneck (1969), Schmid (1972), Coleman (1975), Getty (1975), von den Driesch (1976), Halstead & Collins (1994), Lyman (1994), Leach (1997), Jansen (2000) and in the bone and shell reference collection at La Trobe University. Six bone pieces weighing 5 g and six shell pieces weighing 20 g were too fragmented for accurate identification to a taxa level. The assemblage contains 20 sheep (*Ovis aries*) bones, 19 cattle (*Bos taurus*) bones, seven fish (*Pisces*) bones, four pig (*Sus scrofa*) bones and three chicken (*Gallus domesticus*) bones. All bone is from domestic taxa, except marine varieties.

| Animal | Number of bone pieces | Weight (grams) | Site location |
|---|---|---|---|
| Cattle | 19 | 329 | area 3, 4, TZ |
| Sheep | 20 | 147 | area 1, 3, 4, TZ |
| Pig | 4 | 61 | TZ |
| Chicken | 3 | 2 | area 4, TZ |
| Fish | 7 | 9 | area 4, TZ |
| Unidentified | 3 | 12 | area 1, TZ |
| Total | 56 | 560 | N/A |

Table 6.6 Number, weight and location of recovered animal bones (TZ = tidal zone).

| Animal | Area 1 | Area 2 | Area 3 | Area 4 | Tidal one |
|---|---|---|---|---|---|
| Sheep | 1 | | 3 | 4 | 12 |
| Cattle | | | 2 | 3 | 14 |
| Fish | | | | 3 | |
| Chicken | | | | 1 | 2 |
| Shell | | | | 10 | 4 |
| Pig | | | | | 4 |
| Unidentified | 1 | | | | 2 |

Table 6.7 Faunal distribution across the site (minimum numbers identified).

A brief discussion on the Chinese consumption of meat and the differences between European and Chinese butchering practices provide useful background to the faunal analysis. The diet of overseas Chinese people varied from traditional food practices in southern China. The significance of this variation often remains undetermined in archaeological projects – i.e. it is not clear whether this reflects acculturation or simply a reflection of food availabilities or elements of both (Ritchie 1986: 623–24; Langenwalter 1987: 76; Longenecker & Stapp 1993: 98).

While acknowledging that some dietary variation occurred, it is generally accepted that most overseas Chinese people preferred to maintain their traditional dietary habits which consisted largely of rice, cereals and grains as a staple; a wide variety of vegetables and spicy sauces and in most cases only small quantities of meat (Spier 1958: 130; Anderson & Anderson 1977: 319; Piper 1988: 34). Depending on region, meat eaten in the traditional Chinese diet – in order of importance – has been documented as pork, fish (in areas near large bodies of water fish outranked pork in importance), beef, poultry and mutton (Anderson & Anderson 1977: 336; Langenwalter 1987: 56; Buck 1937: 413). Chinese people eat almost all parts of an animal except feathers, scales, hair and bone, which are generally used in other ways. Carcasses were carefully butchered to assist this maximum-usage pattern (Mote 1977: 201; Wang 1920: 290).

Colonial European butchers commonly used knives, cleavers and handsaws to divide animal carcasses, while Chinese butchers generally used knives and cleavers (Levine 1921: 8; Piper 1984: 35). Levine (1921: 11) and Longenecker & Stapp (1993: 105) suggest that occasionally – and only for cutting the pelvic, breast or vertebrate bone – Chinese people used saws. However, saws are not included in the standard Chinese animal-butchering kit described by Levine (1921) and Longenecker & Stapp (1993) and are usually not discussed in association with Chinese butchering techniques.

Accordingly, when examining butchering patterns in bone assemblages from overseas Chinese sites, the difference between European and Chinese butchering technologies should be identifiable through the presence or absence of saw marks on the bone – except for pelvic, breast or vertebrate bone. Langenwalter's (1980: 107) studies on butchering techniques show that width and depth analysis of chopping marks on bone are also useful in distinguishing between European and Chinese butchering marks. While chopping marks on bone from Chinaman's Point are too weathered to enable this type of analysis, saw marks are common.

## Sheep

In southern China, the Chinese fat-tailed sheep had minor importance as a source of meat, comprising approximately one percent of the standard dietary intake (Levine 1921: 4; Langenwalter 1987: 76). However, the widespread consumption of sheep by overseas Chinese people has been recorded at archaeological sites in the United States, New Zealand and Australia (Piper 1984: 22–23; Ritchie 1986: 621; Longenecker & Stapp 1993: 100; Lydon 1999: 97). Sheep were represented at Chinaman's Point through metacarpi, humeri, ribs and teeth. It is estimated from the presence of four right metacarpis, bone size and tooth maturity that four incomplete individual sheep are represented. The recovered metacarpi distal ends show small, slightly notched, parallel trochlear condyles which, as described by Boessneck (1969: 355), clearly define them as sheep as opposed to the very similar skeletal structure of goat (*Capra hircus*) (figure 6.10). Moreover, goat was considered by the Chinese to be a greatly inferior quality of meat and was not commonly eaten (Levine 1921: 2, 4). One metacarpus displays distinct gnaw marks that are most likely from a rat, demonstrating rodent activity at the site.

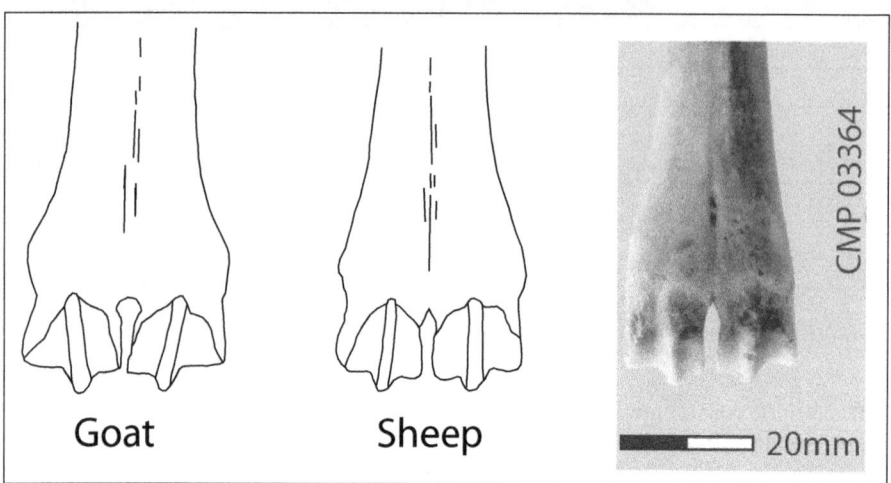

Figure 6.10 Metacarpus from Chinaman's Point showing similarities to sheep as opposed to goat.

The humeri have had either their distal, proximal or both ends removed by saw, which is usually associated with bone-marrow extraction (Piper 1991: 273). A number of rib bones were also sawn through at approximately one third from the head end, similar to European methods of butchering sheep (Piper 1991: 310).

The assemblage of sheep teeth includes a number of worn M2 and M3 molars from animals aged between two and four years. One pre-molar tooth was also present (Getty 1975: 93). The recovery of teeth and a cervical vertebra implies cranium presence, which could reflect on-site slaughter of animals (Schulz & Gust 1983: 48; Longenecker & Stapp 1993: 110). However, as most of the recovered sheep bone display European butchering patterns, it seems more likely that sheep heads were brought to the site and used for meals such as sheep's head soup and those involving tongue, eyes and brain.

One weathered humerus displays a possible cleaver/chopping/cut mark in conjunction with saw marks. This mark could represent bone de-fleshing by a European butcher or a Chinese cook to reduce the size of meat cuts and assist handling with chopsticks (Chinese people did not use knives during meals) (Ball 1925: 149; Chang 1977: 8). Sheep bone from Chinaman's Point shows a consistency with low meat-bearing portions and European butchering practices (Piper 1991: 93–94). This suggests that cheap cuts of sheep were purchased from European butchers, as opposed to sheep slaughtering and butchering occurring on site.

## Cattle

Cattle in Australia have always been used predominantly for meat. During the 19th century in China, cattle were usually only eaten as a luxury item and were considered to be more valuable for pulling ploughs than for consumption (Wang 1920: 292; Langenwalter 1987: 75; Piper 1988: 35). Chinese people with strong Buddhist beliefs avoided eating beef altogether and many others considered it a sacred meal to be consumed only on special occasions (Wang 1920: 289; Mote 1977: 201). Nevertheless, beef did have some role in the Chinese diet and was estimated by Buck (1937: 413) to have contributed between two and seven percent of the animal calories for southern Chinese people.

A total of 19 cattle bones represent a minimum of two incomplete animals. This number was estimated through the presence of two different sized phalanx number two bones. The recovery of cattle phalanxes, carpi, tarsi, tibias, patellas, sawn proximal femurs, longitudinally sawn humeri and pelvis bones indicate that the Chinese tended to eat low meat-bearing portions. One mandible was located and is also a low meat-bearing part. None of the cattle bones display cleaver/chopping marks, but, as with the sheep bone, appear to have been sawn in the European fashion (described by Ritchie 1986: 591).

Two rib bones have been sawn into unusually small 60 mm long sections. Piper (1984: 20) discusses a similar bone assemblage from a Chinese site in New Zealand, suggesting they may represent the purchase of specially requested meat cuts. Cutting ribs (and other bone pieces) into small portions is a common Chinese practice especially for the sweet stir-fry meal of *chue p'aai kwat* and for ease of handling with chopsticks (Levine 1921: 13; Chang 1977: 8). Purchasing ribs pre-cut to this size would minimise the preparation required for Chinese-style cooking.

Larger bones such as the tibia and humerus have had their proximal/distal ends sawn off, or have been split longitudinally (figure 6.11). Similar butchering patterns on cattle bone were noted by Ritchie (1986: 591, 623) at Chinese sites in New Zealand and were suggested to indicate the "distinctly Chinese practice" of bone-marrow extraction. Smith (1998: 151) also noted the same cut patterns from Chinese sites at Kiandra, New South Wales. Marrow bones are very cheap to purchase and are generally used for stock in soups, broths and stews (Piper 1988: 37).

Cattle age at time of slaughter – estimated through size comparisons – was between one and three years, which is a standard slaughtering age for quality beef (Longenecker & Stapp 1993: 115).

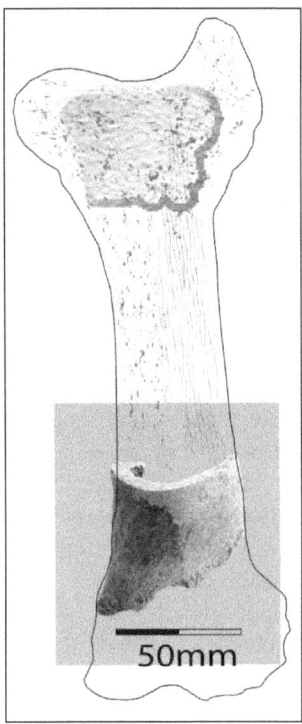

Figure 6.11 Cattle long bone from the Chinaman's Point site showing signs of deliberate sawing most likely for the removal of bone marrow.

**Pig**

There is generally a low representation of pig bone from overseas Chinese sites in Australasia. Pork is the favoured meat in China, accounting for an average 72% of dietary calories (Buck 1937: 413). Its low representation in Australasia is most likely a reflection of the limited availability of pork and its high price compared to beef and mutton during the colonial period (Piper 1988: 36). A lower left-side tusk, two rib bones and a left calcaneus were the only pig elements identified from the bone assemblage at Chinaman's Point. The tusk size and visible fusing on the calcareous indicate that the pig was between two and two-and-a-half years old at time of slaughter. This is a relatively old hog for meat purposes which suggests a female animal, as male hogs were usually slaughtered under one year old and female hogs were kept longer for breeding purposes (Levine 1921: 14; Silver 1978: 286; Longenecker & Stapp 1993: 115). No butchering marks are evident on the calcaneus or tusk and although both ribs appear to have been sawn to approximately 60 mm lengths, the ends are too weathered for a conclusive result.

As with the recovered sheep and cattle bone, the pig components represent low meat-bearing parts of the carcass. Studies of pig cranial remains from overseas Chinese archaeological sites such as those considered by Langenwalter (1980: 107) in California and Piper (1984: 21) and Ritchie (1986: 600) in New Zealand conclude that pig skulls were commonly split open and the brain extracted. Levine (1921: 14) states the most common Chinese use of pig head is:

> for lard, or cut into strips about three quarters of an inch wide and cured or it may be used
> for making sausage or head cheese. The snout, ears and tongue may be used fresh or pickled.

This lack of wastage in the consumption of pig is typical of Chinese eating practices (Peabody 1871: 660). It is not surprising then, that archaeological investigations at overseas Chinese sites – including Chinaman's Point – often recover the lower meat-bearing portions of pig bone (Langenwalter 1987: 75; Piper 1984: 22; Stapp 1990: 194, 200). The older age of the slaughtered pig and the cheaper cuts also suggests that the Chinese were happy and perhaps even thought it desirable (culturally or economically), to consume meat cuts that were considered poor quality by Europeans.

### Chicken

Chicken was represented by one small, broken and fragile section of ulna, a radius in similar condition and a complete coracoid from a single mature bird. Both the ulna and radius may have been chopped with a cleaver, however as discussed by Piper (1988: 38), cleaver blows to chicken bones are difficult to determine, especially on weathered samples. Eggs are common in Chinese cuisine and most Chinese people with a little spare land – in China or overseas – raised poultry for eggs (Wang 1920: 290; Yee 1975: 12). Chicken meat, however, was more for special occasions than as an everyday meal and was consumed much less frequently than other poultry such as ducks and geese (Levine 1921: 4; Buck 1937: 413; Nordhoff cited in Spier 1958: 130; Piper 1988: 35). This may account for the negligible representation of chicken bone from Chinaman's Point.

### Fish

In locations near any large body of water, fish is the most important and widely used protein source in China (Anderson & Anderson 1977: 336). It is therefore surprising (especially as it was a fish processing site) that the fish component from Chinaman's Point contains only seven pieces of bone weighing a total of 9 g. These include the lower mandible and premaxilla from a porcupine fish (*Atopomycterus nictheremus*), two vertebrae from sand flathead (*Platycephalus caeruleopunctatus*), one *Parika scaber* (erectile dorsal spine) from a leather jacket (*Nelusetta vittata*) and three fish vertebrae that are too fragmentary for identification to species level (Wedlick 1980: 48; Roughley 1957: 139).

Port Albert's waterways abound with fish which were even more plentiful during Australia's colonial period. Certainly the occupants of Chinaman's Point fish-curing establishment would have consumed by choice and for economic reasons large quantities of fish. It is possible that a substantial cache of fish remains was missed during the site excavation process. Such 'bone pits' have been discovered at other colonial-period overseas Chinese sites (see for example Longenecker & Stapp 1993: 118). Possibly the cooking methods – steaming or boiling – softened the bones to such a degree that they have not survived in the archaeological record. Fish resources at Chinaman's Point may have been so abundant that only the fleshiest parts were consumed – as with the European 'boneless fillet' – and the wasted portion thrown into the water with the commercial fish offal, used as berley when fishing or possibly taken off site and used as fertiliser, for example at Chin Lang Tip's Chinese market garden approximately two kilometres away. However, as most bone came from the site's tidal zone, the most likely explanation for the scarcity of fish remains at Chinaman's Point is that food scraps were thrown in the rubbish tip area. It is likely that the fish bones were not heavy enough to withstand the tidal currents and were washed away – probably along with other animal bone and light materials from the site.

### Shell

Ten shell pieces weighing 87 g were recovered from Chinaman's Point. This shell represents three bivalves – two from the Mytilidae family (*Xenostrobus inconstans*) and one mud oyster (*Ostraea angasi*) – and one gastropod from the Muricidae family (*Thais baileyana*) (Coleman 1975; Jansen 2000). Of the remaining six shells, all are gastropods that are too fragmented to identify, other than that they are of a conical variety. As only the mud oyster represents a commonly used human food source and as shells occur naturally in the environment, with no definitive connection to human activity (Colley 2005: 75), the site's shell component is not considered to represent a significant dietary source.

## Discussion

The bone assemblage from Chinaman's Point is typical of other overseas Chinese sites in Australasia. Although the sample size is small, meat consumption appears to have mainly consisted of sheep and cattle and to a lesser extent pig, chicken, fish and shelled mollusc. Meat consumption ratios are difficult to determine as fish and other animal bone is suspected to be severely under-represented (due to artefact removal through tidal-based site erosion) and it is unclear what quantities of sheep and cattle bone were purchased for bone marrow rather than for flesh. It is probable that the site occupants had a standard diet of fish, varied occasionally by other meats. The dominance of sheep and cattle bones over pig differs from traditional Chinese dietary preference. However, such a bone assemblage is common at overseas Chinese sites (see for example Piper 1984; Ritchie 1986; Langenwalter 1987; Smith 1998) and can be explained in terms of availability and relative cost of meats, as opposed to a change in dietary preferences.

A preference for lower quality, cheaper meat portions is noticeable in the sheep, cattle and pig bone assemblage. The use of low meat-bearing parts is often viewed as reflecting the site occupants' low economic status (Schulz 1979: 56; Schulz & Gust 1983: 44). Australia's colonial Chinese population is frequently portrayed as being frugal (Gittins 1981: 72), providing a convenient explanation for the cheap meat cuts from Chinaman's Point and other sites. However, Chinese people have a cultural preference for less fatty, lower meat-bearing cuts and marrow bones used in Chinese style cooking. As animal bones from overseas Chinese sites in Australasia and the United States generally indicate a predominance of low meat-bearing parts such as head, rib, leg, shin, knuckle and marrow bones from sheep, cattle and pig (Langenwalter 1880: 107; Ritchie 1986: 593, 600, 602; Langenwalter 1987: 75, 88, 93; Smith 1998: 154, 286), a bone assemblage with a dominance of these types of meat cuts (if associated with other suitable material or documentary evidence) could be considered an indicator of overseas Chinese occupation of a site. The occupants of Chinaman's Point probably purchased these types of meat cuts very cheaply for use in traditional Chinese dishes.

The absence of chopping marks, the dominance of saw marks and a pattern of standard European carcass dissection (described by Ritchie 1986: 591, 610–11) of the bone recovered from Chinaman's Point, suggest that sheep and cattle elements were purchased from European butchers. While no definite conclusions can be made in regard to the butchering of the recovered pig elements, their low representation suggests that pigs were not raised and slaughtered on site.

None of the recovered bones display evidence of burning, which is typically demonstrated by white, often fragile sections of bone (Spennemann & Colley 1990: 57). Together with the style of cooking containers recovered from the site (stewing pots and a wok), this provides further evidence of Chinese cooking techniques, including water-based meals such as soups, broths and steamed foods and quick-cooking stir-fry meals (Ball 1925: 149; Anderson & Anderson 1977: 355, 358; Piper 1984: 12).

## Food storage

Two types of food container were identified from Chinaman's Point – European and Chinese timber casks and stoneware containers.

### European cask

A 2450 year-old Egyptian-built wooden cask on display in New York's Museum of Fine Arts reveals the long history of these storage containers (Hughes 1925: 22). During the 19th century, wooden casks were the most common form of bulk container used to store and transport food and other goods (Staniforth 1987: 21).

Two thousand and fifty six pieces, weighing 131 kg, of hoop iron for cask hooping were recovered from the Chinaman's Point site. Three widths of strap – 38 mm, 32 mm and 25 mm – mostly displaying a uniform curvature, were evident in the assemblage. These measurements are consistent with standard 19th-century regulations for the top, middle and base hoop iron widths for wooden cask containers (Hughes 1926: 20) (figure 6.12). In association with the cask hooping were 62 metal rivets weighing 2231 g, which are consistent with the type of rivet used for securing the end pieces of cask hooping. Recovered rivets display a convex cylindrical head 20 to 35 mm diameter, 6 to 10 mm body diameter and a hammered flat section that forms the stop-end or inner rivet head.

The original function of the casks was probably to hold foodstuffs. They were probably used mainly at Chinaman's Point for brining fish, as metal tubs would have quickly rusted and tainted the flesh. Timber casks could be re-used over long periods and may have been fitted with tight covers to reduce evaporation and dilution of the brine through rain water (Ashbrook 1955: 217). As approximately 76% of cast hooping fragments were recovered from area 1 – believed to have been an industrial area of the site – it is conceivable that barrels were positioned here for fish-brining purposes and in other areas of the site for storage of fresh water and other goods.

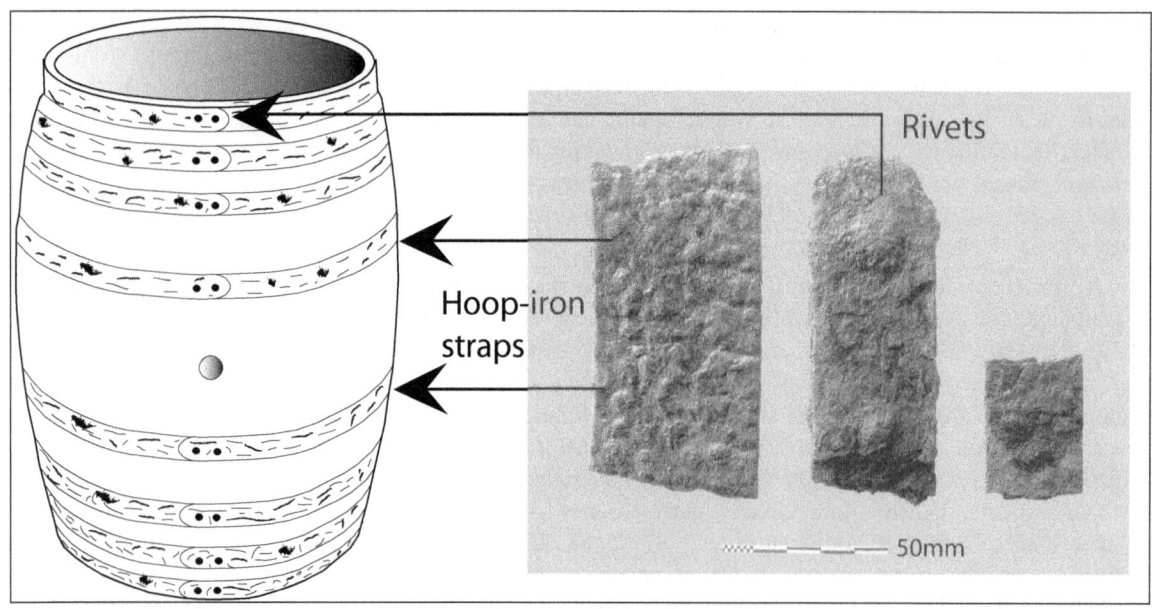

Figure 6.12 Cask hoop (with rivets) from the Chinaman's Point site shown in association with a 19th-century European iron-hooped cask.

**Chinese cask**

A Chinese cask is held at the McCrossin's Mill Museum in Uralla, New South Wales, labelled 'early 1900s dark soy sauce barrel' (Wilton 2004: 78). This cask differs in hoop-iron design from European casks as the horizontal, cylindrical hoops (25 mm wide) are supported by vertical, straight sections of iron (20 mm wide). To unite the vertical and horizontal straps, the vertical iron band has been folded and hammered tight around the cylindrical band.

In area 1 at Chinaman's Point, corroded and fragmented cask hooping was located in association with very fragile timber remains. A section of approximately 20 mm wide hoop iron was bent and hammered flat around another approximately 28 mm wide section of hoop iron to form a 90 degree 'T' angle similar to the cask at McCrossin's Mill Museum. It is probable that this hooping is from a Chinese-style timber cask. The feature was too fragile to be removed without the destruction of material and form. Therefore, it was recorded, drawn, photographed and left *in situ* (figure 6.13).

Figure 6.13 A Chinese-style timber cask (left and insert) and the *in situ* cask hooping from Chinaman's Point. Image of Chinese cask from Wilton 2004: 78.

The storage and transport of Chinese food items is most commonly associated with Chinese-style brown and green glazed stoneware ceramics. It is likely that Chinese casks held a variety of food items other than dark soy sauce. The Chinese cask remains from Chinaman's Point may have contained imported items for use by the site occupants or been used to export commodities such as pickled fish from the site. At the very least, its presence reveals that Chinese-style timber casks were used in colonial Victoria and provides a basis to assist future researchers identify such artefacts.

**Chinese stoneware**

Chinese stoneware vessels specifically designed for food storage include the brown glazed wide-mouthed shouldered jars (and associated lids) and green glazed ginger-style jars. Both vessel types were recovered from the Chinaman's Point site. The ceramics used by 19th-century overseas Chinese people are the subject of increasing amounts of research. Documentary information on Chinese stoneware vessels and other Chinese ceramics discussed below under the heading 'Liquid storage', 'Tableware' and 'Recreational', has come predominantly from Quellmalz (1972; 1976), Chace (1976), Etter (1980), Ritchie (1986), Brott (1987), Wegars (1988; 1998; 1999), Jones (1992), Wylie & Fike (1993), Sando & Felton (1993), Svenson (1994), Yang & Hellmann (1996), Lydon (1999) and Muir (2003).

During analysis of the Chinese ceramics from Chinaman's Point, it became clear that the base and body fragments from wide-mouthed shouldered jars are indistinguishable from those of the Chinese spouted jar (figure 6.14). Ritchie (1986: 234, 238) has also documented this similarity in artefacts from overseas Chinese sites in New Zealand and suggests that the body and base sections "could have been mass produced for both pot types". In a fragmentary assemblage, it is only when rim, spout or shoulder sections of these vessels are represented that the individual items can be identified. For this reason, brown glazed stoneware fragments that could not be clearly identified as either a wide-mouthed or spouted jar are referred to here as being either wide/spouted jars. The minimum number count for wide/spouted jars (table 6.8) has been estimated through base diameter reconstructions. Type, number of sherds, MNI and location for Chinese stoneware vessels is shown in table 6.8.

| Chinese stoneware | Number of sherds | Weight (grams) | MNI | Site location |
|---|---|---|---|---|
| Liquor bottles | 167 | 805 | 7 | TZ |
| Spouted jar | 63 | 545 | 19 | area 4; TZ |
| Wide-mouthed jar | 36 | 176 | 5 | TZ |
| Wide/spouted jar | 2377 | 10 966 | 26 | area 3; 4; TZ |
| Green glaze jar (round) | 31 | 68 | 2 | TZ |
| Lid/shallow bowl | 60 | 168 | 24 | TZ |
| Total | 2734 | 12 728 | 57 | N/A |

Table 6.8 Type, number of sherds, MNI and location for Chinese stoneware vessels (TZ = tidal zone).

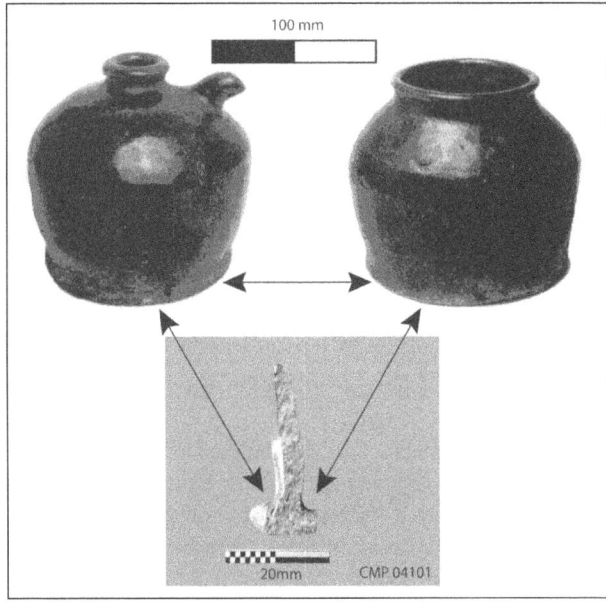

Figure 6.14 The Chinaman's Point base sherd could represent a Chinese spouted jar (left) or a Chinese wide-mouthed shouldered jar (right). Images of complete jars from Muir 2003: 44–45.

**Wide-mouthed shouldered jar**

These utilitarian brown ware vessels are generally recovered in association with seven other Chinese brown ware containers: spouted jar, straight-sided jar, globular jar, liquor bottle, barrel jar and pan and are among the most common artefacts discovered at overseas Chinese sites (Yang and Hellmann 1996: 4–9; Lydon 1999: 215). They were produced in China from coarse stoneware that was shaped on a spinning wheel to a consistent 'idealised form' (Ritchie 1986: 231) and have a thick outer coating of brown iron glaze and a thinner, often uneven inner brown glaze (Muir 2003: 44). Their bases are concave and left unglazed externally (figure 6.15). The minimum number count for wide-mouthed shouldered jars from Chinaman's Point (shown in Table 6.8) has been estimated through rim fragment diameter associations. Interestingly, the usually very common straight sided and globular jars (figure 6.16) were not found in the Chinaman's Point assemblage.

Wide-mouthed jars are commonly between 130 to 150 mm high (Muir 2003: 44), with samples recovered from Chinaman's Point displaying an average 4 mm in body thickness, between 100 and 200 mm in base diameter and 80 to 150 mm in rim diameter. Papers such as Yang & Hellmann (1996) have examined the uses of imported Chinese brown ware vessels in the United States and what their contents may have been, however archaeologists still struggle to ascertain a specific range of contents. It is generally accepted that they were used to store a wide array of preserved and raw foods such as eggs, vegetables, bean curd, fruit, garlic, soy bean, food pastes, salt and sugar. They also had an extremely versatile re-use value (Olsen 1978: 32; Yang & Hellmann 1996: 3; Muir 2003: 44).

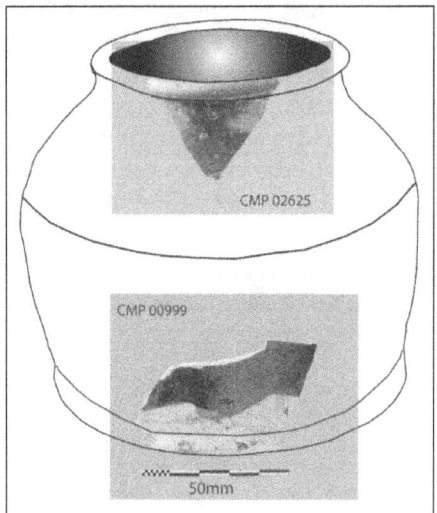

Figure 6.15 Drawing of a wide-mouthed shouldered jar with associated artefacts from the Chinaman's Point site.

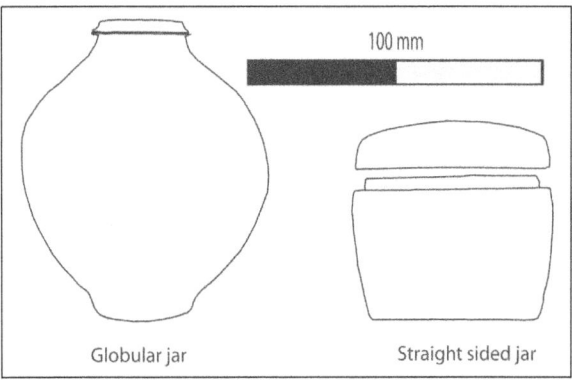

Figure 6.16 Surprisingly, the Chinese globular jar (left) and straight-sided jar (right), were surprisingly not represented at the Chinaman's Point site.

Wide-mouthed jars recovered from other overseas Chinese sites often display burning on the base sections, indicating that they have been used for cooking purposes (Ritchie 1986: 242). No stoneware bases from Chinaman's Point revealed evidence of burning, however two base sherds from wide/spouted Chinese brown glaze vessels had residue adhered to their inner surface. This residue likely represents food remains and although expensive analyses could not be conducted for this project, future chemical analysis of these residues holds potential to reveal further information about the everyday lives of overseas Chinese people in colonial Australia.

**Lid/shallow bowl**

Chinese wide-mouthed jars are often located in association with unglazed, concave, stoneware lids. Ritchie (1986: 242) suggests the lids were fitted to seal the wide-mouthed vessels with soft unfired clay, the remnants of which are still adhere to some lids recovered from New Zealand sites. Yang and Hellmann's (1996: 3–4) discussion on functional re-use suggests the saucer shape of the lids enabled them to be re-used as shallow bowls for sauces and other food.

The minimum number count for lid/shallow bowls from Chinaman's Point (table 6.8) has been estimated through rim fragment diameter associations. The lids range between 80 and 150 mm in diameter, have an average 3 mm body thickness, sit between 10 and 15 mm deep in the bowl and range in colour from cream to buff red (figure 6.17). The lid diameters correspond with the wide-mouthed jar rims, thereby complementing Ritchie's (1986) and Yang & Hellmann's (1996) theory that the two items are associated artefacts.

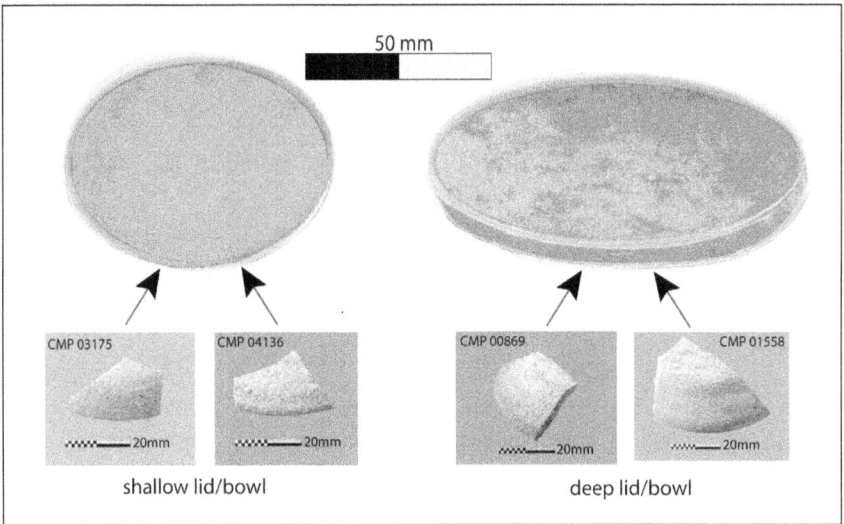

Figure 6.17 Fragments of unglazed lid/shallow bowls from the Chinaman's Point site and pictures of the complete items.

**Chinese green-glazed jar**

Green-glazed Chinese stoneware vessels are generally associated with the term 'ginger jar'. However, as discussed by Olsen (1978: 35), these vessels contained a range of preserved foods other than ginger such as sliced turnip, green onions, green plums and sweet gherkins. Consequently, Ritchie (1986: 259) uses 'ginger jar' as a generic term, further suggesting they may also have contained various types of cosmetic or medicinal creams. Two green-glazed jar shapes are commonly recovered from overseas Chinese sites: the hexagonal and the round (figure 6.18). They are produced from a stoneware material, in a similar fashion to the brown glazed vessels, only their glaze is a glossy light or dark green colour (Muir 2003: 46). Wood (1999: 224) has analysed these green glazes to reveal that they were produced from a mix of ground glass and natural minerals found in river mud.

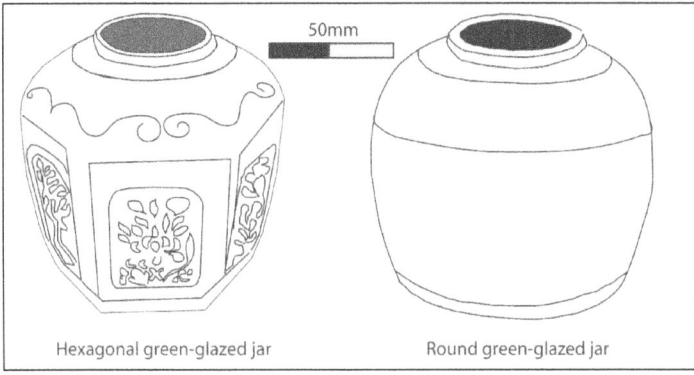

Figure 6.18 The two most common types of Chinese ginger jar: the hexagonal (left) and the round (right).

The minimum number of green-glazed vessels was ascertained through the recovery of three different sized vessel rim diameters – 70 mm, 90 mm and 120 mm (table 6.8). Rim, body and base fragments reveal that each vessel is of the round wide-mouthed variety. In keeping with the green-glazed jars recovered from other overseas Chinese sites such as in Ritchie (1986: 260) and Brott (1987: 245), the green-glazed jars from Chinaman's Point display a thick outer green-glaze that has been allowed to drip down the exterior to leave thick dollops or drips of glaze. They also have a light brown interior glaze (figure 6.19).

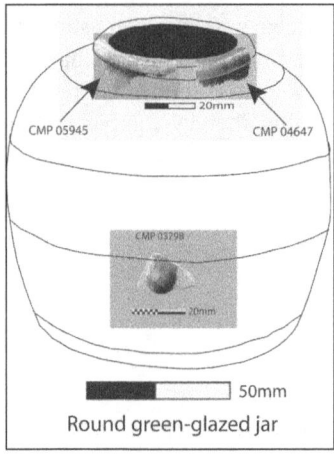

Figure 6.19 Chinese ginger jar rim fragments and a dollop of glaze (centre of jar) from the Chinaman's Point site.

**European stoneware**

Like Chinese stoneware, European stoneware is generally associated with mass produced, heavy, thick-walled vessels that are most commonly used as utilitarian wares and storage containers with a huge range of re-use values (Sharpe 1992: 48). When kiln-fired, stoneware is non-porous and therefore does not require a glaze to seal the vessel. Even so, an external salt glaze and internal slip glaze was commonly applied for aesthetics or to enable easy cleaning for re-use purposes. Stoneware vessels were produced in a huge range of colours although the utilitarian and storage wares were most commonly a white/cream or light tan to dark brown colour (Gleeson 1997: 64). They were often impressed with a potter's mark or had transfers printed with black ink, or were manufactured without markings (Arnold 1989: 111–12).

Eleven dark brown, salt glazed, European-style stoneware sherds, weighing 145 g and representing a minimum number of two food storage vessels were recovered from Chinaman's Point. The minimum vessel count was estimated through the recovery of two similar but separate styles of vessel rim. None of the sherds display any evidence of a manufacturer or trademark. The only recovered base fragment is 80 mm in diameter. The two rim fragments have 60 mm diameters and body sherd thicknesses range from between 3 and 6 mm. These attributes are consistent with the European bung jar, a common storage vessel during the Australian colonial period (Ford 1995: 208). These containers require a large cork stopper to seal their opening, hence the name 'bung jar' and stored anything from pickled foods and preserved jams through to shaving creams and medicinal ointments (figure 6.20). They were also regularly sold without contents, as general storage jars (Arnold 1989: 112).

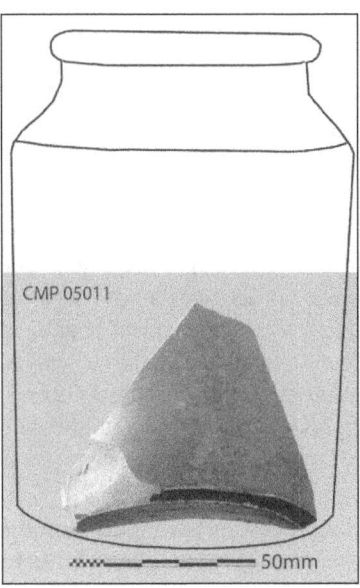

Figure 6.20 Base fragment of common European bung jar from the Chinaman's Point site.

## Furnishings

### Box hasp

A flat, rectangular piece of brass weighing 13 g and displaying strategic circular and rectangular holes was recovered from the tidal zone at Chinaman's Point. It measures 61 mm long, 33 mm wide and although set in one complete piece, has three separate rectangle-shaped sections that form two large enclosed rectangles, one small open-ended rectangle and six cylindrical holes. The item has 2 mm diameter holes in each corner of the rectangle, as if to fasten the object to a flat surface and a 2 mm and 1.5 mm diameter hole in its central region. The artefact's unusual and deliberately constructed proportions suggest it had a specific function, perhaps as a box hasp – a locking mechanism that fits over a fastener and is secured by a pin, bolt, or padlock – on a Chinese luggage or storage chest/box.

Ornate hasps are especially popular in China. Internet sites of dealers in Chinese antiques demonstrate good comparisons, but not an exact match, between the Chinaman's Point artefact and hasps on antique Chinese storage boxes (figure 6.21). For further examples see (www.trocadero.com and www.chinese-furniture.com).

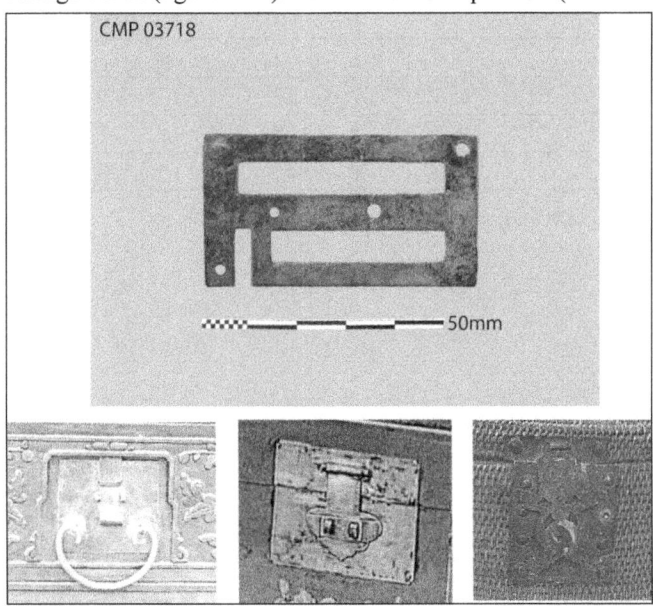

Figure 6.21 Suspected box hasp from the Chinaman's Point site (top) and examples of antique Chinese storage-box hasps (bottom). Picutres of box hasps from web pages www.trocadero.com and www.chinese-furniture.com.

## Liquid storage

The following section provides an outline of the main liquid storage containers recovered from the Chinaman's Point site. These items include two types of material: bottle glass and Chinese stoneware.

### Bottle glass

The popularity of glass containers in colonial Australia and the general durability of glass fragments ensure their regular recovery from historical archaeological sites. Analyses of glass assemblages are useful in identifying site occupation dates (discussed in chapter 7), patterns of consumption, living conditions and providing general insights into site activities. Repeated discoveries of similar bottle types across separate sites can also infer an ethnic site occupation, see for example Wegars' (1993: 223) work on the identification of perfume vials and Ritchie's (1986: 181, 195, 204) discussion on preferred domestic products, pharmaceutical containers and certain types of alcohol bottles. The data below describes the main glass container forms, specific attributes, their most likely original contents (no adhesive labels were recovered), shard quantities and the minimum number of vessels represented and provides some interpretation of the recovered assemblage as a whole.

The high level of bottle-collector activity and site erosion through tidal movements is reflected in the recovery of only four complete glass bottles. Therefore, excluding buttons and window glass, the glass recovered – 13 997 shards, weighing 18.361 kg – represents a very fragmentary assemblage. The glass fragmentation and post-depositional movement of tidal-zone artefacts caused difficulty in analysing the glass bottle assemblage. Nineteenth-century glass bottles have a known colour-to-content association that enables broad patterns to be established. For the above reasons, this bottle glass analysis is structured around glass colour: dark green (often called 'black glass') light green, aqua-green, amber, light blue, aqua-blue and clear. Terms used to describe the basic bottle components from the top down are: finish, neck, shoulder, body and base (after Jones 1986: 34). Through analysing colour, shard form, bottle finishes and fragments of embossed glass, the main bottle styles appear to be beer, wine, aerated water, alcoholic spirits (gin, schnapps and whiskey), condiments (sauces, essences and oil) and medicinal containers.

One hundred and thirty-eight different bottle forms, representing a minimum number of 845 individual vessels have been identified from the Chinaman's Point assemblage (tables 6.9 and 6.10). All minimum number of individual vessel counts have been estimated through an analysis of bottle base fragments. Spatially, bottle glass was recovered from all areas of the site, but most prolifically from area 4 and the tidal zone (table 6.11).

| Glass colour | Number of shards | Weight (grams) | Base types | MNI | Total% |
|---|---|---|---|---|---|
| Dark green | 2993 | 52 641 | 30 | 278 | 32.9 |
| Light green | 6646 | 86 384 | 17 | 247 | 29.2 |
| Aqua-green | 2591 | 25 978 | 36 | 196 | 23.2 |
| Amber | 1236 | 14 617 | 29 | 90 | 10.6 |
| Light blue | 78 | 568 | 3 | 4 | 0.5 |
| Aqua-blue | 168 | 1559 | 17 | 22 | 2.6 |
| Clear | 285 | 1859 | 6 | 8 | 1 |
| Total | 13 997 | 18 3606 | 138 | 845 | 100 |

Table 6.9 Colour, number of shards, number of base types, MNI and MNI percentages for glass containers.

| Glass colour | Cyl MNI | Sq MNI | Poly MNI |
|---|---|---|---|
| Dark green | 231 | 47 | 0 |
| Light green | 206 | 41 | 0 |
| Aqua-green | 171 | 12 | 13 |
| Amber | 76 | 14 | 0 |
| Light blue | 1 | 3 | 0 |
| Aqua-blue | 9 | 8 | 5 |
| Clear | 7 | 1 | 0 |
| Total | 701 | 126 | 18 |
| Total% | 83% | 15% | 2% |

Table 6.10 Colour, form, MNI and MNI percentages for cylindrical, square and polygonal glass containers (Cyl = cylindrical; Sq = square; Poly = polygonal).

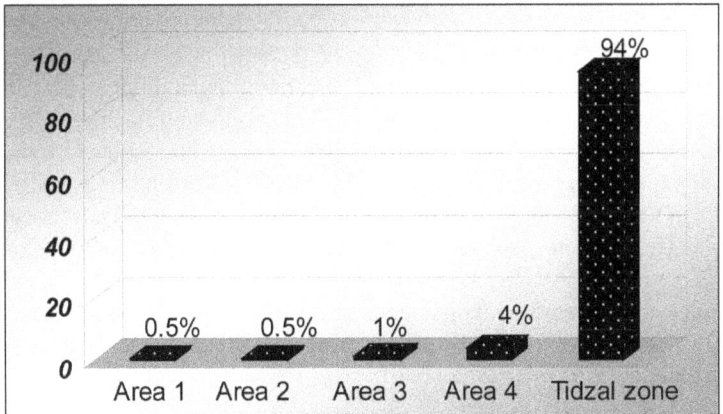

Table 6.11 Chinaman's Point bottle glass distribution.

As there is no available classification of glass colour in historical archaeology, the colour notation system from the Munsell (1966) book of colour standards has been used to provide an indication of the glass colours discussed. A great deal of literature exists on the identification and analysis of glass items. Glass artefacts from Chinaman's Point are interpreted primarily through the aid of Jones (1971; 1981; 1986), Toulouse (1971); Vader & Murray (1975), Hutchinson (1987), Wilson (1981), Miller & Sullivan (1984), Jones & Sullivan (1989), Ritchie (1986), Arnold (1987; 1990), Fike (1987), Stapp (1990) and Boow (1991).

*Dark green*

Dark green glass is often so dark in colour that it appears black, especially in the thicker bottle sections; hence it is often referred to as 'black glass' (Boow 1991: 20). Dark green glass from Chinaman's Point was at its lightest, Munsell hue 7.5GY 3/6, with a middle hue 7.5GY 3/2 and 5GY 2/1 at its darkest shade. Cheaply produced from impure materials – usually with high quantities of natural iron oxides in the sand – dark green glass bottles were manufactured in a range of shapes, sometimes with a globule-type ownership seal on the bottle body and occasionally with embossing (Wills 1974: 16; Dumbrell 1983: 152). These bottles are generally associated with aerated water and alcohols – primarily beer, wine and spirits (Vader & Murray 1975: 37; Boow 1991: 24, 37). Aerated water is unlikely to have been heavily consumed at an all-adult, male dominated Chinese fish-curing site. Imported colonial beer was bulky, which made it expensive to transport compared to its relative sale value, had low alcohol content and went stale during the slow sea voyage to Australia (Dingle 1980: 235). Moreover, for most of the 19th century, Victoria's brewing industry only produced small quantities of poor quality beer, which in turn created a colonial preference for spirits, predominantly rum and brandy (Dingle 1980: 230, 232, 241). Therefore, the dark green bottles from Chinaman's Point most likely contained wine and spirits.

Dark green bottles are the dominant type in the Chinaman's Point glass assemblage by minimum number count. Thirty-five shards reveal evidence of embossing, which in a small number of cases indicated the original bottle contents to have been whisky or schnapps.

One cylindrical dark green bottle base showed evidence of deliberate post manufacture modifications. This base had the push up centre section (the pontil) chipped away to create a small opening in the base centre. Such modifications have been noted – but not analysed – from two other sites in Australia, both with an association to overseas Chinese occupation. This base is discussed in detail in the 'Recreational' section of this chapter, where a plausible function is suggested.

*Light green*

Sometimes called 'forest glass' or 'natural green', light green glass can be produced from only slightly more than the basic glass ingredients of sand and an alkali flux such as lime or soda with the addition of ash from burnt rotten vegetation which reduces the colour impact from iron impurities (Birmingham & Bairstow 1987: 153). Therefore, without the cost of expensive oxides and other compound additives and with more aesthetic elegance than dark green glass, light green glass became favoured among 19th-century glass bottle makers (Proh 1973: 23). Light green bottles had an extremely versatile use in colonial Australia and although they are associated more with wine and aerated water than with beer or spirits, their contents varied widely (Fike 1987: 13).

At its lightest Munsell hue, light green glass from Chinaman's Point is 7.5GY 7/6, with a middle hue 7.5GY 5/4 and 7.5GY 4/6 at its darkest shade. By shard numbers (6646) and weight (86 384 g), light green is the most common glass colour from Chinaman's Point, dominated by the middle hue. Seventeen bottle base designs and seven finish types are present. Seventy-two separate shards have evidence of embossing with 64% of these – representing a minimum number of seven vessels – confirmed to be the square bodied Udolpho Wolfe's Schnapps bottle.

Udolpho Wolf's Schiedham Aromatic Schnapps is a Dutch-produced, gin-based alcohol created from juniper berries and was widely considered to have been a distilled drink of excellent quality and alcoholic value for money (Valder & Murray 1975: 37; Wilson 1981: 75). Heavily advertised through colonial newspapers and pamphlets including in the local Gippsland papers (*Gippsland Standard* 1884, March 21) this bottle is a very common find at historical sites in Australia (Vader & Murray 1975: 40). Gin bottles and to a slightly lesser extent brandy, are also common at overseas Chinese sites (see for example Langenwalter 1980: 106; Ritchie & Bedford 1983: 239; McCarthy 1986: 37; Gaughwin 1995: 235). Whether overseas Chinese people found European gins to be of better quality, cheaper or more easily obtainable than the Chinese distilled equivalents (*mm ga pei* and *mui guai lo*) is uncertain. It is clear however, that overseas Chinese people in Australasia were consuming greater quantities of European alcohol than Chinese alcohol.

Even with bottles that specifically state their contents, there is no way of ascertaining what the bottles at Chinaman's Point had contained, as it is likely that many were purchased as refilled second-hand vessels. Boow (1991: 24) indicates, "there are numerous references to used-bottle sales and part payment for returned empties" and both Ritchie & Bedford (1983: 237) and Staski (1993: 135–36) have recovered European manufactured bottles from overseas Chinese sites that have been pasted with Chinese language paper labels. In some cases, these labels had been pasted over embossing that denotes the original bottle contents. This suggests that the re-use of bottles by overseas Chinese people was a common and organised practice.

The Chinese preference for European gins and brandy over other alcohols is noted in colonial-period texts. Adams (1997: 24–26) compiled a number of original food supply invoices from 19th-century overseas Chinese gold miners in Victoria's Omeo region (figure 6.22). These invoices show gin and brandy as the most frequently purchased alcohols. The Reverend Young's 1868 report into the state of Victoria's Chinese population estimates that overseas Chinese people were spending annually almost as much money on spirits as they were on food. Moreover, Reverend Young states that "Mr Wade, of the Coopers' Arms Hotel, Little Bourke Street, informed me that he sells monthly to the Chinese 40 gallons of gin ... in bottles", an amount equalling the monthly Chinese purchase of all other alcoholic sprits combined (Young 1868 cited in McLaren 1985: 63).

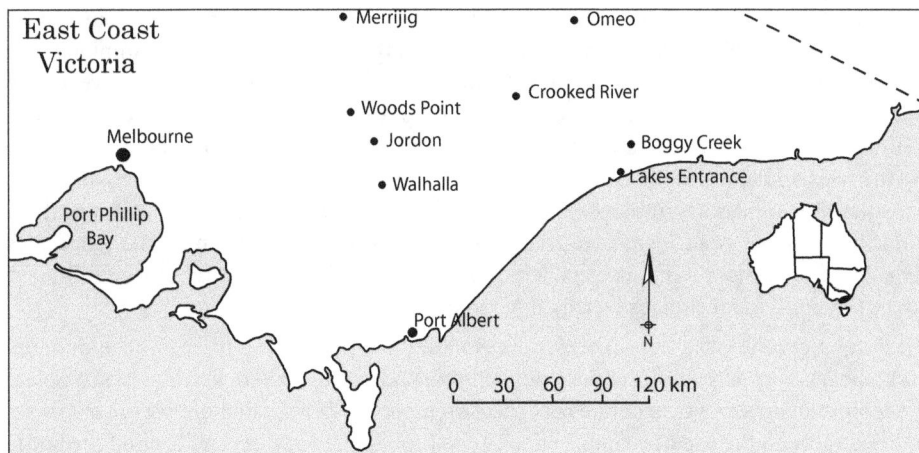

Figure 6.22 Map of Gippsland's main colonial goldfields including Omeo, top right of map (Melbourne, Port Albert and Lakes Entrance are included as reference points only).

The light and dark green bottle assemblage from Chinaman's Point suggests there was a preferred consumption of gin over other sprits. However, the fragmentary nature of the assemblage, the versatile use of green bottle glass and bottle re-use makes this difficult to confirm. It would be fair to say, however, that the occupants of Chinaman's Point consumed considerably more European than Chinese wine and spirits (table 6.12).

| European alcohol bottles MNI | Chinese alcohol bottles MNI |
|---|---|
| 811 | 7 |

Table 6.12 Minimum number of European compared to Chinese alcohol bottles (MNI for European alcohol bottles is an estimate only due to the uncertainty of bottle contents).

*Aqua-green*

Aqua-green glass is a refined version of light green glass. It is produced through mixing good quality sand i.e. low in iron content, with a standard flux and a small quantity of oxide (Arnold 1990: 5). It had an extremely wide range of uses, including as window glass, drinking glasses, decanters, plates and bottles. In bottle form its contents were also wide ranging, holding anything from soft drinks, cooking additives and condiments, to medicinal liquids and alcohols.

A breakdown of aqua-green glass fragment attributes can be seen in table 6.13. The lightest aqua-green coloured shards correspond to Munsell hue 5GY 9/4 and have only the slightest tinge of green. The middle colour range correlates with the Munsell hue 5GY 8/2 and the darkest verge on a light green, but with a more transparent quality correlating with Munsell hue 5GY 8/4.

| Shards | Weight (grams) | Base types | Finish types | MNI |
|---|---|---|---|---|
| 2591 | 25 978 | 36 | 16 | 196 |

Table 6.13 Green aqua bottle glass attributes.

Ninety-eight shards of aqua-green glass show signs of embossing or other identifying marks which reveal a range of original bottle contents including Champion's vinegar, other vinegar or oils, coffee essence, Worcestershire sauce and tomato sauce. A number of manufacturer and trade marks were also recovered such as 'T.B. & Co', 'R.M. Goodfellow & Co', 'J. Lesson's', 'John Kilner & Sons', 'Blogg Brothers' and 'Lea & Perrin'. Many shards were too fragmented to accurately identify the embossed symbol, number pattern or wording.

Lea & Perrin Worcestershire sauce bottles have also been noted from other Australasian overseas Chinese sites by, for example, Ritchie & Bedford (1983: 250) and McCarthy (1986: 35). Worcestershire sauce has similarities to Chinese soy sauce – both are an all-purpose spice, have a strong fragrance and flavour, are very salty and use fermented wheat as a base ingredient. Traditional Chinese cooking ingredients were presumably periodically unavailable to the Chinaman's Point site occupants, therefore European condiments such as Worcestershire sauce may have been used as a 'best fit' substitute.

Similarly, vinegar is a key component of most Chinese food dressings, table sauces, sweet and sour dishes, sautés and stews (Passmore & Reid 1982: 34), which explains the strong representation of Champion's and other vinegar bottles from Chinaman's Point. Likewise, most Chinese cooking requires a quantity of vegetable oil (Passmore & Reid 1982: 34), reflected at Chinaman's Point and other overseas Chinese sites such as those studied by Ritchie & Bedford's (1983: 250) and Blanford (1987: 195) in the recovery of European-style salad oil bottles, most commonly the waisted band and the twist-neck types. Other domestic food and medicinal bottles in the Chinaman's Point aqua-green glass assemblage – sauces, pickles, jams, coffee essence, pharmaceutical cure-alls and other pain killers – have been identified predominantly through bottle form or characteristics as opposed to embossing. The use of these items is considered to represent either a substitute for the Chinese traditional equivalent or purely individual choices based on personal preference.

Thirty-six cylindrical aqua-green bottle base pieces, representing a minimum number of 30 individual bottles show evidence that the push-up sections have been deliberately and carefully knocked out. No complete modified base rims were represented, however accurate base measurements of 75 mm diameters were obtained. Each base has been modified through the use of a centre punch-type tool, tapped at intervals around the bottle base rim, effectively removing the push-up section and leaving distinct markings on the base shards (figure 6.23).

Modified glass artefacts at overseas Chinese sites have been noted by Ritchie & Bedford (1983: 248) McCarthy (1986: 36) and from the Chinaman's Point site (discussed below with opium-related materials). These are usually suggested to be covers for opium heating lamps and are comprised of shoulder and neck bottle sections. However, no overseas Chinese sites display base modifications similar to the type recovered from Chinaman's Point. The Chinaman's Point base modifications are all at the bottle's base, making the manufactured item too long in the body for use as opium-heating lamp covers.

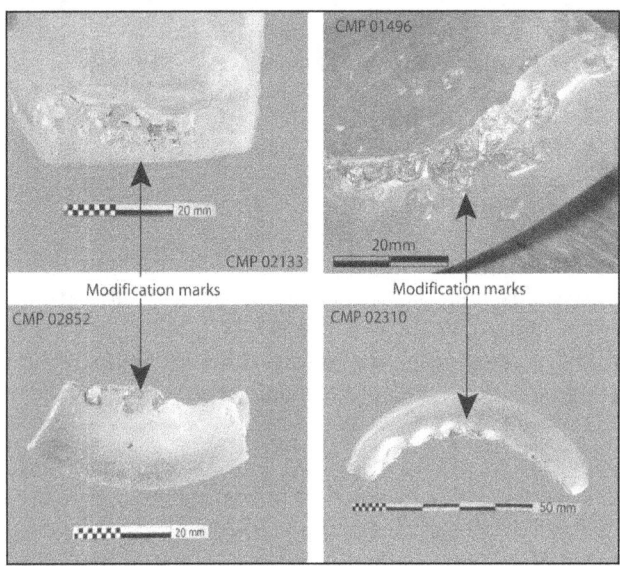

Figure 6.23 Deliberate modification marks are clearly visible on these bottle base fragments.

During Australia's colonial period, domicile lamp bases and lamp chimneys were standard household items used for general lighting. Lamp chimneys are made of thin and delicate glass, with a range of standard base sizes up to and exceeding 75 mm in diameter (Cuffley 1973: 186). By using oil or kerosene lamp bases or any form of solid container to hold a wick or candle base, an aqua-green bottle without a base section would have made a robust lamp chimney (figure 6.24). The occupants at Chinaman's Point may have produced such items for general domestic lighting purposes or for fishing at night.

Figure 6.24 Reconstruction of oil lamps using modified bottles as substitute lamp chimneys.

In Wards's (1954: 198, 203) anthropological study of a Chinese fishing village, she notes that fishermen often work at night using:

> glass globes and mantles for the purse-seine fishermen's bright lights … the bright kerosene lights are used to attract fish … bright cat's-eye lights [can] be seen all around the coast.

An 1888 report to the United States Commission of Fish and Fisheries states that the Chinese fishermen of San Francisco also fished at night using "a boat with a blazing torch at the bow … to attract large schools of squid to the surface" (Collins 1892: 60). On 4 December 1873, the *Illustrated Australian News* reported on the Chinese fishermen at St Kilda, stating, "The fishing is chiefly carried on at night". The method of fishing with lights at night to attract fish, particularly squid, to the surface is common in many parts of the world. In the 1880 royal commission into the New South Wales fisheries, Chin Ateak is asked if he has ever traded in squid. He replies, "The squid … plenty valuable … at Melbourne plenty of that; schooner send plenty up" (*Votes and Proceedings of the New South Wales Legislative Assembly* 1879–80, vol. 3: 1225–26). It is likely that the Chinese fish curers at Chinaman's Point participated in night fishing and therefore required some form of light to attract fish. With a rolling boat, cold water and flapping fish, glass light covers would have broken easily and needed replacing regularly. It is conceivable that the deliberately modified bottle base sections represent the by-products from a candle, oil or kerosene lamp cover-making process.

### *Inkwells*

Fourteen shards, weighing 139 g and representing a minimum number of five inkwells were recovered from Chinaman's Point. Their colour is predominantly aqua-green, but some shards appear to have a subtle blue-green appearance, due to ferrous iron impurities in the glass ingredients (Lockhart 2006: 45). One bottle is a complete short bodied (32 mm high) cylindrical (48 mm diameter) shear-top inkwell, produced in a two-part mould (figure 6.25). Another is represented by the finish, neck and body fragments of a hexagonal-shaped shear top inkwell (possibly a Williams Australia type). Still another displays fragments from a smooth sided, cabin-shaped inkwell and two are represented by sections of a ribbed, shear-top, cabin-shaped inkwell, one of which has an 'R' or a 'B' embossed on its base.

Each inkwell represents a common type recovered from historical sites in Australia. They suggest that at least one occupant of the Chinaman's Point site was literate. Land lease documentation discussed in chapter 7 reveals the English signature of Ah Hoo in association with short passages of ink writing on several colonial period documents. Ah Hoo may have had associates who helped with such official tasks, but the recovery of five individual inkwells suggests that writing (either in Chinese characters or other written language) was undertaken at the Chinaman's Point fish-curing establishment.

Figure 6.25 A cylindrical, short bodied, shear top inkwell from the Chinaman's Point site.

*Amber glass*

Amber coloured bottles generally held beer, wine, tonics and medicines in a liquid, pill or powdered form, but sometimes contained other substances including aerated waters and domestic or industrial goods such as acids and cleaners (Vader & Murray 1975: 56, 58; Boow 1991: 17, 23). As with the greens, amber glass can occur unintentionally through iron impurities in the sand mix (Lockhart 2006: 45). However, by adding carbon to the glass mix a range of amber colours can be deliberately produced (Birmingham & Bairstow 1987: 154). The lightest coloured amber from Chinaman's Point matches Munsell hue 5YR 8/6 and appears as a very pale translucent amber. A middle colour range for amber correlates with Munsell hue 5YR 4/8. The darkest amber could easily be considered a black, especially in the thicker sections. It is only by holding a broken edge up to the light that a dark amber is revealed, correlating best with Munsell hue 5YR 2/2.

A breakdown of amber glass fragment attributes can be seen in table 6.14. Fifty-one shards show embossing, mostly base numbers such as 'M 69' or '38 2 R' or fragments of lettering that don't allow their full meanings to be known.

| Shards | Weight (grams) | Base types | Finish types | MNI |
|---|---|---|---|---|
| 1236 | 14 617 | 29 | 8 | 90 |

Table 6.14 Amber bottle glass attributes.

One embossed shard shows its maker to be 'Hamilton & Pulfer' in 'Bendigo' and the letters 'PHEN' suggest it may have contained phenyl extract. Another amber body shard is embossed with 'NOT TO BE' suggesting it held some form of poison. Other embossed shards include fragments of lettering such as 'Co Pty', 'HT2', 'TASMA' and 'NE &'. However, much of the recovered amber glass is without embossing or other forms of marked identification.

*Aqua-blue/light blue*

When glassmakers made clear and sometimes aqua-green glass, ferrous iron impurities in the glass ingredients often resulted in a very faint aqua-blue or aqua-green colour (Lockhart 2006: 45). Nineteenth-century glass makers accepted such slight colour variation as normal with neither colour actively intended. However, the aqua-blue and blue glass colour discussed in this section is slightly darker than these unintentionally occurring aqua-blue or greens and therefore seem to be a deliberately produced colour. This colour is made by adding quantities of cobalt or copper oxide when preparing a glass mix (Birmingham & Bairstow 1987: 154). At its lightest Munsell hue the aqua-blue is 2.5B 8/4, with a middle hue of 10BG 7/6, which is somewhere between aqua and light blue and the darkest shade of light blue is 2.5B 3/6. These coloured bottles are often oval or rectangular in design and are generally associated with medicines, cosmetics and specialities such as castor and eucalyptus oils (Valder & Murray 1975: 62; Fike 1987: 13; Davies 2001b: 70–71). They were produced with an array of finishes, but were most commonly fitted with applied single collars, formed with a flat, patent or prescription finish (figure 6.26) (Fike 1987: 8, 15; Jones & Sullivan 1989: 93).

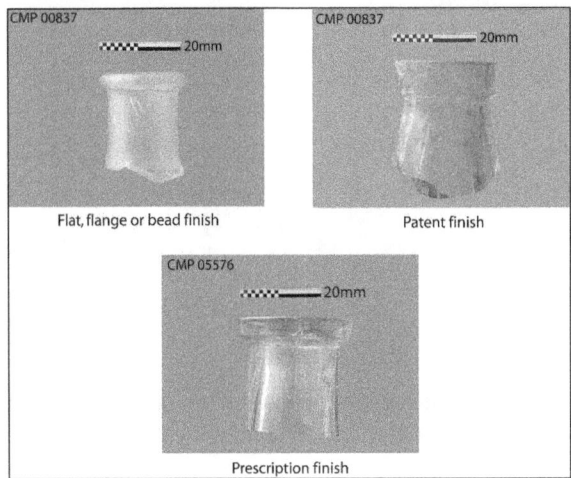

Figure 6.26 Examples of three common types of aqua-blue or light blue applied single-bottle collars or finishes from the Chinaman's Point site.

A breakdown of aqua-blue/light blue glass fragment attributes can be seen in table 6.15.

| Shards | Weight (grams) | Base types | Finish types | MNI |
|--------|----------------|------------|--------------|-----|
| 164 | 2127 | 20 | 6 | 26 |

Table 6.15 Aqua-blue/light blue bottle glass attributes.

Various embossed lettering was apparent such as 'RT & Co'; 'J'; 'RI'; 'IRE'; 'EMP'; 'MEDAL'; 'TTE' (possibly BITTERS); and 'RPE & Co' (possibly Robert Harper & Co Imports of Bendigo). The original contents of these bottles will perhaps never be known more accurately than a medicine, cosmetic or speciality oil. They add to the evidence that overseas Chinese people used some of the vast array of these types of products available in colonial Australia. Mainstream colonial-period medicines usually had an opium and/or alcohol content (Fike 1987: 3), but this was not advertised on the bottle and most consumers would have been unaware of the true contents and so it is unlikely these bottles represent a substitute for opium use. However, European medicines were probably used as alternative drugs, thereby demonstrating sampling, ordinary use or possibly even addiction to the standard medicinal products available during Australia's colonial period.

*Medicinal vials*

In the archaeological literature, a degree of assumption surrounds this small, aqua-green, Chinese-style medicinal vial. Often discussed in the glass section of artefact analyses, it is generally accepted that they contained opium-based medicinal substances.

Numerous styles of Chinese medicinal vials have been recovered from overseas Chinese sites (see for example the appendix in Chandler 2005: 105–10). Ten glass segments weighing a total of 71 g and representing a minimum of five medicinal vials were recovered from the tidal zone at Chinaman's Point. As these small glass bottles are unusual in appearance, artefact collectors often pick them up at overseas Chinese sites. Without exception, all Port Albert residents and artefact collectors interviewed for this project had a collection of these bottles, showing that the vials were once abundant at the site. Only one type was recovered from the Chinaman's Point excavation or found in Port Albert residential collections. Their regular form shows they were made in a dip mould (Blanford 1987: 201), which produced a thick-walled bottle, slightly wider at the shoulder than base. All vials from the Chinaman's Point site were aqua-green in colour. The glass typically contains many air bubbles, is ovoid or rectangular in cross section and generally measures between 55 mm and 62 mm tall and up to 14 by 12 mm wide (figure 6.27). The bottle neck and finish is plain, as if snapped straight from the manufacturer's blower pipe and were possibly fitted after body manufacture. It is likely that a cork stopper – as opposed to a shear top or crack-top finish – was used to seal the bottle contents. These are the most common type of vial recovered from overseas Chinese sites in Australia.

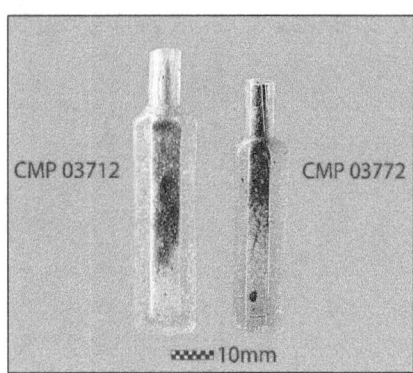

Figure 6.27 Medicinal vials recovered from the Chinaman's Point site.

These vials are believed to have been manufactured in China (Ritchie 1986: 195) and are rarely recovered in a European context. Their association with opium is assumed given that most Chinese medicines (besides herbal medicine) from at least 1100 AD to approximately the mid-1900s contained liberal doses of opium (Zheng 2005: 12). Opium is partially soluble in water and in alcohol and very soluble in vinegar and in oil (Thomson 1845: 96). Opium would have been united with one or more of these substances to produce a range of Chinese medicines, which were then distributed in these small vials.

Evidence from the United States, New Zealand and Australia show that these particular vials contained more than one substance type. A vial recorded in the Asian American Comparative Collection (Catalogue No. Acc-89–45) has a cork seal and a red paper label with black printing that reads "U-I-Oil/Sole Manufacturer/ Wong Cheung Wah/Canton, China" (www.uidaho.edu/LS/AACC/htm). This suggests its contents were at least in part oil-based. From excavations at Cromwell's Chinatown and elsewhere in New Zealand, Ritchie & Bedford (1983: 251–52) and Ritchie (1986: 195) recovered four vials containing visually distinct substances. Yet to be chemically analysed, they are a clear liquid, a dark brown liquid, a red powder and small dry grey pellets. One of Ritchie & Bedford's vials displayed a paper label the same as the American example, reading "U-I-Oil/Sole Manufacturer/Wong Cheung Wah/Canton, China". A further four medicine vials recovered by Ritchie (1986: 195) display Chinese characters that have been translated to indicate they once contained various 'all-purpose' remedies. Chandler's (2005: 43, 106–07) compilation of artefacts from overseas Chinese sites in northeast Victoria – from private collections – includes Chinese-style medicinal vials containing substances that also are yet to be chemically analysed. Each vial is sealed with a piece of cork. Two vials contain a white powder, one contains a 'yellowing' powder (when in powered form, opium is yellowish in colour) (Thomson 1845: 96) and another contains a brown liquid and has an orange paper label again bearing the words 'U-I-Oil, sole manufacturer, Wong Cheung Wah, Canton, China'.

Without knowing the chemical make-up of these vial contents, it cannot be determined what substances they contain – except perhaps something mixed with oil. However, with such visual variation in vial contents, Ritchie (1986: 394) appears correct in stating, "they contained a wide range of medical preparations". That some of the vials had opium content seems almost certain. It also seems likely that some of the vials contained no opium content.

Most of the Australian and New Zealand literature discussing Chinese medicine vials suggests they served as a source of opium for addicted users after the drug became illegal to smoke in 1914 (1901 in New Zealand) (Ritchie and Harrison 1982: 28; McCarthy 1986: 36; Lydon 1999: 101; Galloway 2005: 127). However, as Chinese medicine vials are prolific at overseas Chinese sites where the occupation period ends before 1914, such as Chinaman's Point, it is unlikely the vials represented an alternative source of opium in these cases. Moreover, when heavy tariffs were placed on imported opium for smoking purposes to the United States between 1883 and 1890 (and in Australia after 1901), the result was increased activity in Chinese opium smuggling operations, which created an increase in opium supplies for the general user. This continued well after the banning of opium smoking in Australia (*The Chemist and Druggist of Australasia* 1901: 369; Breacher 1972: 44; Sando & Felton 1993: 169).

Another notable result of the banning of opium smoking in the United States and Australia (in 1914 in both countries) was that it created an opening for the low-priced, purer and more easily smuggled opium variants such as heroin (diacetylmorphine) (Breacher 1972: 46–47; Sando & Felton 1993: 169). Heroin was developed in Britain in 1874 and by the 1890s had become available throughout the world (Manderson 1993: 5; Booth 1996: 77). Heroin may have been among the contents of the Chinese medicinal vials and may have some connection with the modified bottle bases discussed in association with 'chasing the dragon' (see discussion below under the heading 'Alternative smoking method').

The abundance of opium-smoking equipment found at the Chinaman's Point site is evidence that opium for smoking was a readily obtainable item. The recovered medicinal vials most likely represent the use of standard colonial-period medicinal treatments for medical complaints.

A further possible content of the vials is some form of laxative. A side effect of opium use – smoking or otherwise – is constipation. The British army used opium from the 18th century to treat dysentery (Booth 1996: 58) and until the mid 20th century, European doctors prescribed opium-based medicines as a cure for all forms of diarrhoea-related complaints (Muskett 1894: 52).

### Clear glass

The cheapest and most common method of producing clear glass is to use sand that is as pure as possible – ideally 99.9% silica – then to add manganese to the glass mix (Birmingham & Bairstow 1987: 153–54). From the mid 1800s, the manufacture of clear (often called colourless) glass became popular and was used for an extremely wide variety of bottle and other products (Lockhart 2006: 45). A side effect of adding manganese to the glass mix is that with prolonged exposure to sunlight, the clear glass turns a transparent purple colour, with a Munsell hue varying around 5P 8/4 (Proh 1973: 24). Approximately 30% of the clear glass recovered from Chinaman's Point displays a purple tinge.

A breakdown of clear glass fragment attributes can be seen in table 6.16. Sixteen shards display forms of embossing, most of which are unidentifiable single or broken sets of numbers and letters. The embossing 'ON'S', 'GAR', 'ION'S' and 'R' probably represents the London export Champion's vinegar bottles (Boow 1991: 190). Other than vinegar, the original content of the clear glass bottles from Chinaman's Point is unknown.

| Shards | Weight (grams) | Base types | Finish types | MNI |
|---|---|---|---|---|
| 285 | 1859 | 6 | 6 | 8 |

Table 6.16 Clear bottle glass attributes.

Shoulder and neck sections of bottle in the clear glass assemblage have been modified to produce opium heating lamp covers. These bottle sections are detailed with the opium related materials discussed below.

### Discussion

Besides the Chinese medicinal vials and the two separate types of modified bottles, the diverse range of alcohol, medicines, condiments and other bottle types is typical of Australian colonial sites. Through glass analysis, a good insight into patterns of consumption and general lifestyles of site occupants has been obtained. While acknowledging issues of bottle re-use and the fragmentary nature of this assemblage, bottle glass from Chinaman's Point is dominated by the types frequently associated with alcohol, most likely wine and sprits. Without solid reference to actual alcohol volumes consumed at the site – which is unobtainable due to glass fragmentation levels and artefact scavenger-activities – and without a good indication of site-inhabitant numbers, the site occupants cannot be categorised as either heavy or temperate drinkers. Recorded incidences of Chinese drunkenness are not common in colonial Australasia or the United States of America and overseas Chinese populations are referred to in the documentary record as generally sober (Staski 1993: 141; Adams 1997: 23). However, archaeological evidence from the majority of overseas Chinese sites suggests they were consumers of alcohol (see for example Langenwalter 1980: 106; McCarthy 1986: 36; Ritchie 1986: 167; Blanford 1987: 208; Stapp 1990: 194; Staski 1993: 141; Gaughwin 1995: 242; Smith 1998: 127).

It appears that the drinking habits of overseas Chinese people were consistent with Confucian values, which usually recommend moderate behaviour but appear flexible in regard to alcohol consumption, stating, "There is no limit to wine drinking, as long as one does not become disorderly" (cited in Passimore & Reid 1982: 402). Rather than a sustained sobriety, evidence shows that overseas Chinese people drank alcohol just as Europeans did, only the overseas Chinese drank in private, appear to have preferred gin and were rarely intoxicated in public. These findings are consistent with studies on other colonising nationalities, such as the work conducted by Staski (1984) in regard to colonial America's traditional attitudes and the stereotypes of 'drunken Irishman' and sober Jewish Americans. In fact both groups were found to have been heavy consumers of alcohol.

Even though enormous quantities of Chinese domestic goods were exported from China to Australia, the glass bottles from Chinaman's Point and other overseas Chinese sites are of non-Chinese manufacture. Chinese medicinal vials may be an exception. The absence of Chinese-produced glass at overseas Chinese sites reflects China's limited glass-manufacturing industry in the 19th century (Ritchie 1986: 167; Staski 1993: 134).

**Chinese stoneware**

Two types of Chinese brown glazed, stoneware, liquid-storage containers were recovered from the Chinaman's Point site: the liquor bottle and the spouted jar. See Table 6.17 for a summary of item quantities.

|  | Sherds | Weight (grams) | MNI |
|---|---|---|---|
| Liquor bottle | 167 | 805 | 7 |
| Spouted jar | 63 | 545 | 19 |

Table 6.17 Chinese liquor-bottle and spouted-jar fragment quantities.

*Liquor bottle*

Chinese brown glazed liquor bottles, sometimes called tiger whisky bottles due to the occasional display of a tiger pattern stamped into their base, appear as tear-drop shaped containers with a carafe-type flared neck. These ceramic bottles held distilled liquor that is often referred to as Chinese wine, similar, but a little spicier in taste to European gin (observation by the author). It was produced from either a grain or starch base and is commonly associated with two types of very strong Chinese alcohol – *mm ga pei* (also *ng ga Py*) and *mui guai lo* (also *mei guei lo*) – traditionally used in cooking, medicines and for drinking (Anderson & Anderson 1977: 342; Passmore & Reid 1982: 403; Naquin & Rawski 1987: 74; Hellmann & Yang 1997: 182).

Chinese liquor bottles have a glossy, brown glaze that has been double-dipped in the glaze solution and fired at higher temperature to produce a better quality bottle than other Chinese brown ware vessels (Ritchie 1986: 232). They can also display considerable colour variation including light and dark browns, orange-brown, blue-brown, green-brown and black. The liquor bottle is also made of a much finer grain than other Chinese brown stoneware (Muir 2003: 45).

Flared rim sections suggest that a minimum of seven vessels are represented in the artefact assemblage. Base fragments are flat-bottomed as opposed to concave, have a 10 to 15 mm raised basal ring and range in diameter from 80 to 100 mm. Body sherds are on average 3 mm to 5 mm thick and display an internal and external glaze. Flared rim sherds have a 50 to 70 mm external diameter. No embossing or impressed characters were found on any of the liquor bottle sherds, nor do they show any post-production modifications or evidence of re-use.

Joins are clearly visible on the internal side of select sherds, indicating that the base, body and neck sections were separately produced and then joined to form each bottle (figure 6.28). This three-segment manufacture process for Chinese liquor bottles has also been noted by Ritchie (1986: 232) at sites in New Zealand and by Praetzellis & Praetzellis (1979: 22) at sites in the United States. The liquor bottles from Chinaman's Point conform to the standard manufacturing process and typical size ranges of those recovered from other 19th-century overseas Chinese sites. They demonstrate use of alcohol for drinking, cooking and in medicines.

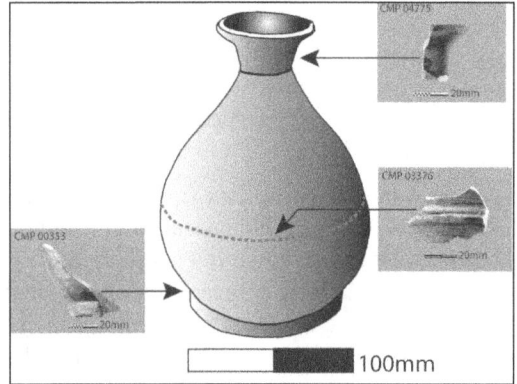

Figure 6.28 Drawing of a Chinese liquor bottle and pictures of artefacts from the Chinaman's Point site (artefact 03376 shows internal ceramic join).

*Spouted jar*

Chinese brown spouted jars are commonly associated with the storage of soy sauce. Yang & Hellmann (1996: 5) have argued, on the basis of oral evidence, that they were also used to hold a range of cooking liquids such as spicy mild alcohols, vinegars, oils and molasses. Examples from Australasian sites show a fairly standard size and cylindrical shape, between 120 and 140 mm high, 140 to 150 mm in base diameter and with a squat body, outwardly rolled rim section and a protruding upper body spout (Ritchie 1986: 234, 237; Muir 2003: 45). Spouted jars of a smaller size have been noted from sites in the United States and square varieties have been recovered from sites in Canada (Quellmalz 1976: 294; Pastron & Garaventa 1981: 405–06; Wegars 1988: 45). Yang & Hellmann (1996: 5) suggest that in some rural areas of China, spouted jars were often re-used as teapots.

Each of the spouted jar fragments from Chinaman's Point are cylindrical and are consistent with the standard squat shape and size recovered from other Australasian sites (figure 6.29). As mentioned above in the 'Food storage' section, base and body fragments from wide-mouthed shouldered jars are indistinguishable from those of the Chinese spouted jar. As only rim and spout sections were counted as spouted jars, there is a low representation of spouted jar sherds from Chinaman's Point and quite a lot of wide/spouted jar sherds.

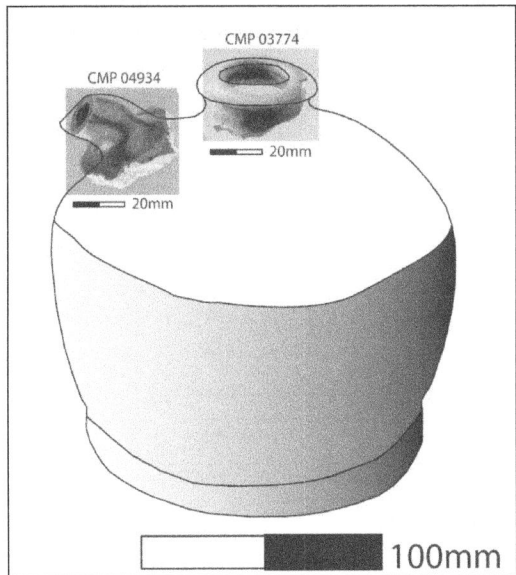

Figure 6.29 Chinese spouted jar and fragments from the Chinaman's Point site.

The minimum vessel count for spouted jars was estimated from recovered rim sections. Rim fragments measured between 30 and 50 mm external diameters, with slight variations noticeable in the rim thicknesses, probably the result of production by hand. Fourteen spout sections were recovered, each approximately 25 mm long and displaying an average internal diameter of 15 mm. As discussed by Ritchie (1986: 237), the spouts appear to have been formed by moulding a short slab of clay around a stick to create a clay tube that was then pressed directly onto the vessel body.

## Tableware

This section discusses objects used for serving and eating food. Ninety-seven and a half percent of the ceramics from Chinamen's Point are of Chinese form, decoration and origin. The remaining 2.5% is European tableware. Similar disparities in the percentage of Chinese and non-Chinese ceramics at overseas Chinese sites are noted by McCarthy (1986: 12), Ritchie (1986: 205, 281), Mueller (1987a: 265), Staski (1993: 138), Gaughwin (1995: 234–35), Smith (1998: 114) and Lydon (1999: 143).

Asian porcelains, many of which are generically classified as Chinese *tz'u* (Medley 1976: 13), are frequently recovered from overseas Chinese sites. All of the recovered Asian ceramics have been identified as accurately as possible to be of Chinese origin. This is opposed to Japanese ware that is also regularly located in association with American overseas Chinese artefact assemblages and occasionally from Australasian assemblages – see Stenger (1993: 323–30) and Wegars (1998). The artefacts discussed below include Chinese bowls, spoons and teapots and European cups, bowls and plates.

Chinese *tz'u* sherds, their weight and minimum number of vessels are represented in table 6.18. European white ware, bone china and stoneware sherds are represented in table 6.21. Minimum number of vessel count was determined through rim and base fragments, design and decorative elements.

| Chinese *tz'u* | Sherds | Weight (grams) | MNI |
|---|---|---|---|
| Bowls | 181 | 580 | 19 |
| Spoons | 16 | 43 | 8 |
| Teapot | 54 | 427 | 2 |
| Total | 251 | 1050 | 29 |

Table 6.18 Type, number of sherds and MNI for Chinese *tz'u* ceramics.

**Chinese bowl**

Recovered Chinese bowls were all Chinese porcelain of plain blue-green celadon, the three friends pattern or the double happiness pattern. These artefacts were recovered predominantly from area 4 and within the tidal zone at Chinaman's Point.

Blue-green celadon, often called wintergreen ware (Olson 1978: 118; Sando & Felton 1993: 157) bowls were recovered in three sizes (figure 6.30; table 6.19).

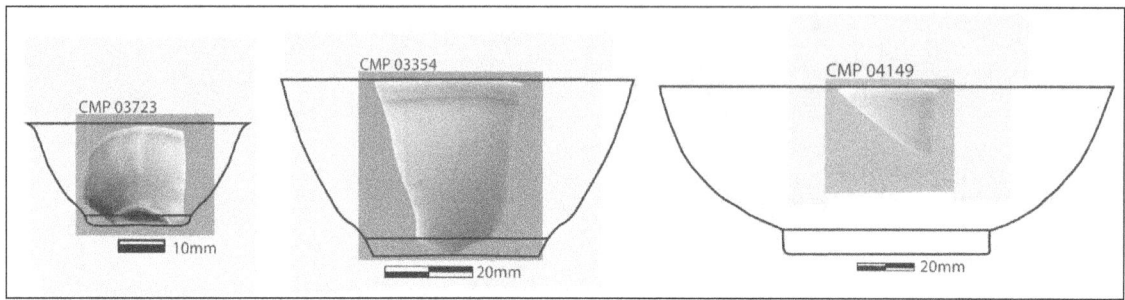

Figure 6.30 Three sizes (50, 100 and 160 mm rim diameters) of Chinese celadon bowl from the Chinaman's Point site.

| Celadon bowl | Rim diam. (mm) | Sherds | Weight (grams) | MNI |
|---|---|---|---|---|
| Wine cup | 50 | 12 | 74 | 4 |
| Teacup/rice bowl | 100 | 91 | 276 | 7 |
| Rice/serving bowl | 160 | 74 | 241 | 6 |
| Total | N/A | 177 | 591 | 17 |

Table 6.19 Chinese celadon bowl rim diameters and quantities.

Seven of these bowls have a manufacturer's mark in underglaze cobalt-blue within the foot-ring of the bowl. Two base-mark types are apparent. The first type is similar to those recovered in New Zealand by Ritchie (1986: 212) which he suggests may be corrupted imitations of traditional Chinese manufacture marks, but still in some instances provide information on artefact date and place of manufacture. Hellmann & Yang (1997: 174) discuss these types of base marks, suggesting they represent Chinese poetry that was produced specifically as export porcelain. Jones (1992: 37) suggests these types of base marks "serve to further illustrate the ambiguities in interpretation of Chinese art and calligraphy". The base marks from Chinaman's Point are fragmentary pieces too small to be useful for specific bowl-type identification other than to confirm they are base marks of a Chinese nature, similar in appearance to those discussed by Ritchie, Hellmann & Yang and Jones. The second type of base mark represents a very basic, hand-painted, cobalt-blue underglaze containing a single or double circle type design (figure 6.31). The meaning of these marks is unknown, but they may represent an individual potter's mark or a hallmark for a particular kiln or ceramic producer.

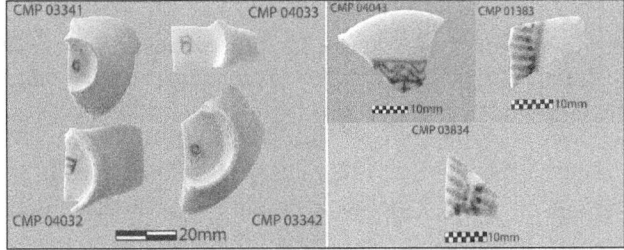

Figure 6.31 Manufacture marks in the foot ring of celadon bowls from Chinaman's Point. Left type is the single or double circle design, right type are similar to those discussed by Ritchie, Hellmann & Yang and Jones.

Fragments of Chinese bowls with what appear to be double happiness or three friends bowl patterns were located at Chinaman's Point (table 6.20). Both of these patterns are commonly found at overseas Chinese sites. Although the designs on the bowls are distinct, the small size of the recovered fragments hinders a definite identification of the pattern (figure 6.32). It is more accurate to identify these artefacts broadly as Chinese *tz'u* sherds.

|  | **Sherds** | **Weight (g)** | **MNI** |
| --- | --- | --- | --- |
| Chinese bowl | 11 | 23 | 2 |

Table 6.20 Chinese bowl fragments displaying either the double happiness or three friends pattern.

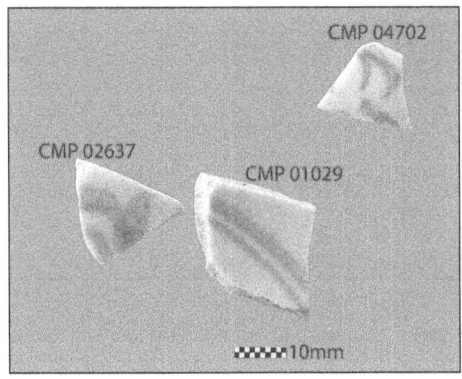

Figure 6.32 Chinese *tz'u* shards (either double happiness or three friends pattern) from the Chinaman's Point site.

**Chinese spoon**

Each Chinese spoon sherd is of plain blue-green celadon, 3 to 4 mm thickness and represents a standard sized (approximately 50 mm across the spoon mouth), traditionally shaped Chinese soup spoon (figure 6.33). Such spoons – which often have an underglaze decorative motif – are used for eating soups and other liquid-based meals. They are commonly recovered at overseas Chinese sites (Muir 2003: 47).

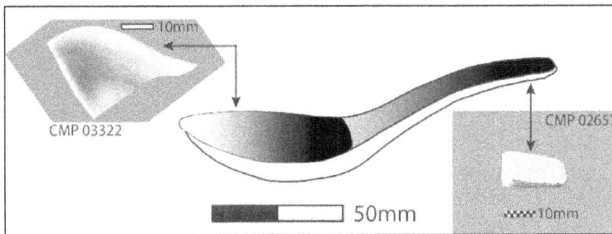

Figure 6.33 Chinese spoon sherds from the Chinaman's Point site.

**Chinese teapot**

Drinking tea could probably be considered a Chinese cultural activity. A Chinese legend states that the Emperor Sheng Nung, c. 2737 BC, observed that people who drank boiled water were less prone to disease than those who did not (Kan & Leong 1963: 229). Consequently, from approximately this period, tea drinking became increasingly popular among Chinese people. Tea was grown extensively in China from the fifth century AD and is often attributed as a major factor in the good health and productivity of Chinese populations (Mote 1977: 199). Ethnographic evidence from Anderson & Anderson (1977: 365) shows the teapot is an essential item in southern Chinese kitchens.

Porcelain teapot fragments represent a barrel shaped teapot, which is typically straight-sided with a central spout, then tapers from a high shoulder with opposing handles to form the smaller rim and lid sections. Two separate decorative forms of the barrel teapot were recovered from Chinaman's Point. One represents a plain white teapot with a base diameter of 120 mm, a body of 2 to 4 mm thickness, a 170 mm long curvy spout, a rim diameter of 60 mm and an external lid diameter of 75 mm (figure 6.34). Only lid fragments remain of the second teapot. The lid sherds have an overglaze polychrome floral motif and an external rim diameter of approximatly 85 mm (figure 6.34).

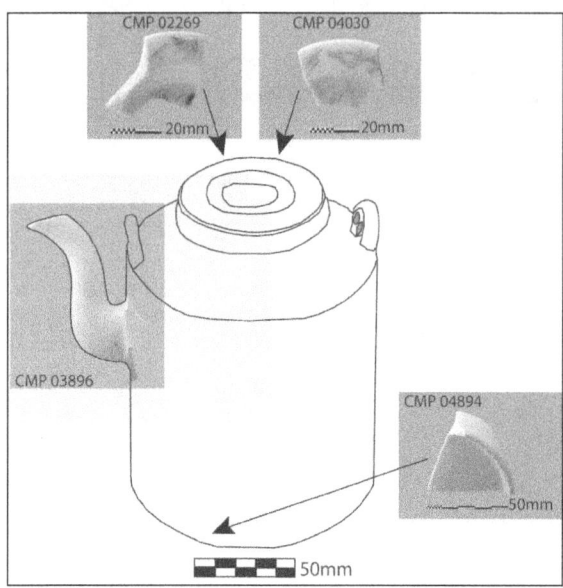

Figure 6.34 Two separate decorative forms (the plain white and the floral motif) of barrel-shaped Chinese teapot sherds from the Chinaman's Point site.

**European ceramics**

Information to identify and analyse European ceramics came predominantly from Sussman (1985; 1997), Cameron (1986), Coysh & Henrywood (1986), Majewski & O'Brien (1987), Arnold (1990), Miller (2000) and Brooks (2005a). The type, number of shards and minimum number of vessels for European ceramics can be seen in Table 6.21.

White ware is a low fired, opaque, porous, mass-produced, affordable and very durable refined earthenware. During the 19th century, white ware was widely used to manufacture a huge range of plain and decorative tableware, toiletries and other basic utilitarian items (Brooks 2005a: 34). Recovered sherds consist of base, foot ring, side, marl and rim (ranging from 180 to 210 mm in diameter) sections and are of 3 to 7 mm in thickness (figure 6.35). The underglaze maker's mark was visible on the underside of one white ware item. This mark represents the B & L beehive symbol from Hill's Pottery in Britain. This artefact along with other white ware sherds is discussed further in the site-dating section of chapter 7.

Bone china is a coarse-bodied porcelain that was first introduced to Britain in 1794 as a soft paste porcelain. From early in Australia's colonial history it was – and still is – imported to Australia in large quantities (Miller 2000: 9). Bone china occurs principally as plain or decorated tea ware and is most easily identified by an off-white body and micro-crazed glaze (Brooks 2005a: 27). Bone china was represented at Chinaman's Point through the recovery of non-decorative cup and plate or saucer sherds (table 6.21). The cup was identified through an 80 mm diameter rim section of 2 mm thickness and the plate or saucer through a small fully glazed foot ring sherd, side sections of 2 mm thickness and a very small section of marl.

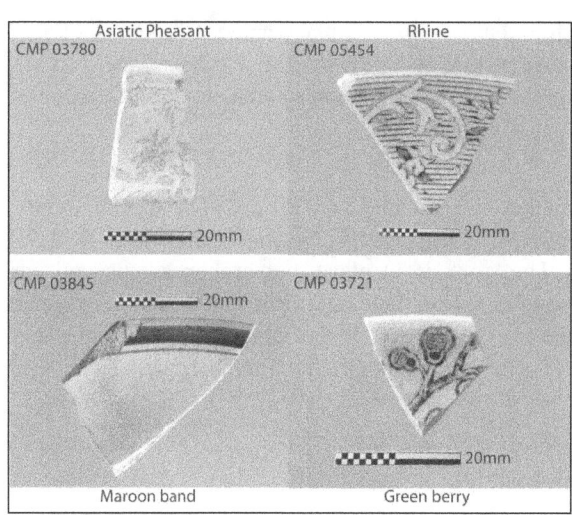

Figure 6.35 European plate ceramics from the Chinaman's Point site.

Most ceramics from 19th-century Australian sites are of British manufacture and the Chinaman's Point European ceramics were most likely also manufactured in Britain, although this can only be confirmed for the B & L beehive symbol artefact. As the recovered European ceramics from Chinaman's Point represent only a small quantity of relatively cheap, functional utilitarian wares, their on-site presence is probably best explained as opportunistic and practical. Networks of Chinese trade extended to Port Albert and beyond, as evidenced in part by the large percentage of Chinese ceramics in the assemblage. The non-Chinese ceramics, along with nails, meat and other items purchased from European stores reinforces the notion that Chinese people had access to sources of supply for their general living requirements.

| European ceramic | Pattern | Number of sherds | Weight (grams) | MNI |
|---|---|---|---|---|
| White ware (plate) | Rhine | 21 | 102 | 2 |
| White ware (plate) | Asiatic pheasant | 6 | 22 | 2 |
| White ware (plate) | Maroon band | 5 | 18 | 1 |
| White ware (plate) | Green berry | 16 | 47 | 1 |
| White ware (plate) | Plain | 10 | 71 | 2 |
| White ware (plate) | Unidentified | 4 | 15 | 1 |
| Bone china (1 cup & 1 saucer) | Plain | 5 | 10 | 2 |
| Stoneware (jar) | Salt glaze | 11 | 145 | 5 |
| Total | N/A | 78 | 430 | 16 |

Table 6.21 Type, number of sherds and MNI for European ceramics.

## INDUSTRIAL

Industrial components from Chinaman's Point include artefacts considered to have an association with the procuring and processing of fish resources.

### Fishing

Port Albert's long association with the fishing industry has left considerable local and regional archaeological remains. There is a slight possibility that some remains relating to fishing from the Chinaman's Point site have a European association. This is because European fisherman regularly visited the site to sell fish and because some items such as boat parts could have drifted with tidal movements from other regions into the site area. Where ambiguity over Chinese or European use of an artefact exists, brief discussion will be provided.

As argued in chapter 1, the Chinese-style artefacts found at the site, the place name 'Chinaman's Point' and primary historical documentation confirm that Chinese people occupied the site. No newspaper reports, land title or other historical literature was located to suggest that European people had at any period occupied the site or near vicinity for fishing or any other purpose.

**Anchor**

A broken, heavily corroded and possibly homemade anchor was located in the tidal zone at Chinaman's Point. The anchor is made of 30 mm round solid steel, with a 320 mm body length that turns at a 75° angle to form another 200 mm of shaft (figure 6.36). The stock is in place, but broken at one end and the anchor arms and flutes are missing. The presence of the anchor helps confirm that boats were a part of the working operations at the fish-curing site. In addition to its function of holding a vessel in place, an anchor was often used to secure one or both ends of a net to the ocean floor for net-fishing purposes (figure 2.4).

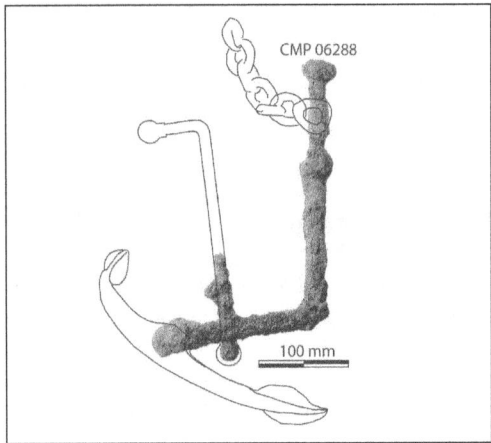

Figure 6.36 Corroded anchor remains from the Chinaman's Point site.

**Boat timbers**

As mentioned in the architectural/structural section above, the remains of a slipway for boat maintenance were identified at the site. Four sections of broken, milled, softwood timber planks were recovered from the tidal zone and area 1 of the site. As with the timber jetty remains discussed previously, no scientific analysis of these timbers was possible due to financial restraints. However, Pearson (1992: 12) suggests that Victorian fishing vessels of this era were usually constructed with New Zealand kauri pine or Tasmanian huon pine for their outer timber planking. The recovered planks have a maximum length of 250 mm and all display nail holes, with one piece containing four square shaft copper nails and two pieces showing the remains of white oil-based paint. The planking, copper nails and oil-based paint are necessary for the construction and maintenance of boats, again suggesting the presence of boats at the site. As some of the boat timbers were excavated from the site's ground layers and were found in the general vicinity of the slipway remains, they are considered to be associated with the Chinese period of occupation.

**Dried paint**

In addition to the painted planks, one white-coloured and two cream-coloured masses of hardened oil-based paint were recovered from the site's tidal zone. These bodies of paint are still in the shape of the tins that once held them, the tin having rusted away (figure 6.37). The cream coloured paint mass is 115 mm in diameter and the white paint mass is 90 mm in diameter. Also within the tidal zone, several paint tin-rims were located, some with cream or white oil-based paint still adhered and matching the respective rim diameters of the hardened masses of paint. Oil-based paint may have been used to paint land structures and is also essential to protect boat timbers from the harsh marine environment. Part of the material evidence identified by Bowen (2004: 83) for early commercial fishing activities on the far South Coast of New South Wales includes "launch repair equipment such as copper nails ... traces of oil-based paint and broken sections of launches". The presence of these items at Chinaman's Point confirms that these are expected items of recovery where early commercial fishing activities have occurred.

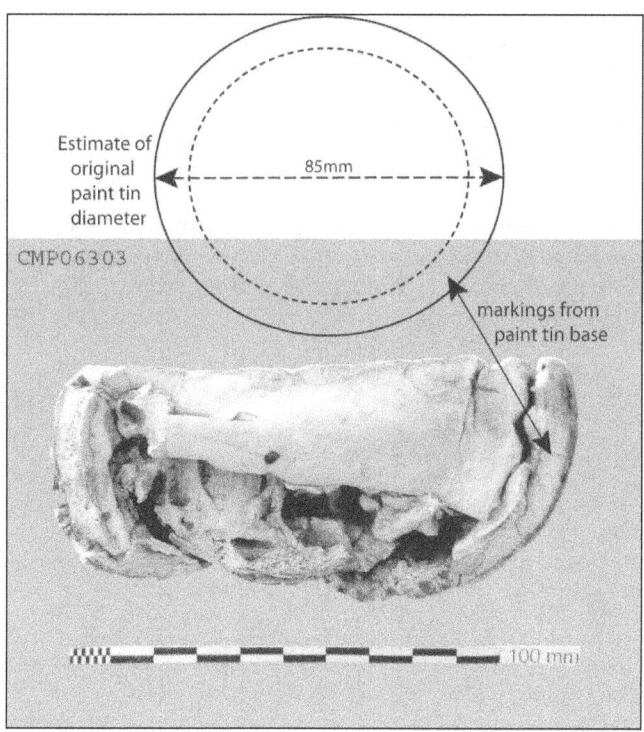

Figure 6.37 Mass of oil-based paint, still in the approximate shape of a paint tin, from the Chinaman's Point site.

## Copper nails

As copper is resistant to the corrosive marine environment, copper nails are often used for boat construction and maintenance purposes. Eight copper nails, weighing a total of 26 g – not including the four previously discussed as embedded in timber – were recovered from the tidal zone at Chinaman's Point. Five of these are square shaft rose head type nails with 2.5 and 3 mm widths and of varying lengths between 25 and 95 mm. Three have 4 mm square shafts, a rose head on one end and a washer and the nail shaft hammered to form a burr on the other end. The smaller shaft copper nails are suitable for securing outer boat planking, which would be simply nailed to the vessel's structural timbers. To secure two or more structural boat timbers together, copper nails were hammered through the timbers so that they protruded through to the outer side. A washer would then be placed over the nail and the end hammered until burred. This process is visible on copper nails from Chinaman's Point (figure 6.38). Copper nails are further evidence of boat use, maintenance and perhaps construction at Chinaman's Point.

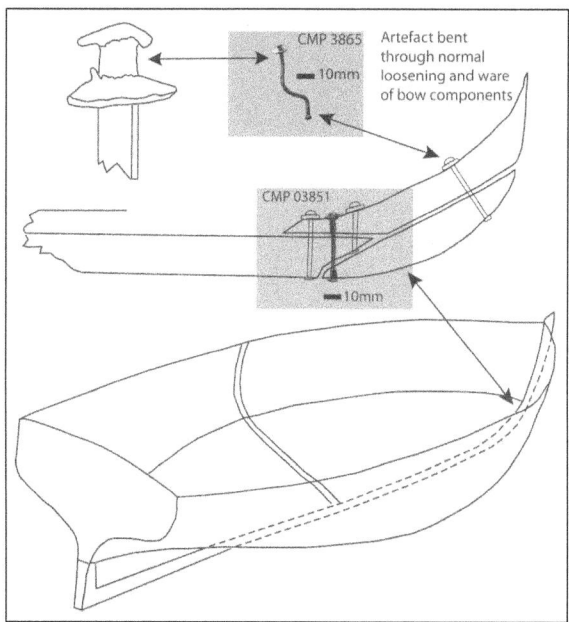

Figure 6.38 Deliberately burred copper nails from the Chinaman's Point site suggesting the on-site existence of boats and boat-construction or maintenance activities.

**Net sinkers**

Fishing nets, either cotton or hemp, require cork or glass net floats on their top rung to keep the upper net sections on the water surface and net sinkers on the lower rung to pull the net downwards. This ensures the fishing net hangs upright in the water. Twenty-two lead net sinkers and one line sinker, weighing a total of 284 g were recovered from the Chinaman's Point site. All the lead sinkers were recovered from the site's tidal zone except for one, which was excavated from area 4. Cut marks on the sinker edges suggested they had been cut with a pair of snips from lead sheeting between 1 and 3 mm thick, to various lengths between 30 mm and 60 mm. The flat lead sheeting was then presumedly rolled around the bottom rung of fishing net or some other cylindrical object to form a tube (figure 6.39). The net sinkers are in various stages of production, showing that they were manufactured on site. This was common among colonial European fishermen, who usually also made all their own nets (Chaplin 1985: 42).

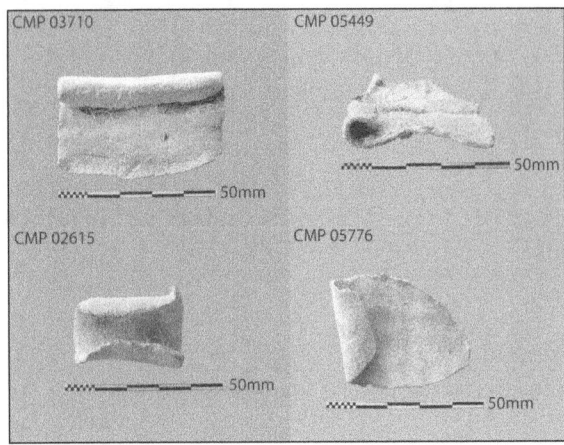

Figure 6.39 Selection of lead net sinkers from the Chinaman's Point site.

The single line sinker is too light in weight to be a net sinker. It appears to be designed to trawl for barracouta (*Thrysites atun*), commercially popular in Victoria from the 1880s to the mid-1900s (Kerr 1985: 49; Evans 2003: 6). If the fishermen judged the fish to be on the surface, trawl lines were rigged with a hook lure. However, if the fish were swimming some distance below the surface, small tubes of lead were placed at approximately 350 mm intervals along the trawl line to sink the lure, enabling them to 'fish deep' (Evans 2003: 187).

The recovery of lead net sinkers from Chinaman's Point provides further evidence of boat use by the Chinese fish curers. Importantly, the sinkers represent strong evidence that the site occupants themselves actually fished, as opposed to simply purchasing the catches of European fishermen. It is possible that some of the net sinkers represent objects fallen from European fishing nets whilst a catch was unloaded. However, dropped lead sinkers would be expected to stay *in situ* (probably around the proposed site jetty area) even with tidal movements. As these items were found in different site locations and in various stages of manufacture, their use is predominantly attributed to the site occupants. The line sinker is also significant as it suggests the Chinese fish curers were fishing with lines, which is not generally associated in the historical literature with overseas Chinese fishing activity in colonial Australia. However, as line trawling was not common in Victoria until the 1880s, well after the peak of overseas Chinese fishing activities in Australia, the recovered line sinker probably means the Chinese site occupants were involved in fishing activities after the 1880s, using the standard methods of the period.

# Recording

### Weighing instrument (balance scale)

Historical records show that during the colonial period – as now – fish were sold and purchased by weight. The Chinaman's Point fish curers would have required some way to weigh each basket of fish they purchased or caught. They would also have needed to keep an accurate tally of basket numbers and weights, the quantities of different fish types and total weights. Evidence from the site suggests that balance scales, slate boards and slate pencils were used for this purpose.

Excavation of overseas Chinese sites occasionally recovers components of small, delicate, manually-operated balance weighing instruments called *li-ding*, which are generally associated with weighing opium or small quantities of gold (see for example Ritchie & Harrison 1982: 24, New Zealand; Stanin 2004b, Butcher's

Gully, Victoria). Chinese merchants and general buyers and sellers of food and other commodities used much larger balance scales, of which there are a great many varieties. Balance scales involve a balanced horizontal bar with an object of known weighted placed on one side of the bar and an object of unknown weight placed on the opposite side. The known weight is either added to or reduced until the bar remains exactly horizontal, thereby establishing the unknown quantity of weight.

The heavily corroded and broken remains of a large balance scale were recovered from the tidal zone at Chinaman's Point. The scale has a T-shape and is made from a 22 mm diameter solid steel bar. The vertical section is 200 mm long and hooked at the end to allow it to be hung from a frame or suspended by rope or chain. The horizontal arm sections are slightly curved. One arm is approximately 200 mm long and ends with a downward-facing hook to hang the item to be weighed. The other arm is approximately 220 mm long with no hooked section, suggesting an arm that held a sliding counter balance weight. The centre T section is thicker, with a diameter of approximately 50 mm – now heavily corroded – possibly indicating where some form of horizontal indicator arrow was positioned (figure 6.40).

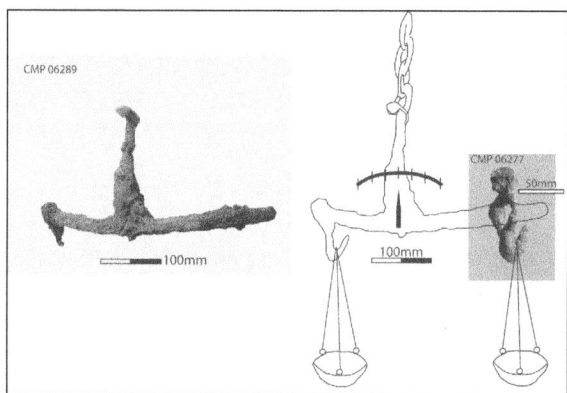

Figure 6.40 Corroded balance scales (left) from the Chinaman's Point site and a reconstruction of the scales with a sliding counter balance hook (right) also recovered from the site.

**Metal hook**

A steel hook was recovered from the tidal zone. At its top is a closed circle with a finger grip and the hook is below (figure 6.40). This design suggests it may have been part of the sliding counter weight section of a balance scale. The hook is 133 g in weight and 110 mm long. The circular top is 30 mm in diameter and, although heavily corroded, displays wear marks as if it has been repeatedly pulled back and forth across a metal pole. It is likely that a rod (the horizontal arm of the balance scale) was fitted through the circle and the hook used to suspend a tray of counter weights.

The balance scales demonstrate the economic importance of the Chinaman's Point site. The scales would have been central to European–Chinese interaction at the site and highly significant to both groups as the fish being weighed was the livelihood of both seller and buyer.

**Slate board and slate pencil**

Slate pencils and writing boards were commonly used during the 1800s and are often recovered from historical sites in Australia. Slate provided a cheap, effective, durable and reusable means of recording information in a temporary form (Davies 2005: 64). By the early 1900s, however, the popularity of slate writing equipment was in decline. It was still advertised for sale in Australia during the 1920s and used in primary schools until approximately 1945 (Mee 1927: 2645; Finlay 1990: 58). Generally, however, by the 1920s, wood-cased graphite pencils and sheet paper had become very affordable and rapidly became the more popular writing implements (Petroski 1990: 29).

One slate pencil and five broken pieces of plain slate writing board were recovered from the tidal zone at Chinaman's Point. Slate writing board can be distinguished from roofing slate by its thickness and smooth polished surface. The pencil is 40 mm long, 6 mm in diameter and weighs 2 g. Each of the slate board pieces are 2 mm thick, blue-grey in colour, weigh 10 g collectively and three of the pieces display a chamfered edge (figure 6.41). These implements may have been used to record the weight of the fish baskets and to calculate how much money fishermen received for their catch.

Figure 6.41 Broken slate pencil and writing board from the Chinaman's Point site.

## Slag

Slag (a by-product of smelting and usually industrial-related) is a complex mixture of inorganic materials that has been exposed to high temperatures and has failed to reach the full molten state of its co-conglomerate substances, eventually becoming a separate body of material (Raymond 1984: 55). Slag is extremely resistant to weathering, difficult to classify chemically and complicated to date (Bachmann 1982: 1). Two hundred and seventy-eight pieces of slag, weighing a total of 420 g were found at the Chinaman's Point site. Most was recovered from the tidal zone, but a small portion was excavated from area 4. The slag consists of angular, black/grey, very porous lumps an average of 25 mm in diameter. As slag from a single smelting process produces "a sizable heap of waste" that is generally calculated by the meter cubed when encountered archaeologically (Bachmann 1982: 5), the recovered slag from Chinaman's Point only represents a very small quantity.

Following Bachmann's (1982) guide to slag identification, the slag from Chinaman's Point appears to be a non-ferrous metallurgical slag with mineral inclusions, consistent with that produced from metal smelting. For the purpose of this project – cost reasons and the likely low value of information to be obtained – it was decided not to pursue chemical composition of the slag. The slag's dark colour, very porous nature, lightweight and lump-like shapes indicate it is almost certainly the product of intentional or unintentional iron smelting. For iron to produce slag it must be heated to a minimum temperature of 1050°C (Bachmann 1982: 30). The heat from a normal surface-level campfire is approximately 500°C, but with a dug ground hearth or a hearth with built-up sides, temperatures can reach 1100°C (Maddin 1988: 264). This suggests the slag at Chinaman's Point was produced in an enclosed hearth.

Nineteenth-century blacksmiths, several of whom operated in the Port Albert district, commonly travelled with a portable clay forge to undertake repair work and small manufacturing jobs (Adams 1990: 39). This 'smithing' produces slag as a by-product from hammering red hot metal, known as 'smithing slag' or 'tap slag' as opposed to smelting which generates lumps of slag (Bachmann 1982: 5, 31). Smithing slag tends to have smooth surfaces, a convex or concave shape, is fine and brittle and, when recovered archaeologically, is usually coated in a brown iron-oxide crust – unlike the slag recovered from Chinaman's Point.

Due to the small amount of slag recovered, a controlled metal smelting operation at Chinaman's Point seems unlikely. As iron smelting temperatures could be reached unintentionally in a ground pit or stone-lined fire, the slag from Chinaman's Point appears to have been produced by metal objects attached to timber (such as nails or other metal objects), being thrown into a large enclosed fire.

## Tools

### Ammunition

Colonial fishermen faced the persistent problem of seals ripping holes in fishing nets. While sharks would opportunistically attack fish-laden nets, seals would deliberately follow fishermen, laying in wait until a net was 'shot' around a school of fish. Then, when the net was being hauled in, the seal would rip into the cotton mesh to get at the fish (Allan in Ellis & Lee 2002: 29). Colonial fishermen in Victoria would shoot seals on sight

(Albert Clark 2003 pers. comm.). This provides a plausible reason for the recovery from the Chinaman's Point site of one rim-fire percussion cap from a shotgun cartridge. As the faunal analysis does not show evidence of native game consumption, it is unlikely the site occupants used a gun for hunting purposes. It is also possible the cap represents a discard from hunters of a later period.

The percussion cap was recovered from within the tidal zone. It is made of brass and is comprised of the inner centre-fire primer section and the outer case head of an ammunition cartridge, most likely (due to diameter) a ten gauge shotgun (White & Munhall 1963: 8). The inner firing pin shows a distinct indentation mark from the striking of a hammer pin, indicating a spent cartridge. As a complete item, the outer ammunition casing would have been made of thin cylindrical brass, measuring approximately 22 mm in diameter, 60 mm long and dating from the 1850s onwards (Winant 1959: 207–08). This type of cartridge could have shot a single lead ball or a cluster of lead pellets. The dimensions of the inner percussion cap recovered from Chinaman's Point are 10 mm in diameter, 5 mm long, 0.5 g in weight and with no evidence of a head stamp or maker's mark (figure 6.42). It is conceivable that the spent cartridge left lying on a boat's decking and had been thrown or somehow displaced from the vessel while docked at the site.

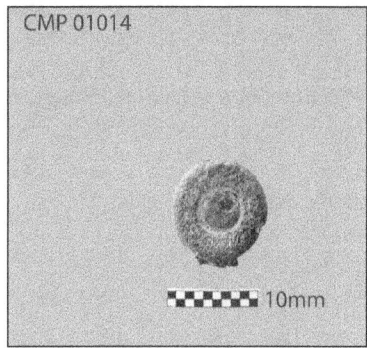

Figure 6.42 Spent bullet cartridge from the Chinaman's Point site.

**Bayonet or sword**

Processing bulk quantities of fish for curing would have required an array of cutting implements. A broken section of what appears to be a bayonet or sword was recovered from the tidal zone of the site. Although heavily corroded, the object can be distinguished from a standard knife through blade thickness, a distinctive tapering to the end point – most of which is missing – and a double-bladed shaft.

The blade is 10 mm thick in the body, tapering on either side to form opposing blades that are 25 mm apart from edge to edge, 114 mm long from the broken tip end to the broken shaft end and 82 g in weight (figure 6.43). As this artefact is associated with a fish-curing site, it probably had an on-site purpose other than weaponry. A full-length bayonet or sword would be too long for use as a domestic or occupational tool. However, the blade is broken at 114 mm long, which could conceivably allow it to be used in tasks such as gutting, scaling, heading and portioning the fish processed at Chinaman's Point.

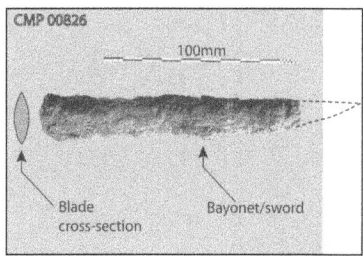

Figure 6.43 Corroded and broken section of a bayonet or sword blade from the Chinaman's Point site.

The blade's corrosion hampers an accurate identification. From pictorial evidence in books displaying common swords of the time, possible matches include early-style British and American cutlass or infantry swords (pictured in Peterson 1956: 263, 275), or 19th-century Australian infantry bayonets from the short rifle, artillery carbine or Martini-Henry rifle (pictured in Skennerton 1988: 15, 18, 36). Acknowledging the ethnic nature of the site, the blade could equally represent one of a number of Chinese iron sabers (see Trousdale 1975: 60).

**Horseshoe**

Three broken sections of horseshoe, representing a minimum number of two complete horseshoes, were recovered from within the tidal zone at Chinaman's Point. During Australia's colonial period, horses were the principal mode of land transport and horseshoes were very common. One horseshoe piece has two complete nails still positioned within the shoe eyelets and a 100 mm outer radius that indicates it came from a pony rather than a horse. The two remaining horseshoe pieces have portions of nail still attached and a 150 mm outer radius. The combined weight of the three pieces is 63 g.

The Chinese fish curers at Metung owned two packhorses that they used to cart cured fish to the Chinese miners on Gippsland's goldfields (Bell in the *Bairnsdale Advertiser* 1955, September 5; Halstead 1977: 32; Tomlin et al. 1979: 101). There was also a great deal of European-operated bullock and packhorse movement between Port Albert and Gippsland's goldfields (Adams 1997: 6; Olsen 1974: 119). It is possible that the Chinaman's Point fish curers had a horse or horses for transport of goods. However, as there is no supporting historical documentation for this and no other horse-related items were recovered from the site, the horseshoe remains seem more likely to have come from horses visiting the site either during or after the Chinese occupation period.

**Cleaver**

Cleavers are used by Chinese people for chopping, slicing and crushing a myriad of items. An anthropological study of foodways in southern China (Anderson & Anderson 1977: 364) observed the versatility of Chinese cleavers, stating that they are used for:

> splitting firewood, gutting and scaling fish, slicing vegetables, mincing meat, crushing garlic (with the dull side of the blade), cutting one's nails, sharpening pencils, whittling new chopsticks, killing pigs, shaving (it is kept sharp enough, or supposedly is) and settling old and new scores with one's enemies.

Cleavers are often recovered from overseas Chinese sites (see McCarthy 1986: 53; Stapp 1990: 209). Although a multi-functional tool, Chinese cleavers are generally described – archaeologically or otherwise – in association with meat butchering and other food preparation (Levine 1921: 8; Passmore & Reid 1983: 33; Longenecker & Stapp 1993: 117). They are easily identifiable from European style cleavers by the Chinese preference for a curved blade: as put by Levine (1921: 13) when describing Chinese butchering practices, "for cutting through the flesh ... a curved blade is best".

One almost-complete, but heavily corroded Chinese-style metal cleaver was recovered from the tidal zone at Chinaman's Point. It is 180 mm long, 55 mm wide, 9 mm thick on the top side which tapers down to the blade section and weighs 367 g (figure 6.44). As it is likely that this cleaver was sometimes, possibly even predominantly, used by the Chinaman's Point fishermen to process fish it is therefore considered an industrial component of the site for the purpose of this project.

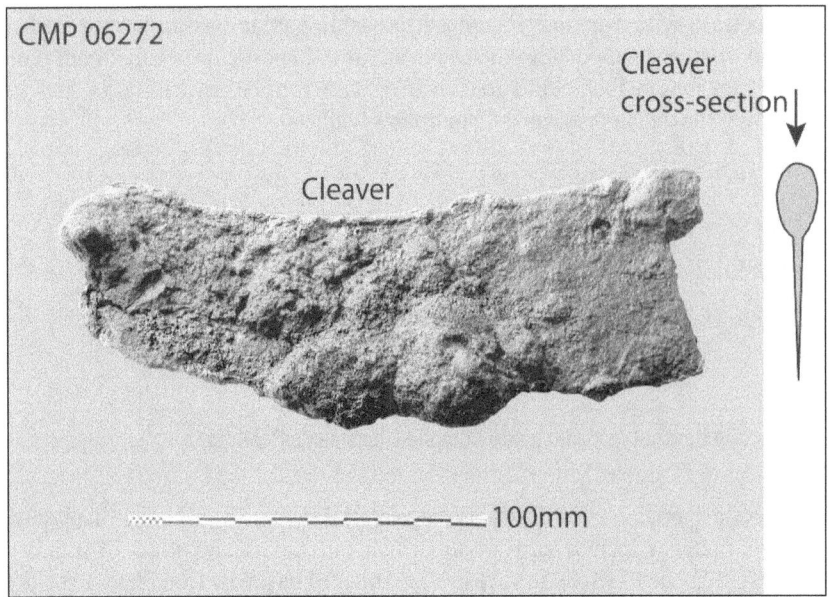

Figure 6.44 Corroded Chinese-style metal cleaver from the Chinaman's Point site.

## PERSONAL

Personal components from the site include artefacts originally manufactured for individual personal use. The only items in this category from the Chinaman's Point site are clothing buttons.

### Buttons

Due to the rapid deterioration of personal clothing, archaeological excavations only occasionally reveal analytically useful items. Buttons, generally the most robust parts of clothing, are the exception and are valuable for dating purposes and in interpreting style, status and gender of the wearer (Lindbergh 1999: 50). Six buttons were recovered from the site (table 6.22). Five buttons were recovered from the tidal zone at Chinaman's Point and one button was derived from excavation area 4.

Five of the buttons are pressed glass, two-hole, undecorated, opaque milk, British-style, utilitarian, 12 mm in diameter and associated with cuff collar and shirt fasteners from clothing such as cotton and linen shirts and underwear (Cameron 1985: 113, 153). The remaining button is a metal copper alloy, four-hole, 14 mm diameter button, stamped with the quality mark 'BEST MAKE' (figure 6.45). This type of button was used in durable trousers, overalls, suspenders and coats (Cameron 1985: 20; Lindbergh 1999: 51–52).

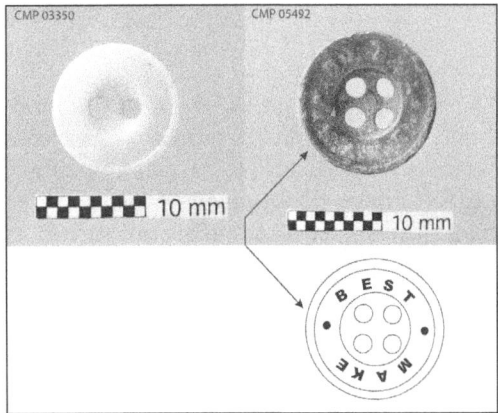

Figure 6.45 Glass (left) and metal (right) buttons from the Chinaman's Point site.

The buttons from Chinaman's Point are consistent with common, utilitarian-type, colonial-period clothing fasteners that were designed typically for men's work clothing. In a study of buttons from 19th-century whaling sites in Tasmania, George (1999: 12, 62) found that whalers favoured bone or copper alloy buttons, as these materials would withstand the corrosive saltwater environment in which they worked. The glass and copper alloy buttons from Chinaman's Point complement George's (1999) findings, showing that the Chinese fish curers also had a preference for non-corrosive buttons. The potential for these buttons to aid in dating the site occupation period is discussed in chapter 7.

| Button material | Number of buttons | Sew holes | Weight (grams) |
|---|---|---|---|
| Milk glass | 5 | 2 | 0.4 |
| Copper alloy | 1 | 4 | 0.6 |
| Total | 6 | N/A | 2.6 |

Table 6.22 Type and number of recovered buttons.

## RECREATIONAL

This category comprises artefacts created originally or through modification for the purpose of individual or group enjoyment. All artefacts that have an association with recreational activities at Chinaman's Point – besides alcohol consumption – are related to opium use. Materials, number of pieces, weight and minimum number of individual ceramic opium smoking bowls, metal opium-bowl connectors, glass opium-lamp covers, opium-can remains and Chinese-style medicine vials can be seen in Table 6.23. Opium use by overseas

Chinese people has been documented through historical accounts and archaeological remains in Australia, New Zealand and the United States. Opium-related artefacts from Chinaman's Point are interpreted primarily through the aid of Etter (1980), Ritchie & Harrison (1982), Ritchie (1986), Hodgson (1999), Sando & Felton (1993), Wylie & Fike (1993), Wilton (2004), Galloway (2005) and Zheng (2005).

| Opium related item | Material | Number of pieces | Weight (grams) | MNI |
|---|---|---|---|---|
| Smoking bowl | Ceramic | 47 | 87 | 32 |
| Bowl connectors | Brass | 2 | 4 | 2 |
| Lamp bases | Glass | 41 | 1540 | 41 |
| Lamp covers | Glass | 19 | 249 | 12 |
| Medicinal vials | Glass | 10 | 71 | 5 |
| Opium can | Brass | 27 | 39 | 2 |
| Total | N/A | 146 | 1990 | 103 |

Table 6.23 Representation of opium-smoking equipment.

## Opium smoking

The opium poppy (*Papaver somniferum*) was introduced to China from southern Europe several centuries ago (Courtwright 1982: 64). This highly addictive drug was initially used for medicinal purposes as it blocks messages of pain to the brain, effectively relieving symptoms associated with coughs, colds, poor respiration, gastric complaints, laryngitis and many other illnesses or painful conditions (Hodgson 1999: 17). However, it is opium's ability to induce feelings of contentment and to alleviate anxiety that rapidly entrenched its popular use in all levels of Chinese society (Zheng 2005: 56), not only as an ingested medicine, but also, by approximately the 1600s, as a recreational indulgence (*Encyclopaedia Britannica* 1981: 1052; Wylie & Fike 1993: 256). By the 1850s and the beginning period of significant Chinese movement into Australia, opium use had become a way of life and many Chinese people were addicted to smoking opium (Wilton 2004: 66).

In Australia, opium was a legal all-purpose panacea of the colonial period and the early 1900s. It was available from general stores and was a component in common remedies such as Allen's Irish Moss Gum Jubes and Mrs Winslow's Soothing Syrup. Opium was also used in medicines such as laudanum and Chlorodyne, which were principally mixtures of opiates laced with a generous dose of alcohol. European addiction to opium was also common in colonial Australia (Phillips 1978: 84; Hodgson 1999: 2).

With the movement of Chinese people to colonial Australia, the Chinese technology for smoking opium was brought to Victoria (Wilton 2004: 68). It was during this second half of the 19th century that non-Chinese people in Australia, including some Aboriginal people, began to smoke opium, as opposed to ingesting the drug through medicines (*The Chemist and Druggist of Australasia* 1901: 85, 241; Manderson 1993: 32; Adams 1997).

It is difficult to estimate accurately how widespread opium smoking was among overseas Chinese people in colonial Australia, especially given that many overseas Chinese people only smoked opium occasionally as a casual social activity (Galloway 2005: 67) and that colonial European accounts of Chinese opium use are ambiguous. Wylie & Fike (1993: 257) suggest that in China between 1870 and 1890, approximately 10 to 30% of Chinese people smoked opium. Ritchie (1986: 365) indicates that in colonial New Zealand, approximately 60% of the overseas Chinese population smoked opium. In the Victorian goldfields in 1868, Manderson (1993: 22) estimates that as many as 90% of overseas Chinese people smoked opium. In 1868, Reverend Young returned from touring each of Victoria's mining districts to report that approximately half the Chinese population in Victoria smoked the "evil ... injurious ... wretched ... wicked ... disastrous ... monster" drug opium (cited in McLaren 1985: 53).

The most common method of recreational opium use by Chinese people was to smoke it through a specially designed implement that was comprised of four main components: a smoking bowl, bowl connector, a 'gee rag' and a pipe (figure 6.46). The bowls are a broad-cupped shape and have a convex lid with a small central hole and a cylindrical base flange/connector that joins to the pipe, which is usually made of bamboo. The 'gee rag' is a piece of cloth that enables a tight fit between the base flange and the pipe, also acting to collect ashes and unburnt opium particles, which were re-used (Etter 1980: 99). A constant flame was required (generally in the form of a specialised opium lamp) and a knitting-needle shaped implement used to pick up and manipulate

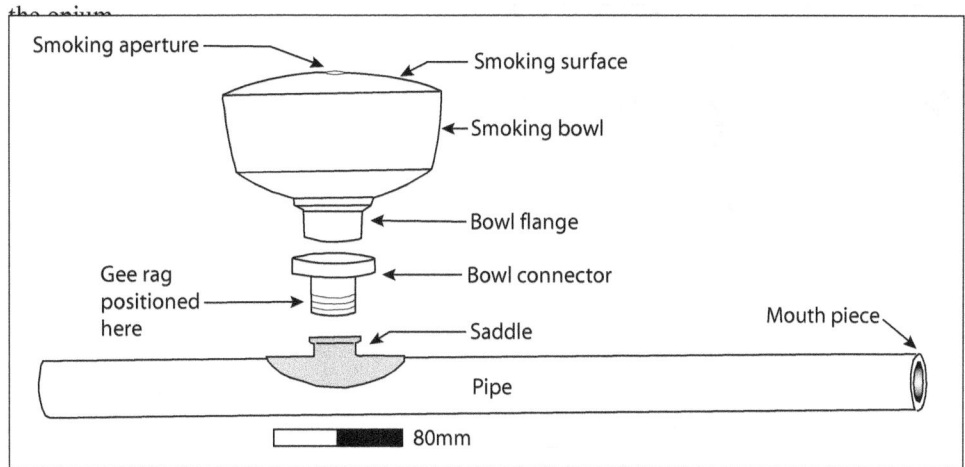

Figure 6.46 Opium smoking pipe, bowl and other parts. Opium is placed over the smoking aperture and then held over a flame.

Etter (1980: 99) provides a good description of the use of an opium pipe:

> Smoking opium was a viscous liquid – like Molasses – and had to be cooked before smoking. A pea-sized portion of opium was impaled on the needle and heated over the cooking lamp until it became soft, like gum, as its moisture evaporated. The smoker then placed the opium-laden needle into the aperture of the pipe bowl and withdrew the needle. The opium remained on the top of the bowl, around the aperture like a small doughnut. Ideally, the smoker reclined on a couch and holding the pipe at an angle to the flame of the lamp, inhaled and sucked the flame against the opium. The opium burned to smoke and the smoker breathed this in, much cooled down through the pipe.

Slight variations to this process have been noted by Ritchie (1986: 367) and Wylie & Fike (1993: 259–60). Both authors quote a description of opium-smoking procedures written in 1881 by Dr. H. H. Kane of New York.

**Opium smoking bowl**

Opium bowl and bowl segments are frequently recovered from overseas Chinese sites. An integral component of the opium-smoking process, bowls are manufactured predominantly from earthenware or stoneware to form an array of shapes, although the basic design (figure 6.46) always remains the same. Opium-bowl sizes are typically between 40 and 50 mm in height and 50 and 80 mm in diameter (Etter 1980: 99).

A fragmentary assemblage of ceramic opium smoking bowl sherds was recovered from the tidal zone at Chinaman's Point. The sherd count, weight and minimum number of individual bowls can be seen in table 6.23. The bowl type was ascertained through smoking surface shape, body shape and decorations. The minimum number is estimated through colour and flange-piece counts. While the assemblage fragments did not reveal how a complete bowl would have looked, they would likely have been similar to the bowls shown in figure 6.47. Eighteen percent of the sherds, representing two separate bowls, are of stoneware and the remainder are earthenware. Etter (1980: 100) and Wylie & Higgins (1987: 346) suggest earthenware bowls were the cheaper variety and more likely to be recovered from worker camps. Twenty sherds display distinct fingerprint marks on their inner surface, which is consistent with Ritchie's (1986: 369) and Wylie & Higgins's (1987: 336) observation that bowl smoking surfaces and body sections were manufactured separately then joined together by hand while the clay was still wet, before firing.

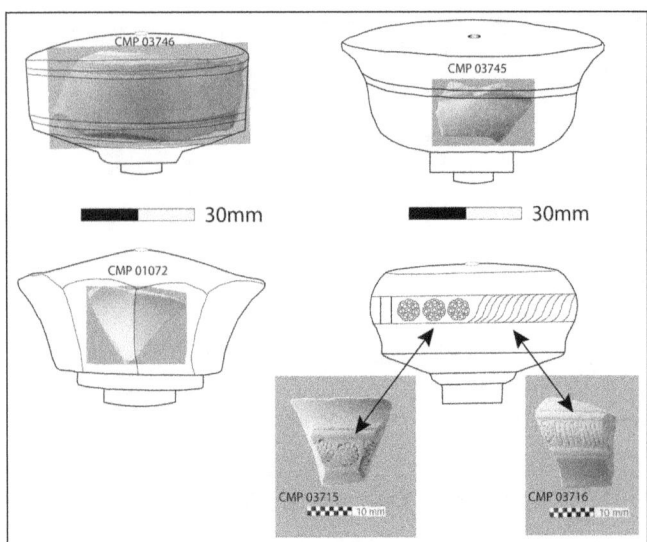

Figure 6.47 Common opium smoking bowl shapes, designs and artefacts from the Chinaman's Point site.

Three different clay colours are evident in the bowls: a black stoneware with an internal and external slip glaze; an orange/tan slipped and un-slipped earthenware (the most numerous type of recovered sherd) and grey earthenware with an external slip glaze. Four variations within the bowl finish are noticeable: no slip, an orange/red slip, a brown slip and a highly fired black glaze.

Charring is apparent on approximately 23% of the bowl lid/smoking surfaces recovered from Chinaman's Point. Ritchie (1986: 367) observed char marks on 50% of the bowl smoking surfaces recovered from his New Zealand study. While Etter (1980: 99) suggests the opium was placed on the outside of the bowl's surface, Ritchie (1986: 367) and Wylie (1980: 3) refer to a method where the prepared opium is placed inside the bowl, therefore requiring the flame to have actual contact with the bowl. This flame contact, they suggest, causes char marks on the smoking surface.

Opium-heating lamps (shown below in Figure 6.49) appear to be designed to prevent the flame from touching the opium or the bowl. As charring is only visible on some of the smoking-surface sherds, it seems likely that prepared opium required only the heat given off from an opium-smoking lamp to emit smoke – as opposed to actual contact with flame – otherwise all shards would display charring.

Moreover, the size of the opium needle inserted through the opium bowl's smoking surface aperture (any tapered implement could be used) appears to be only slightly smaller than the bowl aperture itself (Wylie & Higgins 1987: 325), commonly from 1 to 3 mm in diameter (Wylie & Fike 1993: 263). This would make it very difficult to place a ball of opium inside the bowl. Ritchie did note that some of the apertures had been enlarged up to 12 mm in diameter (Ritchie 1986: 368). However, a later study by Wylie and Fike (1993: 268) shows that worn or damaged bowl aperture was often deliberately enlarged to between 8.5 and 13.5 mm in diameter to enable replacement ceramic or metal aperture inserts to be fitted. The charring on opium-bowl surfaces appears more likely to represent bowls that have been held over the heat for too long, been used with a poorly burning lamp, a lamp with no shade, or with a substitute candle or other exposed flame.

Chinese markings – as opposed to decorations – appear on only one of the Chinaman's Point bowl sherds. These were made by a pressed stamp leaving raised (positive) characters on the lower section of the bowl, near the flange. According to Wylie & Fike (1993: 270), this is a common position for such stampings. They appear as two very faint symbols, almost touching each other but distinctly separate, one enclosed in a square figure. The characters are too faint to be recognisable and even from sites where they are legible such marks are often very difficult to interpret due to ambiguity in their meanings and their frequently fragmented state (Wylie & Fike 1993: 270).

**Opium-bowl connector**

Brass or copper connectors were used to attach the opium bowl to the pipe (Etter 1980: 99). Bowl connectors comprise a stem piece that fits into the pipe and an apron section that houses the bowl flange. Two cylindrical brass bowl connectors were recovered from Chinaman's Point. The flanged sections of both were either broken off or corroded away. One was recovered from the tidal zone of Chinaman's Point and the other was excavated from area 4. Both are 15 mm in diameter, stand 10 mm high, weigh 2 g each and have three concentric, negative (pressed inwards) rings on the outside body (figure 6.48). One still displays a small fragment of 'gee rag' cloth attached to its outer surface and both are internally blackened through use.

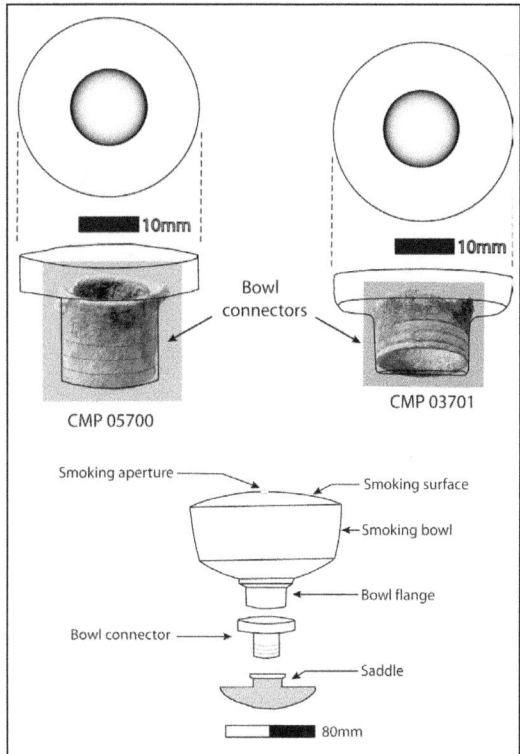

Figure 6.48 Opium-bowl connectors from the Chinaman's Point site (top) and diagram showing the connector's position between bowl and saddle.

**Opium-lamp cover**

Opium lamps comprise four archaeologically recoverable components: a base, a globular fuel reservoir, a wick support and a lamp cover (figure 6.49). An opium lamp's purpose is to provide a constant source of heat through an enclosed flame first to heat and then smoke opium – opium lamps also provided a source of light.

The minimum number of opium-lamp covers (table 6.23) was determined through upper rim/neck sections. Four fragments are of clear glass, one has a purple tinge and the remaining 14 are aqua-green. Five fragments were excavated from the base of the gutter system in area 3 and the remainder were recovered from the site's tidal zone. Lower portion body diameters are unavailable due to the broken pieces. All upper rim sections have a 35 mm outside diameter and range from 1 to 5 mm in neck length – from shoulder to upper rim (figure 6.50).

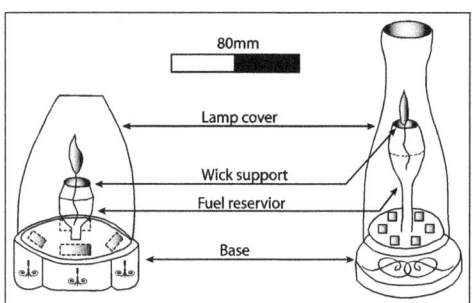

Figure 6.49 Two typical opium-lamp types.

135

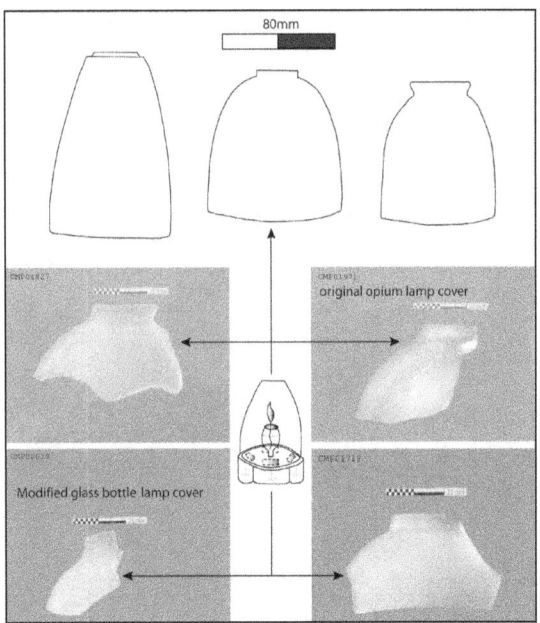

Figure 6.50 Three typical opium-lamp shades (top) and four opium-lamp shade fragments (bottom) from the Chinaman's Point site.

Wylie & Fike (1993: 288) report that glass opium lamps recovered from sites in the United States were probably manufactured in Birmingham, England and then transported to China before going to the United States. The same is probably true of opium lamps recovered from Australian sites. Two of the fragments have a smoothly ground rim surface and are likely to have been originally manufactured as opium lamp covers. The recovered fragments that were not originally manufactured as opium lamp covers are modified glass bottle sections. Such modified lamp covers have been noted at many overseas Chinese sites in the United States (Sisson & Harrison 1983: 4; Stapp 1990: 214) and New Zealand (Ritchie 1986: 369). There are two recorded Australian cases, both from sites in the Northern Territory Palmer goldfield region (Jack et al. 1984: 56; McCarthy 1986: 36). However, as both these are bottle base sections (the upper parts were not recovered) there is some doubt over their association with opium-lamp covers. Lamp covers found Ritchie (1986: 391) in New Zealand appear to have been manufactured by using a hot wire placed around the section of bottle that is to be snapped off – i.e. above and below the bottle shoulder. Hot wire placed around a glass bottle weakens the glass around the heated section and if struck enables a clean break along the fault line. This method appears to have been used to manufacture the opium-lamp covers recovered from Chinaman's Point.

Evidence by Ritchie (1986: 391) indicates that a small reservoir of oil or tallow with a secured wick was positioned inside the glass cover to produce the constant source of heat required to smoke opium.

**Alternative smoking method**

An opium consumer can obtain the desired analgesic effect through a variety of ways. Opium can be taken orally in pill, liquid, powder or raw form (snorted or mixed with water and injected intravenously), or it can be smoked through an opium pipe as pure resin or mixed with tobacco and smoked in a water or dry pipe or in a cigarette. To smoke opium the preferred Chinese way, the techniques for heating the resin and inhaling the fumes vary greatly. A number of distinctly modified bottle bases that are very likely associated with opium smoking have been identified from three separate archaeological sites in Australia – i.e. at Chinaman's Point; Little Lonsdale Street/Casselden Place, Melbourne and Cunningham Street, Sydney.

Archaeologist Lance Wackett recalls that approximately 30 of these bottle bases were excavated in 2003 from the Little Lonsdale Street/Casselden Place sites near Melbourne's Chinatown (Wackett 2006 pers. comm.). At the time of excavation "an old Chinese man" suggested the bases had an association with opium smoking (Wackett 2006 pers. comm.). However, this comment was not followed up at the time and the particular attributes of the bottle bases were not recorded in the artefact catalogue, hampering their retrieval from an assemblage of over 300 000 artefacts just from the Casselden Place collection. Any mention of the modified bases is also absent from the excavation report compiled by Godden Mackay Logan et al. (2004). In June 2006, a physical search – by the author – through a portion of the Little Lonsdale Street/Casselden Place artefact assemblage identified one of these bases.

A further six such artefacts were recovered by Austral Archaeology in 2004 from the Cunningham Street archaeological excavation in Sydney, an area also historically known to have had a large Chinese presence. The land developer for this project went into liquidation before the archaeological work was finished, therefore the artefact catalogue and archaeological report have not been completed (Wackett 2006 pers. comm.). In Galloway's examination of archaeological evidence for opium smoking, she noted these bases, provided pictorial evidence and gave an interpretation of how they may have been used in association with opium smoking (2005: 112–13). She states:

> the pontil was chipped away to make a small hole and the bases were simply broken from the bottle. There was no uniformity in the length of the bottle sides, some were broken at the base, others further up. They may have been used inverted over a tin of fuel with the wick protruding through the hole. The concave shape of the bottle base may concentrate the heat for cooking the opium.

This suggested method of use seems unlikely because, due to the rough break, the bases would be extremely unstable in an inverted position. It is more likely that they were used in a standing bottle position.

Through comparing the bases from each of the three sites, aspects of uniformity have been noted. For example, each modified base was produced from a dark green (black) glass bottle with a deep push-up section. The bottles' centre pontil sections have been chipped away to create a hole consistently between 10 and 20 mm in diameter. The broken bottle sides vary in length, but do have some consistency as each has at least one broken section that traverses to the bottle's base, which in some examples displays a point of impact on the basal rim, clearly indicating a deliberate act of modification (figure 6.51).

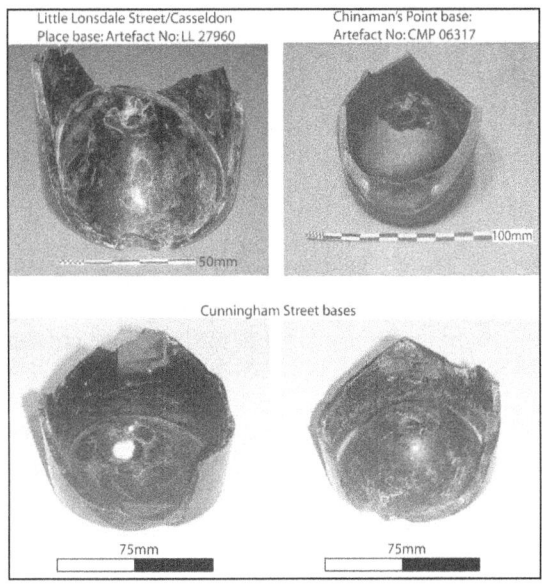

Figure 6.51 Modified bottle bases for the purpose of opium smoking.

An alternative to Galloway's interpretation is that these artefacts were used in a process called 'chasing the dragon'. The term 'chasing the dragon' is presently associated with the smoking of heroin, a powdered derivative of opium. When heroin powder is placed on tin foil and heated from below, it turns a sticky brown and gives off smoke fumes. As thick plumes of smoke fumes rise – giving the appearance of a mythical flying Chinese dragon – they are followed (chased) by the smoker and inhaled through a rolled-up newspaper, magazine or other tube-type object, hence the term 'chasing the dragon' (www.biopsychiatry.com/heroin.htm). This same method can be used to smoke marijuana hashish resin and would also be suitable for smoking opium resin, which is very similar in appearance and consistency.

In the absence of a complete traditional Chinese opium smoking pipe and associated implements, the modified bottle bases would have made a very effective alternative for 'chasing the dragon'. A small oil lamp or candle could be placed under a base with the flame protruding through the hole. A piece of metal such as a reinforcing strip from an opium can (figure 6.53 below) or a 'funs tray' (figure 6.54 below) with opium placed on it could be suspended across the broken bottle sides and heated by the central flame. The section where the bottle sides are broken to the base level would provide easy hand access to position the metal support and opium. Once the opium resin became hot enough to produce smoke, 'chasing the dragon' could begin (figure 6.52). The cost to produce one of these smoking devices would be minimal, they are robust and could be re-used indefinitely. This functional explanation is, however, speculative and open to further interpretation.

Figure 6.52 Potential method of modified bottle-base use. Painting by blaked beans design 2007.

**Opium can**

Opium for smoking was usually exported from China to Australia by the can. With the appearance and consistency of thick molasses (Wylie & Fike 1993: 261), a can contained approximately 186.5 g of opium (Ritchie 1986: 378). Several grades of opium were available, according to the quality of the morphine content and taste when smoked (Wylie & Higgins 1987: 322). In Australia, Jack et al. (1984: 53) and McCarthy (1986: 42) have recorded opium can remains at overseas Chinese sites in the Northern Territory; Smith (2003: 27; 2006: 996) has noted their occurrence in assemblages from New South Wales; Chandler (2005: 62–63) located opium cans in a private collection in Victoria's Upper Ovens district; opium cans were found at Dolly's Creek in Victoria (Lawrence 2007 pers. comm.) and Gaughwin (1995: 235) recovered opium cans from Chinese sites in north-eastern Tasmania. When complete, opium cans typically measure 95 mm tall and 66 by 41 mm in base proportion (Ritchie 1986: 378; Sando & Felton 1993: 167). Made from lightweight brass, they are usually recovered in the form of crushed or segmented containers. Ritchie (1986: 378) gives the best indication of their manufacture, stating that 0.2 mm thick brass sheeting – frequently with impressed Chinese characters on the lid and base – was bent, folded and soldered together to form the base, body and lid sections. A heavier 0.5 mm thick reinforcing strip was used as a rim to seal the interior of the can (figure 6.53). Opium cans are also often recovered with pasted orange Chinese paper labels (Ritchie 1986: 378).

The minimum number of opium cans (table 6.23) was estimated through linear measurements of interior reinforcing strip seals. One section of opium cans was excavated from area 4 and the remainder were recovered from the tidal zone. Six crumpled corner can sections were recovered, but are not sufficient to obtain accurate measurements of the complete article and show no visible paper labels or Chinese character impressions. Twenty-one pieces of reinforcing strip were recovered, many still showing traces of the solder that once secured them to the opium can. The strips are 0.5 mm thick, between 7 to 14 mm wide and of various broken lengths, the longest measuring 50 mm. Two of the reinforcing strips display modification in the form of nail holes and others appear to have been deliberately cut with snips. The purpose of these post-manufacture modifications are unknown, however as noted by Ritchie (1986: 387–90), empty opium cans were often modified, for example to make 'funs trays' used to hold a portion of opium (figure 6.54), brass strip ties (similar to a modern day tie-tag), gambling tokens, brass washers, brackets, candleholders, funnels and lamp-wick holders.

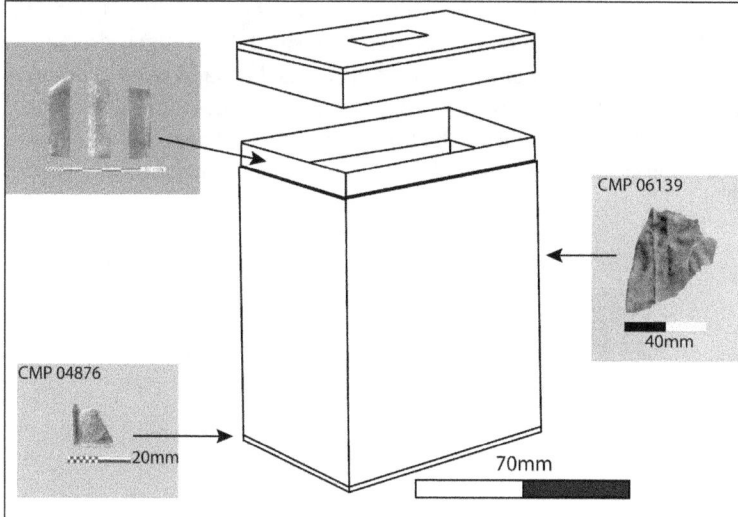

Figure 6.53 Reinforcing strips (top left) and other opium-can pieces from the Chinaman's Point site.

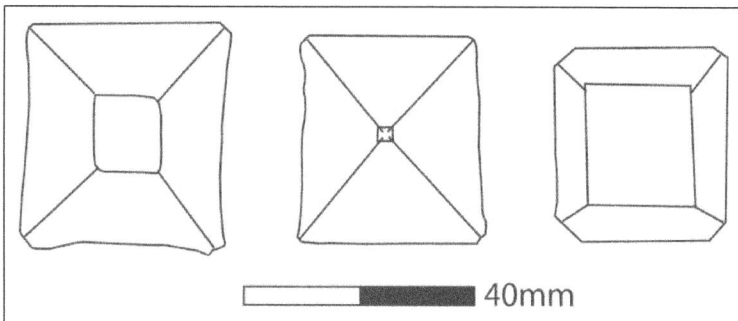

Figure 6.54 Opium cans modified into 'funs trays', used to hold a portion of opium. Drawing after Ritchie 1986: 389.

## UNIDENTIFIED

There are several items recovered from Chinaman's Point whose purpose cannot be determined. The largest group of these are the heavily corroded nondescript metals, likely to be predominantly pieces of cask hoop-iron. Typically in the form of small, flat, thin, corroded metal fragments, it is not possible to determine their original function. These represent 8155 pieces, weighing 16.229 kg. A sample of 150 pieces, weighing 204 g has been retained and subjected to a conservation program to arrest the corroding process and the remainder have been discarded.

Two links of corroded chain, weighing 12.5 g were recovered from the site's tidal zone. The links have 25 by 30 mm oval dimensions and are made from iron approximately 6 mm thick. These pieces could be associated with either domestic or industrial components of the site, but it is not possible to identify them any further.

Two pieces of leather 4 mm thick and weighing 4.9 g were excavated from area 4 of the site. They were recovered side-by-side in a very fragile condition and appear to have been cut from a larger piece. One piece is 35 by 26 mm and the other is 25 by 20 mm. Their appearance is plain with no holes or deliberate markings. Leather is a very versatile material and these artefacts could have been used at the site in a number of industrial or domestic capacities.

## CONCLUSION

Analysis of the industrial and domestic artefacts recovered from Chinaman's Point shows that a range of activities were performed at the site. Information concerning commercial activities, industrial and domestic equipment used, dietary habits and recreational activities have been ascertained.

Comparative analysis indicates that the collection represents a fairly typical colonial-period overseas Chinese site that is broadly consistent with historical documentary records. Analysis of the artefact assemblage has provided further comparative data for overseas Chinese sites and, in some cases, has facilitated alternative explanations for overseas Chinese activities. Industrial components from the site leave no doubt that it was a Chinese fish-curing establishment and that the site's occupants caught fish themselves. The material remains discussed in this chapter form the basis of a general site analysis in the following chapter and facilitate estimates of the period of occupation of the site.

# CHAPTER 7

# OCCUPATION DATES AND SITE INTERPRETATION

This chapter discusses some of the more important information from the artefact analysis, including the dating of the site's material remains. A discussion is advanced on the relationship between the Chinaman's Point fish curers and the larger overseas Chinese community. Evidence of the existence of a controlling force behind the site's operations, composition of the labouring workforce and the possible number of site occupants is examined. The activities performed on site are then summarised, followed by an examination of the site's fish-curing methods and the equipment used. In this chapter, it is necessary to reiterate (as succinctly as possible) some of the historical evidence discussed in previous chapters.

## OCCUPATION DATES

The material remains from Chinaman's Point have revealed much new information for historical archaeology in Australia. However, to obtain accurate beginning and end dates for the site occupation period, a more focused analysis of the artefact collection is required. The following section uses a broad assortment of artefacts from the site to establish – in conjunction with the historical documents discussed in chapter 2 – a site-occupation period.

To aid the site-dating process, two formulas for dating historical sites are briefly discussed, early overseas Chinese activities in Victoria are considered and the methods of dating of Chinese ceramics is explored. This is followed by an examination of the available material remains and documentary evidence.

The exercise results in a very good understanding of how long overseas Chinese people ran a commercially viable fish-curing operation at Chinaman's Point. It was possible to identify the site's abandonment period more accurately than the initial occupation period.

## DATING METHOD

Until recently, South's (1977: 217) mean ceramic date formula was often used in dating historical sites. South's formula uses averages of site-specific ceramic manufacture dates (also adaptable to other materials) to establish possible occupation periods. Recent works by Adams (2003: 30–40) and Brooks (2005: 53–55), however, demonstrate that South's mean ceramic date formula contains a number of unpredictable distortions that undermine the validity of the data obtained. While South's formula does have some useful applications, it will not be applied to material remains from the Chinaman's Point site.

Time lag is defined as the period between when an item was manufactured to when it fell into disuse, becoming part of the archaeological record (Adams and Gaw 1977: 218). In a detailed evaluation of time lag, Adams (2003) notes that sites with a short occupation time or known start period "should be expected to contain few if any ceramics made in that decade because it takes time for these objects to be broken and discarded" (Adams 2003: 38). Storage, transport, item lifespan and recycling are elements that can create time lags, potentially decades long (Brooks 2005: 54). Issues of time lag can only be effectively addressed when artefacts or artefact assemblages display a specific period and place of manufacture. The wide range of artefacts from the Chinaman's Point site seldom reveals such specific dates. While issues of time lag will be considered where applicable, as with the mean ceramic date formula, time lag is unsuitable to aid in dating the Chinaman's Point site.

In order to date this site, recovered artefacts are examined for their own unique dating features. Once artefactual information has been extracted, documentary and material evidence are considered together to establish when and for how long Chinese fish-curing activity occurred at the site.

## HISTORICAL SETTING

When investigating Chinese sites in Victoria, an earliest possible date of occupation can be easily established. Historically, the first group of Chinese people known to have entered Victoria arrived in December 1848 when 219 men were contracted as labourers for the rapidly growing pastoral industry (Cronin 1982: 4). Their activities are reasonably well documented and none, as far as it is known, entered the fishing industry or any other industry during their first few years in the colony. By 1854, Victoria's gold rush had been gaining momentum for three years, enticing many nationalities, including more than 5000 Chinese people to seek a share of the wealth (Moore & Tully 2000: 4). A year later, Victoria's Chinese population had increased to over 11 500 and over the next four years this figure almost tripled (Cronin 1982: 141). Against this background, it is unlikely that historical sites in Victoria could have had Chinese occupation before 1848. Many thousands of Chinese people stayed in Victoria after the gold-rush period, leaving an end date for Chinese sites in Victoria open to site-specific historical and material examination.

An earlier, European occupation of the site is unlikely, as this area was originally uninhabitable swampland that was deliberately channelled and drained by the Chinese to create small (approximately 10 by 10 m), dry working areas. Europeans are not historically known to have undertaken such processes to create only a small working area. However, such methods were and still are the custom in many regions of China (Knapp 1989: 20, 68; Mote 1977: 197). Furthermore, early European settlement in Gippsland was centred on pastoral rather than coastal industry.

## CHINESE CERAMICS

The majority of ceramics (97.5%) recovered from the site were of Chinese form, decoration and origin. Such a large proportion of Chinese compared to European wares justifies a brief discussion of the dating potential for Chinese ceramics.

Much of the knowledge concerning the dating of Chinese ceramics – including earthenware, stoneware and porcelain – comes from work conducted by Jones (1992) and Stenger (1993) at historical sites in the United States. Chinese porcelain is often difficult to date, as the shape and decorative style of some vessels continued unchanged in some cases for up to 17 centuries and it often displays no maker's mark or very ambiguous marks (Lenz 1920: 395; Beals & Steele 1981: 7; Stenger 1993: 315). Stenger (1993), building on the early work of Kaplan (1952), conducted highly magnified visual examinations of Chinese glazes and discovered a broadly datable variation in glaze opacity. During the Song Dynasty (960–1280 AD), Chinese potters used an ash glazing flux produced from bracken ferns to create a barely opaque finish on porcelains. In the Ming Dynasty (1368–1643 AD) potters used feldspar, a mineral flux that produced a noticeably clearer glaze. By the Quin Dynasty (1644–1911 AD) potters had switched back to plant ash as a fluxing agent, only this time the ash left a slight bubble pattern in the glaze (Stenger 1993: 316). Although magnified visual identification is a very useful technique for identifying dynastic periods, it is not accurate enough to be useful when dating Australian historical sites.

Chinese stoneware vessels (brown and green glazed) produced as storage containers, generally display little or no decoration. Like porcelain items, their shape and style was often unchanged for many centuries (Quellmalz 1976: 292). Chinese brown glaze is produced from iron mineral extracted from sedimentary river silt; green glaze differs only in that it has crushed colour extracts mixed with the silt (Wood 1999: 137, 224). Some success in dating Chinese stoneware has been achieved through the use of X-ray fluorescence spectroscopy and optical emission spectroscopy. These two methods identify, source and collate trace elements such as nickel, copper, lead and manganese, which in conjunction with historical records may identify which region and what potter produced an item under examination. These methods are only accurate to within approximately one century and are often too expensive for general site-dating purposes (Stenger 1993: 321). Stoneware vessels dominate the ceramics recovered from most Chinese sites in Australasia and the United States. As yet, no adequate methods have been developed for dating these items. The use of artefact association combined with historical documentation remains the most accessible and appropriate method for dating Chinese (and European) wares from historical sites.

## DATABLE ARTEFACTS

There is a wide range of colonial-period artefacts that have historically documented dates of manufacture. These often provide the only means of ascertaining meaningful occupation dates for a site. The artefacts discussed in this section are metal nails, buttons, window glass, bottle glass and European ceramics.

### Nails

The difficulty of dating nails has been discussed in chapter 6. Of the 76 nails recovered from Chinaman's Point that were recognisable and datable, 20 were machine-cut square/rectangle shaft, rose-head type nails commonly available in Australia from 1810 to the 1870s. The remaining 56 were hard drawn, round shaft, wire rose head type nails generally used in Australia from 1853 to the 1890s (Varman 1980: 108).

Throughout their production periods, cut plate and round shaft rose head nails were imported from England, Europe and the United States and were also produced in Australia (Varman 1993: 169). Initial prejudice by builders, re-use issues and uncertainty over whether the nails were imported or produced locally are factors that create highly variable determinates. Any attempt to apply factors of time lag to an artefact with such highly variable features would result in meaningless estimates of site-occupation periods. In the case of nails from Australian assemblages, it is more practical to simply work within the dates established by Varman (1993: 211) for the period during which each nail type was commonly available (figure 7.1). Varman's estimates suggest that the nails from Chinaman's Point were commonly used in Australia from 1810 to 1890, enabling slightly better than broad dates to be established for the site.

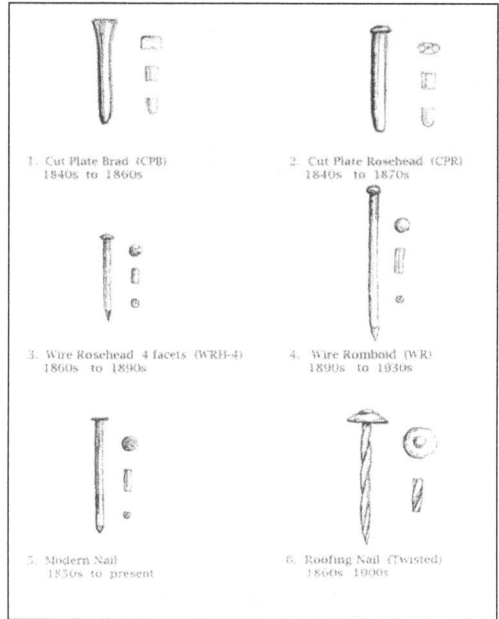

Figure 7.1 Selection of common nail types from Australian sites. Estimated dates by Varman 1993: 211.

## Clothing buttons

Many button types have markings that enable accurate dates of manufacture to be ascertained (Houart 1977: 18; George 1999: 66; Lindbergh 1999: 50). Buttons, like nails, also have a high re-use rate; so at best can only indicate general site occupation dates (Kirk 1975: 299–30; Cameron 1985: 17). Six machine-made buttons were recovered from the site (figure 6.45). Five of these were plain machine-pressed, opaque milk glass, two-hole, British-style utilitarian buttons that fall within the manufacturing period 1880 to 1890. Vast quantities of these machine-made buttons were imported from England during this time (Epstein 1968: 62). The remaining button was a four-hole, pressed copper alloy fastener, with 'BEST MAKE' stamped into the metal. Press manufactured buttons stamped with words denoting quality such as 'best make' have a production period beginning in the early 1800s (Luscomb 1974: 18). Cameron's (1985: 20–27) chronology of metal buttons suggests that this type of button was manufactured in Britain from 1850 to 1900.

## Window glass

The majority of flat glass entering Australia during the colonial period was produced in England (Boow 1991: 102). Jones & Sullivan (1989: 172) give two main reasons for exercising caution in using window glass to date site-occupation periods. Firstly, window glass was often in use at a site for many years before it moved into the archaeological record and secondly, the present methods of dating window glass (generally through a measurement of thickness) can be ambiguous as early glass thickness could vary even within one window pane. Jones & Sullivan, however, suggest that when used with caution, window glass may provide a useful indication of initial site occupation period. The two types of window glass recovered from Chinaman's Point were crown type (1800–70) and improved flattened cylinder type (1834–1910) (Boow 1991: 100–02). Combined with the nail data, this may enable a date for shelter/house construction at the site to be estimated. Window glass can also be safely used to complement other data from the site.

## Bottle glass

Changing methods of manufacture during the mid 19th to early 20th centuries have resulted in a sound chronology of physical characteristics of glass bottles (Jones 1971: 63). From the late 19th to early 20th centuries, newly invented machines began outclassing the existing method of hand-blowing glass vessels (Miller & Sullivan 1984: 104). By 1920, the vast majority of bottles produced in or entering Australia were fully machine made and are easily identified through their characteristic machine mould markings (Boow 1991: 70). Terms used here to describe the basic bottle components from the top down are: finish, neck, shoulder, body and base (after Jones 1986: 34).

Table 7.1 illustrates the fragmentary nature of the glass assemblage. Fragmentary assemblages are not ideal for dating purposes, however bottle attributes such as base, finish, turn marks, embossing, engraving, stamping and seals can still be used to obtain a good indication of period (Dumbrell 1983: 34). See table 7.2 for an assessment of datable glass-bottle shards according to manufacture periods and percentages.

| Glass colour | Nomber of shards | Weight (grams) | MNI |
|---|---|---|---|
| Dark green | 2993 | 52641 | 278 |
| Light green | 6646 | 86384 | 247 |
| Aqua-green | 2591 | 25978 | 196 |
| Amber | 1236 | 14617 | 90 |
| Light blue | 78 | 568 | 4 |
| Aqua-blue | 168 | 1559 | 22 |
| Clear | 285 | 1859 | 8 |
| Total | 13997 | 183606 | 845 |

Table 7.1 Colour, number of shards and MNI for glass bottles.

| Date range | Percentage |
|---|---|
| 1820 to 1920 | 3.9 |
| 1850 to 1920 | 40.2 |
| 1860 to 1920 | 17.2 |
| 1875 to 1920 | 37 |
| 1900 to 1920 | 1.7 |

Table 7.2 Breakdown of datable glass bottle shards.

### Bases

Various forms of English, European and American makers' marks enabled 20-four base shards to be identified as having been manufactured within the period 1860 to 1890. No specific early dates were detected on bottle markings. The latest makers' mark was from John Lesson's Cordial Factory in Alberton. This factory was local to the Port Albert district and was only in operation from 1901 to 1907. As this bottle was produced locally, issues of time lag are considered marginal. Of those bottles datable through stylistic changes, 96% were ascertained as having been manufactured between 1850 and 1920. A small number of bases display a manufacture period between 1920 to present. These most likely represent the discards from picnickers, pleasure walkers and recreational fishing people after the site fell into disuse by the Chinese.

### Mamelons

Mamelons, sometimes called vent marks, are protruding, rounded lumps of glass often positioned in the centre of a bottle base (figure 7.2). Mamelons are formed through the action of molten glass forced out of vent holes in a bottle mould. These holes are designed to allow air to escape the mould as a bottle is formed (Boow 1991: 48). Jones & Sullivan (1989: 47) suggest that bottles displaying mamelons were only produced from 1875 to 1920. Eighteen percent (221 bases) of bases recovered from Chinaman's Point display push ups with mamelons.

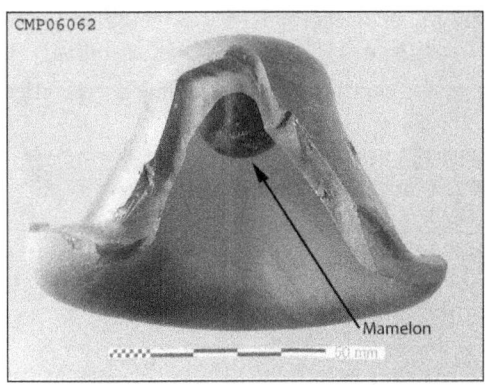

Figure 7.2 Base from Chinaman's Point with a deep push up and large mamelon.

### Finishes

Finishes allow a sequence of datable stylistic changes to be observed (Jones 1986: 36). The crack off and applied single collar types only enable very broad dates, approximately from 1820 to 1920, to be ascertained and represent 14% (43 finishes) of the finishes recovered. The remaining 86% (289 finishes) have various forms of applied finish such as double collar, foil covered, blob top, cod variant, champagne, crown and external screw types each dating to the 1850 to 1920 period (Boow 1991: 117).

### Turn marks

Turn marks are clearly distinguishable on the outer surface of hand-blown bottles that have been rotated in a bottle mould. The inner surfaces of two-piece bottle moulds were often pasted with water or lanolin to create a layer of steam between the molten glass and the mould. The blown bottle was then spun in the mould, leaving distinct turn marks in the glass (figure 7.3). This procedure produced a seam-free, smooth, outer-glass surface (Boow 1991: 8). Paste and turn methods were in use from approximately 1870 to 1920, thereby enabling good manufacture dates to be identified for glass shards displaying these markings. Twenty-five percent (3310 shards) of glass from the Chinaman's Point site show turn marks on their outer surface.

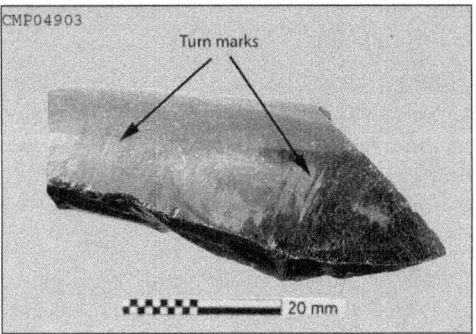

Figure 7.3 Turn marks visible on a shard of amber-coloured bottle glass from the Chinaman's Point site.

Bottle attributes from the site demonstrate the wide range of bottle manufacturing processes used during Australia's colonial period. These basic bottle elements enable a broad indication of the Chinaman's Point bottle production dates and their contents. Bottle dates from the site span a period of 100 years, from 1820 to 1920. The majority of recovered bottles were in common use in Australia from the 1860s to the 1900s.

### European ceramics

The non-decorative and unmarked shards of European bone china and salt-glazed stoneware found at the Chinaman's Point site are not very useful for dating purposes.

The Asiatic pheasant and Rhine transfer print patterns are both commonly recovered from Australian sites. On white ware material, the Asiatic pheasant pattern dates from 1834 to 1890 and the Rhine pattern from 1820 to 1890 (Coysh & Henrywood 1986: 29, 286, 301).

Majewski & O'Brien (1987: 161) and Brooks (2005: 36) suggest that plain white ware with a regular horizontal decorative band (such as the maroon banded white ware from Chinaman's Point) was produced after 1860.

A printed maker's mark was visible on the underside of a ceramic plate shard. This was identified as the B & L beehive symbol from Hill's Pottery in Britain, which was in use from 1862 to 1890 (Godden 1991: 117).

The manufacture dates for European ceramic from the Chinaman's Point site show – as do the glass bottles – broad production periods that begin in the 1800s (table 7.3).

| European ceramic | Pattern | Date range | Percentage |
|---|---|---|---|
| White ware (plate) | Rhine | 1820 to 1890 | 16.4 |
| White ware (plate) | Asiatic pheasant | 1860 to 1890 | 4.7 |
| White ware (plate) | Maroon band | After 1860 | 4.0 |
| Bone china (cup) | Plain | 1800 to present | 4.0 |
| Stoneware (jar) | Salt glaze | 1800 to present | 8.6 |

Table 7.3 Breakdown of datable European ceramics and their percentage of the total ceramic collection.

## Discussion

An examination of the datable artefacts places the Chinaman's Point site confidently within the second half of the 19th century. Nails, buttons, window glass, bottle glass and European ceramics strongly suggested 1850 to 1860 as an initial site occupation period and 1901 to 1907 as the site abandonment period. The greater portion of datable items is from the 1870 to 1900 period. The most rewarding artefacts for determining occupation periods were the glass and ceramics. No artefacts were capable of yielding an exact date of manufacture, however it was possible in several cases to identify good manufacture date ranges, the tightest dating from 1901 to 1907.

As discussed in chapter 2, the relevant non-primary historical documents individually could not be considered reliable sources of information. However, when viewed in conjunction with the site's material remains they – as with the artefacts – suggest an initial site occupation period in the 1860s. The latest evidence of payment of a land residence licence fee (primary documentary evidence discussed in chapter 2) was in early 1904 and allowed legal occupancy until early 1905. This again complements the material record. The land title documents show that payments could be missed for two or three years and then backpayed, making it possible that the Chinese stayed on site for several years after the last recorded payment. A periodic occupation of the site must also be considered probable.

The only item worth discussing in relation to time lag is the Hill's Pottery beehive symbol, dating from 1862 to 1890. As it has a known place and date of manufacture, time lag elements could be applied to estimate when this item arrived on site. However, as many of the other recovered artefacts have a possible manufacture period before 1862 and after 1890, this exercise would not result in the discovery of any significant new information.

During the mid 1860s, Port Albert was in its heyday and thousands of Chinese miners passed through the town on their way to goldfields in the Gippsland region (Lennon 1975: 216). The Chinese on the Gippsland goldfields would also have provided an excellent market for cured fish, which in turn makes the 1860s an opportunistic period for a fish-curing site to have been established.

Through collating general aspects of Chinese activities in Victoria, material evidence and non-primary and primary historical documentation, a good indication of the initial occupation period has been identified for the site at Chinaman's Point. The combination of material and documentary evidence indicates Port Albert's Chinese fish-curing establishment was occupied for approximately 40 years, from the 1860s to the early 1900s.

## SITE INTERPRETATION

### Broader overseas Chinese community

Chinese fish-curing activities represent just one element of a much larger overseas Chinese community in colonial Australia. Identifying Chinese fish-curing establishments in association with the broader Chinese community is important to the overall understanding of early Chinese activities in Australia. The main reason for the existence of fish-curing sites was to supply cured fish to the overseas Chinese gold miners. This satisfied the most culturally important part of the standard Chinese diet (Herklots & Lin 1964: 6; Anderson 1970: 7; Wang 1920: 293) and would have assisted greatly in maintaining Chinese cultural life.

Fish-curing sites were designed to obtain fresh fish, produce a cured product and assemble the merchandise for transport. This required a substantial level of infrastructure and organisation in order to procure workers (especially ones with knowledge of fish-curing processes), equipment, everyday supplies, transport of the cured product and broader distribution and marketing beyond the site. During the peak period of Chinese population in colonial Australia – approximately the mid 1850s to the 1870s (Horsely 1879: 417; Choi 1975: 20, 22) – fish-curing operations were financed by Chinese merchants, as in the case of Chin Ateak (*Votes and Proceedings of the New South Wales Legislative Assembly* 1879–80, vol. 3: 1224). The Chinaman's Point artefact analysis provided further evidence for merchant involvement and was very useful in determining the site-specific aspects of a Chinese fish-curing site in colonial Australia.

The artefacts found at Chinaman's Pont confirm that the residents had regular contact with suppliers of Chinese goods and with the European population to purchase European-manufactured commodities. New information gained from the excavation and artefact analysis explains how the site functioned, how the occupants lived and worked and aspects of their social and economic interactions. It has been established that the site occupants themselves fished (often at night), did their own boat maintenance, brined fresh fish before drying them on racks, weighed and purchased fish, interacted on site with European people in a mutually beneficial manner, prepared and ate meals, socialised and conducted recreational activities all within the site bounds.

Chapter 4 showed that colonial-period overseas Chinese fish-curing establishments were generating substantial sums of money through the sale of cured fish (*Bendigo Advertiser* 1857, January 5; *The Gippslander* 1865, November 10; Parliamentary Debate, *Votes and Proceedings of the South Australian Legislative Council* 1861, 858; *Votes and Proceedings of the New South Wales Legislative Assembly* 1879–80, vol. 3: 1224). However, the artefacts from Chinaman's Point do not display wealth, affluence or any elements of material comfort much above essential requirements. On this basis, the following section examines the evidence for a controlling force behind the site's operations. The likely social status of the site workers is also discussed.

## Site workings

### Merchant involvement

The material evidence for Chinese merchant control of the Chinaman's Point site is indirect. Etter (1980: 100) and Wylie & Higgins (1987: 346) argue that stoneware opium smoking bowls were dearer than earthenware varieties and hence less likely to be recovered from overseas Chinese worker camps. A minimum of two stoneware opium smoking bowls are the only items above basic quality recovered from Chinaman's Point. All other material remains (except perhaps specific site requirements such as weighing scales) are standard utilitarian wares or, like the cheapest meat cuts and home made-net sinkers, reflect the most economical option. Accordingly, the Chinaman's Point artefact assemblage is indicative of lower-class overseas Chinese occupation and shows that large sums of money were not at the disposal of the site occupants.

It is unlikely, due to the large amount of money generated from the sale of cured fish, that these basic living conditions simply reflect the common perception that most income from overseas Chinese activity was shipped back to family in China (Wu 1982: 93; Chou 1993: 76) or that overseas Chinese populations were exceptionally thrifty (Gittins 1981: 72).

A percentage – possibly even the majority – of money earned by individual overseas Chinese workers was obligatorily – and usually willingly – sent back to immediate family in China (Choi 1975: 13; Chou 1993: 76). With the remaining portion, overseas workers could – with the aid of kinship contacts – set about improving their own personal social ranking and through this, that of their family back in China (Hwang 1976: 6; Yang 1994: 123). This traditional Chinese social behaviour has been noted in many overseas Chinese communities such as Wu (1982) and Inglis (1975) for Papua New Guinea, Willmott (1960) for Indonesia, Moench (1963) for Tahiti, Watson (1975) for England and importantly Smith (2006) for New South Wales and – as described above in chapter 3 – in Victoria through the case of Louey Ah Mouy.

Individuals or groups of overseas Chinese people holding status and wealth can be recognised historically and archaeologically from the working classes through a more lavish selection of personal possessions (for example see Horsely 1879; Oddie 1961; Jones 1990; and Gungwu 1992). Pictorial evidence from Australia's colonial period reveals displays of overseas Chinese people striving – through poise and attire – to appear to their Chinese compatriots and to European eyes prosperous and socially advanced (see for example pictorial evidence in www.chia.chinesemuseum.com.au). If the workers at Chinaman's Point were personally earning the large monetary sums associated with fish curing, this would almost certainly be reflected in their personal and occupational possessions, architecture at the site and their presence in the Port Albert community. Instead, the modest nature of the material remains indicates clearly that the site residents themselves were not receiving the large sums of money they were generating. The specific individual (or group) who profited from the fish-curing operations at Chinaman's Point is unknown, but through general historical information on overseas Chinese social systems, Chinese merchant involvement seems highly likely.

Further evidence for Chinese merchant involvement at Chinaman's Point can be inferred through the lack of material house remains. In chapter 5, historical documents were used to show that at least one dwelling at Chinaman's Point was a substantial, sturdy house made of palings (PROV, VPRS 5357/P0000, unit 5899). During the 1850s, ships arriving in Melbourne from Hong Kong and Singapore would carry as many as thirty prefabricated wooden houses per voyage (Syme 1987: 207). On 9 July 1870, the *Australian Town and Country Journal* reported on both of the Chinese fish-curing establishments at Lake Macquarie, New South Wales, stating "They have each two or three very comfortable slab cottages ... which is more than can be said of all the European dwelling-houses on the lake". Evidence from California describes Chinese imported prefabricated houses that were "infinitely superior and more substantial than those erected by the Yankees" and "built chiefly of logs of wood, or scantling [timber palings]" (Frost 1853: 100).

Research on the Chinese gold-rush period migrants generally agrees that the credit–ticket system was active and that participating merchants were under obligation to supply rations and accommodation to their indebted workers (Yong 1977: 1; Wang 1978: 89; Cronin 1982: 19). In remote regions where fish-curing establishments were often situated, such as Chinaman's Point and Lake Macquarie, prefabricated houses would have been ideal for merchants requiring immediate lodgings for a working crew.

The frugal nature of the site's material remains is inconsistent with the substantial (approximately 8.5 by 10m) house at Chinaman's Point. The lack of material remains of a dwelling, the availability of easily constructed (and deconstructed) prefabricated Chinese houses and the likely benefits of such housing for Chinese merchants is good evidence to suggest that a prefabricated house existed at Chinaman's Point. The cost of purchasing or importing a Chinese prefabricated house in colonial Victoria is unknown, but it probably exceeded the financial means of lower-class overseas Chinese workers. Therefore, a Chinese merchant may have supplied the house and removed it at a later period. This provides an explanation for the absence of house-remains at the site.

Strong historical evidence and some archaeological inference suggest that Chinese merchants were behind the founding and management of the Chinaman's Point site (and, very likely, Chinese fish-curing activities in colonial Australia more broadly). The site's merchant would have financed much of the domestic and industrial material remains recovered from Chinaman's Point. The identity of the workers to whom these commodities were supplied is now examined.

**The workforce**

Similarities in artefact assemblages suggest that workers at Chinaman's Point were of the same social standing and had the same economic means as overseas Chinese gold miners or market gardeners of the period. Six utilitarian, men's-style buttons from working clothes were the only artefacts of a personal nature recovered from Chinaman's Point. There was no evidence for the presence of women or children at the site. Similar to the interpretation of the material evidence for merchant activities, a lack of personal artefacts can be used to make inferences about the site workers.

Yong (1977: 1) estimates that 80% of overseas Chinese people in colonial Victoria arrived under the credit–ticket system. Wang (1978: 305) and Cronin (1982: 18) argue that these people were bound to their creditor (under debt bondage) for at least one year, possibly more. For the controlling merchants, this would have created an itinerant workforce and a high turnover rate of workers. Indebted overseas Chinese workers would have likely travelled with only basic, valued and well-guarded possessions and their overseas wage would not have allowed for many purchases of personal items. This theory suggests a reason for the lack of personal material remains recovered from Chinaman's Point.

As argued in chapter 3, it is highly likely that labour for Chinaman's Point was procured through the credit–ticket system. Whatever the employment method, at least some of the workers at Chinaman's Point would have required knowledge of fishing and fish curing. In traditional Chinese society, fishermen are placed among the lowest occupational class (Diamond 1969: 3). Fishing families were generally very poor (Anderson 1970: 7) and often lived in perpetual debt (Ward 1959: 44). Nevertheless, there were a huge number of commercial fishing families living in China's Kwangtung Province due to the region's extensive waterways and demand for fish (Ward 1954: 196; Choi 1975: 5; Brienes 1983: 26). Therefore, among the lower-class Chinese destined for overseas goldfields, especially under the credit–ticket system, there would likely have been a good quantity of fishermen.

Direct, on-site, merchant involvement is not evident from the site's material remains. This suggests that a headman (perhaps a merchant aspirant) was responsible for overseeing the daily operations at Chinaman's Point. The actual site workers appear to have been lower-class overseas Chinese men – probably former fishermen themselves – who were willing to work to pay off their passage for the chance (through gold) to relieve themselves and their immediate family from the hardships of 19th-century life in China.

Smith (2006) has examined the location and structural features of overseas Chinese communities in rural south-eastern New South Wales. He demonstrates that two distinctly separate types of mid to late 19th- century Chinese settlements existed (in his study area and in other Australian regions). One settlement type is a 'central place', broadly defined as a large overseas Chinese community where the infrastructure (such as Chinese temples and cemeteries) and commodities required to sustain a traditional, self-sufficient Chinese community are assembled, held and redistributed to smaller settlements and, importantly, where Chinese merchants resided. The other settlement type represents a much smaller community living in satellite settlements which were usually task specific – generally mining. These communities were self contained but not self sufficient and their Chinese population was largely dependent on the nearest 'central place' for food supplies and other necessities. The highest ranking resident at these satellite settlements was probably a Chinese headman.

Parallels between Chinese mining satellite settlements and the Chinaman's Point fish-curing camp are clearly visible. For example, Chinaman's Point consisted of a small, self-contained, task-specific (fish curing) working-class Chinese community. The site occupants relied on an outside 'central place' (probably the Chinese community in Melbourne) for the commodities required to sustain a traditional lifestyle, and during its peak period of operation the settlement appears to have been run by a Chinese headman. Smith's (2006: 209–52) theories on overseas Chinese organisation of settlements suggest that Chinese fish-curing establishments were part of a broader network of overseas Chinese activities in colonial Australia.

## Number of occupants

Historical evidence (discussed in chapter 4) suggests that where Chinese people fished and cured fish, up to 16 Chinese workers could be employed, but for operations that only cured fish, two to four people were sufficient. The lack of material remains for a domestic dwelling, lack of personal items and the unknown quantity of artefact removal from site-scavenging activities hampers an accurate estimation of occupation numbers at Chinaman's Point. Importantly, it is likely that the residents at Chinaman's Point fished and cured fish for the whole site-occupation period, as opposed to only curing fish (a topic discussed below). After the end of the initial gold rush in the 1870s, the market for cured fish (like Chinese market gardening) was reduced and fish-curing establishments (like Chinaman's Point) tended to be owned by individuals or groups rather than by merchants as discussed in chapter 3. Therefore, from the early Victorian gold-rush period, there was an initial boom in the 1850s to 1870s when many workers would have been required. This was followed by a slower economic period for the Chinese, which continued to dwindle until eventually the site was abandoned.

Evidence for early Chinese fishing (as opposed to just fish-curing) activities at Chinaman's Point can be found in historical documents and inferred through the size of the site's fish-drying racks. During the early 1860s, only a small number of European fishermen worked at Port Albert due to the distance to market. However, the Chinaman's Point fish-drying rack – known historically to have been in place during the 1860s (*Gippsland Standard* 1944, July 7; Olson 1947: 118) – was constructed on a large scale and was capable of supporting many tons of fish. In addition, references in historical documents (such as *Gippsland Guardian* 1867, July 1; *Gippsland Standard* 1944, July 7; Capps 1994: 56) support the idea that Chinese people were using boats and fishing with nets in Port Albert's waterways during the 1860s. Combined with the evidence of merchant control of the site and the availability of cheap, flexible, labour resources who knew how to fish, it seems highly likely that, from the period of initial site establishment, the Chinaman's Point workers were engaged in catching and curing fish. Accordingly, during the first years of operation, up to 16 people may have staffed the Chinaman's Point fish-curing establishment. This number could easily have been accommodated in the 8.5 by 10 m dwelling shown in the 1888 land title document (PROV, VPRS 5357/P0000, unit 5899). Certainly, the building size itself suggests a large group of people were living at the site.

Early official documentary evidence for land-usage fees or fishing-licence payments for the Chinaman's Point site could not be located. However, in the latter half of the 19th century, some licensing records become available. These (which are discussed in more detail in the site dating section) show that from the second half of the 1880s to after the 1900s, official residency rights for Chinaman's Point move back and forth between two Chinese men: Ah Hoo and Hop Sing. As noted by Williams (1999: 85–87) and discussed in chapter 3, Chinese names are difficult to trace through documentary records. Efforts were made to further identity Ah Hoo and Hop Sing through shipping records, mining syndicate papers and official Government registries for Chinese people entering colonial Victoria. However, owing to incomplete records and European difficulties in pronouncing and spelling Chinese names, no direct links could be obtained. After the 1870s, the lower demand for cured-fish products must have significantly reduced occupation numbers at the site. Ah Hoo and Hop Sing's delayed appearance at Chinaman's Point suggests that they are unlikely to have been Chinese merchants and were most likely retired miners, possibly even past workers at the curing site. During this later period, Ah Hoo, Hop Sing and possibly some others probably managed to earn a steady income through fishing and fish curing, but nothing like the sums generated in previous years.

The select committee reports on the fishing industry in Victoria reveal that in 1892, the Chinaman's Point fish curers were still purchasing fish from European fishermen (*Votes and Proceedings of the Victorian Legislative Council* 1892: 111). It is probable that, by this date, the remaining two to four workers at Chinaman's Point were no longer under direct merchant influence but were instead making an independent living as market gardeners, tobacco growers and fish curers in the same manner as other post gold-rush Chinese workers.

## Site activities

From material evidence, the following section provides a summary of the activities at Chinaman's Point.

Architectural and structural materials such as nails, screws, bricks, lead flashing and window glass, along with historical records, show that structures were a feature of the site. It may be that there was one building for living and sleeping, with places for cooking and other less prominent constructions nearby, or just one substantial dwelling where all indoor activities took place. Other on-site construction is evident in the form of a slipway for boat maintenance, a jetty and fish-drying racks. There must also have been an undercover area to store the cured fish awaiting transport to market.

Domestic items show that meals were prepared from European and Chinese ingredients and cooked using traditional Chinese kitchen equipment. Green leafy vegetables, standard in Chinese cooking, may have been acquired from Chin Lang Tip's local Chinese market garden (Langtip 1986) (possibly also part of a merchant network), while meat was obtained from European butchers. Some European ceramic food-storage vessels and tableware were used at the site, but traditional Chinese household ceramics were much more common. For liquid storage, although ceramic Chinese containers were used, the vast majority of containers were made of European-produced bottle glass. This glass was modified to suit a number of secondary functions, including lamp chimneys for night fishing or lighting purposes and two separate types of opium-heating lamps.

Weighing scales, slate writing material and inkwells show that business-related activities were conducted on site. The headman, who may have spoken some English, was probably required to tally fish quantities, make payments to European fishermen, keep transaction records and report to the controlling merchant.

In 1892, the NSW Royal Commission on Alleged Chinese Gambling and Immorality stated, "the Chinese as a community are very largely addicted to gambling" (*Votes and Proceedings of the New South Wales Legislative Assembly* 1891–92, vol. 5: 19, 21). Many overseas Chinese people in Australia seem to have gambled either because of an addiction or casually as a means of recreation, with *fan tan* and *pak kop piu* being the most favoured games (Smith 2006: 28). Archaeological evidence of these games – in the form of black and white ceramic counters, domino disks and dice – are common finds at overseas Chinese sites (Mueller 1987: 385; Ritchie 1984: 101). Ritchie (1986: 39) and Mueller (1987: 385) suggest that gambling was used as a social outlet from the long monotonous days of mining and as a component of Chinese festivities.

It is relatively unusual for an overseas Chinese site like Chinaman's Point to display no evidence of gambling. Perhaps in their period of debt payment, credit–ticket workers at Chinaman's Point lacked the funds to gamble or maybe with dreams and optimism for family security still fresh they were unwilling to risk what little money they did have. However, money was spent on other indulgences, as evidenced through alcohol and opium use. It is possible that the site merchant supplied these items under some form of bonus system, but no evidence of this exists. It is also conceivable that the alcohol- and opium-related artefacts are from a period after the site's most productive times, when there were no credit–ticket workers or direct merchant involvement and so site workers retained the profits from their fish-curing activities. Alternatively, it may be that artefact collectors at Chinaman's Point have already recovered this evidence, although none was noted in the private artefact collections held by Port Albert residents.

### Curing methods

As discussed in chapters 3 and 4, fish cured by overseas Chinese people was either pickled, or salted and then dried in the sun (*Bendigo Advertiser* 1857, January 5; *Votes and Proceedings of the New South Wales Legislative Assembly* 1879–80, vol. 3: 1224–26; Firth 1946: 218–20). Pickling fish required salt, water and an appropriate container. Salting and sun-drying fish required that salt be placed on the fish in a dry form or that fish be placed in salty brine then put in the sun to dry.

An indication of how the Chinaman's Point workers cured fish is known. They "Salt[ed] them and dried them in the sun" on "long tables on trestles" (Legislative Assembly report 1892: 111; *Gippsland Standard* 1944, July 7). Material evidence for these activities at Chinaman's Point includes timber cask remains and timber stumps from the drying rack system. No ambiguity exists over the rack system's purpose – which was to support fish while they dried in the sun. The timber casks, however, could have been used to pickle, dry-salt, or brine fish. Therefore, all of the historically known overseas Chinese fish-curing methods could conceivably have been undertaken at the site.

**Working components**

Fish-curing activities at Chinaman's Point can be confirmed through specific material remains. For clarity and for use by future researchers, the methods and expected material remains of overseas Chinese fish-curing activities are shown in chart form (table 7.4). The chart comprises three components: activities, which represents the essential activities performed at the site; equipment, which represents the items required for each activity; and archaeological evidence, which shows what physical remains of Chinese fish-curing activities may be left for interpretation. The chart has been developed from archival research and material remains from the excavation at Chinaman's Point.

Some of the activities at overseas Chinese fish-curing sites are identical to those conducted at colonial sealing, whaling and fishing sites, as each utilised maritime technology to exploit marine resources from a land base. For this reason, artefacts such as Chinese ceramics and opium paraphernalia – a standard feature of overseas Chinese sites – and other more site-specific remains such as fish-drying racks, are essential for accurate site identification. Possibly (once site ethnicity is established) the most defining feature of a Chinese fish-curing site is location. A colonial-period site displaying Chinese occupation that is positioned on the bank of a salt-water estuary or tidal lake is highly likely to be an overseas Chinese fishing or fish-curing camp.

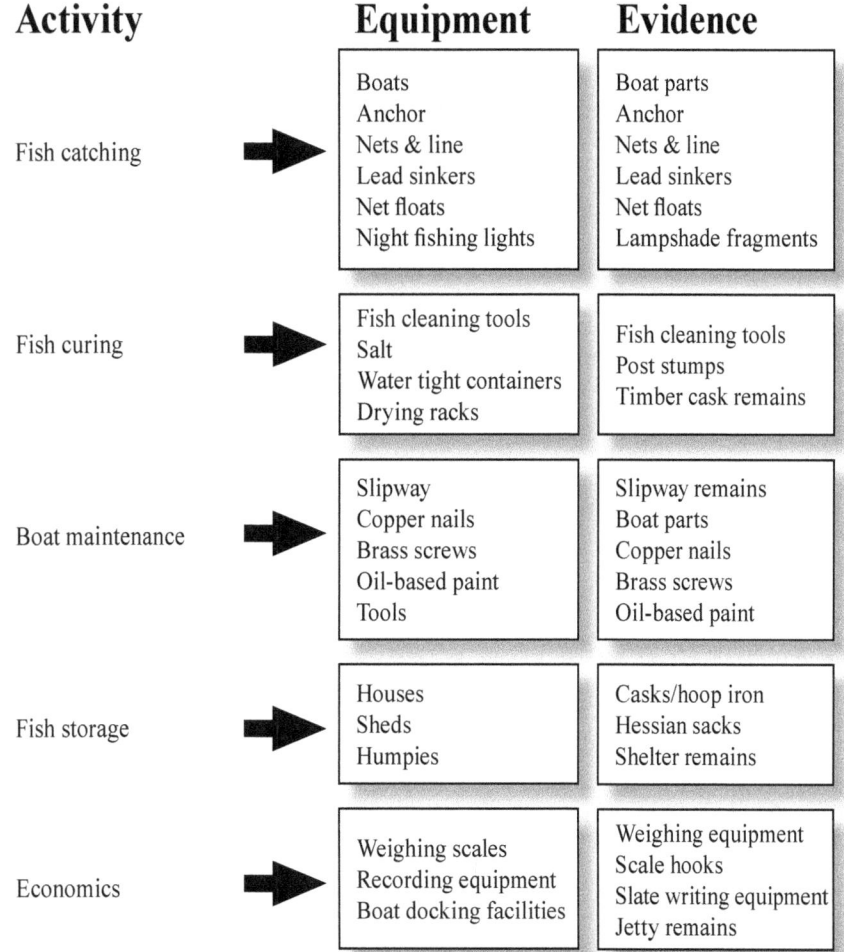

Table 7.4 Theoretical model for the activities conducted, equipment required and the archaeological evidence recoverable from commercial fishing sites. The activity column indicates a range of fishing activities. The equipment column shows a representation of the items required for each activity. The evidence column is a sample of what physical remains may be expected if one or more of the activities occurred.

### After the 1870s

By the 1870s and beyond, historical records suggest that Chinese merchants no longer found Australian-based Chinese fish-curing operations profitable and abandoned their interests in such business (*Votes and Proceedings of the New South Wales Legislative Assembly* 1879–80, vol. 3: 1224). At Chinaman's Point, the original merchant owner appears to have been replaced by Chinese owner-operators who actually worked at the site. The transition details from merchant control to worker ownership are unknown. The Chinese kinship system may have enabled a lower-ranking kin relative of the merchant to take over the site. Some form of monetary payment or product-supply system may have been in place. The site may simply have been abandoned by the merchant, which then enabled an enterprising Chinese person to take up residence and curing operations. Whatever the case, transfer of ownership would have created very little change in the site's physical appearance and is not apparent through the material remains. Site structures would have become worn with age, some would have been propped up and repaired and others would have been left to collapse, or been dismantled and used for repair work or firewood. Fish procurement and curing methods would have remained the same. It is difficult to determine how many men worked the site during this later period. It is likely that the quantities and profit from cured fish were greatly reduced due to the removal of merchant-controlled labour, organisation and distribution networks and because there were no longer the huge number of Chinese people in Victoria to demand the product. Nevertheless, the establishment was still in operation into the early 1900s. Artefacts from the site show the occupants retained many elements of traditional Chinese lifestyle, however, they had probably adopted European clothing and hairstyles.

In the very broadest terms, the occupants of Chinaman's Point participated in a range of colonial fishing-industry activities, cured fish in the traditional Chinese manner, conducted economic transactions with European people, had at least one dwelling with glass windows, used traditional Chinese and European foods and other commodities, drank alcohol and smoked opium.

# CHAPTER 8

# CONCLUSION

This study provides – for the first time – a comprehensive understanding of the Chinese involvement in Victoria's colonial fishing industry and changes historical perceptions of the Chinese experience in colonial Australia. The Australian gold-rush period provides a backdrop to explore the unique character of colonial contact between two diverse cultures. This project demonstrates a much greater complexity of colonial-period social and economic organisation and cross-cultural (Chinese–European) interaction than was previously known to have existed.

By taking a step back from the theoretical framework of changing social organisation which is commonly used to consider the issue of colonial encounters and instead identifying the strategic actions of Chinese individuals and the social structures of small groups that combined to facilitate change, a number of new areas of interest have been identified. Importantly, this approach has also opened avenues for the consideration of interactions between colonial-period Chinese and European people in comparative studies of other complex societies.

Overseas Chinese society in colonial Australia displayed three broad categories of social class rankings: a wealthy minority of influential socially elite (the merchants), a group of middle-class workers or headmen (the merchant aspirants), and the workforce majority (the lower classes). A range of diverse interactions was identified and some of the complexities in Victoria's overseas Chinese social system revealed. This allows a deeper understanding of overseas Chinese systems and opens opportunities further to explore social and economic (beneficial and adverse) organisation and cross-cultural interactions of Chinese and European societies in colonial Australia. Importantly, Europeans are shown to have benefited from interactions with colonial-period overseas Chinese populations a point that has been largely overlooked in previous Australian, New Zealand and American research.

The research approach in this project has enabled a new perspective on overseas Chinese activities in Australia, unlike previous research methodology that generally saw the Chinese as victims of Australia's restrictive laws and persistent racism and whose principal actions were in response to these negatives. Regardless of any restrictive laws or racism, overseas Chinese people were successful in establishing large-scale commerce other than mining. These conclusions highlight the need in modern archaeology for further theory-based thematic investigations.

Evidence for Chinese fish-curing establishments in Victoria, New South Wales, the Northern Territory, South Australia and Tasmania, leaves no doubt that Chinese people were heavily involved in Australia's colonial fishing industry. Documentary evidence shows overseas Chinese activity in Victoria's fishing industry by 1856. However, Chinese people were probably participating in Victoria's fishing industry as early as 1855, with the mass arrival of Chinese goldminers. Primary documentation and material remains have shown the types of fish Chinese fish curers cured, the preferred species, how they obtained them, cured them and even how they were cooked and eaten.

Fish-curing establishments were not general retailers. Chinese cured fish was sold primarily to the overseas Chinese population in Australia, markets in China and other opportunistic bulk buyers. Fish-curing establishments were capitalist endeavours that used the Chinese kinship system of obligation to procure, process and supply bulk-cured fish very cheaply. This provided overseas Chinese people – particularly those working on the goldfields – with an abundant food source and helped to maintain cultural continuity in the Chinese diet and way of life. This study shows evidence to support the notion that financial gain from fish-curing activities went largely to a select group of controlling Chinese merchants, with the lower-class labourers working to pay off their debt bondage and receiving little if any monetary payment for their services.

An examination of how much fish the Chinese fish curers in colonial Australia were processing annually and the profits this generated provides convincing evidence of a far greater level of participation by overseas Chinese people in colonial Australia fishing activities than previously realised. The annual sales from Chin Ateak, just one of the Chinese traders in Australian cured fish (and there were many), amounted to almost ten times the annual quantities of fish sold through Sydney and Victoria's European markets combined. Such figures are far out of proportion to the size of the Australian colonial economy and show the enormous scale of Chinese business in colonial Australia.

Chinese participation in Australia's colonial fishing industry is shown to have greatly aided the growth and continued survival of European commercial fishing activities, especially in regions distant to major markets. Opportunities for European fishermen arose through the Chinese need for bulk quantities of fresh fish for curing. Chinese fish curers established themselves as reliable buyers of the fish European fishermen caught.

The multi-disciplinary approach taken in this study has provided new knowledge of Victorian Chinese fishing sites, their internal workings, structure, functioning, layout and the associated material culture. Material and documentary evidence suggests that Chinese fish-curing establishments in Australia – from the late 1850s to early 1870s – were owned by Chinese merchants and staffed by a headman and a team of credit–ticket labourers. This project identifies for the first time that the credit–ticket system of procuring labour was critical to the establishment of Chinese fishing and fish-curing activities in Australia.

There is no doubt that a proportion of the Chinese population in colonial Australia did not go to the goldfields. Rather, the credit–ticket system was used by merchant bosses to procure labour for their business activities including the supply of food and other requirements to Chinese and Europeans on the goldfields. This cheap, willing supply of labour underpinned early overseas Chinese industry. Moreover, it enabled the overseas Chinese in Australia to be largely self-sufficient, maintain healthy diets and obtain and sustain niche positions in commercial ventures. The strong cultural cohesion of overseas Chinese groups and the authority of a few merchants over the lower-class majority enabled vast amounts of labour to be assembled, moved and utilised (although the internal mechanisms of this remain poorly understood). Through appointing lower-ranking Chinese people to undertake specific tasks – often reflecting kinship relationships – Chinese merchants shaped the early (1850s to 1870s) Chinese communities in colonial Australia.

This system of labour procurement and utilisation was prevalent in Victoria (and Australia more broadly) for only a limited period. After approximately 1870, significant change in the overseas Chinese system of social and economic organisation is apparent. While cultural kinship systems remained, the rush for gold was fading and the number of Chinese people seeking to enter Australia declined. This eroded the market for (and huge profits attained from) supplying primary produce and weakened merchants' grip on cheap overseas Chinese labour resources. By the early 1900s, all commercial Chinese fish-curing activity in Australia had ceased.

As the Australian gold rush continued to lose momentum, individual Chinese people began taking up self-employment opportunities made available through merchants divesting themselves of primary produce business ventures. The self-employed overseas Chinese broadened their market by selling fresh produce to European populations. At Chinaman's Point, Port Albert, in the late 1800s, it appears that at least two Chinese people either moved into an abandoned fish-curing site, or leased or made some other arrangement with the founding Chinese merchant to take over the establishment.

An examination of the material remains at Chinaman's Point assisted to build a picture of the site's history, how it worked and how the occupants lived and has facilitated an understanding of relationships between workers, headmen and merchants. Historical documentation and theoretical hypotheses help explain the links between Australian colonial fish-curing sites and the local, regional and global overseas Chinese community. In their host society, the overseas Chinese fish curers (and overseas Chinese people generally) maintained many aspects of their own cultural system of social and economic organisation, including social classes, interpersonal relationships, support systems and the scope for personal advancement.

The significance of this research is its ability to reveal previously unknown aspects of Australia's colonial past, to shed further light onto the role that overseas Chinese people played in the development of Australia and to demonstrate how archaeology can assist in understanding the complex nature of human interactions during colonial encounters. This has been achieved by examining material remains and the historical documentary record and is a further progression in the interpretation of archaeological research and theory.

The discovery of a Chinese fish-curing establishment presented a timely opportunity to test the value of this methodology, particularly in facilitating a more complete appreciation of the complexities of colonial society. This project has been successful in bringing to light further information on the role of overseas Chinese people in colonial Australia.

## HYPOTHETICAL RE-CREATION

If a newspaper reporter had visited the site during the 1860s and written about his or her experience, the narrative would probably read something like this: Facing forward to obtain the best possible view and rowing in the standing position, the distance from Port Albert Pier to Long Point took only a few minutes. The bay location and mid-summer, early morning light, had, as planned, enabled the best possible view of the Chinese fish-curing establishment. As the boat drew nearer to the working site, three separate areas became apparent – one domestic and two working. Farthest from the water's edge, a large and well-built dwelling takes priority among several otherwise makeshift lean-tos and open-sided shelters. Most of these structures are stacked to the roof with hessian sacks filled to bursting point with sun-dried fish. Next to these sacks are a number of sealed casks containing fish that have been pickled in the Chinese fashion. These closed bags and sealed casks represent the finished cured product ready for transport. Both sun-dried and pickled fish are rumoured to fetch a high price among the Chinese on the goldfields. Dominating the site's central area are several rows of fish-drying tables, 30 ft (10 m) or more in length, 7 ft (2 m) wide and supported by a framework of trestles. On the water's edge, in front of the drying tables, a slipway has been constructed upon which two small boats are receiving repair and general maintenance. To one side of the slipway is a vast number of brine-filled timber casks, a support for hanging fishing nets to dry and a set of weighing scales suspended from a timber frame. A substantial jetty traverses from one side of the slipway and drying tables, over a swamp area and ends near the main channel of the waterways. Apart from the house, the site's appearance is shabby. Local timbers cut roughly from the tree and lashed together by rope or any other means hold structures together. A pile of household waste, un-harnessed by any form of surround, is positioned to one side of the house and spills over a large area.

Contrary to overall site appearances, a closer, on-foot inspection reveals a hive of well-organised human activity at the site. Fourteen or more Chinese men, dressed in the Chinese fashion, displaying shaved heads and ponytails and aged approximately between 18 and 35 years old are working singularly or in groups on tasks associated with the fish-curing operation. Two small sail boats, with two Chinese men in each, can be seen anchored across the bay; both are hauling seine nets. Broad-shouldered European fishermen – standing in their boats – are queued four deep at the jetty, waiting to unload their catch of fish, have it weighed and receive payment. Supplying the seemingly unquenchable Chinese market with fish is a process they have all become familiar with and for the most part, are thankful of.

Four Chinese men unload baskets of fish from the first boat and hurry them across to the weighing scales. Here the boss or headman of the curing operation stands. Occasionally he uses the singsong language particular to the Chinese to give instructions to his working team. Mostly though, he is paying attention to tallying the fish weights and counting out the correct payment to the European fishermen. Relations between the two nationalities seem casual, even friendly. From the weighing scales, the baskets of fish are taken to another group of four Chinese men who crouch at the water's edge scaling fish, splitting them down the backbone, removing the intestines and folding them open to resemble a butterfly shape. Their work is done in a fast, practiced movement. After a final wash the fish are packed into nearby brine filled casks. In this cleaned, split and brined state, the fish remain for four to six days at least.

A short distance away, two more site workers remove already brined fish from their casks and carefully spread them to dry in the sun on the long tables. Beside the rows of drying fish, another Chinese man works at the task of turning each fish so that both sides may receive equal sun, a chore that must be done countless times before the curing process is complete. At the far end of the racks another man nimbly carries out the final process, which is to remove the fully dried fish from the racks, pack them into hessian bags, sew the top and stack them out of the weather to await transport to Melbourne. From Melbourne they will be distributed to Chinese communities throughout Victoria and overseas.

Mid morning arrives and a Chinese man opens a window of the house to yell one unintelligible word at the site workers. All work activity stops and the Chinese men file into the house for a meal break. The house interior contains three areas. Furthest from the door is an arrangement of bunk beds; the central region has a large table and seating; and at the front of the house, to one side and close to the front door, is positioned a sizeable clay hearth and cooking arrangement. A stewing pot and kettle hang over the hearth, with several other pots and deeply curved metal cooking dishes placed nearby. Next to the cooking zone is a meals preparation area. Among other odd equipment (unknown to the European kitchen) is a large cleaver, several brown ceramic jars and a range of preserved and raw foods; all are neatly hanging or positioned on benches in an orderly fashion.

At the main table, a steaming hot, heavily spiced broth of beef bones and green leafy vegetables is served to each man. The headman (speaking in tolerable, but broken English) relates that the curing establishment is owned by a Melbourne-based Chinese merchant. Every two weeks the merchant sends a ship from Melbourne to pick up cured fish and drop off supplies for the operation. The headman himself is paid a wage, but the working crew is made up of men who have had their passage from China paid by the merchant. Each man must now work as directed by the merchant until the cost of his fare, with interest, has been returned – this is the credit–ticket system. The working men are lean and appear eager and in good health. Totally accepting of their situation and the Chinese system of indebted labour, the men talk rapidly, laugh and smile broadly as they eat with wide ceramic spoons from delicate Chinese-style bowls and await, if they are lucky, their chance to strike it rich on the Australian goldfields.

# BIBLIOGRAPHY

Abbott, K, 1883, 'Under the shadow of the dragon'. *Overland Monthly and Out West Magazine*, 2 (11): 449–459.

Adams, A, 1997, *The Chinese ingredient: a history of the Chinese at Omeo 1859–*. A Adams, Bairnsdale, Victoria.

Adams, J, 1990, *From these beginnings: history of the shire of Alberton (Victoria)*. Alberton Shire Council, Victoria.

Adams, R, 1974, 'Anthropological perspectives on ancient trade'. *Current Anthropology*, 15: 239–258.

Adams, WH, 2003, 'Dating historical sites: the importance of understanding time lag in the acquisition, curation, use and disposal of artifacts'. *Historical Archaeology*, 37 (2): 38–64.

Adams, WH, and Gaw, LP, 1977, 'A model for determining time lag of ceramic artifacts'. *Northwest Anthropological Research Notes*, 11 (2): 218–231.

Adams, WY and Adams, EW, 1991, *Archaeological typology and practical reality: a dialectical approach to artifact classification and sorting*. Cambridge University Press, Cambridge.

Anderson, EN, 1970, 'Essays on South China's boat people'. In Lou, T (editor), *Asian Folklore and Social Life Monographs*, 19: 1–9.

Anderson, EN, and Anderson, ML, 1977, Modern China: south. In Chang, KC (editor), *Food in Chinese culture: anthropological and historical perspectives*. Yale University Press, London, pp. 317–382.

Anderson, M, 1920, 'The Story of Pittwater'. *The Royal Australian Historical Society, Journal and Proceedings*, 6 (4): 161–181.

Andrews, E, 1985, *Australia and China: the ambiguous relationship*. Melbourne University Press, Melbourne.

Armentrout-Ma, E, 1983, 'Urban Chinese at the Sinitic frontier: social organisation in United States' Chinatowns, 1849–1898'. *Modern Asian Studies*, 17 (1): 107–135.

Arnold, K, 1987, *Collecting Australian found bottles, part 1*. Crown Castleton Publishers, Victoria.

Arnold, K, 1989, *Collecting Australian found stoneware*. Crown Castleton Publishers, Victoria.

Arnold, K, 1990, *A Victorian thirst*. Crown Castleton Publishers, Victoria.

Ashbrook, GF, 1955, *Butchering, processing and preservation of meat*. Van Nostrand Reinhold Company, New York.

Aspinall, C, 1862, *Three years in Melbourne*. L Booth Pty Ltd, London.

Attwood, BM, 1984, 'Blacks and Lohans: a study of Aboriginal–European relations in Gippsland in the 19th century'. Doctoral thesis, Department of History, La Trobe University, Melbourne

Bachmann, H, 1982, 'The identification of slags from archaeological sites'. *Institute of Archaeology, Occasional Publication No. 6*, Institute of Archaeology, London.

Baggaley, VA, 1984, *Professional fishing at Port Albert to 1907*. Gippsland Maritime Museum, Gippsland.

Bagnall, K, 2000, 'Digging deep: sources for Chinese-Australian history in NSW'. *Locality*, 11 (2): 4–12.

Bahn, P, 1992, *Collins dictionary of archaeology*. HarperCollins Publishers, Glasgow.

Bailliere's post office directory, 1870.

Baker, RGV, 1985, *Historic sofala: a goldfield that changed a nation 1851–1943*. CentrePak Research, Cronulla, Sydney.

Ball, JD, 1925, *Things Chinese; or notes connected with China*, fifth edition. Kelly & Walsh Limited, Hong Kong.

Balme, J, 1983, 'Prehistoric fishing in the lower Darling, western New South Wales'. In Grigson, C and Clutton-Brock, J (editors), *Animals and archaeology: 2. Shell middens, fish and birds*. British Archaeological Reports, International Series S 183, Oxford, pp. 19–32.

Banbury, P, 1975, *Man & the sea: from the Ice Age to the Norman Conquest*. Granada Publishing Ltd, London.

Barker, ML (editor), 1882, *Pears Cyclopaedia*. A & F Pears, Ltd. Isleworth, Middlesex, United Kindom.

Barr, LG, 2000, *Black bream in the Gippsland Lakes: In crisis? Or fallacy? An angler's view*. Delbarr Publications, Swan Reach, Victoria.

Bateson, C, 1963, *Gold fleet for California*. Rigby Limited, Sydney.

Beals, HK and Steele, HW, 1981, Chinese porcelains from site 35-TI-1, Netarts sand spit, Tillamook County, Oregon. University of Oregon Anthropological Papers, No. 23.

Bell, P, 1983, 'Pine Creek: a report to the National Trust of Australia (Northern Territory) on an archaeological assessment of sites of historic significance in the Pine Creek district'. James Cook University (report to the National Trust, Northern Territory).

Bell, P, 1996, 'Archaeology of the Chinese in Australia', *Australasian Historical Archaeology*, 14: 13–18.

Bell, P, Grimwade, G and Ritchie, N, 1993, 'Archaeology of the overseas Chinese in Australia, New Zealand and Papua New Guinea: a select bibliography'. *The Australian Society for Historical Archaeology, Supplement to Newsletter*, 23 (1): 1–18.

Bennett, B, 2002, *The fish markets of Melbourne*. Bruce Bennett, Hawthorn, Victoria.

Bennett, I, 1974, *The fringe of the sea*. Rigby Limited, Sydney.

Berg, M, 1994, *The age of manufacturers, 1700–1820: industry, innovation and work in Britain*. Routledge, London.

Berryman, J, 1999, 'Chinese abalone fishermen on San Clementle Island'. *Mains'l Haul*, 35 (2&3): 14–21.

Bimber, B, 1994, 'Three faces of technological determinism'. In Smith, MR and Marx, L (editors), *Does technology drive history? The dilemma of technological determinism*. The MIT Press, London, pp. 79–100.

Binford, L, 1962, 'Archaeology as anthropology'. *American Antiquity*, 28 (2): 217–225.

Binford, L, 1965, 'Archaeological systematics and the study of culture process'. *American Antiquity*, 31(2): 203–210.

Binford, L, 1972, *An archaeological perspective*. Seminar Press, New York.

Birch, WD, 2003, *Geology of Victoria*. Geological Society of Australia, Victoria.

Bird, E, 1987, *The past, present and future of the Gippsland Lakes – with particular emphasis on Lake Wellington and Lake Coleman*. The Gippsland Lakes Committee, Sale.

Birmingham, J and Bairstow, D, 1987, 'Papers in Australian historical archaeology'. Reprinted from *The Newsletter of The Australian Society for Historical Archaeology 1970–1982*. The Australian Society for Historical Archaeology Incorporated.

Birmingham, JM. and Jeans, DN, 1983, 'The Swiss Family Robinson and the archaeology of colonisations'. *Australian Journal of Historical Archaeology*, 1: 3–14.

Birrell, RW, 1998, *Staking a claim: gold and the development of Victorian mining law*. Melbourne University Press, Melbourne.

Blanford, J, 1987, 'Overseas Chinese ethnicity and Euroamerican glass bottles at the Wong Ho Leun site'. In *Wong, Ho Leun: an American Chinatown*. The Great Basin Foundation, San Diego, pp. 189–232.

Boessneck, J, 1969, 'Osteological differences between sheep (*Ovis aries* Linne) and goat (*Capra hircus* Linne)'. In Brothwell, D and Higgs, E (editors), *Science in archaeology*. Thames and Hudson, London, pp. 331–358.

Bognuda, J and Moorhead, L, 1981, *Between the bays: Mornington Peninsula*. Wilke and Company Limited, Victoria.

Booth, M, 1996, *Opium: a history*. Simon & Schuster Sydney.

Boow, J, 1991, *Early Australian commercial glass: manufacturing processes*. The Heritage Council of New South Wales Research Study, No. 10.

Borthwick, JD, 1857, *Three years in California*. Unknown publisher, Edinburgh, United Kingdom.

Bowdler, S, 1976, 'Hook, line and dilly bag: an interpretation of an Australian coastal shell midden'. *Mankind*, 10 (4): 248–258.

Bowdler, S, 1993, 'Sunda and Sahul: a 30kyr culture area?' In Smith, MA, Spriggs, M and Fankhauser, B (editors), *Sahul in review*. Highland Press, Canberra, pp. 60–71.

Bowen, A, 1999, '"For they were fishers": The archaeology of the NSW south coast fishing industry 1890–1950'. Honours thesis, Department of Archaeology and Anthropology, The Australian National University, Canberra.

Bowen, A, 2003, 'The archaeology of early commercial fishing activities in New South Wales: a theoretical model'. *Bulletin of the Australian Institute for Maritime Archaeology*, 27: 9–18.

Bowen, A, 2004, 'Material evidence for early commercial fishing activities on the far south coast of NSW'. *Australian Historical Archaeology*, 22: 79–89.

Bowler, JM, 1976, 'Recent developments in reconstructing late Quaternary environments in Australia.' In Kirch, LR and Thorne, AG (editors), *The origins of Australians*. Australian Institute of Aboriginal Studies, Canberra, pp. 55–77.

Bowler, JM, Jones, R, Allen, H and Thorne, AG, 1970, 'Pleistocene human remains from Australia: a living site and human cremations form Lake Mungo, western New South Wales'. *World Archaeology*, 2: 39–60.

Bowles, S, 1866, *Across the continent*. Springfield Publishers, Massachusetts.

Breacher, EM, 1972, *Licit and illicit drugs*. Little Brown and Company, Boston.

Bride, TF (editor), 1969, *Letters from Victorian pioneers*. Heinemann, Melbourne.

Brienes, M, 1983, *China camp and the San Francisco Bay shrimp fishery*. California Department of Parks and Recreation, California.

Brooks, A, 2005a, *An archaeological guide to British ceramics in Australia 1788–1901*. The Australian Society for Historical Archaeology and The La Trobe University Archaeology Program, Victoria.

Brooks, A, 2005b, 'Observing formalities: the use of functional artefact categories in Australian historical archaeology'. *Australasian Historical Archaeology*, 23: 7–14.

Brott, CW, 1987, 'Utilitarian stoneware from the Wong Ho Leun site: a pictorial essay. In *Wong, Ho Leun: an American Chinatown*, The Great Basin Foundation, San Diego, pp. 233–247.

Brown-May, A, 1998, *Melbourne street life: the itinerary of our days*. Australian Scholarly Publishing Pty Ltd, Victoria.

Buck, JL, 1937, *Land utilization in China*. University of Nanking, Nanking, China.

Bull, JC and Williams, P, 1967, *Story of Gippsland shipping*. Published by the authors, Metung, Victoria.

Butler, P, 1977, *Opium and gold: a history of the Chinese goldminers in New Zealand*. Alister Taylor, Martinborough.

Butler's Gipps' Land and Wood's Point Directory, 1866.

Byrne, D, 1996–1997, 'The archaeology of disaster'. *Public History Review*, 5/6: 18–29.

Caire, N, 1886, Picture: Shaving Point Metung. Collection: Gippsland Scenery No. 46. Accession No. H27507. La Trobe Picture Collection, State Library of Victoria.

Caldow, W, 2003, 'The commercial inn, Tarraville maritime trade and the early settlement of Gippsland'. *Victorian Historical Journal*, 74 (1): 1–23.

Cameron, C, 1986, *Encyclopaedia of pottery & porcelain. The 19th & 20th centuries*. Faber and Faber, London.

Cameron, FR, 1985, 'Analysis of buttons, clothing, hardware and rextiles of the nineteenth century Chinese goldminers of central Otago'. Honours thesis, University of Otago, Dunedin.

Campbell, J, 2002, *Invisible invaders: smallpox and other diseases in Aboriginal Australia 1780–1880*. Melbourne University Press, Melbourne.

Campbell, PC, 1969, *Chinese Coolie emigration to countries within the British Empire*. Negro Universities Press, New York.

Canada Parks Service, 1992, *Canadian Parks Service classification system for historical collections*. Canadian Parks Service, Environment Canada, Ottawa.

Capps, D, 1994, *A family called Smith 1824–1886 and their continuing story 1886–1940s*. Sylvan Studio, Wilson

Carment, D, 1993, 'Archaeology and history in central Australia'. *Australasian Historical Archaeology*, 11: 139–141.

Casey, M, 2004, 'Falling through the cracks: method and practice at the CSR site, Pyrmont'. *Australasian Historical Archaeology*, 22: 27–43.

Census of the colony of Tasmanian 1881: Tasmanian office of the Government Statist.

Census of the colony of Victoria 1861: Victorian office of the Government Statist.

Census of the colony of Victoria 1871: Victorian office of the Government Statist.

Census of the colony of Victoria 1891: Victorian office of the Government Statist.

Chace, P, 1976, 'Overseas Chinese ceramics'. In Greenwood, RS (editor), The changing faces of Main Street. Unpublished report, Ventura Mission Plaza Archaeological Project, Redevelopment Agency, City of San Buenaventura, California, pp. 510–530.

Chandler, J, 2005, 'Chinese sojourners in Victoria. A collection of artefacts from the Upper Ovens Goldfields'. Honours thesis, the Archaeology Program, La Trobe University, Bundoora, Victoria.

Chan, HD, 2001, 'Becoming Australasian but remaining Chinese: the future of the Down Under Chinese past'. In Chan, HD, Curthoys, A and Chiang, N, *The overseas Chinese in Australasia: history, settlement and interactions*. Interdisciplinary Group for Australian Studies, National Taiwan University, Taipei and Centre for the Study of the Chinese Southern Diaspora, Australian National University, Canberra, pp. 1–16.

Chan, HD, Curthoys, A and Chiang, N (editors), 2001, *The overseas Chinese in Australasia: history, settlement and interactions*. Interdisciplinary Group for Australian Studies, National Taiwan University, Taipei and Centre for the Study of the Chinese Southern Diaspora, Australian National University, Canberra.

Chan, KB, 1997, 'A family affair: migration, dispersal and the emergent identity of the Chinese Cosmopolitan'. *Diaspora* 6 (2): 195–231.

Chan, M, 1995, 'A decade of achievement and future directions in research on the history of the Chinese in Australia'. In Macgregor, P (editor), *Histories of the Chinese in Australasia and the South Pacific: proceedings of an international public conference held at the Chinese Australian Museum, Melbourne, 8–10 October 1993*. Chinese Australian Museum, Melbourne, pp. 419–423.

Chang, KC, 1977, *Food in Chinese culture: anthropological and historical perspectives*. Yale University Press, New Haven, Connecticut.

Chang, S, 1968, 'The distribution and occupations of overseas Chinese'. *Geographic Review*, 58 (1): 89–107.

Chaplin, SE (editor), 1985, *Fishing, sand and village days: an oral history of Frankston from the early 1900s to 1950*. Frankston City Library, Victoria.

*Chinese Repository* magazine, 1849 (January), pp. 100–120.

Choi, CY, 1975, *Chinese migration and settlement in Australia*. Sydney University Press, Sydney.

Chou, B, 1993, 'The Chinese in Victoria: a longterm Survey'. Masters thesis, University of Melbourne, Melbourne.

Chou, B, 1995, 'The sojourning attitude and the economic decline of Chinese society in Victoria, 1860s–1930s'. In Macgregor, P (editor), *Histories of the Chinese in Australasia and the South Pacific: proceedings of an international public conference held at the Chinese Australian Museum, Melbourne, 8–10 October 1993*. Chinese Australian Museum, Melbourne, pp. 191–202.

Chun, A, 1996, 'Fuck Chineseness: on the ambiguities of ethnicity as culture as identity'. *Boundary 2*, 23 (2): 111–138.

Clements, JA and Richmond, WH, 1968, 'Port Albert and Gippsland trade, 1840–66'. *Australian Economic History Review*, 8 (2): 129–138.

Clowes, EM, 1911, *On the wallaby through Victoria*. London.

Cohen, P, 1892, *The marine fish and fisheries of NSW past and present*. Unknown publisher.

Coleman, J, 1980, 'Fish bones for fun and profit'. In Johnston, I (editor), *Holier than Thou*. Department of Prehistory, Australian National University.

Coleman, N, 1975, *What shell is that?* Paul Hamlyn Pty Limited, Dee Why, New South Wales.

Coles, B and Coles, J, 1989, *People of the wetlands*. Thames and Hudson, London.

Collett, B, 1994, *Wednesdays closest to the full moon: a history of south Gippsland*. Melbourne University Press, Melbourne.

Colley, SM, 1983, 'Prehistoric fishing strategies'. In Grigson, C and Clutton-Brock, J (editors), *Animals and archaeology: 2. Shell middens, fish and birds*. British Archaeological Reports, International Series S 183, Oxford, pp. 160–172.

Colley, SM, 1987, 'Fishing for facts. Can we reconstruct fishing methods from archaeological evidence?' *Australian Archaeology*, 24: 16–26.

Colley, S, 2005, 'Marine shell from Australian historic sites: research design and data standardisation'. *Australasian Historical Archaeology*, vol. 23: 71–77.

Collins, D, 1987, 'Tradition and network: interpreting the fish remains from Riverside's Chinatown'. In *Wong Ho Len, an American Chinatown San Diego*, The Great Basin Foundation II, San Diego, pp. 121–132.

Collins, JW, 1892, 'Report on the fisheries of the Pacific Coast of the United States'. In *United States commission of fish and fisheries report to the commissioner 1888*. Washington Government Printing Office, Part XVI: 3–269.

Colquhoun, A, 1883, *Across Chryese: being the narrative of a journey of exploration through the south China border lands from Canton to Mandalay*, vol. 1. Sampson Low, Marston, Searle and Rivington, London.

Connah, G, 1983, 'Stamp-collecting or increasing understanding? The dilemma of historical archaeology'. *Australian Journal of Historical Archaeology*, 1: 15–21.

Connah, G, 1998, 'Pattern and purpose in historical archaeology'. *Australasian Historical Archaeology*, 16: 3–7.

Cooke, M, 1987, *Makassar & Northeast Arnhem Land: missing links & living bridges*. Education Media Unit Batchelor College, Indonesia.

Coolidge, M, 1909, *Chinese immigration*. Henry Holt & Company, New York.

Cooper, JB, 1931, *The history of St Kilda: from its first settlement to a city and after 1840 to 1930*, vol. 1. Melbourne Printers Proprietary Limited, Melbourne.

Cotterell, B and Kamminga, J, 1990, *Mechanics of pre-industrial technology: an introduction to the mechanics of ancient and traditional material culture*. Cambridge University Press, Sydney.

Couchman, S, 2001, 'From Mrs Lup Mun, Chinese Herbalist to Yee Joon, respectable scholar: a social history of Melbourne's Chinatown, 1900–1920'. In Chan, HD, Curthoys, A and Chiang, N, *The Overseas Chinese in Australasia: history, settlement and interactions*. Interdisciplinary Group for Australian Studies, National Taiwan University, Taipei and Centre for the Study of the Chinese Southern Diaspora, Australian National University, Canberra.

Courtwright, DT, 1982, *Dark paradise: opiate addiction in America before 1940*. Harvard University Press, Cambridge, Massachusetts.

Cox, N, 1995, 'Residents of Gipps' Land 1851'. *Gippsland Heritage Journal*, 18: 47–49.

Cox, Rev. G, 1890, *Notes on Gippsland history*, vol. 2. Port Albert Maritime Museum and Yarram and District Historical Society.

Coysh, AW and Henrywood, RK, 1986, *The dictionary of blue and white printed pottery 1780–1880*, vol. 2. Antique Collectors' Club, Woodbridge, Suffolk.

Crawford, JD, 1877, 'Notes on Chinese immigration in the Australian colonies'. In *Davenport, A. to Lord Tenterden*, 15 September 1877, Britain, Foreign Office Archives, 1879–1881, Confidential Print no. 3742.

Cronin, K, 1982, *Colonial casualties: Chinese in early Victoria*. Melbourne University Press, Melbourne.

Crook, P, 2005, 'Quality, cost and value: key concepts for an interpretive assemblage analysis'. *Australasian Historical Archaeology*, 23: 15–24.

Crook, P, Lawrence, S and Gibbs, M, 2002, 'The role of artefact catalogues in Australian historical archaeology: a framework for discussion'. *Australasian Historical Archaeology*, 20: 26–38.

Cuffley, P, 1973, *A complete catalogue and history of oil and kerosene lamps in Australia*. Pioneer Design Studio Pty Ltd, Victoria.

Curthoys, A, 2001, 'Men of all nations, except Chinamen, Europeans and Chinese on the goldfields of New South Wales'. In McCalman, I, Cook, A, Reeves, A (editors), *Gold: forgotten histories and lost objects of Australia*. Cambridge University Press, Melbourne.

Cushman, JW, 1984, 'A 'colonial casualty': The Chinese Community in Australian Historiography'. *Asian Studies Association of Australia: Review*, 7 (3): 100–113.

Cuthill, WJ, 1959, 'The Gippsland Road, 1836–1848'. *The Victorian Historical Magazine*, 29 (1): 8–33.

Cutting, CL, 1955, *Fish saving: a history of fish processing from ancient to modern times*. Leonard Hill Limited, London.

Daley, C, 1928, 'Gleanings from an old day-book, Port Albert', 1845–7. *The Victorian Historical Magazine*, 13: 39–50.

Daley, C, 1932, 'The Chinese in Victoria'. *The Victorian Historical Magazine*, 14: 23–35.

Daley, C, 1960, *The story of Gippsland*. Whitcombe & Tombs Pty Ltd, Melbourne.

Dargin, P, 1976, *Aboriginal fisheries of the Darling-Barwon Rivers*. Brewarrina Historical Society, Queensland.

Darnell, M, 2001, 'Law and the regulation of life: the case of indentured Chinese labourers'. In Chan, HD, Curthoys, A and Chiang, N (editors), *The overseas Chinese in Australasia: history, settlement and interactions*. Interdisciplinary Group for Australian Studies, National Taiwan University, Taipei and Centre for the Study of the Chinese Southern Diaspora, Australian National University, Canberra, pp. 54–68.

Das, M and Kolack, S, 1989, *Technology, values and society: social forces in technological change*. Peter Lang Publishing, New York.

Daumas, M, 1969, *A history of technology and invention: progress through the ages, Volume 1. The origins of technological civilisation*. Crown Publishers, New York.

Davies, M and Buckley, K, 1987, Archaeological procedures manual. Port Arthur conservation and development project. Occasional Paper No. 13, Department of Lads, Parks and Wildlife, Hobart.

Davies, P, 2001a, 'Isolation and integration: the archaeology and history of an Otways Forest Community'. Doctoral thesis, School of Historical and European Studies, Faculty of Humanities and Social Sciences, La Trobe University Bundoora, Victoria.

Davies, P, 2001b, 'A cure for all seasons: health and medicine in a bush community'. *Journal of Australian Studies*, 70: 63–74.

Davies, P, 2005, 'Writing slates and schooling'. *Australasian Historical Archaeology*, 23: 63–69.

Davis, JF, 1844, *The Chinese: a general description of China and its inhabitants*. Charles Knight & Co, London.

Davis, P, 1973, 'Smoke curing of fish: Australian fisheries paper no. 23'. Australian Government Publishing Services, Canberra.

Dew, AT, 1891, 'The fishing industry of Krian and Kurau, Perak'. *Journal of the Straits Branch of the Royal Asiatic Society*, 23: 95–119.

Diamond, N, 1969, *K'un Shen, a Taiwan village*. Holt, Rinehart and Winston, New York.

Dibble, HL. and Pelcin, A, 1995, 'The effect of hammer mass and velocity on flake mass'. *Journal of Archaeological Science*, 22: 429–439.

Dickinson, MG (editor), 1987, *A living from the sea: Devon's fishing industry and its fishermen*. Devon Books, Britain.

Diderot, D, 1959, *A Diderot pictorial encyclopedia of trades and industry*. Dover Publications Inc., New York.

Dietler, M, 2005, 'The archaeology of colonization and the colonization of archaeology: theoretical challenges from an ancient Mediterranean colonial encounter. In Stein, GJ (editor), *The archaeology of colonial encounters*, School of American Research Press, New Mexico, pp. 33–67.

Dimond, G (editor), 1996, *Sweet & sour: experiences of Chinese families in the Northern Territory*. Museum and Art Gallery of the Northern Territory, Darwin.

Dingle, T, 1980, 'The truly magnificent thirst: an historical survey of Australian drinking habits'. *Historical Studies*, 19 (5): 227–249.

Don, Rev. A, 1894–1911, *Annual inland tour diaries*, Hocken Library, New Zealand.

Doran, JT, 1954, *Port Franklin: they called it Bowen*. G.I.A.E. Library Pamphlet, Churchill, Victoria.

Dow, C, 1995, 'The wattle bark industry and the Gippsland Lakes'. *Gippsland Heritage Journal*. 19: 10–19.

Dumarcay, J, 1991, *The house in South-East Asia*. Oxford University Press, Oxford.

Dumbrell, R, 1983, *Understanding antique wine bottles*. The Antique Collectors Club, Woodbridge, Suffolk.

Dunn, B, 1991, *Angling in Australia: its history and writings*. David Ell Press Pty Ltd, New South Wales.

Durand, J, 1960, 'The population statistics of China, 2–1953 AD'. *Population Studies*, 13: 209–256.

Duruz, R, 1973, 'An unusual pioneer in Victoria: a biographical sketch of James McKain Meek'. *The Victorian Historical Magazine*, 44 (1&2, February–May): 40–47.

Egloff, BJ, 1993, *Aboriginal fishing communities at Wreck Bay*. Australian Institute of Aboriginal Studies, Canberra.

Ellis, J and Lee, T, 2002, *Casting the net: early fishing families of the Gippsland Coast*. Lakes Entrance Family History Resource Centre, Lakes Entrance, Victoria.

*Encyclopaedia Britannica*. 1981, Volume 5.

Epstein, D, 1968, *Buttons*, Walker and Co., New York.

Etter, PA, 1980, 'The west coast Chinese and opium smoking'. In Schuyler, RL (editor), *Archaeological perspectives on ethnicity in America*. Baywood Publishing Company Inc., New York, pp. 97–101.

Evans, S, 2003, *Fins scales and sails: the story of fishing at Port Fairy 1845–1945*. Jim Crow Press, Victoria.

Evans, W, S, 1980, 'Food and fantasy: material culture of the Chinese in California and the West, Circa 1850–1900'. In Schuyler, RL (editor), *Archaeological perspectives on ethnicity in America: Afro-American and Asian American culture history*. Baywood Publishing Company, Inc., New York, pp. 89–96.

Fallowfield, T, 2001, 'Polynesian fishing implements from the wreck of HMS Pandora: a technological and contextual study'. *Bulletin of the Australian Institute for Maritime Archaeology*, 25: 5–28.

Fike, RE, 1987, *The bottle book. A comprehensive guide to historic, embossed medicine bottles*. Peregrine Smith Books, Salt Lake City.

Finlay, M., 1990, *Western writing implements in the age of the quill pen*. Plain Books, Cumbria.

Firth, R, 1946, *Malay fishermen: their peasant economy*. Kegan Paul, Trench, Trubner & Co., Ltd, London.

Fitzgerald, S, 1996, *Red tape, gold scissors: the story of Sydney's Chinese*. State Library of New South Wales Press, Sydney.

Flood, J, 1980, *The moth hunters: Aboriginal prehistory of the Australian Alps*. Australian Institute of Aboriginal Studies, Canberra.

Ford, G, 1995, *Australian pottery: the first 100 years*. Salt Glaze Press, Victoria.

Freeman, J, 1888, *Lights and shadows of Melbourne life*. Sampson Low, Marston, Searle and Rivington Limited, London.

Frost, J, 1853, *Frost's pictorial history of New York*. Auburn Press, New York.

Frost, WM and Harvey, CCM, 1997, 'Forest industries or dairy pastures? Ferdinand von Mueller and the 1885–1893 Royal Commission on Vegetable Producers'. *Historical Records of Australian Science*, 11: 431–437.

Frost, W, 2002, 'Migrants and technological transfer: Chinese farming in Australia'. *Australian Economic History Review*, 42 (2): 113–131.

Galloway, M, 2005, 'Chasing the dragon around the Rocks. Opium smoking in the Rocks, Sydney 1870 to 1900'. Honours thesis, Department of Prehistoric and Historic Archaeology, the University of Sydney.

Garran, A (editor), 1886, *Picturesque atlas of Australasia*. Picturesque Atlas of Australasia. Co. Limited, Sydney.

Garratt, D, 1989, 'Sri Lankan fishing technology: past, present and future'. *Bulletin of the Australian Institute for Maritime Archaeology*, 13 (1): 1–8.

Gasco, JL, 2005, 'Spanish colonialism and processes of social change in Mesoamerica'. In Stein, GJ (editor), *The archaeology of colonial encounters*. School of American Research Press, New Mexico, pp. 69–108.

Gaughwin, D, 1995, 'Chinese settlement sites in north–eastern Tasmania: an archaeological view'. In Macgregor, P (editor), *Histories of the Chinese in Australasia and the South Pacific: proceedings of an international public conference held at the Chinese Australian Museum, Melbourne, 8–10 October 1993*. Chinese Australian Museum, Melbourne, pp. 230–247.

George, S, 1999, 'Unbuttoned: archaeological perspectives of convicts and whalers' clothing in nineteenth century Tasmania'. Honours thesis, School of Historical and European Studies, Faculty of Humanities and Social Sciences, La Trobe University Bundoora, Victoria.

Getty, R, 1975, *Sisson and Grossman's the anatomy of the domestic animals*, fifth edition, vol. 1. WB Saunders Company, Philadelphia.

Gilchrist, R, 2005, 'Introduction: scales and voices in world historical archaeology'. *World Archaeology*, 37 (3): 329–336.

Gittins, J, 1981, *The diggers from China: the story of the Chinese on the goldfields*. Quartet Books, Melbourne.

Gleeson, J, 1997 (editor), *Collecting pottery & porcelain: the facts at your fingertips*. Miller's Publishing, London.

Glowrey, C, 2000, *Snake island & the cattlemen of the sea.* Education Centre Gippsland, Warragul, Victoria.

Goddard, J and Spalding, R, 1987, *Fish 'n' chips: the rise and fall of Grimsby – the world's premier fishing port.* Dalesman Books, Lancaster.

Godden, GA, 1991, *Encyclopaedia of British pottery and porcelain marks.* Barrie & Jenkins, London.

Godden Mackay Logan, La Trobe University, Austral Archaeology, 2004, Casseldon Place (50 Lonsdale Street Melbourne) archaeological excavations research archive report. Prepared for ISPT and Heritage Victoria.

Goode, GB, 1884, *The fisheries and fishery industries of the United States, section 1, natural history of useful aquatic animals with an atlas of two hundred and seventy-seven plates.* United States Commission of Fish and Fisheries, Government Printing Offices, Washington.

Goode, GB, 1887, *The fisheries and fishery industries of the United States, Section II to V.* United States Commission of Fish and Fisheries, Government Printing Offices, Washington.

Gosden, C, 2004, *Archaeology and colonialism. Culture contact from 5000 BC to the present.* Cambridge University Press, United Kingdom. Government Printer, Sydney.

Greif, SW, 1974, *The overseas Chinese in New Zealand.* Asia Pacific Press, Singapore.

Gudger, EW, 1926, 'Fishing with the cormorant in China'. *The American Naturalist,* 60 (666): 5–41.

Gungwu, W, 1992 *Community and nation: China, Southeast Asia and Australia.* Allen & Unwin Pty Ltd, St Leonards, Australia.

Gunson, N, 1996, *Reminiscences of the Nelson family and descendants in Australia and New Zealand.* Neil Gunson, Canberra.

Gurcke, K, 1987, *Bricks and brickmaking: a handbook for historical archaeology.* The University of Idaho Press, Idaho.

Halstead, G, 1977, *The story of Metung and its first inhabitants.* MacArthur Press Pty Ltd, Victoria.

Halstead, P and Collins, P, 1994, The taxonomic identification of limb bone of European farmyard animals and deer: a multimedia tutorial. Teaching and Learning Technology Programme, Glasgow.

Haysom, N, 1999, 'Some pioneering personalities of Queensland's fishing industry'. *Journal of the Royal Historical Society of Queensland,* 17 (1): 25–48.

Hellmann, VR and Yang JK, 1997, 'Previously undocumented Chinese artefacts'. In Praetzellis, M and Praetzellis, A (editors), *Historical archaeology of an overseas Chinese community in Sacramento, California.* Anthropological Studies Centre, Sonoma State University Academic Foundation Inc., California, pp. 155–202.

Herklots, GAC and Lin, SY, 1964, *Common marine food-fishes of Hong Kong, third enlarged edition.* The South China Morning Post Ltd, Hong Kong.

Hibbins, GM, 1984, *'A history of the city of Springvale: constellation of communities'.* Lothian Publishing Pty Ltd, Melbourne.

Hill, B, 2004, *The enduring rip: a history of Queenscliff.* Melbourne University Press, Victoria.

Hodder, I, 1982, *Symbols in action: ethnoarchaeological studies of material culture.* Cambridge University Press. Cambridge.

Hodder, I, 1985, 'Postprocessual archaeology'. In Schiffer, MB (editor), *Advances in archaeological method and theory.* Academic Press, New York, pp. 1–26.

Hodder, I, 1986, *Reading the past: current approaches to interpretation in archaeology.* Cambridge University Press, Cambridge.

Hodgson, B, 1999, *Opium, a portrait of the heavenly demon.* Greystone Books Vancouver.

Horsely, Rev. JF, 1879, 'The Chinese in Victoria'. *Melbourne Review,* 4 (16): 415–428.

Horsfall, D, 1985, *March to big gold mountain.* Red Rooster Press, Sydney.

Houart, V, 1977, *Buttons: a collector's guide.* Souvenir Press, London.

Howitt, AW, 1904, *Native tribes of south-east Australia.* Macmillan, London.

Hughes, AC, 1925, 'Cooperage antiquity – a wooden barrel 2450 years old'. *Barrel & Box,* 30 (8): 22.

Hughes, AC, 1926, 'A tight cooperage message to purchasing agents'. *Barrel & Box,* 31 (4): 20–22.

Hughes, TP, 1994, 'Technology momentum'. In Smith, MR and Marx, L (editors), *Does technology drive history? The dilemma of technological determinism.* The MIT Press, London, pp. 101–113.

Hutchins, B and Swainston, R, 1986, *Sea fishers of southern Australia: complete field guide for anglers and divers.* Swainston Publishing, Perth.

Hutchinson, D, 1987, 'Identifying bottles'. In Birmingham, J, and Bairstow, D (editors), *Papers in Australian historical archaeology*, Sydney, pp. 153–60.

Hwang, Y, 1976, *The overseas Chinese and the 1911 revolution.* Oxford University Press.

Inglis, C, 1975, 'Particularism in the economic organisation of the Chinese in Papua New Guinea'. *Anthropological Forum*, 4 (1): 69–76.

Jack, I, 1986, 'The overseas Chinese: recent work in Australia'. *Australian Society for Historical Archaeology Newsletter*, 16 (3): 4–7.

Jack, I, 1993, 'Historical archaeology and the historian'. *Australasian Historical Archaeology*, 11: 130–138.

Jack, I, 1995, 'The contribution of archaeology to the history of the overseas Chinese'. In Ryan, J (editor), *Chinese in Australia and New Zealand: a multidisciplinary approach.* New Age International, New Delhi, pp. 21–29.

Jack, I, Holmes, K and Kerr, R, 1984, 'Ah Toy's garden: a Chinese market-garden on the Palmer River Goldfield, North Queensland'. *Australian Journal of Historical Archaeology*, 2: 51–58.

Jack, SM, 1993, 'Divorce or reconciliation: history and historical archaeology'. *Australasian Historical Archaeology*, 11: 124–129.

Jackson, JC, 1970, *Chinese in the west Borneo goldfields: a study in cultural geography.* University of Hull Publications, Hull.

Jansen, P, 2000, *Seashells of south-east Australia.* Capricornian Publications, Lindfield, New South Wales.

Jansson, J, 2004, End of an Era. Unpublished manuscript.

Jenkins, JK, 1974, *Nets and coracles.* David and Charles, London.

Jarvis, ND, 1950, *Curing of fishery products: research report 18.* United States Government Printing Office, Washington.

Johnston, H, 1993, 'Pleistocene shell middens of the Willandra Lakes'. In Smith, MA, Spriggs, M and Fankhauser, B (editors), *Sahul in review.* Highland Press, Canberra, pp. 197–204.

Jones, O, 1971, 'Glass bottle push-ups and pontil marks'. *Historical Archaeology*, 5: 63–73.

Jones, O, 1981, 'Essence of peppermint. A history of the medicine and its bottle'. *Historical Archaeology*, 15(2): 1–57.

Jones, O, 1986, *Cylindrical English wine and beer bottles 1735–1850.* National Historic Parks and Site Branch Environment Canada – Parks, Canada.

Jones, O and Sullivan, C, 1989, *The parks Canada glass glossary: for the description of containers, tableware, flat glass and closures.* Canadian Publishing Centre, Canada.

Jones, PH, 1992, 'A comparative study of mid-nineteenth century Chinese blue-and-white export ceramics from the *Frolic* shipwreck, Mendocino County, California'. Masters thesis, San Jose State University, USA.

Jones, S, 1999, 'Historical categories and the praxis of identity: the interpretation of ethnicity in historical archaeology'. In Funari, PP; Hall, M and Jones, S (editors), *Historical archaeology: back from the edge*, Routledge, London, pp. 219–232.

Jones, TG, 1990, *The Chinese in the Northern Territory.* Northern Territory University, Darwin.

Kan, J and Leong, L, 1963, *Eight immortal flavours.* Howell-North Books, California.

Kaplan, SM, 1952, 'Towards a classification of Chinese glazes: a preliminary report', *Far Eastern Ceramics Bulletin*, 4 (2): 781–791.

Kardulias, PN (editor), 1999, *World-systems theory in practice.* Rowman and Littlefield, Lanham, MD.

Karskens, G, 1996–97, 'Crossing over: reflections on the integration of history and archaeology at Cumberland/Gloucester Street site, the Rocks 1994–1996'. *Public History Review,* 5/6: 30–48.

Karskens, G, 1997, *The Rocks: life in early Sydney.* Melbourne University Press, Melbourne.

Karskens, G, 1999a, *Inside the Rocks: the archaeology of a neighbourhood*. Hale and Iremonger, New South Wales.

Karskens, G, 1999b, 'Review of: Lydon, J, *'Many inventions': the Chinese in the Rocks 1890–1930'*. *Australasian Historical Archaeology*, vol. 17: 121–122.

Karskens, G, 1999c, *Inside the Rocks: life in early Sydney*. Melbourne University Press, Melbourne.

Kemp, J, 1996, 'Chinese monterey fishing industry'. *Cannery Row Historic Newspaper*. Monterey, California.

Kerr, G, 1985, *Craft and craftsman of Australian fishing 1870–1970: an illustrated oral history*. Mains'l Books, Portland, Victoria.

Kirk, MA, 1975, 'Buttons from the San Buenaventura Mission site, 1974', In Greenwood, RS, *3500 years on one city block, San Buenaventura Archaeological Report*. Report for Redevelopment Agency of the City of San Buenaventura, USA.

Kirkman, NS, 1984, 'The Palmer gold field 1873–1883'. Honours thesis, Department of History, James Cook University, Queensland.

Knapp, GR, 1989, *China's vernacular architecture: house form and culture*. University of Hawaii Press, United States of America.

Kyi, A, 2004, 'Unravelling the mystery of the Woah Hawp Canton quartz mining company, Ballarat'. *Journal of Australian Colonial History*, 6: 59–78.

Lorimer, SM, 1984, 'The technology & practices of the New South Wales fishing industry 1850–1930'. Masters thesis, University of Sydney, Sydney.

Langenwalter, PE, 1980, 'The archaeology of 19th century Chinese subsistence at the lower China store, Madera County, California'. In Schuyler, RL (editor), *Archaeological perspectives on ethnicity in America: Afro-American and Asian American cultural history*. Baywood Monographs in Archaeology, Baywood Publishing Company, Inc, pp. 102–112.

Langenwalter, PE, 1987, 'Mammals and reptiles as a food and medicine in Riverside's Chinatown'. In *Wong, Ho Leun: an American Chinatown*. The Great Basin Foundation, San Diego, pp. 53–106.

Langtip, R, 1986, Ray Langtip: grandson on Chin Lang Tip. Unpublished manuscript, Victoria.

Lawrence, S (editor), 2003, *Archaeologies of the British: exploration of identity in Great Britain and its colonies, 1600–1945*. Routledge, London.

Lawrence, S, 1998, 'An integrated approach to the archaeology of whaling'. In Lawrence, S and Staniforth, M (editors), *The Australasian Society for Historical Archaeology and the Australian Institute for Maritime Archaeology Special Publication*, 10: 111–115.

Lazarus, M, 1975, 'The Rusden papers'. *The Victorian Historical Journal, Journal and Proceedings of the Royal Historical Society of Victoria*, 46 (2): 348–363.

Le Cheminant, M, 1978, 'Who discovered the Gippsland coast and Bass Strait?: Three small boats on the Gippsland coast in 1797'. *Gippsland Heritage Journal*, 2 (1): 14–17.

Leach, F, 1997, 'A guide to the identification of fish remains from New Zealand archaeological sites'. *New Zealand Journal of Archaeology Special Publication*.

Leavitt, TWH (editor), 1888, 'Low Kong Meng'. In *The jubilee history of Victoria and Melbourne,* vol. 1. Duffus Bros, Melbourne.

Lee, CBT and Lee, AE, 1979, *The gourmet Chinese regional cookbook*. Castle Books.

Lee, M, 1999, 'The Chinese fishing industry of San Diego'. *Mains'l Haul*, 35 (2&3): 6–13.

Lennon, J, 1973, 'Wilson's promontory in Victoria, its commercial utilisation in the 19th Century'. *The Victorian Historical Magazine*, 44 (2), pp. 179–200.

Lennon, J, 1975, 'Squatters, merchants and mariners: an historical geography of Gipps' Land'. Masters thesis, Department of Geography, University of Melbourne, Melbourne.

Lennon, J, 1998, 'Whaling at Wilson's Promontory, Victoria in the 1840s'. In Lawrence, S and Staniforth, M (editors), *The archaeology of whaling in southern Australia and New Zealand*. Australian Society for Historical Archaeology and The Australian Institute for Maritime Archaeology Special Publication, 10: 29–31.

Lenz, FB, 1920, 'The world's ancient porcelain center'. *The National Geographic Magazine,* 38 (5): 391–406.

Levine, CO, 1921, 'Butchering and curing meats in China'. *Canton Christian College Bulletin*, No. 27.

Lightfoot, KG, 2005, 'The archaeology of colonization: California in cross-cultural perspective'. In Stein, GJ (editor), *The archaeology of colonial encounters*. School of American Research Press, New Mexico, pp. 207-236.

Lightfoot, KG, Martinez, A and Schiff, AM, 1998, 'Daily practice and material culture in pluralistic social settings: an archaeological study of culture change and persistence from Fort Ross, California'. *American Antiquity*, 63: 199–222.

Lindbergh, J, 1999, 'Buttoning down archaeology'. *Australasian Historical Archaeology*, 17: 50–57.

Little, J, 2004, *Down to the Sea: The true saga of an Australian fishing dynasty*. Macmillan Pty Ltd, Sydney.

Lockhart, B, 2006, 'The color purple: dating solarized amethyst container glass'. *Historical Archaeology*, 40 (2): 45–56.

Loh, M, 1989, *Dinky-di: the contributions of Chinese immigrants and Australians of Chinese descent to Australia's defence forces and war ffforts 1899–1988*. AGPS Press Publications, Canberra.

Loney, J, 1982, *Bay steamers and coastal ferries*. AH & AW Reed Pty Ltd, French's Forest, NSW.

Longenecker, JG and Stapp, DC, 1993, 'The study of faunal remains from an overseas Chinese mining camp in northern Idaho. In Wegars, P (editor), *Hidden heritage: historical archaeology of the overseas Chinese*. Baywood Publishing Company, Inc., New York, pp. 97–122.

Luscomb, SC, 1974, *The Collector's Encyclopedia of Buttons*. Bonanza Books, New York.

Lydon, J, 1999, *Many inventions: the Chinese in the Rocks 1890–1930*. Monash Publications in History, Clayton.

Lydon, J, 2001, 'The Chinese community in the Rocks area of Sydney: cultural persistence and exchange'. In Chan, HD, Curthoys, A and Chiang, N, *The overseas Chinese in Australasia: history, settlement and interactions*. Interdisciplinary Group for Australian Studies, National Taiwan University, Taipei and Centre for the Study of the Chinese Southern Diaspora, Australian National University, Canberra, pp. 117–124.

Lydon, S, 1985, *Chinese gold: the Chinese in the Monterey Bay Region*. Capitola Book Company, California.

Lyman, LR, 1994, *Vertebrate taphonomy*. Cambridge University Press, United Kingdom.

Macgregor, P, 1998, 'Dreams of jade and gold'. In Epstein, A (editor), *The Australian family: images and essays*. Scribe Publications, Melbourne, pp. 25–35.

Mackay, R, 1996, 'Political, physical and philosophical plans. Realising archaeological research potential in Sydney'. In *Nailing the debate: archaeology and interpretation in museums*, NSW Historic Houses Trust, Sydney, pp. 123–128.

Mackay, R and Karskens, G, 1999, 'Historical archaeology in Australia: historical or hysterical? Crisis or creative awakening?' *Australasian Historical Archaeology*, 17: 110–115.

MacKnight, CC, 1976, *The voyage to Marege': Macassan trepangers in northern Australia*. Melbourne University Press, Melbourne.

Maddern, IT, 1965, 'The squatters in Gippsland'. *The Victorian Historical Magazine*, 36 (1): 97–109.

Maddin, R (editor), 1988, *The beginning of the use of metals and alloys*. The MIT Press, London.

Majewski, T and O'Brien, MJ, 1987, 'The use and misuse of nineteenth-century English and American ceramics in archaeological analysis'. *Advances in Archaeological Method and Theory*, 11: 97–209.

Manderson, D, 1993, *From Mr Sin to Mr Big*. Oxford University Press, Melbourne.

Manson, JM, 1982, *Bricks in Alberta*. Alberta Masonry and Co-op Press Limited, Alberta.

Mark, M-L. and Chih, G, 1982, *A place called Chinese America*. Kendall Hunt Publishing Co., Dubuque.

Markus, A, 1979, *Fear and hatred: purifying Australia and California 1850–1901*. Hale and Ironmonger, Sydney.

Markus, A, 2001, 'Government control of Chinese immigration to Australia, 1855–1975'. In Chan, HD, Curthoys, A and Chiang, N, *The overseas Chinese in Australasia: history, settlement and interactions*. Interdisciplinary Group for Australian Studies, National Taiwan University, Taipei and Centre for the Study of the Chinese Southern Diaspora, Australian National University, Canberra, pp. 69–81.

Martin, G, 1978, *The founding of Australia: the argument about Australia's origins.* Allen & Unwin, North Sydney.

May, C, 1984, *Topsawyers: the Chinese in Cairns 1870 to 1920.* History Department, James Cook University, Townsville.

McCarthy, J, 1986, 'Pine Creek heritage zone archaeological survey'. A report to the National Trust of Australia (Northern Territory), Darwin.

McEvoy, FA, 1986, *The fisherman's problem: ecology and law in the California fisheries 1850–1980.* Cambridge University Press, New York.

McGowan, B, 2005, 'The economic and organisation of Chinese mining in colonial Australia'. *Australian Economic History Review,* 45 (2): 119–138.

McLaren, IF, 1985, *The Chinese in Victoria: official reports and documents.* Red Rooster Press, Sydney.

McMahon, A, 1966, 'The convict stations of Norfolk Bay'. *Papers and Proceedings of the Tasmanian Historical Research Association,* 13 (3): 58.

McNeil, W.H, 1988, 'Diffusion in history'. In Hugill, PJ and Dickson, BD (editors), *The transfer and transformation of ideas and material culture.* Texas A & M University Press, Texas, pp. 75–91.

Medley, M, 1976, *The Chinese potter, a practical history of Chinese ceramics.* Charles Scribner's Sons, New York.

Mee, A (editor), 1927, *I see all: the world's first picture encyclopedia,* vol. 5. Amalgamated Press, London.

Mei, J, 1979, 'Socioeconomic origins of emigration: Guangdong to California, 1850–1882'. *Modern China,* 5 (4): 463–501.

Melendy, B H, 1984, *Chinese and Japanese Americans...their contribution to American Society.* Hippocrene Book Inc, New York.

Michael, RL, 1974, 'Cut nail manufacture: southwestern Pennsylvania'. *APT – Canadian-American Bulletin of the Association for Preservation Technology,* 6 (1): 99–100.

Middleton, A, 2005, 'Nail chronology: the case of Te Puna Mission Station'. *Australasian Historical Archaeology,* 32: 55–62.

Miller, GL. & Sullivan, C, 1984, 'Machine-made containers and the end of production for mouth blown bottles'. *Historical Archaeology,* 18: 83–96.

Miller, GL, 2000, 'Telling time for archaeologists'. *Northeast Historical Archaeology,* 29: 1–22.

Minutes, 1894, Port Albert branch Victorian Fisherman's Union 1889–1907. Unpublished, held at Maritime Museum, Port Albert.

Minutes of the Victorian Market Committee, Victorian Public Record Office, February 1866, Series 4030, Unit 2 & 3.

Moench, RU, 1963, 'Economic relations of the Chinese in the Society Islands'. Doctoral thesis, Harvard University, Massachusetts.

Moore, R and Tully, J, 2000, *A difficult case by Jong Ah Siug: an autobiography of a Chinese miner on the central Victorian goldfields.* Jim Crow Press, Daylesford, Victoria.

Mote, WF, 1977, 'Yuan and Ming'. In Chang, KC (editor), *Food in Chinese culture: anthropological and historical perspectives.* Yale University Press, London, pp. 193–258.

Mueller, FW, Jr., 1987a, 'Asian tz'u: porcelain for the American market'. In *Wong, Ho Leun: an American Chinatown.* The Great Basin Foundation, San Diego, pp. 259–311.

Mueller, FW. Jr., 1987b, 'Gaming and gaming pieces'. In *Wong, Ho Leun: an American Chinatown.* The Great Basin Foundation, San Diego, pp. 385–393.

Muir, A, 2003, 'Ceramics in the collection of the Museum of Chinese Australian History, Melbourne'. *Australasian Historical Archaeology,* 21: 42–49.

Muir, A-L, 2007, 'Kitchen ch'ing: Chinese ceramics in Victoria'. Masters thesis, School of Historical and European Studies, Faculty of Humanities and Social Sciences, La Trobe University, Bundoora, Victoria.

Mulvaney, DJ and Colson, J (editors), 1971, *Aboriginal man and environment in Australia.* ANU Press, Canberra.

Munsell Color., 1966, *Munsell book of color, glossy finish collection*. Munsell Color Corporation, Baltimore, Maryland.

Murray, T, 2002, 'But that was long ago: theory in Australian historical archaeology 2002'. *Australasian Historical Archaeology*, 20: 8–14.

Murray, T and Allen, J, 1986, 'Theory and the development of historical archaeology in Australia'. *Archaeology in Oceania*, 21 (1): 85–93.

Muskett, PE, 1894, *Prescribing and treatment in the diseases of infants and children*. Pentland, YJ, London.

Naquin, S and Rawski, E, 1987, *Chinese society in the eighteenth century*. Yale University Press, New Haven.

Nash, J, 1981, 'Ethnographic aspects of the world capitalist system'. *Annual Review of Anthropology*, 10: 393–423.

Nash, RA, 1973, 'The Chinese shrimp fishery in California'. Doctoral thesis, Department of Geography, University of California.

Nicholas, D and Sheehan, M, 2002, *Faint traces: Chinese in Hawthorn before the Second World War*. Hawthorn Historical Society and City of Boroondara Library Services, Victoria.

Nicholson, I, 1998, *Log of logs: a catalogue of logs, journals, shipboard diaries, letters and all forms of voyage narratives, 1788 to 1998, for Australia and New Zealand and surrounding oceans*, vol. 3. Roebuck Books, Yaroomba, Queensland.

Nugent, A, 1980, *The story of fishing at Wreck Bay: as told by the people*. Canberra publishing and printing Co., Canberra.

Oddie, GA, 1961, 'The lower class Chinese and the merchant elite in Victoria, 1870–1890'. *Historical Studies Australia and New Zealand,* 10: 65–70.

Oddie, GA, 1959, 'The Chinese in Victoria, 1870–1890'. Masters thesis, University of Melbourne, Melbourne.

Oliver, A, 1871, 'The fisheries of New South Wales'. In *Industrial progress of New South Wales,* NSW Government Printers, pp. 781–792.

Ollif, L and Crosthwaite, W, 1977, *Early Australian crafts and tools*. Rigby, New South Wales.

Olsen, JW, 1978, 'A study of Chinese ceramics excavated in Tucson'. *Kiva*, 44 (1): 1–50.

Olson, F, 1947, *I loved teaching*. AH Massina & Co. Pty Ltd, Melbourne.

Omohundro, JT, 1977, 'Trading patterns of Philippine Chinese: strategies of sojourning middlemen'. In Hutterer, KL (editor), *Economic exchange and social interaction in Southeast Asia: perspectives from prehistory, history and ethnography*. Centre for South and Southeast Asian Studies, The University of Michigan, pp. 113–138.

Organ, M, 1990, *A documentary history of the Illawarra and South Coast Aborigines, 1770–1850*. Aboriginal Education Unit, Wollongong University, New South Wales.

Orser, CE. Jr., 1988, *The material basis of the postbellum tenant plantation: historical archaeology in the South Carolina Piedmont*. University of Georgia Press, London.

Orser, CE. Jr., 1989, 'On plantations and patterns'. In Miller, GL, Jones, O, Ross, L and Majewski, T (compilers), *Approaches to material culture research for historical archaeologists*. Society for Historical Archaeology, Tucson, pp. 371–384.

Orser, CE. Jr., 1996, *A historical archaeology of the modern world*. Plenum Publishing Corporation, New York.

Orser, CE. Jr., 2002, *Encyclopaedia of historical archaeology*. Routledge, New York.

Orser, CE. Jr., 2004, *Race and practice in archaeological interpretation*. University of Pennsylvania Press, Philadelphia.

Orser, CE. Jr. and Fagan, BM, 1995, *Historical archaeology*. HarperCollins College Publishers, New York.

Palmer, M and Neaverson, P, 1994, *Industry in the landscape, 1700–1900*. Routledge, London.

Passmore, J and Reid, D, 1982, *The complete Chinese cookbook: over 500 authentic recipes from China*. Exeter Books, New York.

Pastron, AG. and Garaventa, D, 1981, 'Ceramics from Chinatown's tables: an historical archaeological approach to ethnicity'. In Pastron, AG, and Ziebarth, M (editors), *Behind the seawall: historical archaeology along the San Francisco waterfront*, pp. 365–469.

Patel, HG, 1989, 'Alternate technologies and socio-economic contexts of adaptation: a study of the coastal fishermen of Saurashtra in Western India'. In Van der Leeuw, SE and Torrence, R (editors), *What's new? A closer look at the process of innovation*. Unwin Hyman, London, pp. 54–61.

Peabody, AP, 1871, 'The Chinese in San Francisco.' *American Naturalist*, 4 (11): 660–664.

Pears' Cyclopaedia, 1905, *Pears' shilling cyclopaedia*, eighth edition. A & F Pears Limited, Glasgow, United Kingdom.

Pearson, A, 1992, *Historic Port Albert*. Port Albert Museum, Victoria.

Pearson, M, 1983, 'The technology of whaling in Australian waters in the 19th century'. *Australian Historical Archaeology*, 1: 40–54.

Pedrotta, V and Romero, GF, 1998, 'Historical archaeology: an outlook from the Argentinean Pampas'. *International Journal of Historical Archaeology*, 2 (2): 113–131.

Peterson, HL, 1956, *Arms and armor in colonial America 1826–1783*. Bramhall House, New York.

Peterson, LM, 1978, *Time and tide at Port Welshpool, Gippsland Coast Victoria*. Gippsland Times Commercial Printing, Victoria.

Petroski, H, 1990, *The pencil: a history of design and circumstance*. Alfred A Knopf, New York.

Phillips, PJ, 1978, *Kill or cure? Lotions potions characters & quacks of early Australia*. Greenhouse Publications, Victoria.

Pike, D (editor), 1974, *Australian dictionary of biography 1851–1890*. vols 4 & 5, Melbourne University Press, Melbourne.

Piper, A, 1988, 'Chinese diet and cultural conservatism in nineteenth-century southern New Zealand'. *Australian Journal of Historical Archaeology*, 6: 34–43.

Piper, AK. S, 1991, 'Butchery analysis in Australian historical archaeology'. Masters thesis, Department of Archaeology and Palaeoanthropology, University of New England, Armidale.

Piper, A, 1984, 'Nineteenth century Chinese goldminers of central Otago: a study of the interplay between cultural conservatism and acculturation through an analysis of changing diet'. Honours thesis, Anthropology Department, University of Otago, Dunedin, New Zealand.

Porter, H, 1977, *Bairnsdale: portrait of an Australian country town*. John Ferguson, Sydney.

Pownall, P, 1979, *Fisheries of Australia*. Billing and Sons Limited, London.

Praetzellis, M and Praetzellis, A, 1979, 'The lovelock ceramics'. In Hattori, EM, Rusco, MK and Tuohy, DR (editors), *Archaeological and historical studies at Ninth and Amherst, Lovelock, Nevada*. Archaeological Services Reports, Nevada State Museum, Carson City, Nevada, pp. 140–199.

Praetzellis, M and Praetzellis, A, 1997, *Historical archaeology of an overseas Chinese community in Sacramento, California*. Anthropological Studies Center, Sonoma State University Academic Foundation Inc., California.

Praetzellis, M and Praetzellis, A, 1990, Junk! Archaeology of the pioneer junk store, 1877–1908. Papers in Northern California Anthropology No 4., Anthropological Studies Centre, Sonoma State University, Rohnert Park, California.

Price, CA, 1978, *The great white walls are built: restrictive immigration to North America and Australasia 1863–1888*. Australian National University Press, Canberra.

Proh, S, 1973, *The Australian bottle collector*. Bottle Collectors Review, Upper Mt. Gravatt, Queensland.

PROV (Public Record Office Victoria), VA 672 Premier's Office, VPRS 5357/P0000 Inwards Correspondence, unit 5899 (Fisherman's residence licence documents).

Quellmalz, CR, 1972, 'Chinese porcelain excavated from North American Pacific coast sites'. *Oriental Art*, 18 (2): 148–154.

Quellmalz, CR, 1976, 'Late Chinese provincial export wares'. *Oriental Art*, 22 (3): 289–298.

Raymond, R, 1984, *Out of the fiery furnace: the impact of metals on the history of mankind*. The Macmillan Company of Australia Pty Ltd, Melbourne.

Richardson, P, 1982, *Chinese mine labour in the Transvaal*. The Macmillan Press Ltd, Hong Kong.

Ridpath, JC, 1899, *History of the world,* vol. 4. The Jones Brothers Publishing Company, Cincinnati, USA.

Ritchie, NA and Bedford, S, 1983, 'Analysis of the glass bottles and containers from the Cromwell's Chinatown'. *New Zealand Archaeological Association Newsletter*, 26 (4): 235–258.

Ritchie, NA and Harrison, AP, 1982, An archaeological analysis of opium smoking and associated artefacts from Chinese sites in central Otago, New Zealand. Unpublished manuscript for New Zealand Historic Places Trust Cromwell.

Ritchie, NA, 1984, 'The excavation of a small Chinese mining settlement and store, Arrowtown, Central Otago. *New Zealand Archaeological Association Newsletter*, 27 (2): 83–103.

Ritchie, NA, 1986, 'Archaeology and history of the Chinese in southern New Zealand during the nineteenth century: a study of acculturation, adaptation and ahange'. Doctoral thesis, Anthropology Department, University of Otago, Dunedin, New Zealand.

Ritchie, NA, 1993, 'Form and adaptation: nineteenth century Chinese miners' dwellings in southern New Zealand'. In Wegars, P (editor), *Hidden heritage: historical archaeology of the overseas Chinese*. Amityville, New York, pp. 335–373.

Robinson, R, 1987, *A history of the Yorkshire Coast fishing industry 1780–1914*. Hull University Press, England.

Roeder, MA, 1993, Selected fish remains from Chinatown. Cultural Resources Impact Mitigation Program Los Angeles Metro Rail Red Line Segment 1. RS. Greenwood. Los Angeles, Los Angeles County Metropolitan Transport Authority: 240–244.

Rogers, JD, 2005, 'Archaeology and the interpretation of colonial encounters'. In Stein, GJ (editor), *The archaeology of colonial encounters*, School of American Research Press, New Mexico, pp. 331–354.

Rohe, RE, 1982, 'After the gold rush: mining in the Far West 1850–1890'. *Montana, the Magazine of Western History*, 32 (3): 2–19.

Roughley, TC, 1953, *Fish and fisheries of Australia*. Angus and Robertson, Sydney.

Said, E, 1978, *Orientalism*. Routledge and Kegan Paul, London.

Sando, RA and Felton, DL, 1993, 'Inventory records of ceramics and opium from a nineteenth century Chinese store in California'. In Wegars, P (editor), *Hidden heritage: historical archaeology of the overseas Chinese*. Baywood Publishing Company Inc., New York, pp. 151–176.

Schafer, EH, 1977, 'T'ang'. In Chang, KC (editor), *Food in Chinese culture: anthropological and historical perspectives*. Yale University Press, London, pp. 85–140.

Schmid, E, 1972, *Atlas for the identification of animal bones*. Elsevier, Amsterdam.

Schmidt, D, 2006, 'Subsistence fishing at Jamestown, 1607–24'. *Post-Medieval Archaeology*, 40 (1): 80–95.

Schreiber, K, 2005, 'Imperial agents and local agency: Wari colonial strategies'. In Stein, GJ (editor), *The archaeology of colonial encounters*. School of American Research Press, New Mexico, pp. 237–262.

Schulz, PD, 1979, 'Historical faunal remains from Panamint City: notes on diet and status in a California boom town'. *Pacific Coast Archaeological Society Quarterly*, 15 (4): 55–63.

Schulz, PD and Lortie, F, 1985, 'Archaeological notes on a California Chinese shrimp boiler'. *Historical Archaeology*, 19 (1): 86–95.

Schulz, PD and Gust, S, 1983, 'Faunal remains and social status in nineteenth century Sacramento'. *Historical Archaeology*, 17 (1): 44–53.

Schuyler, RL (editor), 1980, *Archaeological perspectives on ethnicity in America*, Baywood Publishing Inc., New York.

Schuyler, RL, 1970, 'Historical archaeology and historic sites archaeology as anthropology: basic definitions and relationships'. *Historical Archaeology*, 4: 83–89.

Secomb, N, 1995, 'Breaking the fish famine: bringing food to the tables of the people of New South Wales 1880–1925'. Honours thesis, Faculty of Humanities and Social Sciences, University of Western Sydney, Sydney.

Sharpe, D, 1992, *Remember that heavenly ginger beer? A history of Sharpe Bros*. Island Graphics Pty Ltd, Melbourne.

Shen, Y, 2001, *Dragon seed in the antipodes: Chinese-Australian autobiographies*. Melbourne University Press, Melbourne.

Silver, IA, 1978, 'The aging of domestic animals, approaches to faunal analysis in the Middle East'. In Meadow, RH and Zeder, MA (editors), *Peabody Museums Bulletins*, 2. Harvard University Press, Cambridge, Massachusetts, pp. 283–302.

Singleton, OP, 1973, 'Geology of south Gippsland'. In McAndrew, J and Marsden, MAH (editors), *Regional guide to Victorian geology*. School of Geology, University of Melbourne, 14: 129–138.

Sisson, D and Harrison, R, 1983, Chinese occupation in the Lower Salmon River canyon of central Idaho. Paper presented at the 16th Annual Meeting of the Society for Historical Archaeology, Denver.

Sisson, DA, 1993, 'Archaeological evidence of Chinese use along the Lower Salmon River, Idaho'. In Wegars, P (editor), *Hidden heritage: historical archaeology of the overseas Chinese*. Baywood Publishing Company Inc., New York, pp. 33–63.

Skennerton, I, 1988, *200 years of Australian military rifles & bayonets*. Skennerton Margate, Australia.

Smith, LM, 1998, 'Cold hard cash: study of Chinese ethnicity in archaeology at Kiandra, New South Wales'. Masters thesis. Department of Archaeology and Anthropology, The Australian National University, Canberra.

Smith, LM, 2003, 'Identifying Chinese ethnicity through material culture: archaeological excavations at Kiandra, NSW'. *Australasian Historical Archaeology*, 21: 18–29.

Smith, LM, 2006, 'Hidden dragons: the archaeology of mid to late 19th century Chinese communities in southeastern New South Wales'. Doctoral thesis, Department of Archaeology and Anthropology, The Australian National University, Canberra.

Soule, F, 1855, *Annals of San Francisco*. Auburn Press, New York.

South, S, 1977, *Method and theory in historical archaeology*. Academic Press, New York.

Spennemann, D and Colley, S, 1990, 'Fire in a pit: the effects of burning on faunal remains'. *Archaeozoologia*, 3 (1–2): 45–63.

Spier, RFG., 1958, 'Food habits of nineteenth-century California Chinese'. *California Historical Society Quarterly*, 37 (2): 129–136.

Sprague, R, 1980–81, 'A functional classification for artifacts from 19th and 20th century historical sites'. *North American Archaeologist,* 2 (3): 251–261.

Staniforth, M, 1987, 'The casks from the wreck of the *William Salthouse*'. *The Australian Journal of Historical Archaeology*, 5: 21–28.

Staniforth, M and Nash, M, 1998, *Chinese export porcelain from the wreck of the* Sydney Cove *(1797)*. Brolga Press for the Australian Institute for Maritime Archaeology, Adelaide.

Stanin, Z, 2004a, 'From Li Chun to Yong Kit: a market garden on the Loddon, 1851–1912'. *Journal of Australian Colonial History,* 6: 14–34.

Stanin, Z, 2004b, Preliminary archaeological investigation of Chinese residential sites on the Mt Alexander diggings. Report prepared for Heritage Victoria and Parks Victoria.

Stapp, DC, 1990, 'The historic ethnography of a Chinese mining community in Idaho'. Doctoral thesis, American Civilisation, Faculties of the University of Pennsylvania, USA.

Staski, E, 1984, 'Just what can a 19th century bottle tell us?' *Historical Archaeology*, 18 (1): 38–51.

Staski, E, 1993, 'The overseas Chinese in El Paso: changing goals, changing realities;. In Wegars, P (editor), *Hidden heritage: historical archaeology of the overseas Chinese*. Baywood Publishing Company, Inc. New York, pp. 125–149.

Stein, GJ, 2002, 'Distinguished lecturer: from passive periphery to active agents: emerging perspectives in the archaeology of interregional interaction'. *American Anthropologist*, 104: 903–916.

Stein, GJ, 2005, The comparative archaeology of colonial encounters. In Stein, GJ (editor), *The archaeology of colonial encounters*. School of American Research Press, New Mexico, pp. 3–32.

Stenger, A, 1993, 'Sourcing and dating of Asian porcelains by elemental analysis'. In Wegars, P (editor), *Hidden heritage: historical archaeology of the overseas Chinese*. Baywood Publishing Company Inc., New York, pp. 315–331.

Stevens, RW, 1894, *On the stowage of ships and their cargoes*. Longmans, Green & Co., London.

Stockman, N2000, *Understanding Chinese society*. Polity Press, Cambridge, UK.

Stuart, I, 2005, 'The analysis of bricks from archaeological sites in Australia'. *Australasian Historical Archaeology*, 23: 79–88.

Sussman, L, 1985, *The wheat pattern, an illustrated survey*. Studies in Archaeology, Architecture and History, Parks Canada, Environment Canada.

Sussman, L, 1997, *Mocha banded, cat's eye and other factory-made slipware*. Studies in Northeast Historical Archaeology No. 1, Boston University, Boston.

Svenson, GV, 1994, 'Marginal people: the archaeology and history of the Chinese at Milparinka'. Masters thesis, Department of Archaeology, University of Sydney.

Syme, AM, 1987, *Shipping arrivals and departures: Victorian ports*, vol. 2, 1846–1855. Roebuck Society Publications, Victoria.

Synan, P, 1989, *Highways of water: how shipping on the lakes shaped Gippsland*. Landmark Press, Victoria.

Tao, LK and Leong, YK, 1915, *Village and town life in China*. Unknown publisher, London.

The Chemist and Druggist of Australasia. 1901, Volume 16.

The Living Age, 1876, (September 23), 'An excursion in Formosa', 130 (1685): 769–824.

Thomson, AT, 1845, *A conspectus of the pharmacopoeias of the London, Edinburgh and Dublin Colleges of Physicians; being a practical compendium of materia medica and pharmacy*, fifteenth edition. Longman, Brown, Green and Longmans, Paternoster-Row, London.

Thomas, N, 1994, *Colonialism's culture: anthropology, travel and government*. Polity Press, Cambridge.

Tomlin, OF, Bosa, M and Chamberlain, PG, 1979, *Gold for the finding: a pictorial history of Gippsland's Jordan Goldfield*. Hill of Content Publishing, Melbourne.

Toulouse, JH, 1971, *Bottler makers and their marks*. Thomas Nelson Inc., New York, Camden.

Townrow, K, 1997, *Sealing and whaling sites in Victoria*. Heritage Victoria and the Australian Heritage Commission, Melbourne.

Trigg, HB, 2003, 'The ties that bind: economic and social interactions in early-colonial New Mexico, AD 1598–1680'. *Historical Archaeology*, 37 (2): 65–84.

Trousdale, W, 1975, *The long sword and scabbard slide in Asia*. Smithsonian Institution Press, Washington.

Upton, D, 1996, 'Ethnicity, authenticity and invented traditions'. *American Antiquity*, 43 (2): 231–244.

Vader, J and Murray, M, 1975, *Antique bottle collecting in Australia*. Ure Smith, Sydney.

Varman, RVJ, 1980, 'The nail as a criterion for the dating of building and building sites (Late 18th century to 1900)'. *Australian Society for Historical Archaeology Newsletter*, 10 (1): 104–112.

Varman, RV. J, 1993, 'Bricks and nails, building materials as criteria for dating in Sydney and environs from 1788: a documentary survey and assessment of dating potential'. Doctoral thesis, Department of Prehistoric and Historical Archaeology University of Sydney, Sydney.

Vaughan, H, 1987, *The Australian fisherman's companion*. Lansdowne Press, Sydney.

Vivian, H, 1985, Tasmania's Chinese heritage: an historical record for Chinese sites in north east Tasmania. Report for the Australian Heritage Commission and the Queen Victorian Museum, Victoria.

von Brandt, A, 1972, *Revised and enlarged fish catching methods of the world*. Fishing News (Books) Ltd, London.

von den Driesch, A, 1976, *A guide to the measurement of animal bones from archaeological sites*. Peabody Museum of Archaeology and Ethnology Harvard University, Massachusetts.

Voss, BL, 2005, 'The archaeology of overseas Chinese communities'. *World Archaeology*, 37 (3): 424–439.

*Votes and proceedings of the New South Wales Legislative Assembly:*

——1879–80, vol. 1. Minutes of the proceedings of the parliamentary debate on the state of the fisheries of this colony.

——1879–80, vol. 3. Report of the royal commission to inquire into and report upon the actual state and prospect of the fisheries of this colony; together with minutes of evidence and appendix, pp. 1101–1265.

——1891–92. Papers laid upon the table during the session of 1891–92. Fisheries, pp. 273–288.

——1891–92, vol. 5. Report of the royal commission on alleged Chinese gambling and immorality and charges of bribery against members of the police porce, together with the minutes of evidence of the committee.

——1891–92, vol. 7. Report of the royal commission into the fisheries of New South Wales. Legislative Assembly, during the session of 1891–92. pp. 282–394.

——1891–92, vol. 8. Minutes of the proceedings on the report of the royal commission into Chinese gambling and immorality 1891–92. pp. 467–977.

*Votes and proceedings of the New South Wales Legislative Council:*

——1858, vol. 3. Report from the select committee on the Chinese Immigration Bill, together with the minutes of evidence taken before the committee. Session commencing 23rd March 1858.

——1892. Report from the fisheries commission, February 23, pp. 5588–5594.

——1894. Report from the fisheries commission, March 13, pp. 1438–1450.

*Votes and proceedings of the South Australian Legislative Council:*

——1861. South Australia parliamentary debates, September 26, 1861, during the second session from April 26 to December 3, pp. 854–868.

*Votes and proceedings of the Tasmanian Legislative Council:*

——1866, vol. 13. The third parliament of Tasmania, journals of the House of Assembly, sixth session.

*Votes and proceedings of the Victorian Legislative Council:*

——1868, vol. 3. Report on the condition of the Chinese population in Victoria, by the Rev. William Young. Presented to both houses of parliament by his Excellency's command, John Ferres.

——1892. Progress report from the select committee upon the fishing industry of Victoria.

——1919. Report of the royal commission on Victorian fisheries and fisheries industries. Presented to both houses of parliament.

Wakeman, F, 1966, *Strangers at the gate*. University of California Press, Berkeley.

Wallerstein, I, 1974, *The modern world-system, vol. 1: capitalist agriculture and the origin of the European world-economy in the sixteenth century,* Academic Press, New York.

Walsh, NG, & Entwisle, TJ, 1994, *Flora of Victoria: ferns and allied plants, confiners and monocotyledons,* vol. 2. Inkata Press, Melbourne.

Walters, I, 1987, *Prehistoric fisheries in Australia – a long diverse pedigree.* Australian Fisheries, March: 21–24.

Wang, CC, 1920, 'Is the Chinese diet adequate?' *The Journal of Home Economics*, 12 (7): 289–293.

Wang, G, 1988, The life of William Liu: Australian and Chinese perspectives. In Hardy, J (editor), *Stories of Australian migration*. New South Wales University Press, Sydney.

Wang, G, 1991, *China and the Chinese overseas*. Times Academic Press, Singapore.

Wang, G, 1992, *Community and nation: China, Southeast Asia and Australia*. Asian Studies Association of Australia in association with Allen & Unwin Pty Ltd, Sydney.

Wang, G, 2003, *Don't leave home: migration and the Chinese*. Eastern University Press, Singapore.

Wang, S, 1978, *The organisation of Chinese emigration 1848–1888, with special reference to Chinese emigration to Australia*. Chinese Materials Centre Inc., San Francisco.

Ward, BE, 1959, 'Floating villages: Chinese fishermen in Hong Kong'. *Man,* 59 (March): 44–45.

Ward, BE, 1954, 'A Hong Kong fishing village'. *Journal of Oriental Studies*, 1: 145–214.

Watson, I, 1984, *Caledonia Australis: Scottish highlanders on the frontier of Australia*. William Collins Pty Ltd, Sydney.

Watson, JL, 1975, *Emigration and the Chinese lineage: the man in Hong Kong*. University of California, Berkeley.

Wedlick, L, 1980, *What fish is that?* Wedneil Publications, Newport, Victoria.

Wegars, P, 1988, 'The Asian comparative collection'. *The Australian Journal of Historical Archaeology*, 6: 43–49.

Wegars, P (editor), 1993, *Hidden heritage: historical archaeology of the overseas Chinese*. Baywood Publishing Company Inc., New York.

Wegars, P, 1998, *Asian American Comparative Collection Newsletter*. 15 (2): 1–6.

Wegars, P, 1999, Chinese artefact illustrations, terminology and selected bibliography. Paper prepared for the Chinese and Japanese Artifacts Workshop, Society for Historical Archaeology, Salt Lake City, UT, January 1999.

Wegars, P, 2003, 'From old gold mountain to new gold mountain: Chinese archaeological sites, artefact repositories and archives in western North America and Australasia'. *Australasian Historical Archaeology,* 21: 68–81.

Wells, J, 1986, *Gippsland: people, a place and their past* Victoria, Landmark Press.

Wells, J, 2001, *Tooradin 125 years of coastal history: Blind Blight, Cannon's Creek, Sherwood, Tooradin North, Warneet.* South East Print and Design, Victoria.

Wells, P, 1998, 'Culture contact, identity and change in the European provinces of the Roman Empire'. In Cusick, J (editor), *Studies in culture contact: interaction, culture change and archaeology.* Occasional Paper 25, Centre for Archaeological Investigations, Southern Illinois University, Carbondale, pp. 316–334.

Wheelwright, HW, 1861, *Bush wanderings of a naturalist: or, notes on the field sports and fauna of Australia Felix / by an old bushman.* Routledge, Warne and Routledge, London.

White, HP. and Munhall, BD, 1963, *Cartridge headstamp guide.* HP White Laboratory, Bel Air, Maryland, US

Wilcox, WA, 1893, 'The fisheries of the Pacific Coast'. In *Report on the fisheries of the Pacific Coast of the United States*, United States Commission of Fish and Fisheries, pp. 143–257.

Willard, M, 1923, *History of the White Australia policy.* AP Publications, Melbourne.

Williams, M, 1999, Chinese settlement in NSW: a thematic history. Report for the NSW Heritage Office of NSW.

Willmott, DE, 1960, *The Chinese of Semarang: a changing minority community in Indonesia.* Cornell University Press, New York.

Wills, G, 1974, *English glass bottles 1650–1950 for the collector.* John Bartholomew & Son Ltd, Edinburgh.

Wilson, RL, 1981, *Bottles on the Western Frontier.* The University of Arizona Press, Tucson.

Wilton, J, 2001, 'The Chinese history and heritage regional New South Wales'. In Chan, HD, Curthoys, A and Chiang, N, *The overseas Chinese in Australasia: history, settlement and interactions.* Interdisciplinary Group for Australian Studies, National Taiwan University, Taipei and Centre for the Study of the Chinese Southern Diaspora, Australian National University, Canberra, pp. 91–101.

Wilton, J, 2004, *Golden threads: the Chinese in regional New South Wales 1850–1950.* New England Regional Art Museum in association with Powerhouse Publishing, Armidale, Australia.

Winant, L, 1959, *Early percussion firearms: a history of early percussion firearms ignition – from Forsyth to Winchester. 44/40.* William Morrow & Company, New York.

Wolf, ER, 1982, *Europe and the people without history.* University of California Press, Berleley.

Wood, N, 1999, *Chinese glazes, their origins, chemistry and reaction.* Craftsman House, London.

Wu, DY. H, 1982, *The Chinese in Papua New Guinea: 1880–1980.* The Chinese University Press, Hong Kong.

Wylie, J and Fike, RE, 1993, 'Chinese opium smoking techniques and paraphernalia'. In Wegars, P (editor), *Hidden heritage: historical archaeology of the overseas Chinese.* Baywood Publishing Company Inc., New York, pp. 255–303.

Wylie, J and Higgins, P, 1987, 'Opium paraphernalia and the role of opium at Riverside's Chinatown'. In *Wong, Ho Leun: an American Chinatown*, The Great Basin Foundation, San Diego, pp. 317–383.

Wylie, J, 1980, Opium pipes and other Chinese artefacts from Boise Basin, Idaho. Idaho Cultural Resource Notebook. Review Draft, USDA Forest Service Intermontaine Region.

Yang, J and Hellmann, V, 1996, 'What's in the pot? An emic perspective on Chinese brown glazed stoneware'. Paper presented at the Annual Meeting of the Society for Historical Archaeology Conference on Historical and Underwater Archaeology, Cincinnati, Ohio.

Yang, M, 1994, *Gifts, favors & banquets: the art of social relationships in China.* Cornell University Press, London.

Yangwen, Z, 2005, *The social life of opium in China.* Cambridge University Press, New York.

Yarwood, AT and Knowling, MJ (editors), 1982, *Race relations in Australia. A history.* Methuen Pty Ltd, Australia.

Yee, RF, 1975, *Chinese village cookbook: a practical guide to Cantonese country cooking.* Yerba Buena Press, California.

Yong, CF, 1977, *The new gold mountain: the Chinese in Australia 1901–1921.* Raphael Richmond Arts Pty Ltd. South Australia.

Young, F and van Barneveld, N, 1997, *Sources for Chinese local history and heritage in New South Wales.* Young and van Barneveld, Kareela, New South Wales.

Yü, Y, 1977, 'Han China'. In Chang, KC (editor), *Food in Chinese culture: anthropological and historical perspectives.* Yale University Press, London, pp. 53–84.

## NEWSPAPERS

*Australian Town and Country Journal*
*Bairnsdale Advertiser*
*Bendigo Advertiser*
*Every Week*
*Geelong Advertiser*
*Gippsland Guardian*
*Gippsland Mercury*
*Gippsland Standard*
*Gippsland Times*
*Hobart Town Advertiser*
*Illustrated Australasian News*
*Illustrated Australian News*
*Peninsula Post*
*Port Phillip Herald*
*Port Phillip Patriot*
*San Diego Union*
*San Francisco Weekly Bulletin*
*Sydney Morning Herald*
*The Argus*
*The Australasian Sketcher*
*The Examiner*
*The Gippslander*
*The Newcastle Chronicle*
*The Northern Territory Times*
*The Port Phillip Patriot and Melbourne Advertiser*
*The Sydney Mail*
*The Wesleyan Chronicle*
*Warrnambool Examiner*

## PERSONAL COMMUNICATIONS

Johnstone, Arthur. Tooradin, Victoria, 2002, November (retired fisherman).

Woolley, John. Port Welshpool Victoria, 2003, January (retired fisherman).

Findlay, Les. Phillip Island, Victoria, 2003, January (retired fisherman).

Osterlund, Jim. Phillip Island, Victoria, 2003, January (retired fisherman).

Walton, Ted. Phillip Island, Victoria, 2003, January (retired fisherman).

Greenaway, Jock. Hedley, Victoria, 2003, February (farmer and naturalist).

Rossiter, Norie. Hedley, Victoria, 2003, February (farmer and naturalist).

Bury, Peter. Metung, Victoria, 2003, March (shipwright).

Clark, Albert. Port Albert, Victoria, 2003, June (retired fisherman).

Robinson, Jimmy. Port Albert, Victoria, 2005, May (retired fisherman).

Muir, Anne-Louise. Melbourne, 2005, February (archaeologist).

Morphett, Ben. Tasmania, 2006, June (Asian studies researcher).

Wackett, Lance. Sydney, 2006, December (archaeological consultant).

Lawrence, Susan. Melbourne, 2007, June (senior lecturer in archaeology).

## WEB PAGES

Agriculture, Forestry and Fisheries Australia. www.affa.gov.au 7 May 2007.

Antique Chinese storage boxes. www.trocadero.com and www.chinese-furniture.com.

Asian American Comparative Collection. www.uidaho.edu/LS/AACC/htm.

Chasing the dragon, www.biopsychiatry.com/heroin.htm.

Harrison, AJ, 2006, The Tasmanian abalone fishery: a personal history, members. www.users.on.net/~ahvem/Fisheries/Abalone/abalone1.html.

Making of America. moa.library.cornell.edu/.

Images of Chinese people in colonial Australia. www.chia.chinesemuseum.com.au,

Schulz, PD and Allen, R, 2004. 'Archaeology and architecture of the overseas Chinese: a bibliography'. Society for Historical Archaeology. http://www.sha.org/documents/research/Bibliography/arch_artchit_chinese_biblio.pdf.

Shipping intelligence news concerning the Wonga Wonga, a 681-ton coastal steamer. www.pbenyon.plus.com/Gazette/Shipping_Steam/Wonga_Wonga_Maiden_Trip.html.

www.ingramcontent.com/pod-product-compliance
Lightning Source LLC
Chambersburg PA
CBHW080909230426
43664CB00017B/2762